INEXHAUSTIBLE

PRESENCE:

THE MYSTERY

OF JESUS

INEXHAUSTIBLE

PRESENCE:

THE MYSTERY

OF JESUS

J. Patrick Gaffney, s.m.m.

Dimension Books, Inc.
Denville, N.J. 07834

First American Edition 1986 by Dimension Books Inc.,
P.O. Box 811, Denville, NJ 07834.

Copyright © 1986 J. Patrick Gaffney, s.m.m.

ISBN: 0-87193-249-0

TABLE OF CONTENTS

PREFACE

An earlier version of the following text was "published" several years ago through an international telecomputer information center. Anyone with a home computer and telephone attachment (modem) could, at any time and from any place in the world, hook into the telecomputer center and take part in this christological study. Many *hundreds* of people did so; its success went beyond anyone's expectation. It penetrated into offices, homes and also into numerous schools, colleges and universities which have made use of it in whole or in part. In the telecomputer "conferencing" on this subject, the many participants criticized and discussed the "course" point by point. After repeated requests for "hardcopy," it was decided to publish it so that it would not only be available to those who have hooked into the text via telecomputer but also to an even wider audience. This present version has been quite thoroughly updated and the format radically changed to accommodate its transfer from pixels to print. My thanks to all who took part in the telecomputer version, most of whom are known only through an ID or some sort of handle. In a special way, I would like to express my gratitude to a pioneer in telecomputer conferencing, Father Hal Stockert of the Ruthenian Eparchy of Passaic, without whose theological and technological assistance little if anything could have been accomplished.

The text, in a variety of versions, has also been used in university undergraduate courses, in catechetical centers (especially the Paul VI Catechetical Center of the Archdiocese of Saint Louis), in charismatic bible study sessions (at San Antonio and at San Francisco), and by many hundreds who downloaded it from the telecomputer center for their own private reading. It is a basic, *introductory* course on the mystery of Jesus. It presumes little except a desire to seriously reflect upon the person of the Lord. The water gets deep at times but I have found that the serious reader — no matter the age — wants to be challenged. It is hoped that this "hardcopy" will also be of service to many others: parents of college students who "want to know what their youngsters are studying," those involved in ministry who would like to review their basic christology, and all who would desire to study, in an academic fashion, the person of Jesus Christ. Through my ministry of teaching and telecomputer conferencing, I have been surprised to discover that there is such a widespread and deep interest in solid study on the meaning of faith in Jesus. It also became apparent that in the dialogue concerning Jesus, whether it be in a classroom or via telecomputing, the "student" expected the "professor" to express himself in all honesty from within his own situation. It was taken as an insult if I would try to camouflage that I am a Christian, a Catholic priest. The text does, then, reflect my "situation."

The following pages cannot cover the subject adequately but it is hoped that it will inspire the reader to move on into "deeper waters." Words or phrases which may not be understood by the ordinary reader are — for the most part — explained either in the text or in the footnote connected with such a word or phrase. There is a bibliography in the footnotes for the major topics covered and also a general bibliography at the end of the book for those who would want further reading on a subject. The index may also prove helpful.

My thanks to my religious community, the Montfort Missionaries, for permitting me to spend a few months tidying up the text, and to Saint Louis University for the permission to take a semester's leave of absence from the classroom to complete this work and to begin the writing of a text in mariology. The pastor and parishioners of

Saint Barbara's Church in Witt, Illinois, kindly put up with me as a "hermit in residence" as I completed the text. I would also like to publicly acknowledge the generosity and kindness of Eleanor West, now deceased, and of others from Tulsa, Oklahoma, who have been so supportive of this work.

I would like to dedicate this book to the memory of my deaf parents who first taught me to hear the word of God.

J. Patrick Gaffney, s.m.m.
St. Louis University
Department of Theological Studies
St. Louis, Missouri 63108
July 4, 1986

INTRODUCTION

In its broadest connotation, christology is the study of the mystery who is Jesus Christ. Its etymology stems from two Greek words: *christos* (Christ) and *logos* (discourse). However, christology is not any discourse about Jesus. As a division of the academic discipline theology — etymologically a discourse about *theos* (God) — it takes on all its characteristics as an academic, critical, systematic reflection on divine revelation accepted through faith. Christology can, therefore, be defined as a critical, systematic, academic reflection on faith in Jesus Christ, the climactic revelation of God. Although it is not intended to describe in any detail the nature of theology, the following points about its central study, christology, will help clarify the nature of the discipline and indicate the general methodology to be followed.

1. Christology is, first of all, an ACADEMIC study. Christology is not faith in Jesus; rather, it is a scholarly reflection on that faith.

In general, faith is one's free affirmative response, on every level of personality to that person, event or thing which gives ultimate meaning to life. That person or thing *claimed with such ultimacy,* qualifying all aspects of life is called revelation; our lived-out acceptance of this revelation is faith. Anything or anyone can become revelation for an individual: money, power, prestige, pleasure, drugs, alcohol. Even doing good, striving to be a saint can become the idols of one's life.

A christian is someone who accepts as ultimate meaning of his/her life, God's Love Incarnate, Jesus the Lord. More precisely, christian faith, essentially trinitarian, is the dynamic acceptance of the Father's empowering call — embedded in human nature itself — to enter into an all-encompassing relationship with Him through Jesus in the power of the Spirit. A person of such faith sees everything, measures everything, judges everything in the light of the Incarnate Love of the Father, Jesus the Lord.

There is a difference in approach to christology between someone who has freely accepted Jesus as the ultimate meaning in life and the non-christian who does not live such a commitment. For a Christian, christology is a formal, scholarly reflection upon one's own total "Yes" within the christian community to the person of Jesus Christ (always understood in trinitarian context). When the christian formally surfaces this faith in order to reflect upon it academically, it necessarily entails a profoundly personal involvement. For someone who does not look upon Jesus as ultimate meaning, christology is a formal, scholarly reflection on the person and nature of Jesus whom so many others have accepted as the way, the truth and the life.

Nonetheless, for both the believer and non-believer, christology is not faith itself, nor the practice of faith (religion), nor preaching, nor meditation. However, being eminently practical, theology is oriented to acts of hope and love resulting in the intertwining of orthodoxy and orthopraxis. In other words, although a scholarly, academic discipline, theology in the fullest sense of the term is not merely a "head-trip" but calls for an integration of its findings into the daily life of the student.

All who study christology are bound by all the rigorous parameters of an academic discipline as understood by any institution of higher learning. Christology is not studied on one's knees. It demands serious, arduous research and reflection before reaching any conclusions.

2. Christology is a CRITICAL study. The term critical is taken here to mean that nothing is to be considered so sacred that it is not to be scrutinized, examined, studied, with all the tools of modern research.

Did Jesus really exist? If the answer is simply: "Of course, otherwise christianity would be in trouble," then it is not a theologian who is responding. Did Jesus actually speak all the words attributed to him in the Gospels? If without reflection the answer is: "Of course, because the words are in the bible," then, again, it is not a student of christology giving such an answer. Theology is a questioning discipline. As St. Anselm of Canterbury wrote centuries ago, it is "faith seeking understanding." It is human to think, it is human to question, it is human to reflect and draw conclusions. The faith of human beings has intrinsic to it this reflective element as all human relationships have an in-built, on-going evaluation. Christology, however, is the formal, explicit critical reflection on faith in Jesus Christ.

3. Christology is a SYSTEMATIC study. In any system, one part does not contradict another for each statement is interlocked with all the others. If a contradiction is accepted, then the system crashes. Christology must, therefore, weigh its statements, not only against other theological conclusions but also against the findings of other disciplines. Christology cannot tolerate absurdities, square circles. Christology is systematic, well-ordered.

An essential element of this "system" is the on-going life, teaching and worship of the christian community. Since faith is essentially ecclesial, inserting us into the Body of Christ, the christian theologian does not theologize outside the ecclesial community of which he/she is a member. Otherwise, the reflections would be nothing more than subjective insights, as excellent as they may be. In reflecting on christological faith within the context of the community's faith in Jesus, the parameters set by the Spirit-filled community must form part of this "system." Another way of stating this point is to declare that christian theology is essentially related to the teaching office (magisterium) of the church and must recognize the life, teaching and liturgy of the christian community as part of the "system." It must be noted that "theology does not thereby lose its critical function with regard to the Church and its life of faith. Indeed, it is only because it is an ecclesiastical science and hence an element of the Church itself that theology can and must exercise its function as the Church's self-criticism, the constantly renewed effort to purge the faith from all that is merely human and questionable or historically transient."[1]

Since the faith of the community is necessarily linked to the historical word of divine revelation, theology is necessarily dependent on Scripture/Tradition. Scripture/Tradition form, therefore, part of the "system." It may be well to underline from the outset that Tradition is the life, teaching and worship of the Christian community which flows from the word of God (which is the Tradition of the early christian community committed to writing) and which, in turn, clarifies and elucidates the depth of meaning of the word of God.

Theology is not, therefore, the compilation of conclusions reached by strict philosophical reasoning processes or by what can be strictly deduced in syllogistic fashion from the word of God. Thanks to the indwelling Spirit of truth, the word of God flowers in ways which defy strict syllogistic logic. The Immaculate Conception and the Assumption are two evident examples of this reality, for they blossom from the Scriptures actualized through the living faith of the community standing under the word of God. The roots of these dogmas are firmly embedded in the word of God; the actual flowering is through the mysterious power of the Spirit who animates the Church.[2] The theologian, must, of course, carefully scrutinize these "flowerings" distinguishing what may be only cultural and ephemeral from what is truly of the fabric of the faith.

Although theologians differ concerning the essentials of the "system" and the role these elements play, nonetheless, ecclesial theology would appear to demand the points outlined above. To ignore these aspects of the "system" is to place oneself

Inexhaustible Presence

outside the community and turn theology into a "wayward spirituality of the individual."[3]

4. Finally, the contemporary world situation calls for christology. It can, therefore, be termed a NECESSARY study. In today's fearful, questioning times, each one instinctively although for the most part implicitly reflects upon his/her faith. So that healthy questioning does not become a hodgepodge of emotions, hearsay and cynicism, reflection upon ultimate concern should be done critically and systematically, utilizing all the advantages of modern scholarship. In other words, the situation of today's world whose future appears to open up to an atomic wasteland, demands that each one, in varying manners and degrees, be a theologian. To ignore this study enfeebles one's belief and withdraws it from daily living, thereby increasing the danger of either discarding the faith for childish reasons or desperately holding on to it like a voodoo charm.

An unreflecting faith does not relate to the questions of the age in a meaningful way. No wonder that many today would hold that christianity belongs in a museum. And some practicing christians would hold that religious faith does belong in a special (artificial?) compartment of life, divorced from this scientific age, separated, for all practical purposes, from day-to-day human experiences. An unreflecting faith can all too easily become a placebo (some would call it opium) taken at regular/irregular intervals to calm us down in this nervous nuclear age.

The theologian strenuously fights against such a schizophrenic stance. As a critic of the faith, he/she is not out to destroy the faith but to elucidate it in terms which are new, beautiful, original, lived-out and understandable. A theologian is stereophonic: one ear constantly alert to the community's understanding of the faith, the other ear attentive to the needs and mindset of the times. In this border situation, balance does not come automatically nor without healthy personal struggle.

The nature and necessity of theology will become more apparent as this study unfolds. For the believer, it will prompt healthy questioning about Jesus as the center of meaning; for the non-believer, it will not only clarify some questions about Jesus, who in various ways has such influence upon this world, but it will also be an incentive to examine one's own ultimate concern.

A final word before the first chapter begins. Take a risk and open yourself to serious, formal reflection on faith in Jesus Christ. Isn't all life "risk-taking?" In theological jargon, "raise the question," the question which many call the most important of the day, a question which is being scrutinized by more people of all ages than ever before: "Who is Jesus?" If you are hesitant to undertake this study then how strong is your faith or how strong is your non-belief? Or how can one be called educated if he/she fails to study — and on this point it would be hard to find a scholar who would disagree — the person who has the greatest impact upon this world?

SECTION ONE
INTRODUCTION TO THE GOSPEL PORTRAITS

CHAPTER ONE
THE EXISTENCE OF JESUS

The question which should be broached is a fundamental one: is it possible that Jesus never existed?[1] With what grounds can it be said — or not said — that a man named Jesus actually did live? After all, could he not be a fairytale, an invention of the human mind yearning for an ideal human being? Or could he not be a *literary form*, i.e., a neat piece of literature describing love of God and neighbor by personifying this love and calling the personification by a name: Jesus? How many reasons can be raised which would make the reality of Jesus' existence questionable?

In this first chapter of christology, some reasons will first be presented to substantiate the belief that Jesus did NOT exist,[2] followed by some arguments which appear to uphold the existence of Jesus of Nazareth. The conclusion, of course, will be yours.

ARGUMENTS DENYING THE EXISTENCE OF JESUS

William Benjamin Smith, writing in 1927 concerning the authenticity of the Gospels, declares: "The story of Jesus, is therefore, an idealization of the destiny of the nation of Israel in its universal inclusiveness."[3] There never was a Jesus; he is a personification, an idealization of many facets of personal or communitarian dreams for the perfect human being.

Some rather imposing arguments can be mustered up to support this thesis. To mention but a few:

There are no written records concerning Jesus until the letters of Paul of Tarsus (+ 67?). The earliest of these mostly off-the-cuff epistles dates from the early fifties of the first century of the Christian era (the two letters to the Christians of Thessalonika). As far as the Gospels are concerned — which deal with the life of Jesus far more than Paul ever does — there are even later dates, starting at about 67 A.D. for the Gospel of Mark, and ending at about the year 95 A.D. for the Gospel of John.[4] There existed, therefore, a rather prolonged period of ORAL tradition about Jesus before these stories were ever put into writing. For if Jesus dies somewhere around 33 A.D., there is a long time-spread (20 years? 30 years?) before anyone wrote anything down about the so-called Jesus. Should not this fact alone make us doubt the existence of Jesus? After all, when a story is passed around the office or school, within a few days it is unrecognizable! Is it not possible (probable?) that Jesus is an invention which began innocently/maliciously and took on credence as the years went by?

There are also contradictions among the Gospels. Try to outline a chronology of the life of Jesus. For the most part, an impossible task. Try to discover the precise words of Jesus. At least for the most part, beyond scholarly competence, for the divergences are too great. For example, how are we to know if the Ascension of Christ into heaven took place near Jerusalem (the south of Israel) or in Galilee (the north of Israel)? Luke opts for Jerusalem, Matthew for the north. And as far as the words of Jesus are concerned, even the ONE prayer which Jesus is said to have taught his disciples — the *Lord's Prayer* — is found in two rather different versions:

one in Luke, (chapter eleven, verses two to four — or as it ordinarily written, 11:2–4) another in Matthew (6:9–13). Many examples of these differences among the Gospels can be easily discovered. Moreover, try to compare the Gospel of Mark (or Matthew or Luke) with that of John. The divergences are so great that some ask if John is describing the same Jesus whom we meet in Mark's Gospel.[5] There is no Agony in the Garden in John's Gospel, no cry of dereliction from the cross; the Johannine Jesus is never taken by surprise, and his words — so simple in Mark's Gospel (cf. chapter four) — are elegant discourses according to John (cf. chapters 14–17).

Moreover, it is apparent that the Gospels portray a primitive world view. Mark is chock-filled with exorcisms. Devils abound who cry out acknowledging that Jesus is the *Son of God*. Jesus raises people from the dead, changes water into wine, walks on the lake, feeds thousands and thousands with a few loaves of bread and a few fish. Many today cringe at the thought that such primitive stories would be considered historical. (How the miracles of Jesus are understood by contemporary christology will be seen in chapter sixteen.) Not only do the genealogies of Jesus as found in Matthew (1:1–17) and Luke (3:23–38) disagree, but Luke actually traces Jesus' ancestors back to Adam himself, "the son of God."

The question does not deal with the possibilities of discovering the *real* Jesus. The query is much more basic: did he or did he not exist. The contradictions within the Gospels, its primitive world view, its long period of oral tradition and a host of similar examples bring G. Wells to the conclusion that ". . . the rise of Christianity can, from the undoubtedly historical antecedents, be explained quite well without him; and reasons can be given to show why, from about A.D. 80 or 90, Christians began to suppose that he had lived in Palestine about fifty years earlier."[6]

ARGUMENTS SUPPORTING THE EXISTENCE OF JESUS

For the time being, any biblical support for the thesis that Jesus did exist will be put aside. Our focus is on one point: the evidence in non-biblical writings for the existence of Jesus.

First the Roman documents will be examined, then the writings of the Jewish historian, Flavius Josephus and finally, the Talmud. The three Roman "witnesses" ordinarily brought forward to attest to the existence of Jesus are Pliny the Younger, Tacitus and Suetonius.

The Roman Documents

PLINY THE YOUNGER. Writing to the Emperor Trajan about the year 110 A.D., Pliny, the governor of Bithynia, a Roman province on the coast of the Black Sea, asks his superior what he is to do with a band of people called Christians whose influence is so strong that many temples of the gods were being abandoned. About eighty years, therefore, after the death of Jesus, Pliny not only admits to the great number of believers in this new religion but also adds these strange words about Christians in his letter to the Emperor:

"Carmen Christo quasi deo se invicem cantant."

Which means that the Christians are singing back and forth among themselves (innocent enough!) — singing a hymn to Christ as if he were god (not so innocent according to the governor!). Pliny requests information from Rome concerning what action he should take.[7]

The existence of someone called the Christ is presumed, although the practices of this new religion mentioned by Pliny reveal nothing about the life of Jesus. The text is directly a proof of the rapid spread of Christianity and its tenet concerning the divinity of Jesus.

SUETONIUS. In his well-known *Lives of the Twelve Caesars,*[8] this Roman historian, a contemporary of Pliny, speaks of the expulsion of the Jews from the city of Rome under the reign of Claudius who ruled from about 41–54 A.D. The reason for this action of Caesar is because: "the Jews were constantly making disturbances at the instigation of Chrestus."

It is commonly agreed that Suetonius is referring to "Christ" (using the Latin form of the Greek *Christos*) and probably attesting to the fact that many a Jewish community was the scene of heated discussion concerning Jesus as the Christ, i.e., the Messiah. Again, the existence of Jesus is not contested, although the basic thrust of Suetonius' statement is that as early as 49 A.D. there was a group of followers of Jesus among the Jewish community in Rome.

TACITUS. *The Annals of Tacitus* (+117?) has a rather lengthy section on the burning of Rome during the reign of Nero.[9] While vividly narrating the fire which destroyed so much of the city, Tacitus writes:

"(Nothing) could dispel the belief that the fire had taken place by order i.e., of Nero. Therefore, to scotch the rumor, Nero substituted as culprits and punished with the utmost refinements of cruelty, a class of men, loathed for their vices, whom the crowd styled Christians. Christus, the founder of the name, had undergone the death penalty in the reign of Tiberius, by sentence of the procurator Pontius Pilate."

Tacitus then paints a literary picture of Nero holding a cocktail party in his gardens with impaled, tarred Christians aflame, serving as illumination. However, this Roman historian — who presumably had access to official documents — does declare that the Christ was executed during the reign of Tiberius, when Pontius Pilate was procurator of Judaea, probably about the year 29 A.D.

So much for Roman documents. Although Pliny and Suetonius attest only indirectly to the existence of Jesus, the historian Tacitus directly states that the Christ, i.e., Jesus, definitely lived and gives the time of his execution. It is improbable that Tacitus, considered a true historian, is merely repeating rumors that he heard from the Christian rabble, although that possibility cannot be ruled out. The texts, in the final analysis, are of questionable value as a strict "proof" that Jesus existed. Nonetheless, it is fair to say that it is at least the "solid presumption" of the documents. Howard Clark Kee goes even further in his analysis of the value of these quotes from Roman authorities: "The writings of the Roman historians are, however, important evidence for Jesus' existence as a historical person: They show that non-Christian historical writers, and by inference their audiences, believed Jesus to have existed, and that they considered his death and his continuing influence after death to be significant enough to rate a few brief sentences."[10]

THE JEWISH HISTORIAN, FLAVIUS JOSEPHUS

There is one other historian around the time of the New Testament who speaks of the existence of Jesus: the famous Jewish author, Flavius Josephus, who died at the end of the first century.

Josephus, although at first a reluctant leader in Galilean skirmishes against the Roman invaders, became a *quisling* when he saw that there was no hope of victory over the armies of Titus and Vespasian who ultimately did conquer the Holy City, Jerusalem, in 70 A.D. Often regarded as a traitor to his country, Flavius (his adopted Roman name) Josephus never betrayed his Jewish heritage and beliefs. His writing (in Greek) on the history of his people, called *The Antiquities of The Jews,*[11] twice refers to Jesus; sometimes these references are called "the shorter quote" and the "longer quote." The longer quote contains surprising details:

"Now, about this time (*Josephus is speaking about Pilate, so the "time" would be approximately 26–36 A.D.*) there lived Jesus, a wise man, if indeed one ought to call him a man. For he was a doer of wonderful works, a teacher of people who accept the truth gladly. He won over to himself many Jews and many of the Greeks. He was the Messiah. When Pilate, upon hearing him accused by men of the highest standing among us, had condemned him to be crucified, those who had come to love him did not give up their affection for him. On the third day he appeared to them restored to life, as the holy prophets of God had foretold these and ten thousand other marvelous things about him. And the group of Christians, so called after him, has still to this day not disappeared."[12]

The quote has some intrinsic difficulties. First, how could Josephus, a Jewish believer, call Jesus the Messiah? And how could Josephus the Jew speak of the resurrection ("he appeared to them restored to life")? There is no evidence whatsoever that Josephus himself held that Jesus was the Christ. Quite the contrary.

Another point which must be considered in evaluating this "longer" quote. Who would be copying the manuscripts of Josephus? The Jews? Would an American bother with the writings of Benedict Arnold? Who, then, would show such interest in Flavius Josephus to go to the labor and expense of copying his works? The Christians are a possible, if not likely answer. And would it not be possible (likely?) that a Christian copyist would attempt to clarify some of Josephus' ambiguous statements about Jesus?

This "longer quote" of Josephus probably does contain direct reference to Jesus, whose existence is never doubted by this Jewish historian. Although it is possible that Josephus is merely narrating the views of Christians and not professing them,[13] it does appear that the details, e.g., "He was the Messiah," are probably a Christian addition or clarification of an ambiguous statement. Yet the point remains: Josephus in no way denies the existence of Jesus; rather, he affirms it.[14]

The "shorter quote" gives no indication of any Christian interpolation.

". . . so he assembled the Sanhedrin of the Judges and brought before them the brother of Jesus who was called Christ, whose name was James. . ."[15]

In speaking about James, a relative of Jesus highly regarded by the Jewish population of Jerusalem, Josephus mentions the relationship between James and Jesus in order to identify James. Which does imply that Jesus is well-known, and a reference to him could be made with no need of further clarification. Although giving us no information concerning Jesus, Josephus' "shorter quote" again is evidence that Jesus truly existed. Kee aptly concludes: "There is no hint here of a Christian interpolation, which adds more weight to this as an important historical allusion and renders untenable the allegation that Jesus was a fictional figure invented by the Christians. Since mention of Jesus at this point in his narrative serves only to identify James and contributes nothing substantial to his account, Josephus certainly leaves his readers with the impression that Jesus is a historical person. . ."[16]

The Talmud

The Talmud is the complex compilation of the ORAL law of the Jewish people as opposed to the WRITTEN law, the Scriptures. The two divisions of the Talmud are the MISHNAH[17] (the text of the oral law) and the GEMARA (a commentary on the Mishnah, which in a sense, it supplements). The codification of the *Mishnah*, which comprises statements of rabbis of the first two centuries A.D., took place under Rabbi Judah ha Nasi in the third century. The Talmud of Jerusalem — the oral law plus the commentaries of rabbinic scholars of Palestine — dates from about the fifth century, the Talmud of Babylon (three times the length of the Palestinian Talmud and which has become the authoritative work) dates from about the sixth century; it contains the oral law plus commentaries by the renowned rabbinic scholars of Babylon.

Joseph Klausner, author of *Jesus of Nazareth,* summarizes in his well-known statement the earliest strata of tradition concerning Jesus (probably dating from the third century) found in the Babylonian Talmud:

"There are reliable statements to the effect that his name was Yeshu'a of Nazareth; . . . he 'practised sorcery' (i.e., performed miracles) and beguiled and led Israel astray; . . . he mocked at the words of the Wise (the officially sanctioned interpreters of the Law); . . . he had five disciples; . . . he was hanged (crucified) as a false teacher and beguiler on the eve of the Passover which happened on a sabbath. . ."[18]

Other sections of the Talmud, understandably polemical in character, state that Jesus was the illegitimate son of an adulteress — a hairdresser named Miriam — by a Roman soldier, Panthera. (Could this be an allusion to the claimed virginal conception, since Panthera may be a corruption of the Greek term for virgin, *parthenos*?) Later on, often impelled by anti-semitism of so-called Christians, some Jewish works went to great lengths to discredit Jesus. However — and this is the important fact — never does the Talmud deny his existence (it rather supports it) or fundamental facts connected with his life, like his ministry of preaching, of healing, and his final execution.

From this brief survey of non-biblical historical sources, it appears legitimate to conclude that Jesus actually did exist. The objections mentioned in the first segment deal more with the possibility of penetrating into the personality of Jesus than with the existence of Jesus itself.

Summary

It is academically sound to accept the reality of the existence of Jesus. Even if the Gospels were never written, this conclusion would still stand firm.

HOWEVER, this does present a more serious problem: what can be known about Jesus? Little from the non-biblical sources, as we have seen. What can be known about Jesus in the New Testament? Can this series of pamphlets be termed HISTORICAL, i.e., do they deal with events which actually occurred? Or should they generally be called HISTORIC, i.e., their teachings are significant yet abstraction is to be made whether the narratives/sermons actually took place or not?[19] Jesus himself is historical and historic: he actually lived and his life has resounding significance for humanity. However, as one example among many, is the raising of Lazarus from the dead historical? Or is it a *parable-miracle* created by the early Christians to show that Jesus is Life, and therefore the incident can be called historic (it has great significance) but not historical (it actually never happened)? Generally speaking, the East would consider both the historical and historic *real*; however, western thought with its insistence on the scientific, makes a clear distinction between a *story* and a *fact*. How much of the Gospels can be termed historic yet not historical? Is it even possible to discover? And more importantly, of what value are the Gospels in describing Jesus? The next chapter will begin to deal explicitly with the question.

CHAPTER TWO

THE TRUSTWORTHINESS OF THE GOSPELS

In the first chapter arguments were brought forward to demonstrate, first of all, that Jesus did NOT exist; these reasons were countered with evidence that Jesus actually did live around the time when Pontius Pilate was procurator of Judaea. Christology is not the study of a mythological character, of an invention of the human mind, of a projection of the spirit's search for the ideal man. By no means. On this point there is no need to quibble: Jesus definitely existed.

If modern calculations are correct, Jesus is born sometime around 6 B.C. It does sound strange that Jesus Christ is born six years before Christ; however the monk who invented our calendar (dating from the time of Christ and not from the founding of the city of Rome) miscalculated. Herod the Great probably dies around 4 B.C.; Jesus is born shortly before the death of Herod, so 6 B.C. is a good guess. The date on which Mary gave birth to Jesus is unknown.

BUT the question remains: WHO is he? What can we know about him?

The non-Christian sources examined in the last chapter disclose precious little about WHO he is; certainly not enough to give anyone the right to describe his character, personality development, etc. Anyone interested in the study of Jesus is, therefore, forced to go to the only other source possible: the New Testament of the Bible, especially those booklets which deal more explicitly with the words and deeds of Jesus: the four Gospels: Matthew, Mark, Luke and John.

Theological honesty now demands that a critical question be raised: CAN WE TRUST THE SCRIPTURES? Or to be more precise, can it truly be said that the Gospels do present an authentic picture of Jesus? In this chapter some of the principal problems connected with the trustworthiness of the Gospels will be examined. Reasons will be brought forward to support the opinion that the Gospels are *not* an authentic picture of Jesus. After a study of the history of this question in chapters three and four, several points which uphold the authenticity of the Gospel portraits will be probed in chapter five. It the reader's task to weigh all sides carefully before coming to any conclusion.

PROPOSAL: The Gospels Do Not Present A True Picture of Jesus

SOME of the reasons which appear to substantiate the opinion that the Gospels are not faithful witnesses to the so-called *real* Jesus would include the following:[20]

The Period of Oral Tradition

First of all, the long period of *oral* tradition must be seriously considered. If Jesus dies about the year 30 A.D. and the Gospel of Mark is dated at about 67 A.D., there is quite a L O N G period of oral tradition before the stories about Jesus were put into writing. News about Jesus circulated by word of mouth, not in any published form. The time of oral tradition can well be called *the tunnel period* and it appears to be a dark one at that.

At the beginning of the tunnel stands the JESUS OF HISTORY. But at the end of the tunnel, the CHRIST OF FAITH. The difference? The *Jesus of History* is usually identified as the earthly Jesus, the itinerant Jewish preacher who lived for about 35 years, two millennia ago and who was crucified under Pontius Pilate as a revolutionary of sorts. Whether or not this is the meaning of *The Historical Jesus* will be seen in following chapters but for the time being we can stay with the general understanding of the term.

The Christ of faith? He is the INTERPRETED JESUS, or the GOSPEL JESUS, the PROCLAIMED JESUS — the Jesus found in the pages of the New Testament. Is the Christ of faith the Jesus of History? Does not the long period of oral transmission force us to answer with a resounding NO?

How would it ever be possible to preserve the *real* earthly Jesus among generally illiterate people over a period of about 40 years? Even in this computer age, a story can be totally twisted around within a few minutes as news circulates in an office or a home. How much more would the news about Jesus be distorted in a society which had no TV, no newspapers, no evening news, no computers. Does not honesty demand an admission that for the most part, the REAL Jesus (the Jesus who walked the streets of Galilee) is lost and that the Gospels (the Christ of Faith) are exaggerated, story-filled accounts of a simple Jewish preacher?[21] The conclusion is that the long period of oral tradition in the generally illiterate society of the times is the first reason why the Gospels cannot be trusted as an authentic picture of Jesus.

Contradictions within the Gospels

The contradictions within the Gospels themselves form the second reason why the Gospels cannot be used as a reliable source for christology. It would be well nigh impossible to list all the contradictions found in the Gospels. A few will be mentioned; many more can be found by just skimming through the pages of the New Testament.

Profound contradictions between Matthew, Mark & Luke (called *synoptics* because they generally see Jesus from the same *optic,* i.e., point of view) and the Gospel of John:

— Did Jesus go up to Jerusalem once during his ministry (synoptics) or several times (John)?

— Was Jesus executed on Passover (synoptics) or on the eve of the Passover (John)?

— Was Jesus the preacher of long, elegant discourses (John) or the preacher of simple, folksy sermons (generally the synoptics).

— John puts great importance on the resuscitation of Lazarus; the synoptics do not even mention it.

— The synoptics attribute ignorance of some things to Jesus (e.g., Mark 13:32: Jesus admits he does not know the time of the end of the world); never in John's Gospel is he even taken by surprise.

Profound contradictions among the synoptics (Matthew, Mark and Luke) themselves:

— Did the Ascension take place outside Jerusalem (Luke) or on a hill in Galilee (Matthew)?

— The first two chapters of both Matthew and Luke deal with the infancy narratives concerning Jesus. They contradict each other as a perusal of these chapters demonstrates.

— What is the exact version of the Lord's Prayer, the only prayer Jesus taught the disciples? Luke and Matthew do not agree.

— The Easter appearances as given in the Gospels are impossible to harmonize. If they can be arranged in a chronological, historical order, a feat has been accomplished which excels the capabilities of the most erudite scholars.

The contradictions among the Gospels form the second reason which can be given to substantiate the thesis that the Gospels cannot be a valid source for christology.

The Gospels Are Propaganda Literature

Thirdly, are not the Gospels propaganda literature? The Gospels are produced by

BELIEVERS who openly state that one of the reasons they are writing is to entice people to believe (Jn 20:31). The Gospels are therefore not the product of a cool, objective, academic mind. They have been composed by people (whose actual identity is uncertain) filled with burning zeal for Jesus and determined to bring others into faith in Christ. Should propaganda literature be believed?

The very nature of the Gospels — written by believers to make others believe — surely raises the question of the validity of using the Gospels in an academic study of Jesus.

The Progressive Enhancement of the Person of Jesus

There is, also, a progressive enhancement of the person of Jesus as we move chronologically from one Gospel to another.

— The Jesus of Mark's Gospel is called "beside himself" (Mk 3:21) which means that his family thought him to be out of his mind. Even though Matthew and Luke apparently depend upon Mark's Gospel as a principal source of their own writings, they will polish up the picture of Jesus and omit this bold realism of Mark. By the time John's Gospel is composed, it appears that Jesus does not even touch the ground when he walks.

— Another example of this progressive enhancement of Jesus is found in the story of the rich young man who in Mark's Gospel, after calling Jesus "Good Teacher," hears the reply from Jesus: "Why do you call me good?" (Mk 10:19). Matthew will tone down the response of Jesus in order to enhance Jesus' person: "Why do you ask me about what is good?" (Mt 19:17). Quite a difference. And in John's Gospel, written at the end of the first century, Jesus is actually called "God" (Jn 1:2; 20:28) which never occurs in the synoptics.

The evident progressive enhancement of the person of Jesus from the earliest Gospel, Mark, to the latest Gospel, John, also raises serious questions concerning the possibility of using the Gospels as academic sources for an insight into Jesus.

The Primitive Culture of Jesus' Time

The Gospels are written in a non-scientific age. Devils appear to be prowling everywhere in Mark's Gospel; sickness was thought to be caused not by germs but by wrongdoing, culpable or not; the world was believed to be flat, supported by pillars plunged deep into the muddy bottom, the sky an inverted plastic cup (the *firmament*) from which dangled stars, sun, moon; rain was produced when God (who sits above the firmament) opens the sluices and lets the torrents flow. Without a scientific support, it is easy to see how wild stories — so some would say — like multiplication of loaves of bread, walking on water, virginal conception, could be invented and believed.

The non-scientific age in which the Gospels were written is an additional reason to doubt the validity of using the Gospels as solid sources in christology.

Summary

The long period of oral tradition, the contradictions among the Gospels, the preaching character of the Gospels, the progressive enhancement of the person of Jesus from one Gospel to another, the non-scientific age in which the Gospels were composed, have led many people to the conclusion that the Gospels cannot be trusted as a source for an authentic christology.

Are there additional reasons? Are all the reasons adduced logical? Are there some reasons why the Gospels can be used as valid, academic sources for the study of Jesus?

CHAPTER THREE

THE QUEST OF THE HISTORICAL JESUS:
THE OLD QUEST AND THE NO QUEST PERIODS

This third chapter of christology begins a short trip through history . . . a fascinating voyage through the human mind as it searches for an answer to a question raised during the *Age of the Enlightenment*: HOW RELIABLE IS THE NEW TESTAMENT IN PORTRAYING JESUS OF NAZARETH?

True, as we have seen, Jesus existed. But is that basically all that can be known about him? Previous chapters have pointed out that Roman and Jewish documents do not supply enough information to probe into the personality or character of Jesus. The only other possible source is the New Testament, and more specifically, the Gospels. But the last chapter demonstrated(?) that to claim the Gospels are reliable appears quite naive in today's scientific world.

When DID all this questioning arise concerning the historicity of the Gospels? Who instigated these doubts concerning the validity of the Gospels, claiming that they give us only an interpreted Jesus, embellished — so they say — with all sorts of mythological stories like incarnation, walking on water, rising from the dead and ascending into heaven like a modern-day rocket from Cape Canaveral?

No, we are not making a mockery out of scripture . . . A theological study has to be critically honest, examining all sides. To respond to the last chapter by merely saying:

> "Well, who cares, I just believe."

or by blurting out without any further investigation:

> "I always knew the Gospels were fake!"

is to abdicate rational thought which characterizes us as human beings. Does it show a hesitancy to examine the person of Jesus critically because of a fear of what the answer may be?

As surprising at it may seem, until the latter part of the 18th century, there actually was little doubt about the reliability of the Gospels: a LONG stretch of time. That there were problems concerning the picture of Jesus in the synoptics vs. the picture in John was recognized; that there were problems among the synoptics themselves was recognized. But for the most part, the problems were solved by *forced harmonies* or speaking of the *mystical/spiritual* sense of the Scriptures.

The forced harmonies abounded and still do in many books which are entitled *The Life of Jesus Christ*.[22] Usually one account of an event is accepted and others suppressed (for example, the date of the Last Supper, the number of times Jesus travels to Jerusalem) or an event is said to have occurred twice, e.g., the Ascension took place first in Jerusalem (Luke), and then there was another final appearance of Jesus up in Galilee (Matthew).

If the forced harmonies appeared evidently *too forced* then recourse was had to a *mystical/spiritual* meaning of the event. In other words, no need to become upset by the contradictions, since the event is but a symbol of a deeper mystical truth. A miracle of restoring sight to a blind man could mean, in this thought, the opening of the eyes of the spirit to the truths of the faith, actually having nothing to do with bodily seeing.[23] The early church itself was well aware of these differences in the

Gospel portraits of Jesus and searched for ways to reconcile the apparent contradictions.[24] But generally, there was absolutely no doubt that the Gospels are valid pictures of Jesus Christ.

How, then, did the question of the trustworthiness of the Gospels even arise? Centuries ago, studies were already being made of the various manuscripts of the Gospels especially since none of the original have survived, only numerous copies. This helped to produce a more faithful text. Then detailed studies were made of the Greek language in which the Gospels were written. This helped to produce a better understanding of the text.

However, at the end of the 18th century — in the Age of the Enlightenment — a number of SCHOLARS seriously challenged the traditional trust in the authenticity of the Gospel picture of Jesus. The scholarly QUEST OF THE HISTORICAL JESUS — the Jesus at the beginning of the tunnel — HAD BEGUN.

One of the more famous German Deists,[25] H.S. Reimarus (+ 1768), is considered the founder of the *Quest of the Historical Jesus*. A professor of oriental languages, he seems to have been a church-going man, respected by everyone. However, gnawing inside of him was the growing conviction that the Gospels were really the biggest hoax ever put over on humankind.

He secretly wrote thousands of pages to demonstrate his point. At his death, his wife discovered the papers and decided to hide them to preserve the good name of the family. However, another German deist, influential in the German Enlightenment, G. Lessing, was given the papers and published them anonymously as *The Wolfenbuttel Fragments* claiming that they were accidentally found in the back room of the library of the little town of Wolfenbuttel.

The opinion of Reimarus expressed in his work — filled with hate — is that Jesus is a political Messiah and a total failure. The disciples invented the resurrection and created the figure of Jesus whom we have in the Gospels. And thus we have the beginning of the QUEST OF THE HISTORICAL JESUS, or a an academic search for what westerners would call the REAL Jesus with all its implications concerning the reliability of the Gospels.[26]

We can conveniently divide this QUEST into three sections:

— The Old Quest (roughly, the 19th century)
— The No Quest (roughly the first half of our century)
— The New Quest (the stage of present study)

What follows is a schematic overview of this important search for the *Real Jesus*. Only by reviewing this material can we grasp how the Gospels are generally understood TODAY. We can then ask ourselves if the Scriptures can be employed as valid sources for christology. The study is also a fascinating insight in the development of human thought.

THE OLD QUEST: THE 19th CENTURY[27]

Characteristics

The Old Quest for the Historical Jesus is basically a German Protestant endeavor. The Gospels were studied with scholarly precision in the hopes of finding the "real Jesus" which would have the effect, so it was thought, of restoring the simple religion of Christianity without the accretions of dogmas and ecclesiastical formulas. Considering history as chronicle, facts and figures, the quest attempted to scour the Gospels to release the historical Jesus from the fetters of imposed beliefs which, they were assured, were to be found in the Gospels themselves and not only in later church formulations. This rediscovery of Jesus would mark the return to the simplicity of Christianity. The "original" Jesus would be again the norm of the christian faith and of its theological enterprise.

These studies were done by theologians of the greatest competence. Thanks to them, it is a generally accepted conclusion that Mark is chronologically the first Gospel; that Matthew and Luke depend upon Mark and that Matthew and Luke also had access to some other source since there is so much material in their Gospels which is common to them but not found in Mark. This hypothetical oral/written source is called: *Q*, probably from the German word for source, *Quelle*.[28] It was especially through a study of these two sources that the hoped-for *earthly* Jesus would reappear.

However, this search for the *real* Jesus turned out to be highly subjective: the Jesus discovered seems to personify the desires or the theological stance of the investigator.

Some Principal Characters

What ties the following theologians together is that they were involved in the energetic German theological movement of the 19th century. In one way or another they are bound up with the *Old Quest* even if it be by spurring the *Quest* on, in their defense of contrary views.

Friedrich Schleiermacher (+ 1834). This father of modern theology, founds theological investigation on a new basis, i.e., human experience. Religion is essentially feeling. But what Schleiermacher means by feeling is not that clear; he calls it "immediate intuition." Religion is this feeling of absolute dependence on God.[29] Who is Jesus? In keeping with his basic understanding of religion and with his Moravian pietistic background (and reducing a complicated response of Schleiermacher to a few words) it could be said that what is so special about Jesus is his unique "God-consciousness," his "experience" of God, which gained perfect control of his entire person.

Subjective experience was central for Schleiermacher and the effects of his teachings are still a strong element of theological speculation. Schleiermacher was more interested in the inspiration which Christ gives to the present, than he was in the historical Jesus. He is part of the *Romantic Movement* which produced geniuses like Beethoven, Chopin, Balzac, Byron. Not that the *Movement* was anti-Enlightenment but it did hope to broaden the view of humankind to include not only rational thought but also — and primarily — feeling, intuition. His influence is still profound within theology and the *questers* of the historical Jesus were affected by him even though Schleiermacher's interest was not with the Jesus of History — whom he felt was an unattainable goal — but with the present experience of him.

David F. Strauss (+ 1874). When 27 years old, David Strauss wrote his famous *Life of Jesus*.[30] He insists that the Gospels are a texture of myths, and that it is impossible to arrive at the *real* Jesus because of the inconstant oral tradition. Strauss does have in common with the *questers*, a disdain for any religious and dogmatic presuppositions and a desire to liberate Jesus from the legends with which his followers enveloped him.

Ludwig Feuerbach (+ 1872). For Feuerbach, God is the projection of human-kind's infinite self-consciousness. Feuerbach believed that human knowledge is limited to the empirical, the material; religion is nothing more than a "dream." Jesus *as found in the Gospels* is only a projection of man's natural hopes and psychological needs. Feuerbach's thought has played a major role in the thinking of K. Marx and

F. Engels not only concerning their social theories but also in their critique of Christianity.[31]

Ernest Renan (+ 1892). One of the few Catholics involved in this Old Quest, Renan declares that there is scarcely one page of history in all the Gospels put together. His *Life of Jesus* is a romantic fantasy of a simple, charming, attractive young man called Jesus who spoke of the Kingdom of God with deep emotion and feeling. Renan's *Life of Jesus* quickly went through ten editions and was translated into eleven languages.[32]

Adolph Von Harnack (1851–1930). One of the greatest of the Protestant Liberals of the late nineteenth century, Harnack was a specialist in the history of the early church. Early in his career he was acclaimed as an expert teacher, a superb organizer, a critical researcher. As an historian, he — like so many of the German Liberal theologians of the age — strove to liberate Jesus from the shackles of dogmatic "sophistry" and thereby come to the *real* Jesus. In his popular lecture series published as *What is Christianity*, Harnack considers Jesus as the preacher of the Fatherhood of God, the brotherhood of man and of the infinite value of the human soul.[33]

Albert Schweitzer (1875–1965). Many know of Albert Schweitzer as the great organist, the publisher of Bach's works, the famous medical doctor of Lambarene in French Equatorial Africa (present day Gabon). Yet his influence in theology is also renowned primarily because of his book, *The Quest of the Historical Jesus*. His work reviewed the results of the questers and, in fact, brought the *Old Quest* to an end. Analyzing the work of the great theologians who preceded him, Schweitzer reveals the high subjectivity in their writings and then he himself seems to fall into the same trap. His Jesus — stripped of all the garnish — is a man who came to believe that the Kingdom would come through him (he pictured Jesus as thoroughly permeated by an *apocalyptic* [end-time] view.) Yet, Jesus dies a failure in this sense that the end-time does not come with his crucifixion. It was the early church which then created a Jesus who would one day come at the end of the world. R. Bultmann maintains that for Schweitzer, "not only the preaching and the self-consciousness of Jesus but also his day-to-day conduct of life were dominated by an eschatological expectation which amounted to an all-pervading eschatological dogma."[34] His book was a clear indication that the nineteenth century attempt to find the *real* Jesus had not succeeded; it was apparently impossible to work through the tunnel and discover the Jesus who walked the streets of Galilee. For Schweitzer himself, the historical Jesus is no more than an enigma; what truly remains is his message of love.[35]

Many other theologians were also involved in this *Quest*. For example, Eisler declared that Jesus was a proletarian leader attempting to start a revolution against the Roman overlords of his time; Wrede believed that Jesus was the teacher of morality. Again, it was Albert Schweitzer who brought an end to this Old Quest by demonstrating how highly subjective all these *quests* were. Perhaps the works of these great men can be summed up by the famous quote of the English modernist, George Tyrrell (+ 1909): "The Christ that Harnack sees, looking through nineteen centuries of Catholic darkness, is only the reflection of a liberal Protestant face, seen at the bottom of a deep well."[36]

A Few General Conclusions

It is important to keep in mind that the *Old Quest* insisted that Jesus is truly an historical figure, even though so clouded in myth that his voice can scarcely be heard. Attempts to pierce the cloud proved to be failures. The first of the questers had attempted to push aside the proclamation of the Church in which Jesus is found. Their work proved that there was no way that the "purely historical" Jesus could be uncovered, not even through Mark and *Q* for even these early sources were already theological interpretations of Jesus. The *Historical Jesus* then is NOT a facts and figures, time and place historical object. First of all, he is a *person* and like all human beings is shrouded in mystery and cannot be treated as an "object." Secondly, the Gospels are faith proclamations concerning Jesus and although, as we will see, authentic portraits of Jesus, it is impossible to construct a "biography" of him. We can — as we will do — try to clear away the dust from the portraits and thereby clarify the portrait. But the Jesus of History can only be found in portraits done with the colors of the faith-filled interpretation of the early Church. The *Old Questers*, striving to eliminate the colors — the faith-interpretations of the church — destroyed the portrait itself and projected their own image into the Gospels. It becomes apparent that the authentic historical Jesus is mediated to us through the normative experiences of the early Church; that experience is continually mediated down the ages through the on-going experiences of those who encounter him and in dialogue with the scriptural portraits, let themselves be interpreted by him.[37]

THE NO QUEST PERIOD (roughly, the first half of the 20th century).

Characteristics

The *Old Questers* had tried — unsuccessfully — to work with the Gospels as historical documents in their attempt to arrive at an objective, "historical" Jesus. Their scholarly endeavors were marked by a disdain for the interpretations of the early church which are not only embedded in the portraits but which are the material of the portraits. Instead of the "proclaimed, interpreted Christ" they wanted the *real* Jesus. The subjective results of their work, creations which so often mirrored themselves, marked the entrance into the *No Quest* period. If the *Old Quest* had stressed the historical, the *No Quest* stresses the interpretation at the expense of the historical. Little if any interest is shown in historical data, in the Jesus at the beginning of the tunnel. It is the kerygmatic Christ — the proclaimed Christ, the Christ of the Gospels, the Christ at the "end of the tunnel" — who gives meaning to life, even if the facts narrated about him, like Incarnation, Resurrection, miracles are all myths. Coupled with a rejection of the "miraculous" was a growing change in the meaning of history. No historian is an impartial observer; rather, personal presuppositions are intrinsic to the study of the past. This resulted in despair about any possible historical study of Jesus who is known only in the interpretations of the early Church. There was no possibility for a *Quest of the Historical Jesus*; in fact, it was even wrong to attempt it since that would give a *foundation* to faith which in their opinion, destroys faith itself.

A general tenet of the *Old Quest* — to oversimplify — is that the object of Christian faith is NOT Jesus, but WHAT is proclaimed about him in the Gospels. The New Testament actually begins at Easter which is the interpretation in mythological terms of the Jesus-event; faith is a blind surrender. It should be noted that myth is generally understood by these scholars as a narrative-tool which speaks from and to the culture of the age, symbolically expressing a profound theological truth. For example, the virginal-conception can be called a myth in the sense that it is a narrative which symbolically expresses the profound truth that Jesus is unmerited, the gift of the Father to humankind. In speaking about the narrative-tool as myth, abstraction is made of its historicity; the stress is on the deep theological truth conveyed. It is another question to consider the historicity/non-historicity of the narrative tool, although myths are not generally considered to be historical. Someone could, however, theologically discuss the virginal conception as myth and strictly speaking, still uphold its historical and not only historic character although this is evidently not so in common parlance. The concept *myth* has been extensively studied in modern times and today has a variety of meanings; care must, therefore, be had when employing the term which is understood differently by different authors.[38]

Some Principal Characters

The principal character of the *No Quest* period is R. Bultmann. Mention should also be made of Dibelius, Schmidt, Kierkegaard, Barth, Tillich; however to examine the complex thought of all of these modern authors would be too extensive a task for our present endeavor and would take us far afield. We will briefly review the principal stance of R. Bultmann; a resume of the thought of the other early 20th century theologians can be found in *Modern Christian Thought* by James C. Livingston and in *Jesus Christ Through History* by Dennis C. Duling; a brief overview of this period is had in J. Kselman's article on "Modern New Testament Criticism" found in the *Jerome Biblical Commentary*, 41:32–63.

Rudolf Bultmann (1884–1976)[39]

Whether one agrees with him or not, it must be admitted that Rudolf Bultmann has exercised a profound influence on theology in this century. Not only christology but present day scripture studies especially are stamped, and probably indelibly, with aspects of his thought. The goal of Bultmann was not to destroy the scriptures or christology; rather, he wished to rescue them from the morass of subjectivism of his 19th century liberal professors. His hopes were to make the scriptures and especially, then, Jesus Christ, understandable and acceptable to modern men and women so that they could see that the Christ event alone can give them meaningful, *authentic* existence.[40]

Bultmann's positive attempt to "modernize" the scriptures and christology for contemporary society took him through the "negative" path of radical demythologization. It was his contention that the abyss separating today's world from the scriptures and Christ was the mythical understanding common in New Testament times and the enlightened scientific world view of our era. The abyss could only be bridged by demythologizing: stripping the scriptures of all mythological content and translating it all into existentialist terms. Bultmann's demythologization process did not only include cosmology (i.e., the structure of the universe), but also any aspect of the supernatural, any notion of pre-existence, incarnation, resurrection, the sacraments. Just as the world-view of the New Testament community was "mythical," equally so were their beliefs in the historical reality of the miracles, the redemptive incarnation, etc. He therefore shows little if any interest in the Jesus of history and would not be disturbed if the teachings attributed to him were really those of another person.[41] With this lack of interest in the personality of Jesus and insisting on the thrust of the teachings attributed to Jesus, Bultmann proves himself a true existentialist: ". . . the ideas (of Jesus) are understood in the light of the concrete situation of a man living in time; as his interpretation of his own existence in the midst of change, uncertainty, decision; as the expression of a possibility of comprehending this life, as the effort to gain clear insight into the contingencies and necessities of his own existence. When we encounter the words of Jesus in history . . . *they* meet *us* with the question of how we are to interpret our own existence."[42] Bultmann's demythologizing was coupled with a keen interest in "form criticism" (to be seen later) which is the study of the oral traditions concerning Jesus before they were put into writing.

Because of Bultmann's lack of concern for the person of Jesus, for the Jesus of History, it can be said that he is the founder of the *No Quest* period in the *Quest of the Historical Jesus*. His thought, as is evident, has profoundly affected modern understanding of scripture and of christology and of the christian faith itself. There is *much* to commend it: the insistence that the text of the word of God "interrogate us" which is a favorite theme of linguistic scholars today; his attempt to clarify the portraits of Jesus by pointing out the embellishments, adaptations which are intrinsic to them; his stress on integrating the Christ event with our lives so that we are truly changed. But there is also much in Bultmann's thought which is questionable: an unconscious arrogance in making what he believes to be contemporary scientific thought the paradigm through which he judges the "mythical" world of the New Testament, or as Rene Marle states it: "No doubt he rejects any idea of making modern man the measure of all things. Yet it is certainly on the basis of modern man, or more exactly of his rationalist illusions, that he defines and criticizes the allegedly mythical world of thought inhabited by the men of the NT."[43] Bultmann works from the presuppositions that miracles, incarnation, resurrection are all "myths" — basing himself on the contemporary scientific world view as he understands it. Is he truly permitting the text of scripture to "interrogate" him and perhaps divest him of some of his own presuppositions? Moreover, the entire demythologization process is extremely oversimplified: how is it possible to lump together the New Testament view that the world is flat with the belief of the followers of Christ that he is truly the Son of God? Because they may have a "mythical" view of the structure of the planet does not necessarily mean that they also have a "mythical" view of Jesus Christ. Finally, Bultmann appears to abhor any foundation for faith in Christ and therefore rejects any claims of "historicity" as prompting faith. He appears to be advocating an extreme form of Luther's "sola fide" (by faith alone) tenet.[44]

In an extreme form, demythologization can easily lead to *dekerygmatization* which ignores the *kerygma* — the saving proclamation of authentic existence by faith in Jesus Christ — and turns the scriptures into nothing more than another philosophy of existence, couched in mythical terms. Without a clear foundation in the PERSON of Jesus Christ who IS the victorious epiphany of God, the teachings of Jesus are up for grabs. It is precisely because Jesus IS the Lord that we see in him the meaning of life, the way to the Father in the power of the Spirit.

Summary

The Quest of the Historical Jesus has gone through several stages: the first sought for a Jesus whose words and deeds would be precisely known. The final conclusion was that the Jesus of History was so highly and freely interpreted by the early christians that the Jesus of the Gospels is but a faint shadow of the reality. The No Quest period stressed, therefore, the Gospel Christ, paying scant attention to any historical Jesus, claiming that the strictly historical facts concerning Jesus are few and far between in the Gospels and in reality play a minor role if any in christian faith. The scholars involved in these searches were highly competent and through their studies advanced the understanding of the Gospels and of christology.

The so-called No Quest Period lasted until the middle of the 20th century. Its conclusions led the way to a third stage, called *The New Quest of the Historical Jesus* which, although so diversely understood, is the stage of present day scholarship in christology. The nature of this New Quest and some of its possible ramifications are the subject of the following chapters.

CHAPTER FOUR

THE NEW QUEST OF THE HISTORICAL JESUS

It was Bultmann's disciples who brought an end to his *No Quest* and inaugurated the *New Quest of the Historical Jesus*. Since this is the present period of christology, it is difficult if not impossible to fully describe or analyze. Nonetheless, if we date the *New Quest* from W. Kasemann's 1953 assessment of his 'mentor', Bultmann, we can see certain directions already in place and others in formative stages which characterize this *New Quest*. We will, therefore, in this chapter briefly examine the following points in order get a handle on the current situation:

— The input of the post-Bultmannians to the New Quest.
— A critique of post-Bultmannian Thought.
— The divergent routes of present day Jesus research.

THE INPUT OF THE POST-BULTMANNIANS TO THE NEW QUEST

The contributions of the post-Bultmannians[45] — the disciples of Bultmann who inaugurated a new phase in the *Quest of the Historical Jesus* — form the core of the strictly so-called *new* quest. The following section will give an overview of their work which, in a certain sense, brought the *New Quest of the Historical Jesus* into such divergent routes that it can scarcely be called a specific movement in contemporary christology.

Broadening of the Historical Foundations

Kasemann's famous article, *The Problem of the Historical Jesus*,[46] is credited with inaugurating this *New Quest*. Kasemann went beyond Bultmann by stressing that there must be some type of identity between the Jesus of History and the Christ of faith; if there is none, then, Kasemann concludes, there is the serious danger of proclaiming a *non-historical* kerygma, no more than a fairytale. Secondly, Kasemann wondered out loud why, if the early Christians had no interest in the historical Jesus, did they even bother to write a Gospel. Surely they themselves firmly believed that the Jesus they were proclaiming was substantially identical with the Jesus who proclaimed the Kingdom. Finally, Kasemann expressed his opinion that the christian faith itself — an historical religion and not merely a set of moral teachings — demands some type of identity with the Jesus of History.

Kasemann was joined in this new quest by E. Fuchs[47] who extended the interest in historicity to the *deeds* of Jesus (Bultmann had stressed the *words* of Jesus) especially his effective love for the poor, for the sinners of the day. G. Bornkamm contributed to the movement by demonstrating that the authority of Jesus so highlighted in the Scriptures is an historical truth and not the product of the creative faith of the early christians.[48] An American post-Bultmannian, J. M. Robinson, in his *New Quest of the Historical Jesus* expressed the thought that there is some access to the "selfhood" of Jesus through a study of his lived-out commitments.[49] G. Ebeling, although primarily interested in the meaning of faith, also widened the elements of historicity in the teachings of Jesus.[50]

Basically, this *New Quest* declares that not only the teachings of Jesus are open to more extensive historical underpinning but also that the person of Jesus himself can to some degree be known. This surely exceeded the teaching of Bultmann who, as we have seen, showed little if any interest in the Jesus of History.

Criteria of Authenticity

The conclusion that there is a connection between the Jesus of History and the Christ of Faith, that there is far more historicity in the Gospels than Bultmann would claim, led to a search for *criteria of authenticity*, a set of rules by which one could distinguish the "authentic" Jesus from the accretions of the early Church.[51] The primary rule, already outlined by Kasemann in 1953, is termed the "principle of dissimilarity," i.e., what is distinctively different from Judaism and/or the early Church does stem from the historical Jesus. An example of this "rule" is Jesus' use of "Abba" (a study of ABBA will be seen later). This criterion of "dissimilarity" had others added to it, e.g, "multiple attestation," i.e., themes or concerns expressed in a variety of strata concerning Jesus are considered historical (example: Jesus' table-fellowship with the outcasts of the day); "consistency" i.e., material concerning Jesus which is consistent or generally in accord with the preceding criteria may also be considered authentic (example: Jesus' forgiveness of sinners); "Palestinian culture," i.e., what is NOT in accord with the language and environment of Jesus cannot be considered authentic. An example of this latter criterion is the explanation (called *allegorizing*) of the parable of the sower in Mk 4. Since it uses "ecclesiastical" language of the early Church it is not considered "authentic," i.e., it does not stem from Jesus but from the early Church. Others add what could be termed a "principle of embarrassment," i.e., what is embarrassing to the early Church may be considered authentic. Examples of this criterion would be Jesus' baptism by John the Baptist (Mk 1:9–11), his acknowledgment of ignorance (Mk 13:32).

If one or better several of these criteria are fulfilled by some Gospel words or events, they may, according to this system, be considered "authentic." Following J. Jeremias, *authentic* elements of the Gospel are divided into either *ipsissima verba* *(et facta)* (the precise words and deeds of Jesus) or the *ipsissima vox* (the precise voice — mind — of Jesus). For example, ABBA used by Jesus in the Agony in the Garden (Mk 14:36), would be considered among the rare "ipsissima verba," i.e., Jesus actually used that precise word at that precise time. His table-fellowship with Simon the leper (Mk 14:3) would be considered among the precise "ipsissima facta," i.e., Jesus actually did eat with Simon. The "ipsissima vox" is "a way of speaking preferred by Jesus" and we could add, a way of acting preferred by Jesus.[52] The general use of *Amen* at the beginning of a sentence is an "ipsissima vox," but we cannot say that *every* use of it by Jesus as narrated in the Gospels is an "ipsissimum verbum," — a genuine saying (Greek: *logion*) — i .e., in *every* instance where we find it on the lips of Jesus he actually said it; rather, it could very well be a "formation" by the church for that particular setting. Fellowship with the outcast is also a way of acting preferred by Jesus; however, it does not follow that every instance of Jesus' expression of love for the sick and the marginalized is a specific action which Jesus performed; it may be an embellishment of the early Christian community in keeping with Jesus' general attitude.

The New Hermeneutic

Two of the post-Bultmannians, G. Ebeling and E. Fuchs — prominent figures in the *New Quest* — are credited with developing what is termed the *New Hermeneutic*.[53] The Greek word, *hermeneuein*[54] means "to interpret." *Hermeneutike techne* means the art of interpreting, from which we derive the term "hermeneutics." The *New Hermeneutic* implies a new way of interpreting the Scriptures. The goal of this endeavor is not just *theory* — the traditional understanding of hermeneutics — but the practical interpretation of the text itself which makes the New Hermeneutic akin to exegesis.[55] More specifically, the New Hermeneutic first considers the formulation of the text and attempts to express it in a way that will have the clout and power of the original message of Jesus. Neither Ebeling nor Fuchs want to merely theorize concerning a text, to merely study it *academically*. They insist that true knowledge or understanding demands an integration of the text with the reader, or better still, that the text interpret the reader. The New Hermeneutic, therefore implies — and some say it explicitly — a criticism of scripture studies which are arid, abstract, with little if any personal involvement on the part of the scholar and little if any challenge to the reader to live the text.[56] Learning is not to be merely a head-trip; it must personally involve the experiences of scholar and student.

The New Hermeneutic disregards Descartes' theory of knowledge in which a person "looks out on the world as passive object."[57] In fact, the new hermeneutic turns Descartes' theory on its head. *The student is the object, not the textbook; the text grasps the person reading*. This is most evident in the Gospel parables: as the hearer or reader of the parable, the person enters the "world" of Jesus, finds a new vision of God and of the world which is shared with Jesus. The life of the reader is transformed by the word of God for the text interprets the student. For Fuchs this means especially the abandonment of self-assertion even to the point of death which is the repetition of Jesus' own decision to go the way of the cross and the way of love. There is a clear connection between the new hermeneutic and the new quest for the historical Jesus, for Fuchs is advocating that faith in Christ essentially means repeating Jesus' decision to abandon all self-assertion.

The new hermeneutic stresses the "performative" aspect of language, i.e., the scriptures actually change reality by their very proclamation, as the "I do" at a wedding ceremony changes reality by creating a permanent bond of union between man and woman.[58] For such a change to take place, the one who hears or reads the Gospel proclamation must be open to dialogue with the Good News and ready to be transformed by it.

A CRITIQUE OF THE POST-BULTMANNIAN NEW QUEST

We have examined three essential elements of the *New Quest* by seeing how they are developed by the post-Bultmannians: the broadening of the historical base for the words AND person of Jesus as found in the Gospels, the criteria for discovering authentic sayings of Jesus, and finally the New Hermeneutic. There are positive and negative elements in these three aspects of the New Quest:

Broadening of the Historical Foundations

To some degree the skepticism of Bultmann has been reduced by the new quest. In fact, at one point, Bultmann himself thought it time to intervene and respond to this broadening of the historical base of the kerygmatic Christ.[59] Generally speaking, the new questers have taken the principles of Bultmann and extended them to additional sections of the Gospels and to the person of Jesus himself. As welcome as this "opening" is, it is not much different from the stance of Bultmann. Keeping well within the Bultmannian camp, the new questers have discovered that there IS a connection between the Jesus of History and the Christ of Faith. While claiming that an encounter with Jesus was an eschatological encounter with God, the new questers share their mentor's skepticism concerning the central points of christology, the incarnation and resurrection. We do have an "advance" but we must be careful not to exaggerate the differences between Bultmann and the post-Bultmannians. The new quest as seen by the post-Bultmannians who inaugurated it is not a *major* shift from the thought of Bultmann. J. M. Robinson himself states in the preface to the latest edition of *A New Quest of the Historical Jesus* (a title which he calls an "afterthought"): "It was not intended to suggest the presumption latent in the current short title '*the* new quest.' Nor was it intended to ignore Rudolf Bultmann's *Jesus and the Word* . . . as a valid precursor. Rather the book argues that the kind of quest there exemplified, though not carried forward by Bultmann himself, was a possible and legitimate development of the Bultmannian position."[60]

Criteria of Authenticity

The criteria themselves are useful tools but no more than that. They are often ambiguous. For example, the principle of dissimilarity presupposes that the only authentic things Jesus said or did were neither in accord with Jewish culture nor that of the early Church. Yet Jesus is clearly a man of his times, definitely and clearly a Jew and it is to be expected that what he does is within the culture of his Jewishness and within the understanding and thought patterns of his Jewish religion. Jeremias aptly declares: "Indeed it has to be said that the way in which the criterion of dissimilarity is often used today as a password is a serious source of error. It foreshortens and distorts the historical situation, because it overlooks the continuity between Jesus and Judaism."[61] There also appears to be quite a degree of subjectivism in the criteria themselves and in their application which may be a reason why hardly two authors agree on the number and interpretation of these criteria. Within bounds, understanding that they have inherent limitations and can usually give no more than probability, these criteria prove useful in trying to clarify the scriptural portraits of Jesus. But in no way are these criteria air-tight. All things considered, it would appear more reasonable to state that it is NOT the authenticity of the *synoptic* sayings attributed to Jesus — in the sense of ipsissima vox — that needs to be demonstrated; rather it is the unauthenticity which has to be shown. Joachim Jeremias sums it up: ". . . we can say in conclusion that the linguistic and stylistic evidence . . . shows so much faithfulness and such respect towards the tradition of the sayings of Jesus that we are justified in drawing up the following principle of method: In the synoptic tradition, it is the inauthenticity, and not the authenticity, of the sayings of Jesus that must be demonstrated."[62]

Another problem connected with these criteria is the use of the technical term "authentic." As Ebeling remarks in another context, "The same word can be said in another time only by being said differently."[63] And for "ordinary people" the word *authentic* applied only to the "ipsissima verba"[64] and to the "ipsissima vox," gives the impression that only those sections of the New Testament are "true"; the rest are "false." The New Testament scholar does not intend this conclusion; yet for the "uninitiated" into the jargon of academia, "authentic" is not apt in a "popular" context because of the "it's not true" implications for the bulk of the Gospels which are not considered by the scholar to be ipsissima verba or ipsissima vox. The word "authentic" in this context is confusing and has led some to falsely accuse the scripture scholars of denying the *general authenticity* of the scriptural portraits of Jesus, especially since "there is no way to prevent ordinary people from becoming aware of the kinds of questions that are being asked in scholarship today; for whether the scholars consent or not, their views are picked up by the media and often sensationalized."[65] It would appear more in keeping with the mindset of "ordinary people" that the entire Gospel portraits be spoken of as "authentic," i.e., they present to us a "true" *portrait* of Jesus Christ. Within this portrait, as will be seen in more detail in the following chapters, there are many adaptations and embellishments by the early Christian community. Yet these church interpretations which form part of the Gospels are "authentic," in the sense of clarifying the person/ message of Jesus for a variety of communities. Just as the salvific truth content of the Scriptures "is not primarily quantitative (certain passages are salvific; others are not), but rather qualitative, that is, *all* the statements of the Bible are free from error *to the extent* that they convey the truth 'which God wanted to put into the sacred writings for the sake of our salvation',"[66] so too "authentic" should not be used quantitatively but qualitatively: *all* the Gospel portraits are authentic inasmuch as they present us with the *saving* Person and Message who is Jesus. In no way does this imply that there is no value in attempting to distinguish an original word/deed of Jesus from the embellishments and adaptations of the early Church; it is rather to insist that not only the ipsissima verba and the ipsissima vox are "true."

The New Hermeneutic

There are clear advantages in the teachings of the New Hermeneutic. Many welcome its insistence on the "experience" or integration of the text. As a theory of knowledge, it also has its plus factors, insisting that learning is not the accumulation of facts and figures but an effective dialogue with the subject matter. Thiselton well says: "Moreover as he (i.e., *the reader*) 'listens' to the text he will not be content only to use stereotyped sets of questions composed by others but will engage in a continuous dialogue of question and answer until his own original horizons are creatively enlarged."[67] (Which is why a set of "canned" questions at the end of every chapter can never be more than a help in formulating our own dialogue with the text; at times they do more harm than good, restricting the student to one specific route of thought.)

Yet the New Hermeneutic also has its shortcomings. Although Fuchs and Ebeling insist on solid academic work, the stress is clearly on the *experiential* side of learning to a point where some have taken an either/or position: either academic study OR experience. The answer is not an either/or but a BOTH. The New Hermeneutic can imply a move away from information, knowledge, in exchange for an emphasis on participation, engagement and experience at the expense of content. Moreover, as Thiselton points out, Fuchs and Ebeling base their understanding of the power of the text to transform us on what could be called a "magical" theory of language: words have a psychic power of their own and so carry out what is spoken.[68] The true basis for the *performative* aspect of the scriptures, i.e., they accomplish what they signify, is because they are, in Christian thought, God's word (cf. Is 55:10–11). Moreover, the New Hermeneutic appears to disregard the serious question of ascertaining whether or not one's "experience" of the text is within the boundaries of legitimate Christian experience. The result can be highly subjective. The word of God as mediated through the life of the community also sets parameters for an authentic experience of the bible; not everything that one personally "integrates" from the scriptures is necessarily correct.[69]

THE DIVERGENT ROUTES OF THE NEW QUEST

The New Quest of the Historical Jesus has lost any clearly delineated direction. Dennis Duling, after reviewing the situation, comments: "With the 'new quest,' much of the discussion within the Bultmannian camp reached a stalemate; new studies are being written, but they are either not concentrating on the historical Jesus or are taking altogether new directions."[70] William Thompson, basing himself on David Tracy's thought, sees the "Quest" as serving "as a kind of contemporary reformulation of the kerygma itself, if it is done in such a way that it surfaces the substantial identity and continuity between the historical Jesus and the Christ of the New Testament kerygma."[71] This is not something wholly negative: the "Quest" may very well have completed its *specific* task of clarifying the relationship of the Jesus of History to the Christ of Faith. In fact, there appears to be, thanks to the *Quests*, a general consensus on fundamental issues concerning the role of scripture in the study of christology. Basically, there is agreement that there is substantial oneness between the Christ of Faith and the Jesus of History: the Christ of Faith is the interpreted, proclaimed Jesus of History, seen in the light of his resurrection and in light of the different needs of diverse audiences. No biography strictly so called is possible, since the followers of Jesus were not very interested in precise, historical time/place categories or in any description of the psychological growth of Jesus or in many of the other ingredients essential for the literary genre "biography." Their interest was in Jesus as the personal "salvific truth" of the Father; this was proclaimed through adaptations and embellishments of the words and deeds of Jesus seen in the hindsight of the resurrection and in the light of the needs of the audience. Moreover, it is generally recognized that the attempt to eliminate the "Christ of Faith" for the newly-discovered pure and simple "Jesus of History" is impossible. To throw out the one is to throw out the other. The biases of the early questers is also generally recognized for they began with the conviction that all dogmas had to be destroyed, that miracles are incredible in this scientific age, etc. And most importantly of all, there appears to be general agreement that the norm for christian faith is not a facts and figures, time and place Jesus of History, but the proclaimed Jesus — the kerygmatic Christ — as authentically mediated by the continued experience of the Christian community.

With a broadly based agreement on these fundamental issues, it is understandable that the *new quest* has for the most part taken on a wider meaning: the attempt to clarify for modern men and women the scriptural portraits of Jesus the Christ as mediated down through the ages in the Christian community. In this way, a response is given to the yearnings and needs of this beleaguered contemporary world. In order to achieve this goal, christology studies Jesus in a variety of ways. Although there must be specialists for these various fields, an overall contemporary understanding of Jesus should involve at least the following factors:[72]

First of all and most basic of all, SCRIPTURE. In any attempt to clarify the authentic Person of Jesus the scriptures must always have primary place.[73] There is no christology without the word of God; this hardly needs saying. It has to be constantly recalled, however, that scripture is not an entity in itself, any more than a "soul" exists of itself. Scripture is the core experience of the *community* of Israel and of the Church which, for a variety of reasons, was put into writing. Present day Christian life lives from this core experience as it is mediated through the living experience of the *community* down through the ages.

PHILOSOPHY. Philosophy here is taken in a broad sense, meaning the cultural thought patterns by which and through which authentic christology is expressed. Scripture must, as the new quest insisted, speak to contemporary men and women in their language and culture, using the thought patterns of the people addressed. There is, therefore, not only a plurality of christologies in the scriptures themselves but there must also be a plurality of christologies at the contemporary "end of the tunnel," the modern world. Even in one city, Jesus cannot be proclaimed in the identical manner in the upper class white suburbs and in the black ghetto; the disenfranchised, the oppressed must hear the authentic Jesus proclaimed in their culture, in response to their situation. The "sympathetic" proclaimer, appreciating the culture and specific life-situation of the audience, must present the *authentic* Christ as challenge, joy, forgiveness, hope, true freedom.

Any philosophical theology which loses its biblical moorings can only be ersatz. To begin with certain principles and deduce a Jesus from those ideas is not clarifying the portrait of Jesus; it is to fall into the trap of the Old Quest and invent a Jesus to our liking: Jesus the revolutionary, the pacifist, the social worker, the teacher, the outcast, etc.

THE AUTHORITATIVE EXPERIENCE OF THE CHURCH. The experience of the Christian community (i.e., the Church) also exercises a normative role in the mediating of the experience of Jesus Christ. Christians form the *Body of Christ*, a community (Greek:*koinonia*) sharing the one Spirit of Truth (cf. 1 Cor 12:4–30; Jn 14:16–17, 15:26–27, 16:12–15). The Body of Christ is not one individual: it is a society, a gathering together in the one Spirit. The privileged means of mediating the experience of Christ is this community with its normative written experiences, the scriptures, lived and shared through its life, teaching and worship. This experience of the community enlarges and deepens one's personal experience of Christ through word and sacrament while at the same time acting as a guard-rail against possible aberrations. The Church, endowed with the Spirit of Truth (cf. 1 Tim 3:15) expresses its life in Christ in a variety of ways: through teachings of varying authoritative weight,[74] through its liturgy, through its evangelical life.

However, to "freeze" even tentative teachings of the Church, thereby denying the authentic development of dogma,[75] can end up in "ecclesiastical-fundamentalism."[76] Scholarship has advanced in its healthy critical analysis of the word of God; it has been slow to analyze the historical, linguistic, cultural circumstances of the pronouncements of the church and to study the degrees of certitude by which the church expresses herself.

LINGUISTIC STUDIES. Christology has taken seriously the work done by those involved in linguistic studies and also those who have attempted to penetrate the processes of oral culture.[77] The discipline is incredibly complex and in a certain sense in its infancy.

The study of oral transmission can be of great help in trying to understand the rather short period when the Good News of Jesus was proclaimed orally and no written Gospel had as yet arrived on the scene. Moreover, since the culture which produced the Gospels was fundamentally a non-literary society,[78] the studies of cultures committed to the spoken word can give new insights into the meaning of the Gospels. Yet it can also lead to some rather strange understanding of the scriptures. Kelber is so insistent on the loss incurred by a *written* Gospel,[79] that his exegesis appears controlled by it: he upholds that Mark's Gospel is fundamentally a rebellion against orality; Mary, the mother of Jesus is downplayed by the Marcan Jesus precisely because she is a symbol of oral authority, of oral transmission and of its malfunctioning.[80]

Those who dedicate themselves to a study of the written word, the text,[81] insist that it is within the Gospel *text* that Jesus is made known and yet remains unknown. For many linguistic scholars, the modern quest of the historical Jesus has taken place within a certain set of prejudices which have resulted in creating a blindness to the true Jesus.[82] The solution offered is to interpret the *written* materials, entailing a study of how language functions. This is now called the *New Criticism* and takes on a variety of forms: structuralism, reader-response criticism, narrative criticism, deconstructionism, etc. This *New Criticism* seeks to help the reader make sense of texts by exploring the relationship between text and reality, the "world" of the written text and the so-called "real world" outside the text.[83] Some of the difficulties of this linguistic route are the complexity of its thought, the incomprehensible jargon employed by some of its proponents and the widely divergent opinions of this rather young discipline. Moreover, some have gone to the extreme of disregarding the historical referent of the text[84], Jesus of Nazareth. Finally, one wonders if some of the theologians involved in a linguistic study of the New Testament texts accept the importance of the historical development of the text; their studies appear at times to be *ahistorical*.[85]

On the other hand, the advances and insights made by students of language, of oral and literary cultures, have important repercussions on the text of scripture for although inspired, they come from the pen of inspired HUMAN authors and the writings must be analyzed by all the tools of modern research. However, this emphasis of modern scholarship will have value only if used in conjunction with other elements of contemporary theological thought.[86]

EXPERIENCE. A sign of our contemporary world is the stress on "experience." We have seen its role in the *New Hermeneutic* and in the understanding of scripture itself as the experience of the early Christians of their encounter with Christ. Contemporary christology recognizes that one's experience of Christ is mediated through the experience of this early Christian community as it has been passed down through the ages, all in light of contemporary experience. It is evident that we are not speaking about sense experience which is more properly predicated of the strict sciences. Rather, the experience which so characterizes the modern world is founded upon lived-out relationships with God, the universe, our brothers and sisters on this planet. There is a "sensitivity" which is a mark of these relationships: a sensitivity to the fact that the majority of the world goes to bed hungry, to the millions of homeless, disenfranchised, prejudiced members of the human family which itself is under threat of extinction through its own misuse of creation and the stockpiling of planet-destroying weaponry.

Christological studies have been affected by this stress on experience. It is the "humanity" of Jesus which is accentuated in contemporary theology, insisting that Jesus is "like his brethren in every respect . . . for because he himself has suffered and been tempted, he is able to help those who are tempted" (Heb 2:17–18). Strict philosophical theology based upon metaphysical principles is — whether one likes it or not — in disfavor.[87] A charismatic spirituality is a striking imprint of modern times: Jesus is to be "known" in the depths of one's heart, through a living relationship of presence, praise and contemplative prayer. The majority of Christians are not seeking a Jesus who is entombed in metaphysical speculation but the Risen, glorious Lord who inserts himself with power into our history.

That there are dangers to this stress on experience is also evident. It can lead to a renewal of some of the failures of the *Old Quest*, building up a Jesus according to our own subjective "feelings." It can neglect the need for difficult, wearying research which must undergird these experiences. It can also lead to a disregard for the normative life of the Christian community, opening the door to a so-called philosophy of *do your own thing* or *if it feels good, do it*. These excesses have their evident repercussions in christology. While accepting the new depth of *authentic* humanness brought to light by the modern stress on experience — the longed-for harmony with God, the cosmos, our brothers and sisters, ourselves — we must not tear *experience* out of its necessary setting, the normative experience of the christian community as expressed in word and sacrament. The contemporary stress on experience is a call, a challenge to a difficult if not at times heroic life of *harmonious, faithful* relationships with the Ground of All, our God, with this universe, with other nations and peoples and with ourselves.[88]

Summary

An authentic christology must take the scriptures as lived within the Christian community as the hub of all reflection on the person of Christ; yet it must not neglect other aspects outlined above which help to clarify the meaning of the Word of God in itself and for us today in our specific set of circumstances. Theology attempts to play a mediating role between the authentic Christ and the authentic yearnings of modern men and women. The danger is to take one of these aspects mentioned above and disengage it from the others: the end-result is bibliolatry, or an exaggerated personalism, a subjective creation of a Jesus-for-me, a disregard for the experience of the Christian community itself, an ignorance of the biblical portrait of Jesus. In spite of these potholes which can cause so much damage, can it not be said that no other age in the history of the Church is so filled with yearning to know the Lord and has so many resources at its disposition to accomplish the task?

CHAPTER FIVE

THE SCRIPTURES AS PRIMARY SOURCE
FOR CHRISTOLOGICAL RESEARCH

The Scriptures — most especially the Gospels of the New Testament — are the primary source for a critical reflection on Jesus the Christ. Before embarking on this study itself, it is essential that we clarify how this source is to be understood; the tools for New Testament christological research must also be examined. The chapter will, therefore, be divided into the following sections:

— The Gospels are AUTHENTIC PORTRAITS of Jesus
— The Tools for New Testament Christological Research

THE GOSPELS ARE AUTHENTIC PORTRAITS OF JESUS

Thanks to the scholarly work of the Old Quest and the No Quest theologians, it is generally agreed that the Gospels are PORTRAITS of Jesus, i.e., interpretations of the Jesus of History. We will first examine this aspect and then attempt to show that the Gospels give us AUTHENTIC portraits of Jesus.

The Gospels are PORTRAITS of Jesus

Portraits: the term is in the plural. There is no such thing as a monochrome Gospel Christ; there is no such thing as THE Gospel christology, there is no such thing as THE interpretation of Jesus. To declare that Mark's portrait of Jesus is THE authentic one is to forget that there are three other equally authentic — though different — Gospel portraits in the New Testament. At times, this lack of insistence on the plurality of the portraits of Jesus results in the forced — and impossible — harmonizations of the four Gospels; as we have seen, this tendency is at the source of many of the books which claim to be *The Life of Christ*. This is not to deny that some principal revelatory lines may be found in all the portraits enabling us to come to some general conclusion, or is it a denial of a progressive development of the portraits within the Gospels themselves. Nonetheless, the context, the purpose of the Gospels do differ and leave their differences embedded in the portraits.

Ignoring the plurality of the portraits and attempting an implicit or explicit wholesale harmonization of the various Gospels is an ever present trap. And there is a second one: letting our imagination (or our hidden desires and yearnings) run wild and painting a picture of Jesus which is not who HE is, but who WE are or DESIRE to be.

What is primarily being underlined is that the Gospels are not snapshots, not videotapes, not recordings, not computer-printouts but INTERPRETATIONS. Even if Mark and Q are considered by most theologians to be the earliest documents chronologically, they are definitely interpretations of Jesus. The term *portraits* is synonymous with *interpretations*.

We therefore can never know the color of Jesus' hair, his height, the manner he walked, the contours of his face (and even if we did, this would have nothing to do with the salvific truth who is Jesus),[89] details about his years at Nazareth before he began his public ministry, notwithstanding apocryphal Gospels[90] and visions.[91] These FACTS are for the most part lost and we will have to live with these missing pieces which would serve more to satisfy human curiosity than advance the cause of the Christian faith.

In fact, we should CELEBRATE the fact that we have PORTRAITS and not snapshots of Jesus; that we have interpretations and not computer-printouts. Why? The response can be clarified by asking another question: Is it good sense to hire someone for a responsible position on dossier-evidence alone?

If a candidate for a job sends his prospective employer his university file, the search committee may come to the conclusion, judging from the attached photo, that the job-seeker is tall, dark and handsome. It may also be evident that his grade-point average is above average. Should the person be hired on this evidence alone? Even if the candidate revealed his marital status, his past experience as an executive officer, his place of birth and travels abroad — is there enough material for the company to make a decision? By no means. The employer still does not know the applicant. All he has is nothing more than a snapshot and pages of facts and figures. This may arouse interest in the candidate, but is not sufficient data to hire him for a responsible position. For the candidate is not KNOWN.

Thanks to the labors of the *questers*, it is generally accepted that we do not have a dossier on Jesus, and many christians bemoan the fact. Jesus' *file* is an embellished, adapted portrait of the man, with RELATIVELY few unaltered facts and figures to go by.

Then why celebrate? Thanks to other disciplines (e.g., psychology, anthropology, history, literature, archaeology, languages) it is becoming clearer that what the Gospels *do* reveal about Jesus is what is most important: his lived-out commitments, founded upon his relationships. And this is what constitutes selfhood, or personhood. As J.M. Robinson puts it: "Selfhood is constituted by commitment to a context, from which commitment one's existence arises . . . Selfhood results from implicit or explicit commitment to a kind of existence and is to be understood only in terms of that commitment, i.e., by laying hold of the understanding of existence in terms of which the self is constituted."[92] Schillebeeckx, after underlining the difficulties in any search for that which constitutes someone as this particular person, explains that, "the mystery of each person is only accessible to us *in his behaviour* which . . . is just the inadequate sign of the person manifesting himself in it and at the same time conceals him. It is more than his several actions and yet is disclosed only *in* this activity. This does not stop us from acquiring through these acts a slant on the mystery of the person of another individual human being . . ."[93] And the 1983 Pontifical Biblical Commission Report states: "The ultimate explanation, or rather the mystery, of Jesus lies essentially in *his filial relation to God.*"[94]

Portraits do reveal in an accentuated fashion one or several characteristics or commitments of a person. And commitments, expressing lived-out relationships, constitute selfhood, the "person." The Gospel portraits are not so much factual accounts since everything (as repeatedly noted) is filtered through the hindsight of the resurrection and the experiences of various christian communities. Nonetheless, presuming the authenticity of these interpretations of Jesus, these portraits do reveal the fundamental commitments of Jesus of Nazareth which enable us to have an insight into what could be termed the mystery of the selfhood or person of Jesus. What has been preserved for us in the Gospel portraits, therefore, is what is most essential in order to come to a deeper knowledge of the mystery of Jesus the Christ.

For as the new quest maintains, there are embedded in the portraits, important, revelatory facts, disclosing these commitments, these relationships. The ipsissima verba et facta, the ipsissima vox (e.g., Jesus addresses the Father as "Abba," his table fellowship with sinners, etc.) present a deep insight into the person of Jesus.

Exactly when things were said, where they were done, precisely how, etc., is for the most part lost. Presuming again the authenticity of the Gospel portraits, there is an historical core at the source of these interpretations.

The portraits themselves, as authentic ADAPTATIONS and EMBELLISH-MENTS, accentuate the lived-out relationships or commitments of Jesus. The Gospels, by no means a dossier on Jesus, are revelatory of what he lives for and dies for and therefore are revelatory of what can be termed his personhood. These embellishments/adaptations which are of the essence of a portrait stress or at least are founded upon some facet of the character of Jesus.

An *embellishment* is a story formed by the christian community to clarify the person of Jesus or to resolve a problem of their times basing themselves on some historical aspect of Jesus' life. For example, the insistence that John the Baptizer is definitely NOT to be regarded as the Messiah (found in John's Gospel especially),[95] indicates a situation in a post-Easter church and does not reflect any battle which Jesus had with the Baptizer. But Jesus believed himself to be the final word of the Father; therefore the christian community can embellish their understanding of the stance of Jesus thereby *forming* a situation in the life of Jesus or of the Baptizer which would reflect and solve the problem which exists in their time (the followers of John the Baptizer claiming to be the real christians) and which did not exist *as such* at the time of the Lord. It is apparent that an *embellishment* is not a "fabrication out of whole cloth."[96]

An adaptation, on the other hand, would not be the *formation* of a story, but a *modification* of the circumstances/words/deeds of an historical situation to suit the needs of the hearers. For example, there was a farewell Easter appearance of the Lord. It cannot be known where it took place since Matthew locates it in Galilee (for theological reasons based on the needs of his hearers) and Luke (for theological reasons also) locates it just outside Jerusalem. Each author adapts the situation to his own theological slant based upon the needs of the audience. That Jesus taught his disciples how to pray is recognized as a fact; but Luke adapts the words of Jesus to his hearers, Matthew to his.

These stories are not formed out of nothingness. These adaptations do not appear out of thin air. Adaptations and embellishments are based *in some manner* upon the words/deeds of Jesus. To understand them correctly the situation of the community which composed the Gospel must be known, the intention of the community must be deciphered, the meaning that the community wanted to be conveyed must be grasped. If a conclusion does not cohere with the overall portrait of Jesus (often difficult to determine), then it may be presumed that the intention of the christian community was NOT to so portray the Lord, but to express its own situation basing itself on its understanding of some aspect of the life of Jesus (as in the above example concerning the Baptizer). The great difficulty in interpreting the portraits of Jesus is clearly evident.

It is the consistent teaching of the christian churches that the Gospels are authentic portraits of Jesus, truly describing his *salvific* person and message. As the *Decree on Divine Revelation of the Second Vatican Council* declares: "Holy Mother Church has firmly and with absolute constancy maintained and continues to maintain that the four Gospels just named whose historicity she unhesitatingly affirms, faithfully hand on what Jesus, the Son of God, while he lived among men, really did and taught *for their salvation*, until the day when he was taken up . . . The sacred authors, in writing the four Gospels, selected certain of the many elements which had been handed on, either orally or already in written form, others they synthesized or explained with an eye to the situation of the churches, the while sustaining the form of preaching but always in such a fashion that they have told us the *honest truth* about Jesus."[97] The words "honest truth" are the best that can be done with the official Latin text which has "vera et sincera de Jesu" which does not imply *historical* truth, for the object of the Gospels is not ultimately *historical* but "salvific" truth. That this entails a fundamental historical basis is accepted; but the Council is not teaching that everything in the Gospels is historical. It is rather declaring that Jesus, *the salvific truth of the Father* is faithfully proclaimed.

The Gospels are AUTHENTIC Portraits of Jesus

The preceding quote from the Second Vatican Council leads us to examine this specific topic of the general authenticity of the Gospel portraits. The question comes down to this: what reasons can be adduced for the church's stance that the New Testament does present an interpretation of Jesus which truly corresponds with the "honest truth about Jesus" in the sense explained above.

Is it not possible, that the Gospels are whole cloth inventions? Is it not possible, that the general lines of the portraits are nothing but *distorted* embellishments created by the early christian community which drew up a 'new' Jesus? The answer hinges on the statement that these portraits disclose the "honest truth about Jesus" as clarified above.[98]

It should be noted that there is no scholar who denies that there are certain historical facts in the Gospels. Bultmann himself and more especially the post-Bultmannians insist on a basic core historicity. Generally speaking, while Bultmann limits this core to relatively *few* sections of the Gospels, his disciples widen the historical base somewhat. The statement made here goes beyond the post-Bultmannians: the Gospel portraits as a whole — the kerygmatic Christ — are reliable, authentic interpretations of the Jesus of History. That there is, at times, a disregard for geographical precision (e.g., Mk 7:31), for historical accuracy (e.g., Lk 2:2, the worldwide census under Quirinius),[99] for precise Old Testament references (e.g., Mk 2:26 which erroneously speaks of the priest Abiathar in contradiction with 1 Sam 21:1–6) can scarcely be denied. But that does not concern us and is not involved in the *inerrancy* or truth-content of the Scriptures which deals with the purpose of the word of God, *salvific* truth. No one should ever use Mark's Gospel as an AAA triptik just because his Gospel is inspired. It is not inspired as a guidebook, but as *Gospel*, the proclamation of the salvific Lordship of Jesus.

The statement deals with the saving Person — and therefore work — of Jesus. What we have in the Gospels is an authentic, reliable interpretation. With what grounds does the Church declare them reliable in this sense? Parenthetically, it is somewhat strange that the question should even be raised, for there is some truth in F.Bruce's comment: "If the New Testament were a collection of secular writings, their authenticity would generally be regarded as beyond all doubt. It is a curious fact that historians have often been much readier to trust the New Testament than have many theologians."[100] Also, to declare with Bultmann that in general the Gospels are inventions of the early Church is to imply that the Gospel authors "were unaware of the distinction between history and faith . . . If the Gospel writers were, on the contrary, sensitive to what was historical and what was kerygmatic (as there are real grounds for supposing), it is unlikely that they would have treated their traditional sources for the words and works of Jesus with anything but respect . . . (especially) if (as is probable) eyewitnesses were still around."[101]

Eyewitnesses were surely around when Paul wrote his first letter to the Christians at Corinth (early 50s) as he states clearly in 15:6. And not only were eyewitnesses present who with their dedication to the Lord would hardly permit distortion to be proclaimed about the Savior but there were also certain of the disciples of Jesus who were "in charge" (like Paul, Peter, James the relative of the Lord) who would also be loathe to permit distortion to rule. Paul's vehement demands for orthodoxy in the transmission of the *Gospel* (cf. Gal 1:6–9) can be considered typical of those who exercised positions of authority (cf. the Pastoral Epistles, i.e., 1 & 2 Timothy and Titus). In fact, the *apocryphal* Gospels themselves attest to a certain filtering process by which the early christians recognized some Gospels as faithful representations of their faith and others as "apocryphal," i.e., not acceptable.

However, it must be constantly recalled that the New Testament was written in a predominantly oral culture[102] and it is a principle of oral societies that they "live very much in a present which keeps itself in equilibrium . . . by sloughing off memories which no longer have relevance."[103] In other words, the early Christians remembered and transmitted what was important for their lives as followers of the Christ, leaving much of the rest aside. Adaptations, embellishments are typical of oral societies as they live the proclamation in their particular circumstances. Nonetheless, oral societies, with their great respect for the spoken word are likewise marked by "a highly traditionalist or conservative set of mind that with good reason inhibits intellectual experimentation."[104] It appears that judging from the conclusions of the experts in the field of oral cultures, the Good News of redemption in Christ Jesus was adapted, embellished to fit present-day circumstances but not *substantially* modified. And was not the first proclaimer in this oral society Jesus himself whom his followers held in awe? His salvific words and actions would have a special sacredness which the proclaimers of the Good News would hardly distort. 1 Cor 15:3–5 appears to substantiate this, for Paul is careful to repeat — in a vocabulary which is not his — what he was taught when he first became a christian; he prefaces this with a traditional formula of the semitic people: "I delivered to you . . . what I also received." The application of this principle to the tunnel period is evident. The salvific proclamation about Jesus would not be distorted, betrayed; adapted, embellished to clarify, to speak to the problems of the day, yes. But distorted? Hardly.

When we consider the written Gospels, composed after a relatively short period of oral transmission, there are several reasons to claim that they are reliable portraits of the one whom the evangelists regarded as the redeemer. It appears to be too much to say that the disciples, for the most part from the "rabble" despised by the religious leaders of the day, created these stories about Jesus. The incarnation of the Word, the resurrection from the dead (these will be explained in later chapters) were not expected by the Jewish people. They are God's surprise to the world — especially to the Jews of Jesus' time — hardly attributable to the creative imagination of the early christians. Moreover, there are signs of their fidelity to the person of their Lord: in spite of Paul's developed theology about the Christ, the earliest written Gospels, Mark, Matthew and Luke, "did not read his theology back onto the lips of Jesus or in other ways impose Paul's theology on the story of the ministry and passion."[105] Moreover, the disciples did not discard from Jesus' lips expressions which were neither current in the christian communities of their time nor tools of evangelization: terms like "Son of Man," the "Kingdom of God." Apparently the Gospel authors felt obliged to use these out-of-style expressions since they *were* from the lips of Jesus.

Other points could be added: the fact that so many early christians died for the truth of the Gospels, that no one — as far as we know — came forward to "let out the secret" that they were "forgeries."

Inexhaustible Presence

ON THE OTHER HAND, it appears that we can go too far in upholding the authenticity of the portraits if we would claim with the Scandinavian school (represented especially by B. Gerhardsson) which "envisioned Christian disciples, on the analogy of Rabbinic students, taking notes and using notebooks for the purpose of writing down 'parts of the tradition concerning Christ.' Such written materials, together with oral traditions, furnished the sources out of which the Gospels were fashioned." [106] It is doubtful that the Rabbinic method of teaching goes back to the time of Jesus and there is no indication that Jesus taught in catechism-memorization fashion. That there may have been some note-taking by those who encountered and heard Jesus, is a possibility but there is little to substantiate the opinion.

All things considered, it can be said that we have reliable portraits, authentic interpretations of Jesus the Savior. After the skepticism of Bultmann, more scholars have investigated the topic and have reached the conclusion that the Gospels are in substance trustworthy. They do present us with an authentic portrait of the salvific truth of the Father, Jesus.

SCRIPTURAL CRITICISMS: TOOLS FOR NEW TESTAMENT RESEARCH

Thanks to the scholarship of the last few centuries, a number of valuable tools for New Testament research have been developed by which the Gospel portraits may be analyzed. These "criticisms" [107] — to use the professional jargon — are indispensable for a basic study of christology. The principal scriptural criticisms or analyses would include the following:

HISTORICAL Criticism:[108] "What actually happened?" Basically, that is the question that historical criticism has to answer. It is a peculiarly modern, if not particularly western interest; in earlier times, there reigned what we would call today a certain "fundamentalism" in the study of Scripture since questions concerning historicity were rarely raised. And in the East, the "real" is not attributed solely to the factual. The scientific western mind seeks to know if Jesus "actually" walked upon the water, whether he "really" fed thousands of people with a few barley loaves and some fish. Yet what should first be considered is "why is this episode narrated?" and "what is it trying to say to me?" This is not to derogate from the importance of seeking to discover the underlying reality. Modern day Christians are not satisfied to hear that there is a "core historicity" or that the scriptural portraits are authentic in their portrayal of Jesus the Savior. They want to know the "details." And these "details" are important in trying to clarify the portraits of Jesus. The scripture scholar, wisely employing the criteria of authenticity, attempts to search the word of God in order to surface — if possible — the original setting, the original words, the original event. If a "nature miracle" like walking on the water is reported to be a "miracle-parable," i.e., an embellishment in order to clarify the Lordship of Jesus, we not only have a better understanding of scripture itself but a deeper insight into the person of Jesus. For an example of historical criticism applied to one of the more difficult sections of the Gospels, the Infancy Narratives of Matthew and Luke, read Raymond Brown's *The Birth of the Messiah*.[109]

SOURCE Criticism:[110] In a broad sense, source criticism seeks out the sources for any of the booklets of the Scriptures. Strictly speaking, however, source criticism is an analysis of the *literary* interdependence of the Synoptic Gospels: Matthew, Mark

& Luke. We can schematically summarize the generally accepted conclusions of this study as follows:

```
        MK ── ? ── Q
M \      \      / \      L
   \      \    /   \    /
    \      \  /     \  /
     MT            LK
```

The above football play means that Mark and Q are primary sources, in the sense that they are the least theologized (but definitely theologized/interpreted nonetheless) and chronologically probably the earliest — MK being dated about 67 A.D. and Q perhaps somewhere around the early 50s. Matthew (late 80s?) and Luke (late 80s?) depend upon both Mark and Q (whether Mark had access to Q is highly doubtful). Both Matthew and Luke have sources which are specific to them, which are termed, respectively, M and L. An example of an L source would be the parables of the prodigal son, the lost sheep, the lost coin. These parables form an L source since found only in Luke's Gospel and are presumed to be part of a tradition to which only he had access; Matthew's infancy narrative (first two chapters) is an example of an M source for although it has some affinities with the Lucan infancy narrative, it clearly comes from a different source.

FORM Criticism:[111] the study of the *oral* traditions about Jesus before they were put into writing. The key word is ORAL. To put it in descriptive terminology, it is the study of *the tunnel period*.

- - - - - - - - - - - - -

Jesus of History   Christ of Faith

- - - - - - - - - - - - -

(20? 40? year tunnel period)

It is generally agreed that during this period[112] there were adaptations, embellishments; the life of Jesus arranged itself into units or forms: parables, sermons, miracles, dispute-stories (sometimes called 'pronouncement stories' since they usually end with a pithy concluding statement or punch line by Jesus) which in turn became quite stereotyped, stripped for the most part of time/place categories. This is a common phenomenon in the narration of the life of any important person. Even a superficial reading of the Gospels indicates that it also occurred in the handing down of the traditions about Jesus. The artificial connectives which abound in the Gospels ("at that time," "on the next day," "at the seashore," "immediately") plus the contradictions among the Gospels concerning time and place demonstrate that chronology and topology were not of paramount importance to the early christians and quickly — for the most part — were forgotten.

Moreover, it is agreed that during this tunnel period, the preaching of the early Christians about Jesus was done in the light of the belief in the resurrection and adapted to the needs and experiences of the hearers. Small wonder there are such diverse portraits of Jesus in the New Testament! In other words, Jesus was seen in the hindsight of the resurrection and filtered through the problems of THEIR TIMES.

It was as if even the first word spoken presumed the last chapter — the victorious resurrection. Not only was this proclamation adapted to the needs and mindset of the various christian communities, but often artificially arranged to aid the memorization of the good news and also, as we shall see, to bring out the particular theological slant of the author (or the community he represented). Form criticism is a literary tool; it oversteps its field and becomes illogical when it concludes that because of artificial arrangements of the stories of Jesus, the stories themselves are artificial.

LITERARY Criticism: a highly important study of the type of literature to which we should assign Gospel. Is this "GOOD SPEEL," "GODSPEL," "Gospel," — this Good News — to be classified as 'history' or 'short story' or perhaps 'historical novel?' The type of literature is important, since EACH TYPE OF LITERATURE HAS ITS OWN TYPE OF TRUTH.[113]

This is evident when we consider that we would not accuse the sports page editor of deception if he resumed yesterday's football game by headlining: ST. PETER TROUNCES ST. MARY. BUT it would be nonsensical in a theology manual. Likewise, a St. Valentine's Day card will lovingly declare:

My heart so pines for you today
That 'ere it cracks
Your lips must say:
I love you!

BUT — such a ditty would sound stupid in a cardiology textbook.

In previous ages it appears that just about everything in the Bible was lumped into the literary form *history*. If the scriptures said that Jonah was in the belly of a big fish, then that is where he lived for three days . . . if the Israelites coming out of Egypt were about ten abreast and therefore stretched from Egypt to Palestine (yet the Egyptians could not find them!), then that is the way it happened . . . if the first account of creation (there are two: cf. Gen 1:1 ff and Gen 2:4 ff) declares that God created the world in three days, decorated it in three and so rested on the seventh, then that is exactly the way it happened.

The problem with all of these examples is that everything is considered to be *history*. And to complicate matters, history is understood as we know it TODAY (which is not the biblical literary form history — as even a superficial reading of the books of Kings and Chronicles will demonstrate).

Moreover, to insist that every book of the Bible is history (even that beautiful love story, the Song of Songs and the cryptic apocalyptic writings like Daniel and Revelation?) is to severely cramp the creativity of the human author whose literary style, culture, mindset and artistry are not changed but rather enhanced by what christians term inspiration.[114]

The Bible is a series of inspired booklets exemplifying diverse styles and types of literature; *the truth content is to be judged by the literary type*. If Jonah — as we believe from a study of the book itself and from comparative literature — can be compared to an historical novel, then there is no need whatsoever to measure the bellies of whales to see if a man could live there for three days. In other words, the Book of Jonah is a divinely inspired *historical novel* (or some similar literary form). Since the Book of Exodus is a narration of events seen in the pervading atmosphere of YHWH's victorious providence, it can hardly be called history in our sense of the term. Examples can be multiplied. However, the fundamental lesson to be learned is both negative: *inspiration is not synonymous with historical truth* and positive: *there are a variety of types of inspired literature* which make up the Bible.

Thanks to the work of theologians of previous decades, the conclusion has been reached that we cannot classify Gospel in any set literary form (the technical term is *genre*). What does literary criticism tell us about the type of literature called Gospel? On the response depends the understanding of the Gospels' truth content for again,

EACH TYPE OF LITERATURE HAS ITS OWN TYPE OF TRUTH. When we examine the literary form *Gospel*, we can quickly conclude that it is NOT biography, it is not short story, it is not novel, it is not history. But we are a little hard pressed to give a positive definition of this unique form of literature. Actually, it is eludes any specific traditional classification, even though there are points of contact with the literary form *aretalogy* which is a compilation of often fantastic stories about an heroic individual (e.g., Appolonius of Tyana) in order to edify and amaze the reader; however the differences between *aretalogy* — somewhat comparable to a pagan life of a saint — and Gospel are far greater than any similarities.

Gospel can be considered a unique literary genre which through an historical core of words and deeds of Jesus, embellished and adapted in the light of his resurrection and of the experiences of diverse audiences, is the faith-proclamation that the ultimate meaning and fulfillment of life is found in Christ the Savior.

There is no literary genre precisely comparable to Gospel because of the uniqueness of the events described (incarnation, resurrection) in view of proclaiming that the ultimate meaning of life is found in the saving event of the Father, Jesus the Lord.

REDACTION Criticism:[115] This type of analysis deals with the particular theological slant of each evangelist. In other words, what did e.g., the author of Matthew's Gospel (at least the edition we have, which is the only one extant) want to get across to his particular audience? In the hypothesis that Matthew's Gospel was written as a response to the reorganization of the Jews after the destruction of Jerusalem, we can better understand Matthew's theological slant: Jesus is the New Moses, the New Israel, the King, the Messiah, the fulfillment of the Law and the Prophets. Matthew will arrange his book accordingly.

The study of redaction criticism reveals the theological bias of each of the Gospels. This, in turn, determines the manner in which the evangelist will compose his Gospel, how he will organize and embellish the variety of oral traditions coming out of the tunnel, perhaps via Mark, or via Q or via some direct contacts with oral traditions; at times this study of the composition of the Gospel is called composition criticism. "Caution is obviously needed in the analysis of any editorial activity, particularly when, as in the case of the Gospels, we are not always sure who the 'editor' is, or the exact nature of his sources."[116] Used with care, this type of analysis gives the reader an insight into the Gospel as a whole. However, since so much is unknown about the living context of each Gospel, redaction criticism can easily slip into a rather subjective approach to the Gospels.[117]

These tools of New Testament Research, developed over the course of the past century, help us to understand the three stages in the Gospel formation as outlined by the Pontifical Biblical Commission[118] and the Second Vatican Council.[119]

I. Jesus preaches. teaches, acts, according to his own Jewish mindset, using the language, the imagery, the thought patterns of his time. He does not speak like a New Yorker, nor a Parisian; nor does he think like a westerner; nor is his philosophy to be considered Aristotelian-Thomistic; he is a Jew, a fervent Jew, raised in the Torah, the Prophets, the Holy Writings. To claim otherwise is, as we shall see, to destroy the christian understanding of incarnation where the Infinite Word of God, while remaining the Word of God, externalizes Himself in and through the limitations of our humanity. (In spite of what some overzealous christians claim, he never converted to Christianity!). The analysis connected with this period is called historical criticism : an attempt to discover the thought patterns, the words, the deeds of the historical Jesus. Here in stage one, we have the *ipsissima verba et facta* of Jesus.

II. The Proclamation By the Community of Jesus the Christ. This second step in the Gospel formation is the *tunnel period*. The followers of Jesus preach him, always through the hindsight of the resurrection, with adaptations and embellishments expressing the experiences of the hearers. "The Commission seeks to stress that the New Testament writings, for all their proclamation of Jesus as Lord, assert the fundamental continuity between Jesus of Nazareth and Jesus Christ as Lord." [120] The study of this period belongs especially to form criticism.

III. The final step in the formation of the Gospels begins when the proclamation is put into writing (starting with Paul in the early 50s, ending with 2 Pet about 125 A.D.). Each author has his own theological slant which greatly determines the composition of his pamphlet.

Why was the proclamation written down? Eyewitnesses dying off, the realization that the end of the world was not imminent and therefore some organization was needed, the desire of some of the communities to have a reading about Jesus in the liturgy corresponding to the Old Testament reading. The analysis of this third phase — when the proclamation is put into writing by creative evangelists — is called redaction/composition criticism. [121]

Summary

Although academic studies can give some foundation to faith in Jesus, it is important to understand that faith is a gift and not the result of any syllogistic reasoning. In other words, an A + in theology does not make someone a christian. By no means. Theology is not faith; it is a critical reflection on the faith.

Faith in itself does not *ultimately* mean that a list of propositions is true (propositional faith). To uphold propositional faith as ultimate is tantamount to saying this: presented with a list of statements — a creed — and signed on the dotted line, lo and behold, a christian is born. Rather, faith in its ultimate analysis is the total commitment through Jesus the Lord, in the power of the Spirit, on every level of personality to a Person — to the Ground of All Being, whom we term God — so that everything is seen, done, measured, planned in the light of this Person, Love itself. (Always remembering the ancient dictum: "God is more UNLIKE anything we say about him than he is like it.")

As friendship cannot be forced, as love between two people cannot be forced (forced love is a square circle) so faith cannot be forced by any reasoning process nor by any spectacular event whatsoever, not even by an appearance of the Risen Christ.

There is a risk involved in faith, a personal risk, as there is in any interpersonal relationship. Even for those who have taken that risk of faith, the risk of being totally open to the OTHER, that relationship must be examined, probed, clarified. For those who would say that they are NOT people of faith, theology does clear the air, clarify problems, answer questions, but it is impossible for it to produce faith, for again, faith demands a personal free choice and cannot be foisted upon anyone.

Christian theology would say that God — dynamic, redeeming Love — is always present within us as tug, as call, as lure. When we respond to this dynamic call, which is intrinsic to our very being, we can speak of the presence of God as sharing. For a gift only becomes real when it is accepted; God's gift of himself becomes real when it is freely accepted (faith), when we accept acceptance, when we accept that we are accepted, loved, by the Ground of All Being, Love itself.

Faith is, then, a dynamic, personal sharing-with. Can we not call faith a sharing in the omnipotence of God? And his omnipotence is Love. His presence as CALL empowers us to respond. His presence as OFFER enables us to accept. His presence as LOVE strengthens us to surrender.

Christology may knock down a few walls which have been impeding that relationship; theology may answer questions which have stood in the way of any true acceptance of the Lord. But there it stops. Christology must know its limitations and so must all students of christology: theology (whose central component is christology) cannot produce faith, no matter how clear the arguments, no matter how conclusive the reasoning.

SECTION TWO

THE DISCLOSURE WORDS OF JESUS

Much of what has been studied thus far is actually a partial resume of a *General Introduction to the New Testament*, a prerequisite of christology. A review of the content of the preceding chapters is the first step in any course on Jesus.

Now that we have some basic tools at our disposal, we can begin our bold attempt to clarify the portraits of Jesus in the hopes of arriving at a better understanding of the mystery of his person. Following the principles outlined in the previous chapters, a few disclosure words will be studied in this section, the more important revelatory titles will be the subject of section three, Jesus' basic theme, the Reign of YHWH, is the topic of section four and the culminating disclosure of Jesus, the resurrection, will be the subject matter of the final section.

Through this study, Jesus relationships to us and most especially to the Father should surface more clearly, revealing to some degree the mystery of his person.[1]

The task of these sections can be compared to an attempt to clarify an ancient Byzantine icon of Mary holding the Christ Child in her arms. What do the crowns on the heads of Jesus and Mary mean? Did they actually ever wear golden crowns? Why is the face of Jesus that of an adult? And why the configuration of the fingers of the child Jesus? And why that strange, melancholy gaze in the eyes of Mary? And what do those weird scribblings mean which are on both sides of the icon? I will never fully understand this portrait unless someone clarifies it for me. And when I'm told, e.g., that the crown on the head of the child Jesus is an embellishment to clarify, to indicate that he is the LORD of all and that Mary also wears a crown because she is the uniquely faith-filled Mother of the Lord, then I begin to see that there is far more in that portrait than I thought at first glance. In fact, if my conclusion was: Jesus is wearing a golden crown in the Greek icon, THEREFORE he wore a crown during his life, I would be guilty of a type of icon-fundamentalism. For an eastern icon is a spirit filled portrait-lesson, but a lesson I cannot understand correctly unless someone well versed in iconography clarifies it for me. I learn that I must make a distinction between the art-form and the truth conveyed. Undoubtedly I do get quite a bit out of its beauty even if I don't understand it fully; but gazing at it in the light of my own western culture, there is ever present the danger of rejecting it as stupid, of misunderstanding the beauty of the icon, of making the art-form the truth conveyed (e.g., accepting that Jesus actually wore a golden crown at least as a child). I must walk into the culture which painted the icon and find out what the artists were trying to say through these rather strange, ancient, non-western symbols which so strongly convey the power of whom they represent. And what is being said through these ancient religious art-forms often comes as a surprise.

Likewise with the Gospels. They are something like an eastern icon. Jesus is portrayed authentically, yet in style, words, actions, symbols, which can easily elude me if I don't walk into the culture which produced these beautiful portraits of Jesus. Undoubtedly, quite a bit can be gained by just reading the Gospels. But reading them in the light of my own western culture, there is ever present the danger of rejecting them as stupid, of misunderstanding, of misinterpreting the real meaning of these portraits. There is, especially, the danger of confusing the literary tool with the truth conveyed. For example, does the ascension mean that Jesus is sailing up through the skies? Or is it a literary form to denote that the Risen Christ is Lord of the entire cosmos? At the nativity scene in Bethlehem (cf. Lk 2) there are angels in the sky caroling an early christian creed: "There is born to you today . . . a Savior Who is Christ the Lord." When I understand that everything is said of Jesus in the light of the resurrection, then this proclamation of the Lordship of Jesus is much like the golden crown on Jesus' head in the Greek icon. It is authentic, yes — in this sense that it proclaims, in the light of the resurrection, that Jesus is the Lord. But does that mean that angels caroled the creed that first Christmas night? There is no necessity of upholding the historicity of that point. Is it not an embellishment in order to clarify, a beautiful literary tool to convey a profound truth? However, if someone still would want to insist that there were angels on that first Christmas night, fine — provided that they do not get so caught up in the beauty of the literary-form that they ignore the truth to be conveyed! To take the literary-form and squeeze it into the truth-to-be-conveyed is a type of fundamentalism. It ignores the unique genre of literature we call Gospel; it is confuses step number three of the Gospel formation with step number one.

It must be admitted that clarifying the Gospel portraits in the light of the characteristics of western culture (which is highly pragmatic, scientific) appears foolish to fundamentalists and also quite useless to mystically-minded christians. But it is of utmost importance in our present age.

In this scientific western culture, there is a need to clarify the icons — i.e., to explain them in terms that are "new, beautiful, original, and comprehensible," as Paul VI said of his *Credo of the People of God*.[2] We cannot permit the icons to be tossed aside because people do not believe that the child Jesus ever wore a golden crown! And we cannot stand by and watch so many people toss out the Gospel icons of Jesus because they so misunderstand them. On the other hand, we cannot ignore the fact that there is a growing tendency to seek cover under the dangerous security-blanket of extreme fundamentalism. There is a need today which apparently was not felt as much in previous generations, to clarify the Gospel-portraits of Jesus.

In order to polish the portrait of Jesus — use whatever metaphor you wish — three steps will be followed in the next two sections:

1. What does this word/title/action mean AT THE TIME OF JESUS. Following the insight of the Pontifical Biblical Commission's 1983 *Report*, the words/titles of Jesus are taken in a very broad sense, encompassing Jesus' deeds, conducts or habits which "reveal what is most profound about a person."[3] The primary interest is not what these deeds, words, habits, mean NOW; rather, what did they mean THEN. For example, the title *Son of God* is used in a powerful way by christians today to designate what is termed the divinity of Jesus. But we must start off with the understanding that *Son of God* was, at the time of Jesus, one of the weakest titles which someone could give to Jesus (as will be seen in detail). For in itself it designates a Jew who in the light of the Covenant on Mount Sinai[4] believes that all Jews are in a special relation with YHWH.

The actions of Jesus have to be clarified. For example, in western culture, to share a meal with someone can mean nothing more than sitting next to a stranger at McDonalds. But in Jesus' time, by the very fact that a meal was eaten with others, a type of covenant was believed formed among the guests, entailing a sharing of life, with all of its practical consequences of brotherhood, sisterhood.

As much as is possible, a student of christology must try to enter the culture, thought-patterns of Jesus. A difficult task although made easier by the expertise of archaeologists, historians, linguists, etc.

2. The second step is to ask if Jesus accepted such-and-such a title, if he actually spoke such-and-such a word, accomplished such-and-such a deed in that particular context. Or could it be that these words/deeds/titles, etc., are adaptations/embellishments to clarify the person of Jesus or in order to solve — within the general context of the mind of Christ — a difficult situation in the early church which wrote the Gospels? At times (quite often?) the student of christology will have to admit with academic candor that only a probable opinion can be given to these complex questions.

EXAMPLE: the parables appear to be the closest one can ever get to the actual preaching of Jesus. However, most probably the allegorizing of the parable (which means identifying each point of the story) is not from Jesus but is a homily of the early Church, applying the parable to its own situation. This seems to be most evident in the parable of the sower (cf. Mk 4).

3. Finally, the developments which took place in the early christian community concerning the person of Jesus must be examined. These clarifications of Jesus begin before the Gospels were ever put into writing, and have left their traces, at times very clearly, on the New Testament pamphlets. Why these developments occurred, the meaning of these further clarifications, must be examined. The early history of christology as seen in the decisions of the early ecumenical councils must also be studied in order to see how the portrait is clarified and enhanced by the christian community. For sacred scripture cannot subsist independently; it is inextricably one with Tradition,[5] the scripture-based, on-going life, teaching and worship of the Church which reaffirms with clarity what is rooted in the word of God.

The student of christology must familiarize him/herself with the New Testament portraits. All the booklets must be thoroughly examined, the Gospels especially. If at all possible, each booklet of the New Testament should be read at one sitting in order to gain a better understanding of it. And since the New Testament cannot be taken out of its Old Testament context, at least the principal books of the Old Testament must also be read.

Our examination of the scriptural portraits begins with a study of some of the more important Aramaic words found on the lips of Jesus in the Gospels (which were all written in Greek). Can these terms reveal something to us of the relationships, the commitments of Jesus and therefore clarify his personhood? Can a study of these Aramaic terms which the christian community respectfully retained in their original language, clarify the portraits of Jesus?

CHAPTER SIX

THE DISCLOSURE WORD: ABBA

The task ahead is to clarify the authentic portraits of Jesus as given to us in the scriptures. The interpretations of the Jesus of History must be scrutinized in an attempt to understand a little more deeply these Gospel-icons of the Lord. The intention is to accentuate — as far as is possible — the lived-out commitments, the fundamental relationships, which constitute the mystery of the person of Jesus.

One of the ways by which the portraits of Jesus may be clarified is to critically examine some disclosure words, i.e., terms which would reveal him, which would manifest in some way the basic relationships which constitute his person.[6] (Words like today, and, seashore, blue eyes, moustache, etc., would not be considered disclosure terms!) We will understand these revelatory words broadly, i.e., in the context of the life, actions, deeds of Jesus, always keeping in mind the limitations of such a venture. This section will be divided into a study of the following Aramaic words: Abba; Amen; Talitha cumi; Eloi, Eloi, lama sabachthani. *Abba* will be studied in this chapter, the other Aramaic terms in the following chapter.

ABBA

Joachim Jeremias summarizes the importance of this term, when he writes: "The complete novelty and uniqueness of 'Abba' as an address to God in the prayers of Jesus shows that it expresses the heart of Jesus' relationship to God."[7]

Following the methodology given above, the study of ABBA will be divided into three sections:

— The meaning of ABBA at the time of Jesus.
— The possible use by Jesus of ABBA.
— The development of ABBA in the early Christian community.

THE MEANING OF ABBA AT THE TIME OF JESUS

In order to answer this question, we will have to rely not only on the the scriptures but also on extra-biblical sources which disclose the culture of the time of Jesus. The term in itself will be examined and then its use in the Judaism of Jesus' age.

The Meaning of the term ABBA

ABBA is an Aramaic term found only once in the Gospel portraits (Mk 14:36) and twice in the Pauline letters (Rom 8:15 and Gal 4:6).

ABBA comes from the root AB, meaning "Father." ABBA is not declinable, admits of no possessive suffixes. It is a babbling sound, as it has been called, comparable to the term IMMA used for one's mother. It is basically child's talk, a term of a youngster for its own father. Some scholars translate it in English as Dad, or Papa; others would say that there is no strict English equivalent. ABBA denotes not only respect and obedience to one's father (the authoritative aspect) but also affection, intimacy, total confidence. Moreover, comparative literature indicates that the term was used at the time of Jesus not only by children of all ages for their father but also was a term of endearment for an elderly, respected person. It is everyday "family" talk; certainly not the language of prayer.[8]

— The term ABBA, therefore, recognizes the authority of the father whom the children are bound to obey. There is no argument concerning the father's authority in the Judaism of Jesus' day, as we read in the Book of Proverbs:

"Hear O sons, a father's instruction .. for I give you good precepts and do not forsake my teaching" (Prov. 4:1–2).

The note of authority and instruction is the basic reason why the term father was at times applied to Israel's teachers and priests.

Being a son meant *belonging to* and is demonstrated by carrying out the father's instructions and tasks even, at times, being sent on a distant mission. The words of the representatives of King Ahaz to Tiglathpileser join together the concept of son and servant: "I am your servant and your son" (2 Kgs 16:7), as if they were synonyms.

— Yet ABBA has another connotation. It describes love, intimacy, closeness, affection, trust. Originally the first words of a little child for his father, it was at the time of Jesus, a title of respect and love for the venerable elderly; but it always retained that childlike attitude of endearment, intimacy, closeness. Affectionate, trusting obedience is the underlying characteristic of this familiar term.[9]

To summarize: ABBA indicates qualities both in a father and in a child:

— The FATHER has true authority yet this is penetrated by care, tenderness, closeness, simplicity, active love.

— The CHILD is characterized by obedience, penetrated by total trust, tenderness, closeness, simplicity, active love. It is the loving authority of the ABBA which calls forth this ABBA experience in the child.

Use in the Judaism of Jesus' day.

Although not an expression of the protocanonical books[10] of the Old Testament, God is called FATHER in the Judaism of Jesus' day. That God is called FATHER is apparent from the Greek text of Sirach 23:1,4 (the original Hebrew may have had a different reading):

"O Lord, Father and Ruler of my life"
"O Lord, Father and God of my life"

"But it is thy providence, O Father, that steers its course"

and from other literature, e.g., the apocryphal third book of Maccabees 6:3,8 (written in Greek). God is, therefore, addressed as Father in Judaism prior to Jesus both in a collective and personal sense. This is certainly true for the Jews in the Greek world (the diaspora); perhaps, by the time of Jesus, the custom had already penetrated into Palestinian Judaism. If it did, it would be far more rare indeed in this conservative milieu and as far as we can ascertain, does not take the vocative, childlike form, ABBA.

The stress, notice, is on ADDRESSING God as Father, for no one disputes that God is often STATED to be Father in the Old Testament. Even this, however, appears to be done at first with some reluctance, since it has the connotation of biological relationship with God, a concept abhorred by Judaism.

To avoid any notion of physical generation, it is taught, e.g., that God is "LIKE a Father" (Psalm 103:13). With the understanding that God is Father because he has chosen Israel for his own, the term is applied to God more extensively, e.g., Is 64:8 declares:

"Yet, O LORD, thou art our Father; we are the clay,
and thou art our potter; we are all the work of thy hand."

This tenderness of God is forcefully expressed in Is 43:4:

"For you are precious in my eyes and honored and I love you."

However, there is no *certain* record that God was being addressed as ABBA in the Palestinian Judaism of Jesus' time.

In fact, it can be inferred from the Aramaic Targums (paraphrases of the Old Testament text in Aramiac, the language of the post-exilic Jews) that there is a deliberate determination to avoid calling God by such a familiar, intimate, childlike term. If at the time of Jesus, the proper name of God — YHWH — was unpronounceable, how disrespectful (bordering on blasphemy in the mind of some Jews?) would it appear in that culture to call the transcendent, mighty God, by the term of such childlike, trustful intimacy: ABBA. There may be some rare exceptions,[11] but it is safe to say that God is not addressed as ABBA at the time of Jesus. In other religions as well, an equivalent intimate, childlike term for the transcendent God appears to be absent.

THE USE OF ABBA BY JESUS

It is the considered opinion of scholars that Jesus definitely did call the mighty God ABBA. If there is an ipsissima vox in the New Testament, it is ABBA. On this point there is general agreement: the Aramaic term ABBA comes from the lips of Jesus.[12]

Why? Here is a case where we can invoke the principle of dissimilarity. To call God ABBA is against the culture and mindset of the people of Jesus' time. It is difficult to imagine it being invented by the Jewish community. It is a revolutionary way of addressing the Creator of the heavens and the earth. It would appear difficult to be considered an observant Jew at the time of Jesus yet customarily call God by the familiar, intimate, childlike term ABBA. However, it is explicitly stated in Mark (written, of course, in Greek) that Jesus used this Aramaic term in prayer to the Father: "And he said, 'Abba, Father, all things are possible to thee; remove this cup from me; yet not what I will but what thou wilt' " (Mk 14:36).

It is an altogether striking statement, this ABBA on the lips of Jesus. To address YHWH in such a manner is definitely not part of the culture of his people; shocking, therefore, to those who who followed him, and possibly even considered to be deserving of death according to his enemies (cf. Jn 5:18).

Yet, it can be presumed that this was Jesus' ORDINARY way of referring to God.[13] What leads to this conclusion is the constant variations in the Greek of the NT for FATHER as an address to God on the lips of Jesus (with/without the definite article, used as a nominative, as a vocative) which would indicate an underlying, difficult to translate, ABBA.[14]

Also, the fact that in two of Paul's letters (written in Greek) he uses the Aramaic ABBA (Rom 8:15, Gal 4:6), substantiates the awe and respect with which the early Christians pronounced this word. Paul underlines the fact that it is in the Spirit of Jesus that Christians address God as ABBA, implying that its use dates from the historical Jesus himself. That this custom was widespread in early christianity is indicated by the fact that Paul uses it in his letter to the Christians at Rome, a church he had not as yet even visited.

As far as can be deciphered, Jesus' co-religionists in Palestine never call YHWH, ABBA. Yet this is the customary address of Jesus for YHWH. The precise times/ places when Jesus used this term can, of course, never be determined. But that Jesus dared to use ABBA can be declared not just historic but historical. It is the an ipsissima vox of Jesus, i.e., the customary speech of Jesus. We can well imagine that in the Agony in the Garden it was definitely used by Jesus and in that mysterious context, may be called, according to Jeremias' classification, an ipsissimum verbum. In fact, so important is this term, that Schillebeeckx can claim: ". . . without this *Abba* experience the picture of the historical Jesus is drastically marred, his message emasculated and his concrete praxis (though still meaningful and inspiring) is robbed of the meaning he himself gave it." [15]

How did Jesus ever came to use this term? Jesus is — like all human beings — caught up in the alienation of language; speech not only expresses us but also limits us, boxing us into the language spoken. It reveals us and at the same time conceals us for it can never disclose us completely. We search for finite terms to express what appears to be the depth of our being. At times, in moments of great emotion — death of a loved one, joy, betrayal — we are moved to silence. Yet, we must at sometime, in some manner, give vent to our emotions, our feelings. Loving, obedient intimacy with the Father is apparently a deep experience of Jesus, his radical relationship. In his culture, this is best expressed by the childlike use — considered incredibly disrespectful by others — of the word ABBA. Although not fully expressing his deep experience (what word ever does for any person?) nonetheless, it is to some degree, an expression which frees him, it is a liberating cry for it corresponds, at least somewhat, to the reality of his being.

The reverence that Jesus had for this word is expressed in the admonition (which if from the early church, expresses the respect of Jesus for ABBA): "Call no man your father on earth, for you have one Father who is in heaven" (Mt 23:9). Surely Jesus is not prohibiting people from addressing their physical fathers as *abba*. He is rather referring to the custom of addressing distinguished people, especially older men, as ABBA. The term belongs to God.

THE DEVELOPMENT OF ABBA IN THE EARLY CHURCH

(The development of the concept Son of God as applied to Jesus will be studied when we examine that title).

Scarcely used today by Christians in liturgical prayer, the term ABBA for YHWH was apparently prevalent in the early Church. This would explain the fact that Paul, never having been to Rome, could use the expression in his letter to them as he does to the Galatians. And even when its explicit use faded away, it was understood to be intrinsic to any cry to God as Father. We notice in the ancient eucharistic liturgy that the *Lord's Prayer* is prefaced with the phrase: "We dare to say," indicating the boldness in calling God: Father, ABBA. It is far more probable that the beginning of the Lord's Prayer should follow Luke's rendition — shorter than Matthew's — and that *Father* probably refers to an original ABBA.

Although ABBA strictly refers to father, it goes far beyond the English phrase with which Christians so often preface liturgical prayers: "O God Our Father." *Father* in our present culture does not always imply love, fidelity, affection, intimacy, which are intrinsic to ABBA. Moreover, from one perspective, ABBA even transcends *father* and accentuates a loving, sharing, intimate, so personal, dynamic source of life. From this precise standpoint, it goes beyond the distinction between mother — father, for it includes both. True, ABBA stands for a male, a *father*. But used in English by the ordinary faithful, ABBA does not have the "gender stress" of *mother, father*. It was Pope John Paul I who surprised the church by stating of God: "He is our Father; even more, He is our Mother." [16] ABBA would appear to be a scriptural way to approximate this truth both in community and personal prayer.

Summary

Placing the term *ABBA* in the entire context of the New Testament and presuming its particular use by Jesus, this expression does clarify the Gospel portraits:

— *ABBA* opens up a clearer vision of what Jesus means by the theme of his discourses, the Reign of YHWH. For if God is ABBA, his reign is one of love, of intimacy. God's lordship is a lordship of love.

— *ABBA* gives a deeper insight into the parables of Jesus. The simplicity of the parables reflects the simplicity of Jesus' understanding of the Father. Ordinary things — the farmer's sowing, the housewife's baking — all become parables of "thy kingdom come." [17]

— *ABBA* gives a deeper insight into Jesus' self-understanding. It expresses, it reveals a deep experience of his life and put in context of the entire portrait, the overriding experience of his life: nothing can stand in the way of his loving intimate obedience to his ABBA, THE relationship which constitutes, as we will see, his person.

— *ABBA* appears to contradict the traditional philosophical understanding of God. Aristotelian thought comes to a knowledge of God through the Greek deductive process, concluding that God is pure act (i.e., there is no potential in God), unchangeable, the unmoved mover, the uncaused cause. Rather, for Jesus, God is close to humankind in love.

— *ABBA* reveals more clearly who we are: children of a loving Father. To be a child becomes the mark of the kingdom: "Unless you turn and become like little children you will never enter the kingdom of heaven" (Mt 18:3). [18]

— *ABBA* clarifies John's statement (which can be called the basic principle of all Christian theology): "God is Love" (1 Jn 4:8). ABBA *IS* love, and the only thing God can do is love. Sin is its own punishment: to walk out of the Light into the darkness gives no one the right to condemn the Light for it is still on (cf. Jn 3:20 ff).

— *ABBA* sheds some light on the INSCRUTABLE mysteries of suffering, of death. These riddles are seen in a new context when reflected upon in the conviction that the Ground of all Being is ABBA. He is the Power of the Future, which draws, lures in the mysterious ways of Love.

— *ABBA* helps clarify the christian meaning of redemption. For mankind is healed through that cry of love to the Father, ABBA, that offering in love which Jesus makes even in death upon a cross. Jesus' dying implies the surrendering by ABBA of his "beloved" to the destruction of death so that He may fill His "only begotten" with the glory of the resurrection. Since, in Christian theology, Jesus is the climactic point of God's self-disclosure, the summit then of all creation, his cry of ABBA is the loving cry of the universe. The resurrection-response by ABBA, is our certain hope. To share through faith in the life-giving Spirit of Jesus so that God may be known as ABBA, is to be a Christian.

Yet — is it possible that this ABBA experience is the great illusion of Jesus' life? Such a reaction is surely possible from an individual's point of view. But an attempt at an answer should only be made when the entire portrait is studied, for it ultimately asks whether Jesus was the great deceiver/the sincere fool or the truth.

A fitting close to this chapter are the words of the contemporary theologian, Edward Schillebeeckx, who in his book *Jesus: An Experiment in Christology,* discusses the possibility that:

"such an ABBA experience may be disqualified as an illusion. On the other hand for someone who acknowledges and in faith confesses this trustworthiness of Jesus . . . his faith then perceives Jesus' trustworthiness in the material, the biographical data, which the historian can put before him regarding Jesus of Nazareth. This material at any rate confronts us all with the question: Could this person have been right?"

CHAPTER SEVEN

THE DISCLOSURE WORDS: AMEN; TALITHA CUMI; ELOI, ELOI, LAMA SABACHTHANI

AMEN

Christology in a nutshell is what some call it. Such a complicated discipline and there's an insight which epitomizes the whole of the study? The answer given by a number of scholars is "Yes." The nutshell? The term: AMEN. Writing in the *Theological Dictionary of the New Testament* (*TDNT*), H. Schlier states that Jesus' use of AMEN at the beginning of his sayings is "to show that as such they are reliable and true, . . . because Jesus Himself in His Amen acknowledges them to be His own sayings and thus makes them valid. These sayings . . . all have to do with the history of the kingdom of God bound up with His person. Thus in Amen preceding the 'I say to You' of Jesus, we have the whole of Christology *in nuce*."[20] Which means that all christology is contained in the use of *Amen* as in a "nutshell." Other theologians have other "NUTSHELLS," e.g., Jesus' table-fellowship with sinners, or ABBA or some other word or deed of Jesus which they believe highly revelatory of his character. They become the christological nutshells. How important — how much of a nutshell — is AMEN? To discover this, three points will be examined:

— The meaning of AMEN at the time of Jesus.
— Jesus' use of AMEN.
— The use of AMEN in the early Christian community.

THE MEANING OF AMEN AT THE TIME OF JESUS

The topic seems so simple that it's almost ridiculous! YET — what does *Amen* mean? What is really being said when a person shouts *AMEN!* to a statement whether it be liturgical or not?

Amen (an Aramaic term taken over from the Hebrew) derives from the verb *emet*, which means to confirm, to validate; in the passive, then, it means to be firm, to be solid, to be valid, to be binding, to be true. Amen is an expression of the individual or the community, acknowledging a statement which is held to be valid, binding, true. Semitic literature indicates that the AMEN (the YES) validated a contract, accepted the responsibility of a vow, concurred in a statement. It is the active, knowing, affirmative response and therefore participation, in the acts or words of another, by which those words or actions are made mine. In worship, for example, the triple AMEN of the congregation to the blessing of Aaron (cf. Num 6:22) would make it operative since it is being freely accepted through the AMEN.[21]

At the time of Jesus — as today — AMEN is not to be uttered as a formality; its consequences are too binding. In the rare instances in semitic literature when it is said as the conclusion of one's own prayer, it is an expression of hope that what was prayed will be realized.

THE USE OF AMEN BY JESUS

Undoubtedly at the time of Jesus AMEN is commonly used in worship and also, as mentioned above, in some types of agreements. It is basically a concurring, validating response.

In the Gospels, AMEN is NEVER used as a response by Jesus. Rather, it comes at the BEGINNING of some of his words: 30 times in Matthew, 13 times in Mark, 6 times in Luke and 25 times in John's Gospel, where it is doubled, following the Jewish/Christian liturgical usage of the author's time:

"Amen, Amen, I say to you. . ."

This strange use of AMEN is common to all the portraits. Keeping in mind the use of the term at the time of Jesus, its significance would be that he himself is the assurance of the truth of his statements. He needs no AMEN response by others to declare his words true. His own AMEN renders his speech valid.

Did Jesus actually use AMEN in such a strange way, denoting such authority? Does he believes Himself to be the truth so that there is no need for anyone else to Amen what he is saying? It is puzzling, is it not, that in the Gospels, AMEN at the beginning of a phrase is strictly confined to Jesus Himself; no one else in the Gospels ever declares: "Amen, Amen, I say to you. . . ." In fact, this specific usage of Amen is not repeated by any apostle or prophet of the early Church. It is unique to Jesus.

This usage is similar to the "Thus says the Lord. . ." by which the Old Testament prophets introduce their proclamations. But Jesus never says in the Gospel portraits "Thus says the Lord. . ." Rather, the Aramaic word AMEN at the beginning of a phrase is retained in all the Gospels, in all strata of tradition, as a novel usage of Jesus alone. As Fitzmyer states: "So far the exact Hebrew equivalent of the NT Greek formula has not yet turned up . . . and this makes some NT commentators think that the prepositive use of Greek amen, whether single or double, in such a phrase is 'an authentic reminiscence' of Jesus (so R. E. Brown, *John, I–XII, 84*)."[22]

In light of these facts — the principle of dissimilarity, repeated attestations in the Gospels, a uniqueness in language — many theologians declare that AMEN at the beginning of a phrase, is a precise word of Jesus. Reginald Fuller, in *The Foundations of New Testament Christology*, sums up the status of the question: "In this 'Amen,' Jesus pledges his whole person behind the truth of his proclamation. This has certainly been added secondarily to some of Jesus' sayings, as a synoptic comparison will show. But it cannot be doubted that it was characteristic of the historical Jesus."[23] BUT — there is one other fact concerning this prepositive Amen, which is, so it seems, rarely considered:

SIMILAR expressions, e.g., Dan 2:45: "This . . . is certain and its interpretation is sure"; Rev 21:5;22:6: "These words are trustworthy and true" are found in apocalyptic writings to demonstrate the authority of the author and the truth of what is being disclosed. In fact, formulas much like "Amen, Amen, I say to you. . ." are found in Hellenistic (Greek)-Jewish apocalyptic writings. They are typical expressions of the validity of the apocalyptic discourse. And as Fuller notes "one of the two main contexts in which Jesus uses the formula ["Amen, Amen"] is in sayings which speak of the polarity of the presence of the kingdom and its futurity: 'accept the kingdom now in my message and you will be accepted in the kingdom; reject it now and you will be rejected then' (e.g., Mt 10:15,42)."[24] This manner of speaking which is restricted to Jesus in the Gospels, appears to be an apocalyptic expression, declaring that the words to be said are validated by God.

Although *apocalyptic* will be reviewed when *End-Time Prophet* is studied, it may be well to briefly describe it here since the topic has been raised in conjunction with Jesus' use of "Amen, Amen I say to you. . ." Apocalyptic is both a type of literature and also a unique world vision. Someone may employ the literary form of apocalyptic and not necessarily accept its world vision. As a type of literature, it is marked with cryptic, often bizarre symbols, visions, angelic guides, cosmic cataclysms; the often anonymous author artificially places himself at an earlier age in history and then from that vantage point, explains the events which have transpired up to his time. As a world-vision, it looks principally, if not solely, to the future and almost despairs of the present situation which is ordinarily one of alienation, persecution, because of the great evil of the times. Most often the utter discouragement with the present is caused by the fact that the seer believes that God's people are observing his commands, are suffering for him, and yet they are not being helped. The only solution is a future new world, a new heaven, a new earth, a new age, when evil will be conquered. Because of a misunderstanding of apocalyptic literary form, some people today use both Daniel and the Book of Revelation to foretell events, especially concerning the superpowers. Hand-in-hand with the true apocalyptics of centuries ago, they predict that the end of this world is coming soon. As at the turn of the first millennium, so as we approach the end of the second, more and more apocalyptic groups will tell us that the end of the world is here and Jesus is coming today — if not today, then tomorrow. Or the day after.

"Early Christian apocalyptic does not challenge us to gather together on a hillside to await the coming of Jesus . . . or to identify the Beast [of *Revelation*]; it challenges us to recognize the importance and significance of the myths and symbols it uses so dramatically to express hope in the midst of despair."[25]

The content — at least — of the expression "Amen, Amen, I say to you. . . ," is not, therefore, unknown at the time of Jesus. It is widespread in apocalyptic circles. The fact that the words "Amen, Amen" are in Aramaic (Hebrew) cannot be used as an apodictic proof that these words form part of the ipsissima vox of Jesus. Nor does the fact that they are only found on Jesus' lips in the Gospels. Since Greek speaking Jewish Christians used similar expressions, there is the possibility that the prepositive Amen is an embellishment created by the early Christians as their apocalyptic hopes intensified. The formula would express, therefore, not only the early church's belief in the authority of Jesus but the fact that he is the inbreaking of God's judgment upon this world which the early Christians believed was soon coming to an end.

NONETHELESS, in spite of what has been said above, it still appears that this formula is is part of the ipsissima vox. After studying the use of AMEN in the scriptures and its "substantial analogy" with the "Thus says the Lord" used by the prophets, J. Jeremias concludes: "The novelty of the usage, the way in which it is strictly confined to the sayings of Jesus, and the unanimous testimony by all the strata of tradition in the gospels show that here we have the creation of a new expression by Jesus."[26]

Accepting the authenticity of the portraits, we have every reason to believe that prefacing a statement with AMEN — granted that at times this manner of speaking may have been supplied by the early Christians — goes back to the historical Jesus himself. Jesus proclaims with authority. This is the reaction of people to Jesus (cf. Mk. 1:22,27; 2:10;11:23; Mt 9:8;28:18; Lk 4:32,36, etc.), people who heard him, who knew him and, as we will see, is corroborated by many other sections of the portraits. In this sense, it discloses his relationships, his commitments: a fundamental relationship to YHWH whose Word He speaks — as John tells us, whose Word He IS (Jn 1:14) — and flowing from this relationship to his ABBA, a relationship to all people: Jesus, one of us, is THE Teacher, THE proclaimer of the will of the Father. Jesus' usage of the prepositive AMEN is revelatory of the mystery of his person.

Probably the early Christians multiplied the occurrences of this AMEN on the lips of Jesus, demonstrating how strongly apocalyptic hopes flared in the early ages of the church since the expression is typical of apocalyptic circles. Notice that the earliest New Testament writings — First & Second Thessalonians — are an attempt (among other things) by Paul to squelch the exaggerated apocalypticism of the times.

This entire question raises many others. For example, did Jesus think the end of the world imminent? Are the ethics of the Gospels based on an erroneous belief that Jesus is coming soon bringing a new age? Does Jesus fit into the mold of an apocalyptic preacher? The subject will be reviewed when Jesus as End-Time Prophet is examined and when the disclosure theme of Jesus is studied: The Reign of YHWH.

THE USE OF AMEN BY THE EARLY CHRISTIANS

There are at least equivalent phrases of "Amen, I say to you. . ." in the early church, like "the saying is true" (Rev 21:5;22:6;3:14, often in the Pastoral Letters [i.e., the Letters to Titus and Timothy]).

Moreover, AMEN is actually a title given to Jesus by the author of the Book of Revelation (3:14), boldly imitating the prophet Isaiah (65:16) who calls YHWH "God-Amen," translated in the Revised Standard Version as "the God of truth." And Paul in his Second letter to the Corinthians (1:19) speaks of Jesus as the "Yes" (the equivalent of AMEN). The Book of Revelation ends up with the wish that all will respond "Amen" — which means accept the Risen Lord as the meaning of all history, as the fundamental insight into life — and thereby hasten the transformation of this world into the victory of the Risen Christ.

Today, Amen is not only NOT used as a title of Jesus, but even as a response has become more of a formality for most Christians. Amen ("Hear, Hear!" would the Englishman say) is not to be used lightly, especially during the eucharist. For in the Liturgy when the GREAT AMEN is acclaimed the community is not only identifying with the real presence of Christ as the eternal offering — THE AMEN — to the Father but also expressing yearning and willingness to participate fully in His Life, the Victorious Power of the future which breaks into our present.

TALITHA CUMI

Talitha cumi[27] is an Aramaic phrase, found only in Mark 5:41, which signifies, as the evangelist himself explains, "Little girl, I say to you, arise"! Spoken to the daughter of Jairus who is declared dead by her family, it expresses tenderness, care, not only power.

In the light of some of the rabbinical stories of the age, no one can say whether the Jews of Jesus' time would consider the raising of the dead a sign of the power of God Himself. Nonetheless, it would be generally held with Rabbi Yohanan: "Three keys are in the hand of the Holy One, blessed be He, and they have not been entrusted to the hand of an emissary, and they are: the key of rains, and the key of birth, and the key of the resurrection of the dead."[28]

IS THIS EXPRESSION, *talitha cum* exemplifying such tenderness, care and power from the lips of Jesus? Most probably so.[29] For the evidence does lean heavily toward this expression as an ipsissimum verbum. Not only is it kept in Aramaic — which is definitely strange in a Gospel written in Greek (although not a sufficient criterion in itself for an ipsissimum verbum) — but we must remember a belief of many at the time of Jesus (and some today?) that wonder-working words lose their power if translated. As it has been noted by some scholars, when Greek-speaking Christians attempted to work wonders after the example of the Lord (cf. e.g., Acts 8:6 ff, 9:36 ff, 20:7 ff, 1 Cor 12:10,28) they may well have felt it important as citizens of their culture, to preserve the miracle-words in their original form (cf. Mk 7:34 where Mark has retained the Aramaic word — *Ephphatha* — used when Jesus heals a deaf person).

However, in no way are we speaking of Jesus as a "magician," using *magical* terms to effect the cure of the daughter of Jairus. "The fixing of a saying (i.e., *talitha cum*) might seem to suggest that it is regarded as a magic formula. But in reality there is no such idea as all our knowledge of primitive Christianity shows beyond doubt. . . Healings are performed in the name of Jesus Christ (Acts 3:6). It is never suggested, however that the miracle is magically performed merely by the utterance of the name."[30]

There is then the greatest likelihood that we are dealing here with a word truly spoken by Jesus, an expression which in its present context does show interest, tenderness, concern, power, authority. These are traits which the early Christians wanted remembered, for in their eyes, they do speak of the *WHO* of Jesus.

ELOI, ELOI, LAMA SABACHTHANI

This expression — "My God, My God, why hast thou forsaken me" — is often called the cry of dereliction uttered by Jesus as he hung upon the Cross. It is found both in Mark (15:34) and in Matthew (27:46). Matthew speaks of Eli, Eli, (Hebrew), Mark uses the Aramaic (Eloi, Eloi).

Is this really a cry of despair? It is the first verse of Psalm 22, a psalm of the ultimate victory of the suffering, devout Jew. (The entire psalm must be read to grasp its total meaning.) Now, "there is some evidence that among the ancient Jews the opening of this Psalm was interpreted in the light of the rest of it and recognized as an effective form of prayer for help in time of trouble, and according to many commentators, that is the way St Mark understood the words here. He saw Jesus as . . . making his own the Psalmist's expression of complete faith and confidence in God."[31] In other words, we must judge these words by the entire Psalm 22. What we have here, then, is a death-cry of suffering, yes; but it is at least equally, a cry of trust in ABBA, a belief unto death of that experience — loving, tender, strong, obedient — of ABBA.

Mark, the most unpolished of all Gospels, will keep the prayer in the original. Matthew, writing primarily to Jewish Christians who know of the meaning of reciting the first verse of the psalm, retains these words. But Luke, writing to a predominantly Gentile-Christian audience, knows that these words could be easily misunderstood by his people and so paraphrases (an example of redaction) the final words of Jesus as "Father, into thy hands I commend my spirit" (Lk 23:46). John's Gospel, so highly theologized, has Jesus cry out, again an example of theological editorializing, "It is finished" (Jn 19:30).

Or is it possible that the attitude of Jesus at his death was of such trust in God that the early Christians placed Psalm 22 on his dying lips to manifest this surrender? Surely a possibility. This psalm seems to have been one of the favorite passion-psalms of the early church.

Nonetheless, it appears more plausible — but by no means certain — to see in this psalm the actual final expression of Jesus as he dies upon the cross. As embarrassing as they may have been to some readers, (and as embarrassing, these words retained in Aramaic, do have a ring of historicity) they do explain to a persecuted congregation that the horror of martyrdom gives way to glory. There are grounds, therefore, for the inclusion of this Aramaic expression as one of the ipsissima verba. Yet, whether we consider the final words of Jesus as given by Matthew/Mark or Luke or John, or whether the early Christians are expressing his attitude in death by Psalm 22, basically the same truth is being taught: from the incredible pain and suffering of death upon the cross, Jesus offers himself to his loving Father. This is in keeping with the entire context of the portraits as will become more evident.

This first verse of Psalm 22 is then not EITHER a cry of dereliction OR a cry of victory; it is BOTH. Again, it expresses that deep, unique relationship between Jesus and His ABBA. Jesus is obedient "unto death, even death upon a cross" (Phil 2:8). This relationship of trust in His ABBA knows no limits. It is THE commitment of His life, the relationship which, as we will see, constitutes his person. It also expresses the Father's surrender of His Incarnate Word to the radical experience of human finitude: death. And at the same time, it demonstrates that victorious relationship of Love, for the Father bestows new life, new being, victory upon His Enfleshed Word, torn and mangled in death.

Summary

These disclosure words reveal a different facet of the personhood of Jesus. *Amen* especially accentuates his authority; *Talitha cumi* his power and loving kindness; *Eloi, Eloi*, his total surrender in love to his ABBA. The portrait becomes more meaningful as we examine these revelatory words (not to be separated from his actions) which form an expression of his very being. Jesus is remembered as a man of unique oneness with God and also of unique oneness with us. He experiences the depths of human emotions in life and in death and at the same time experiences an intimacy with the Father which he cannot identify with anyone else's knowledge of God. The portrait is developing: in Jesus, the power of God is personally disclosed. In Jesus, God is revealed as a God for humankind. In Jesus, the universe offers to the Father a worship of praise and through his cry of surrender to Infinite Love, we are healed.

SECTION THREE

THE TITLES OF JESUS

After having briefly examined some of the disclosure Aramaic words found in the Gospels, one of the most intriguing topics in christology will now be reviewed: the revelatory character of the more important titles attributed to Jesus in the New Testament portraits. Beginning with the most popular title of all, *Messiah*, the study will encompass *Lord, Son of God, Son of Man, Suffering Servant, End-Time Prophet.*[1]

Working from the assumption that authentic titles encapsulate a person's relationships, disclosing the self, we can already understand the importance this section must hold in christology. As Vincent Taylor remarks, "The question, who Jesus is, is approached best by considering how men named Him, for it is by His names that He is revealed and known."[2] This is especially true in the semitic culture of Jesus where a title or name is not an extrinsic label but "an essential constituent or kind of counterpart of its bearer."[3] A few introductory words concerning the use of titles in christology will bring us to our first topic: Is Jesus the Messiah?

How do you profile yourself when asked, "Who are you?" Which titles do you automatically choose to describe yourself? Many users of telecommunications systems identify themselves not by proper name but by titles, like lawyer, renaissance man, priest, teacher, professor, computer programmer, Christian, stockbroker, university student, home-maker . . . the list seems endless. A profile on a popular telecommunications system contains the following titles: Catholic priest, Montfort missionary, teacher, computer-nut. The profile identifies the author. Perhaps you do not know the color of my eyes, or the length of my beard, or my weight, or where I was born. Nonetheless, through these titles always presuming they are lived-out, you do know *me*, at least to some degree.

Not all titles are important, not all are equally revelatory. Yet when we do identify ourselves through lived-out titles, we *give ourselves away*, we disclose ourselves. Not all titles are *self-designations*. Often they are sincerely given to us by others who know us well. These too can be highly revelatory, especially when the identical title is applied to us by most of our friends even though many of them are unknown to one another. These titles pinned on us by our acquaintances reveal at times an aspect of our *WHO* which for a multitude of reasons we may not be able to verbalize or which we may have unconsciously implied by actions and/or speech. All titles have to be weighed, studied, and to the best of our ability, verified concerning both the intended meaning and applicability to a specific person.

It is this apparently simple process which is followed in trying to wipe off some of the grime and dust from the portraits of Jesus so that we have a clearer view of him. Or to put it another way, we are trying to check his profile.

It is an *apparently* simple process. For, in reality, the task is delicate and difficult. Delicate, since we are treading here on what some people call sacred ground. Many can be easily turned away by what appears to be a flippant remark or a lack of respect. Others may, regrettably, show an unwillingness to examine the situation critically, fearing the conclusions. The task is even more *difficult* than delicate, for christology deals with interpretative titles of two thousand years ago, within a culture so alien to our own that is is impossible to fully penetrate. The difficulty is compounded when we accept the fact that each person is a mystery not only for others but also for oneself. So too with Jesus. Guided by the Christian community's understanding of the portraits, we must cautiously and creatively attempt to underline the principal thrusts of Jesus' character through this study of his titles.

As the Gospel titles for Jesus are being scrutinized, it is important to recall that the task is not the study of a scientific formula, or the composition of a legal brief, or the programming of a computer. Christology probes the *WHO* of this human being, Jesus; it can never be put under a microscope never reduced to a mathematical formula, never neatly packaged in a sealproof plastic bag, never diagnosed by surgical biopsy. What is deepest and most important in life cannot be scientifically proven. It is manifested, revealed, disclosed by our lived-out relationships. The Gospel portraits, painted by the early Church, attempt to disclose the *WHO* of Jesus by pinning titles on him. They form an essential element of these Gospel paintings of Jesus and must, therefore, be closely investigated.

CHAPTER EIGHT

JESUS THE MESSIAH (1)

It is fitting to begin with THE title of Jesus, the magnet title which quickly entwined all others (and therefore so difficult to disentangle), a title so beloved by Christians that they have used it not so much as a *title* for Jesus but as his own *proper name*: CHRIST . . . which is derived from the Greek, *christos*, synonymous with the Hebrew term *mashiach* which in its anglicised form is MESSIAH. Both CHRIST and MESSIAH mean THE ANOINTED ONE.[4] Every book of the New Testament except *2 John* (i.e., the Second Letter of John) designates, in some way or another, Jesus as the Christ. This is, then, a title strongly stressed in all the portraits even though not with the same nuances, as will become evident. As explained above, the study will be in three stages:

— What does the title Messiah mean at the time of Jesus?
— Did Jesus accept/reject the title as far as we can discern?
— What is the history of this title within the early Christian community, i.e., was it invented by the post- resurrection community? Did it take on new meanings? Did the title continue to be applied to Jesus or was it dropped — and why?

THE MEANING OF MESSIAH AT THE TIME OF JESUS

Today, if the question is posed to a group of Christians (i.e., followers of the Anointed One), "What is the meaning of Messiah?," the answer usually received is "Savior." The danger is that the present-day meaning may be retrojected into the time of Jesus. In our *dialogue* with this title we must try to listen to the word *Messiah* as it was understood by Jesus' own people. Such dialogue is extremely difficult for there is no such thing as total objectivity. We are a *situated* people and therefore consider everything from within our situation, with our pre-understanding, with our inbuilt prejudices. Pure objectivity, even in the hard sciences, is not consonant with an authentic understanding of the actual human person. We can, therefore, only hope to approximate in modern terms the force of *Messiah* at the time of Jesus.

In order to grasp, as far as possible, the meaning of Messiah in Jesus' milieu, we must — all too briefly — review the meaning of Messiah in the history of Israel.[5] Fundamentalism immediately equates this task with a study of messianic prophecy. It declares that from the very start — from the first book of the bible — there are a number of messianic foretellings which clearly indicate the coming of the Savior, Jesus. A review of messianism in the Old Testament is, according to this opinion, identical to a narration of all the prophecies concerning Jesus found in the history of Israel (some would even say in secular literature, e.g., Virgil's Eclogues,[6] The Sybylline Oracles[7]). We must, therefore, begin with a necessary tangent: is the Messiah *foretold* in the Old Testament? In answering this question, a few terms need to be clarified, and a brief outline sketched of the meaning of messianism in the Old Testament. Only then will we have the wherewithall to draw the correct conclusions concerning Jesus-the-Messiah-foretold and at the same time have a clearer understanding of *Messiah* at the time of Jesus.

Strictly speaking, *MESSIANISM* deals with a future within our earthly history entailing that final intervention of YHWH by which Israel is established religiously and politically as the hub of the world. Essential to messianism is the figure of a

SAVIOR and more specifically, as we will see, a royal figure of King David's line who will terminate the Davidic dynasty and realize the reign of YHWH within an earthly framework. That the term took on broader meanings will become evident in the course of the study.

Messianism strictly-so-called, must be distinguished from *MESSIANIC FEVER* which is nothing more than the yearning and the striving for a more capable leader, an ideal king. Messianic fever is found throughout the times of the kings for the Jewish people do not seem to have been blessed with the best of rulers. Messianic fever does not look into that end-time (called *eschatology*; apocalypticism can be regarded as a type of eschatology) which is essential to messianism. It deals with the *today*, the *as soon as possible*, which is implied, for example when people exclaim: "When will we get an outstanding leader!"

It cannot be overstressed that until the 2nd century B.C. there is no strictly-so-called *messianism* found within Israel.[8] Messianic fever is found much earlier, yes; messianism, no. Is it being said that Jesus is *not* foretold in the Old Testament considered by itself? Is it being stated that there are no strictly-so-called messianic hopes in the history of Israel before the second century B.C.? Correct. This point cannot be clarified until the history of messianism is first resumed. Only then can the question be raised about Jesus-foretold. The term Messiah, in its strict sense, deals with the monarchy. The Messiah or the Christ denotes someone anointed with oil[9] (either literally or also figuratively, i.e., filled with the Holy Spirit) who as delegate of YHWH carries out a special function in Israel. THE anointed one of YHWH is then, to be strict of terms, the reigning monarch, who probably exercised some priestly functions at various points in Israel's history.[10]

To ask someone around the time of King David, "Where does the Messiah live?" would be a strange question, indeed. The anointed of YHWH is the reigning monarch and the guide would merely point to the royal palace.

When the history of Israel was edited after a generation or so of Babylonian exile (beginning with the fall of Jerusalem 587 B.C.) a greater stress, so it would appear, was placed on the role of the kings in the history of Judah than actually is warranted. With the hindsight of the utter defeat at the hands of the Babylonians, there is what is called a *deuteronomic editing* of history[11] which means that many books of the Old Testament (e.g, Joshua, Judges, Kings, 1 & 2 Samuel) were emended to stress the principal points of the book of Deuteronomy: centralization of worship in Jerusalem, obedience to the law as found in the book of Deuteronomy, avoidance of any kind of apostasy, a rigid system of reward and punishment and — this is its relationship to the topic — giving importance to the Davidic dynasty. The famous proclamation by the prophet Nathan that the throne of David will last forever (2 Samuel 7:8-16) has been enlarged, emended, overstressed by deuteronomic editing.[12]

Nonetheless, after the exile, what appears even stronger — in actual fact — than this royalist hope is the purely theocratic movement stressing that YHWH ALONE is King, and his anointed one (*the Messiah, the Christ*) can be the nation as a whole (cf. Is 55:3-5), or even a foreign, pagan ruler like Cyrus of Persia who is called the Messiah of YHWH in Is 45:1. As far as can be reconstructed, messianism only truly appears within Israel in what is termed by many "Late Judaism" (i.e., 2nd and 1st centuries before Christ, which strictly speaking should be called "Early Judaism") when we do meet a genuine messianic expectation in the literature of the age. This messianism is neither a systematic outgrowth of any restorative monarchism, nor any hopes for the rebirth of the dynasty of David.[13] A son of David, yes, but without any fixed genealogy.

Messianism is more the result of anti-Hasmonean (the unlawful dynasty which ruled Judaea from about 135 B.C. to the conquest by the Romans under Pompey in 63 B.C.), anti-Roman, anti- Herodian tendencies than any scriptural hopes for an ideal king. It is principally the hope of liberation, the yearning for freedom, the reaction against the abuse of power and the breaking of the Law, which in "late Judaism" gave rise to the conviction of Israel's God-given destiny to conquer all enemies through an anointed Davidic leader to come, thus ushering in the final deliverance.

AS NEW TESTAMENT TIMES APPROACH, the Messiah, strictly-so-called, is definitely to be understood in earthly context; he is not a superhuman figure dwelling in eternity. However, strict messianism also exists side by side and often intertwined with a wide variety of beliefs in a coming salvific figure in close ties with YHWH:

— On the threshold of the New Testament, one can speak of priestly messianism, for after the disappearance of the Davidic monarchy, the priest is the anointed one and during the Hasmonean dynasty, king and priest were joined in one person. The Messiah is to be someone of the line of the High Priest Aaron, who will restore Israel as the religious center of the world.

— There is also a type of prophetical messianism, looking forward to an end-time prophet who will usher in the Reign of Yahweh.

— There is also the double messianism in the writings of the Essenes.[14] These highly structured rigorists awaited a Messiah of David and a Messiah of Aaron — a king and a priest (which may be incorporated in one person?) accompanied by a prophet.[15]

— Strict davidic messianism (The Son of David) becomes even stronger after the destruction of Jerusalem in 70 A.D. The Psalms of Solomon,[16] probably of Pharisaic origin, attest to this militant movement which also insisted upon a spiritual renovation of Israel.

— In the apocalyptic literature of the age, there is strictly speaking no place for an earthly Messiah, since the concern is with a "new heaven and a new earth," an other-worldly state. Yet when messianism does infiltrate apolcalyptic literature (e.g., the Ethiopian version of the book of Enoch, 4th Esdras [c.100 A.D.])[17] the strange mixture gives rise to what is called millenarianism (also termed *chiliasm* from the Greek word for a thousand, *chilioi*), where the Messiah is placed upon an earthly throne for a thousand year reign before the final apocalyptic close of the age. Millenarianism becomes a stock apocalyptic symbol of victory, as we see in the *Book of Revelation* (cf. Revelation 20:1-6).

— There is also a transcendental messianism of "late Judaism," when the notion of earthly Messiah strangely coalesces with the pre-existent Son of Man (cf. Dan 7:13) who appears to be a symbol for Israel.

— Finally, there is the pervading *general* notion of Messiah: any liberator, any charismatic leader of a rebellion against Rome who will free God's people and secure their rightful destiny.

IT IS THIS ENTANGLED, COMPLEX UNDERSTANDING OF MESSIAH WHICH IS FOUND IN ISRAEL AT THE TIME OF JESUS. Yet whatever form it takes — strict davidic messianism or transcendental messianism of Son of Man, or an apocalyptic messianism, or priestly or prophetic messianism, or what we have termed a general messianism — or any combination of these — *it does have political overtones*. For even if we speak of a spiritual Messiah, he must overthrow Rome which has placed its standards within the temple itself. A Messiah does, for the ordinary people, involve some type of victory over the Romans. For many, the Messiah would necessarily be a person of prestige, worldly power and domain.

NOW a response can be given to the question raised at the beginning of the chapter: are there messianic prophecies in the Old Testament? Is Jesus foretold? Some Christians who strongly hold the affirmative, point first of all to Genesis 3:15, called the *protoevangelium*, i.e., the first Gospel, the first announcement of the good news of salvation: "Behold, I place enmities [says YHWH-God to the satan-snake in paradise] between thee and the woman, between thy seed and her seed. He[18] shall crush your head and you shall crush him in his heel."

According to the *Jesus-foretold* theory, the "He" is Jesus and the crushing of the head of the snake is the destruction of satan.[19] The proponents of *Jesus-foretold* claim that the line of messianic prophecy continues throughout the Old Testament, with lacunae here and there but with clearer outlines as the centuries go on.

Is not the Savior Jesus announced in the famous prophecy of Balaam in Numbers 24:17: "I see him, but not now; I behold him, but not nigh; a star shall come forth out of Jacob, and a scepter shall rise out of Israel."

Is not his pre-existence and even his birth-place designated in the prophet Micah 5:2: "But you, O Bethlehem Ephrathah, who are little to be among the clans of Judah, from you shall come forth for me one who is to be ruler in Israel, whose origin is from of old, from ancient days."

Is not the virginal conception clearly foretold in Isaiah 7:14: "Behold a young woman shall conceive and bear a son and shall call his name Immanuel."

Are not the qualities of the Messiah-to-come given in Isaiah 9:1-7;11:1-10, who tells us that this Messiah (Jesus) is God: "For to us a child is born, to us a son is given; and the government will be upon his shoulder, and his name will be called 'Wonderful, Counselor, Mighty God, Everlasting Father, Prince of Peace.' "

These are some of the principal prophecies[20] of the Messiah in the Old Testament. WHY THEN IS IT that the Jews did not recognize Jesus, since he is so clearly foretold in the Scriptures? Why is it that they were not ready for him, since even the date (?) of his arrival is given in Daniel 9:24-27? (It should be noted that v.25 is probably the first clear scriptural reference to a future anointed figure who will be of David's lineage; the book of Daniel is written somewhere around 165 B.C.) WHY? For one basic reason: considering the Old Testament ALONE, there are NO foretellings of any Messiah-God, there are NO foretellings of Jesus. It would take a separate book to examine all of the above texts.[21] But when each of the so-called Messianic prophecies is examined critically, there is no reason to see any Old Testament foretelling of Jesus, understanding the Old Testament as a unit in itself. At times the texts refer not to messianism but to messianic fever, or make no reference to any anointed liberator to come, bringing the final deliverance; at times the texts when studied in context have no relationship to the question of Messiah.

Perhaps a more detailed explanation of one of the principal "prophecies" may be of some help. Consider the prophecy of the virginal conception: Jesus is to be born of a woman without any concurrence of the male seed.[22] Is this found in Isaiah 7:14 quoted above? A sign involving the Syro-Ephramite war of 734 B.C. is given to King Ahaz by Isaiah: the young girl in his harem conceives and bears a child. The text in Hebrew does not say *virgin* but a *young girl*. The Greek translators (the LXX [Septuagint]) rendered young girl by the Greek term for virgin, *parthenos*.[23] The verb, however, is formulated in the future: "will conceive"; the translators may have meant, therefore, that the young girl who is NOW a virgin will — by normal means — conceive a child Immanuel, signifying that God is still with us. Neither the Hebrew nor the Greek text of Is 7:14 deals with messianism. And neither text seems to speak of a virginal conception as understood in the Infancy Narratives of the New Testament. As far as can be ascertained, the prophet is probably alluding to the birth of Hezekiah, a son of Ahaz.[24] In the sole light of the Old Testament, there are *no* prophecies of Jesus, no messianic foretellings; there is, in fact, no strict messianism until the second century B.C.

THEN WHY, especially in the portrait painted by Matthew is there such a stress on fulfillment of the scriptures? Why does Matthew repeatedly employ a stereotyped phrase like: "And this was done to fulfill what was spoken of by the prophet. . ." And most importantly, why does Matthew even declare that the virginal conception of Jesus is found in that verse of Isaiah 7:14 (cf. Mt 1:23)?

The answer is that the early Christians *christologized* the entire Old Testament. Starting off with their belief that Jesus is (in 20th century terminology) the eschatologically (i.e., end-time) victorious personal epiphany of God's Word, the climactic point of creation, they logically see in Jesus the fulfillment of all that is hoped for in the Scriptures. The meaning of history is disclosed through its summit, Jesus; therefore, the Old Testament can only be fully understood, say Christians, when it is read through its fulfillment, the New Testament.

Following, therefore, the exegetical method of the time, they see Jesus as the ultimate meaning of "what was spoken by the prophets. . ." especially in those texts which deal IN ANY WAY with salvation, liberation, joy, hope, yearning for deliverance. For deliverance, salvation, has come, proclaim the Christians, in and through Jesus.

It is only with these provisos that we speak of Jesus as foretold: by reading the Old Testament in the light of the New, by looking at the earlier history of Israel in the light of what Christians believe its fulfillment. And for Christians, this is the way that the Old Testament is to be prayed and fully understood. There is an "excess of meaning" hiding in the Old Testament which is only revealed by the New, as it is lived and prayed within its context, the Christian community.[25]

Summary

The title Messiah is an ambiguous one at the time of Jesus, with overtones of ridding Israel of the Romans. Strict messianism is a late phenomenon in Israel but was unusually intense — in its variety of forms — around the time of Jesus.[26] Messianism usually makes the Christian think of all the texts of the Old Testament which foretell Jesus. Yet, the Old Testament of itself does not explicitly look forward to Jesus; but in the light of the New Testament, Jesus is clearly seen by Christians as the fulfillment of all the yearnings and hopes of the Old Testament. Since Christians consider the bible as one book — two testaments — the follower of Jesus understandably reads into the Old Testament of the bible God's climactic self-disclosure, Jesus.

Joachim Becker, in his *Messianic Expectation in the Old Testament*, after declaring so forcefully throughout his book that "there is no such thing as messianic expectation until the last two centuries B.C." ends up his study by stating:

"The fulfillment was an astonishing act of God, which made unbelief possible for Israel . . . If . . . we found it easy to caricature the traditional picture of messianic expectations, we must now retract. To find Christ at every stop on our way through the history of Israel and the Old Testament is not only no deception but also a duty imposed on us by the inspired testimony of the New Testament. . ."[27]

Did Jesus accept/reject the name THE CHRIST? How did this title evolve within the early Christian community? These will be the topics of the following chapter.

CHAPTER NINE

DISCLOSURE TITLE: MESSIAH (2)

Keeping in mind the complex notion of Messiah at the time of Jesus as described in the previous chapter, there are two additional problems which must be studied. Following the methodology outlined above, attention must now focus on:

— Did Jesus accept/reject the title Messiah?
— The development of the title in the early Christian community.

In examining the PROFILE on Jesus in the Gospels one title stands out above all the rest: CHRIST/MESSIAH/ANOINTED.

We know for certain that it was put in his PROFILE by his friends, many of whom did not even know one another. Why they did that and what they meant by that title, is to be seen in step three. For the moment, a more difficult problem must be faced: is it possible that Jesus himself put it in his PROFILE, i.e., is it possible that Jesus accepted the title MESSIAH? And if so, how did he understand it? Or did he reject it? Is it even possible to discover the answer?

Since there are political overtones in the messianism of Jesus' time, since there are implications of victory over the Romans, of power, dominion, prestige, can we *a priori* dismiss the absurdity (?) that Jesus accepted messiahship? However, since the conclusion — Jesus Christ is NOT the Christ — is a startling one, for ALL the portraits insist he IS the Messiah, the question of his messiahship deserves closer inspection. The method? Investigate the portraits where they accentuate that Jesus IS the Christ and see if there are any telltale prints which could give us a possible inkling into Jesus' reaction to this title.

All roads lead first to *Mark* and *Q*, for they are considered the earliest portraits, and the least theologized. We must examine the sections where Jesus is explicitly faced with the question: "Are you the Messiah?" and see if the portrait artists left any clues whether the response is their interpretation or the Lord's. This distinction is needed in light of today's understanding of the nature of the literary from "Gospel," although it was not even considered by the early Christians or even seriously discussed until our modern times.

The search quickly narrows, for nowhere in *Q* is Jesus explicitly faced with the question of messiahship. But there are, surprisingly, THREE references in Mark where Jesus himself responds to this central issue:

— The Confession of Peter (MK 8:27–33).
— The Trial Before Caiaphas (Mk 14:60–64).
— The Trial Before Pilate (MK 15:2–5).

The three episodes will be briefly examined, always keeping in mind not the present day notion of MESSIAH but what it meant at the time of Jesus: Son of David, liberator, representative of the people, the end-time reign of YHWH, politics, prestige, honor, power, a national hero. And even if we take in other hybrid forms of messianism which were flaring up around the time of Jesus, the notion of politics and expulsion of the Romans are intertwined with them. The CONFESSION OF PETER[28] takes place in the north around Caesarea Phillipi. Jesus asks his disciples "Who do men say that I am?" Finally, after declaring that many people think he is some kind of prophet, the blustering Peter speaks for the close followers of Jesus and says, "YOU ARE THE CHRIST!"[29] According to Mark, Jesus "charged them to tell no one about him."[30]

Often in Mark Jesus tells those who call him the Christ to keep silent. W. Wrede terms this the *messianic secret* which he considers no more than a literary device of Mark to explain why the disciples and the Jews did not recognize Jesus as the Messiah.[31] However, considering the political situation in Israel, the confused understanding of Messiah at the times, the automatic condemnation by the Roman overlords of any pretender (Messiah) to a Jewish throne, it does appear to be an historical fact that Jesus did make some attempts to stop people from calling him the Messiah or equivalently, from trying to make him king (cf. Jn 6:15). That there is some discussion among the disciples about the *WHO* of Jesus is thought to be historical, whether it took place at Caesarea Phillipi or not, for it appears to be called for by the circumstances of Jesus' ministry.

The present debate, therefore, concerns Jesus' acceptance or rejection of an ambiguous title which a number of people, including the disciples, were giving him. Is it possible to go beyond the fact that Jesus is so depicted by his followers? Did *he* accept the title, Christ?

In trying to exegete a section of scripture like the *Confession of Peter*, it is important that it be read in its entire context. Ultimately the *context* must include the experience of the Christian community as was seen in the *Introduction*. Moreover, chapters/verses were placed in the text in the 16th century and do harm as well as good, inasmuch as they at times break the flow of thought. For example, from the description of the scene at Caesarea Phillipi described above, no judgment can as yet be made for we have not completed the entire context. Taking a text out of context to prove one's already decided-upon belief (called proof-texting) is quite common. It is, therefore, the *entire* episode (called technically, *pericope*) of this *Confession* which must be examined.

Peter, who would understand *messiah* as a victorious conqueror of sorts, is dismayed when Jesus responds that he, the Son of Man, must suffer. Suffering, dying, is not an integral element of the triumphalistic davidic messianism at the time of Jesus. Peter, according to Mark's description, becomes furious. He has given up all things to follow Jesus, and Jesus speaks of dying? Defeat? Even if there is a mention of ultimate vindication (expressed by "after three days rise again"), Peter, a man of his day, would not understand it. He, therefore, blows up at Jesus and in turn, we find the harshest reaction of Jesus recorded in the Gospel: "But turning and seeing his disciples, he rebuked Peter and said, 'Get behind me, Satan! For you are not on the side of God, but of men.' "

An embarrassing situation, indeed. This community with the Son of God at its head is having a battle royal, with name calling and shoving ("and Peter took him") included. Moreover, this is being preached after the resurrection when Jesus is clearly recognized as the Word of God Incarnate. There is a ring of historicity in the entire episode, taken in its general outlines.

The presumption, therefore, leans heavily on the side of some confrontation between Jesus and his disciples concerning his role. The leader of the apostles cannot understand a "suffering Messiah," a contradiction in terms for poor Peter. And the response of Jesus appears to be a downright rejection of messiahship — at least the way Peter apparently understands it. For Jesus, it is nothing less than a diabolical temptation.[32]

This appears to be verified by the *Letter to the Hebrews* which categorically states that Jesus has been tempted in every way just as we are (4:15) and most especially, by what is called the *Q* temptation narrative (Lk 4:1–13; Mt 4:1–11).[33] In symbolic language, Matthew and Luke vividly describe the fact that Jesus encountered true temptation in his life and not just on one occasion. As G. B. Caird points out, "A man of fervent and dedicated spirit, feeling himself called to liberate the oppressed and to establish the reign of justice and peace, would be open to three types of temptation: to allow the good to usurp the place of the best, to seek God's ends by means alien to God's character, and to force God's hand by taking short cuts to success. And these are the three temptations of Jesus."[34]

Although the temptations are "presented to Jesus in his capacity as Heaven's emissary and Son (3:22)"[35] the devil entices Jesus to accept worldly power, fame, land, dominion: the makings of the davidic messiah. This Q tradition about Jesus' temptation in the desert implies quite strongly that Jesus was truly tempted to become a Jewish messiah of the day. The historicity of this man Jesus, tempted by wealth, grandeur, power, is difficult to deny. The implication of the radical possibility of Jesus sinning — although in fact, always sinless — appears to be an integral part of the synoptic depiction of Jesus' anguished struggle with the powers of evil.[36] The force of the temptation is evident as Jesus loses his temper when Peter wants him to be a Messiah who will not suffer but who will victoriously conquer for Israel. Peter is like satan in the Q temptation narrative, dangling before Jesus messianism without suffering, a messianism of adulation, political victory, power, praise.

The probable conclusion of the study of this episode at Caesarea Phillipi is that Jesus is *tempted* by messiahship. Only with deep anguish and personal struggle does Jesus reject messiahship or at least certain aspects of it in obedience to the Father's will.

THE TRIAL SCENE OF JESUS[37] poses insurmountable problems. The first is the fact that the modern reader has an almost irresistible tendency to turn Gospel into biography, to read these interpretations as a *Life of Jesus*, not as authentic proclamations of faith. Step three in the Gospel formation becomes automatically identified with step one: the pitfall of fundamentalism.

Concerning the general historicity of a trial before Pilate preceded by a type of hearing before the Jewish leaders, there is little if any doubt. And no scholar denies that Jesus died by crucifixion and that messiahship ("King of the Jews") played some role in his execution. But beyond those assertions of basic historicity it is not easy to go, considering the nature of our sources.

Moreover, we must remember the strange (to our way of thinking) use of Scripture by the people of the time. If Jesus is God's emissary, then it must be found in scripture; no Jew could have thought otherwise. So convinced are the early Christians that ALL is found in scripture, that when a psalm (e.g., Ps 22) or a section of the Prophets (e.g., the Suffering Servant of Isaiah, cf. Is 53) is christologized, there is a tendency to transform the details of the psalm or prophecy into historical facts concerning Jesus. Also, some aspects of the trial before the Jewish court, the 71 member *Sanhedrin*, do not tally with Jewish custom although it must be admitted that what we possess today concerning these procedures dates from sometime after the death of Jesus but possibly (probably?) refers to earlier customs.[38] Finally, recall that we are projecting the trial of Jesus on situations which existed years after his death/resurrection, when the tension between church and synagogue was intense. The Gospels, especially Matthew and John, stress, therefore, that the Jews have rejected the messiah. The lack of a scholarly reading of these accounts has sadly led to anti-semitism among some Christians.

Caution is needed, therefore, in trying to decipher any telltale prints on the portrait. On many points, we can only reach probable conclusions since authentic interpretation, not videotape fact, was the goal of the evangelists. With this in mind, we approach the two episodes in the trial scene where Jesus is accused of being a messiah.

Mark tells us that Jesus was tried first by the Sanhedrin which is most likely. That the question of messiahship arises, considering the atmosphere of the times, is most probable. How was the question about messiahship phrased by the High Priest? How did Jesus respond to it? We can only examine each evangelist's *interpretation* of the entire scene which he received from others.

When, according to Mark, Jesus responds "I AM" to the double question "Are you the Christ, the Son of the Blessed One?" the High Priest accuses Jesus of blasphemy. Strict blasphemy involves uttering the divine name. Jesus has not done that (cf. Lev 24:10–23).[39] It is significant that Jesus inserts into his reply: "And you will see the Son of Man . . . coming on the clouds of heaven." Jesus modifies his "I am" to the double question by declaring that he is the Son of Man which would probably make the Sanhedrin think of Daniel 7, of this divine-like Son of Man of apocalyptic literature. Would that be considered, at least in some broad sense, blasphemous? Considering the times, quite possibly.

In Mark's understanding, then, Jesus admits clearly during his preliminary hearing before the Sanhedrin that he is the messiah[40] — an ambiguous concept — but immediately modifies it with the reference to the Son of Man. However, when we compare this Marcan text with the way it is interpreted by Matthew and Luke, we notice that Luke (22:67–68) has Jesus give an ambiguous reply to the High Priest, and Matthew also has the ambivalent "You have said so" (26:64). There appears to be a conviction among the early Christians that Jesus at best accepted "messiah" in a modified form in responding to Caiaphas. Neither Matthew nor Luke repeat the affirmative answer found in Mark's account.

It is, then, a probable conclusion that in the preliminary hearing before the Sanhedrin, the early Christian community believed that Jesus modified his accept-ance of the title *messiah* by speaking of himself as *Son of Man* and/or by giving an ambiguous answer to an ambiguous question.

When confronted with the Roman manner of expressing messiahship, "Are you the King of the Jews?," Jesus responds with the ambiguous, "You have said so" (Mk 15:2). That this should not be understood as a clear affirmation, Mark makes clear by telling us that "Pilate wondered" (15:5). If Jesus affirmed messiahship, Pilate's response of condemnation would have been automatic. Before Pilate, then, Jesus never accepts the title *messiah*; he rather gives an ambiguous answer to what was in reality, an ambiguous question.

From a study of these primary texts concerning Jesus' acceptance or rejection of the title *messiah*, it appears that Jesus never accepted messiahship in the strict davidic sense of the term, but always modified it in some manner, if not rejecting it outright. There are other aspects of the Gospels which lead us to this same general conclusion. Not only do the portraits as a whole militate against any notion of Jesus being a strictly davidic Messiah but two other episodes should be briefly pointed out which substantiate the opinion proposed.

FIRST, in a polemical passage, Jesus, according to Mark (12:35–37), interprets Psalm 110:1, "The Lord said to my Lord, Sit at my right hand, till I put thy enemies under thy feet," as meaning that since David calls the Messiah "Lord," then the Messiah is even greater than David. It appears that the statement is directed against the nationalistic forms of Jewish messiahship prevalent at that time of Roman occupation. Jesus is disclaiming that the notion of messiahship is to be determined solely by sonship of David "according to the flesh" rather than by a unique relationship with God. Again, it appears that Jesus — or the Christian community authentically interpreting him — rejects messianism in any strict sense, replacing it with a highly modified and rather novel version of Messiah which corresponds, as we will see, with the rather novel understanding of Kingdom of God.

There is question, however, concerning the historicity of this episode, since Psalm 110 was one of the favorite texts used by the early Christians in evangelization and it appears to contradict the messianic secret, unless Jesus is speaking of messiahship in a speculative manner which appears highly unlikely. Nonetheless, there is again expressed the belief of the early Christians that Jesus rejects davidic messianism or, at best, reinterprets it.

SECONDLY, the thesis proposed above appears to be substantiated by the pericope of the final entry of Jesus into Jerusalem (Mk 11:1-11) which Christians celebrate as Palm Sunday. Mark appears to allude to Zechariah 9:9: "Shout aloud, O daughter of Jerusalem. Lo, your king comes to you; triumphant and victorious is he, humble and riding on an ass, on a colt the foal of an ass."[41] Historically, as far as can probably be reconstructed, Jesus enters Jerusalem with his small group for the celebration of the Feast of Dedication, when palm branches were waved. It is a small incident in itself, creating only a ripple on the surface of Jerusalem; otherwise, the Romans would have intervened. Yet it does appear to be a symbolic action of Jesus which joined to his general lifestyle indicates a reformulation of the nationalistic davidic messiahship. He comes in triumph on a donkey. There is here a core historicity which would appear to indicate again Jesus' revulsion for the strict messianism of his age. The early Christians will embellish this incident and transform it into a joyful proclamation of their belief that Jesus Christ is Lord, he is the King. In reality, it would appear to be a minor incident which has the character of a prophetical sign demonstrating what Jesus believes his destiny: not to be a davidic Messiah as understood in "late Judaism" but one who in a depth of union with the Father surrenders to the Father's Love, even in death. Hardly the messianism of the times.

Did Jesus accept or reject the title Messiah? The probable conclusion is that in the highly confused and ambiguous understanding of the term, he either utterly rejects it as a diabolical temptation or at least modifies it so that it cannot be understood as involving any triumphalistic, nationalistic, political victory with all that entails. In short, he does NOT accept messiahship in its classical connotation of the term. That Jesus himself was truly tempted to messianism and that he had a difficult time trying to rid his disciples — which included some zealots — of any hope that they were following a messiah of the times, Mark appears to strongly affirm.

DEVELOPMENT OF THE TITLE MESSIAH IN THE EARLY CHRISTIAN COMMUNITY

Presuming that our response to step two is the correct one, then the response to step three is evident: the early Christians are responsible for giving Jesus the title, *Christ*.[42] In fact, it is one of the ironies of history that a title which Jesus rejected or at least substantially modified — as far as we can ascertain — has become his name. This happened because the Christians apparently changed the definition of Messiah. The title on the cross, the reason for the execution of this criminal, Jesus, is: "The King of the Jews." King = the Roman manner of saying *Messiah*. Jesus dies as a failure, a Messiah crucified, a Messiah executed. But in the light of the resurrection, Jesus is not a failure; in the light of the resurrection, Jesus is the conqueror; in the light of the resurrection, Jesus is the leader of his people who liberates the world —

not from the Romans — but from sin and death. Since Jesus is sarcastically called the *King*, the Messiah of the Jews (cf. Lk 23:37), and his followers also called sarcastically the *Christians*, the faithful see this in a new light. Yes, say the followers of the Crucified and Risen One, Jesus is the Messiah in the sense that he is the *Savior* of the world, the *Redeemer*, not in any nationalistic davidic sense but as the summit of creation itself who saves humankind from sin and death.

This redefining of Messiah took place shortly after the death/resurrection of Jesus. For we read in one of the earliest formulations of Christian faith (1 Cor 15:3–7 where Paul narrates what he was taught after his sudden conversion as a young man while on the road to Damascus), "that CHRIST died for our sins. . ."

That is why Jews are correct when they say Jesus is NOT the messiah.[43] How could he be, when shortly after his death (a messiah crucified!) Jerusalem itself is destroyed. And Christians are also correct when, according to their faith, they say Jesus IS the Messiah. For his death/resurrection is the victory, in principle, of the entire cosmos, over all the forces of estrangement, disharmony, sin. Jews and Christians are not defining messiah in univocal (i.e., precisely the same) terms.

Yet, in a certain sense, Christians also declare that Jesus will become fully the messiah when he comes again in glory (called *parousia christology*), even though he is established as messiah through his death/resurrection (called *exaltation christology*).

Reflecting on their experiences, Christians grasp that Jesus is, in his very person the Savior, the Redeemer, for he is the Love of the Father personally manifested in this estrangement; the Yes expressed in and through our No; the obedience, revealed in and through this disobedience. He is the Messiah, therefore, by his incarnation, he is the savior because the light of God is now expressed in our darkness and the darkness cannot overcome it (cf. Jn 1:5). It is this belief of the early Christians which prompted them to give Jesus the title of messiah from the moment of his incarnation, or as Luke has the angels sing in the sky at the nativity: "There is born to you today, in the city of David, a Savior who is CHRIST, the Lord" (2:11). Incarnational messiahship contains within it its flowering: the death/resurrection with its consequence of the parousia. It is only faith which enables the Christian to call Jesus the messiah, the Anointed One, the Christ, in this redefined manner.

But the study is not complete. As with every title, the text of the scriptural portraits must now question you, the Church, the nations of the world. For example, does the Christian community reject davidic messianism as forcefully as Jesus did? Considering Jesus' temptations, does Jesus identify with us? Does he understand us? How does Jesus the Christ challenge and interpret us? What does a study of messiahship say to the value systems of this world? After the study of each title, we must let the enhanced scriptural portraits depict us.

CHAPTER TEN

THE DISCLOSURE TITLE: LORD

The importance of this title would be difficult to exaggerate, for one of the earliest proclamations of Christian faith is the simple: Jesus is Lord! (Rom 10:9; 1 Cor 12:3; Phil 2:11).[44]

Quickly scanning the various portraits of Jesus, it is immediately noticeable that the title stands out in Luke where as a post-resurrection title it is often retrojected throughout the life of Christ even into the Infancy Narratives: "For to you is born this day . . . a Savior who is Christ the Lord" (2:11; cf. 1:43).

Yet for Mark, chronologically the first Gospel, the title is so rare (used only once [11:3]in the absolute sense, THE Lord) that it can be said that it is carries little weight with his community which for one generation has been awaiting the imminent return of Jesus: it is then Jesus will be exalted as LORD.[45] Matthew, following Mark in this use of Lord only once in the absolute sense (Mt 21:3), nonetheless often substitutes Lord when Mark uses the title Teacher. John does not employ the title often (cf. its use in the Lazarus story, chapter 11, and also in the post-resurrection narratives in chapters 20 and 21). When we look at the earliest writings of the New Testament, the letters of Paul, we find the title approximately 150 times. Undoubtedly, it is his most common and also his most telling title for Jesus.

The importance of this title is especially stressed in Luke and Paul. Luke, who is also the author of the *Acts of the Apostles*[46] proclaims that this is THE NAME — meaning Jesus as LORD — in which alone is salvation (Acts 4:12). In fact, it is only through the Spirit, i.e., with the gift of faith, that anyone can even proclaim that "Jesus Christ is Lord" (cf 1 Cor 12:3). Through the invocation of THE NAME, the power of Pentecost is again renewed to strengthen and encourage the followers of Jesus (Acts 4:31). Baptism, which is the entry into the Christian community, is in the "name of Jesus" (Acts 2:38, 10:48, 1 Cor 1:13) which probably means that the person seeking admission into the community must profess that "Jesus is Lord." Paul so underlines the importance of Lord that he can say: "If you confess with your lips that Jesus is Lord and believe in your heart that God raised him from the dead, you will be saved" (Rom 10:9). This is echoed in the Acts 16:31: "Believe in the Lord Jesus and you will be saved."

There is nothing *magical* in Paul's words. He stresses the living out on every level of one's personality that ultimate meaning is found in the epiphany of God's Love, Jesus. NOR is it to be understood that only formal Christians are saved. In accepting sincerely one's own humanity as best as one can, the reality of salvation history is being implicitly accepted, and the climactic point of this reality for Christians is that Jesus is Lord.[47] Our study of the title will follow the three steps we used when examining Christ:

— The Meaning of LORD at the time of Jesus.
— The Possible Use of LORD by Jesus.
— The development of the title LORD within the early Christian communities and, in particular, at the Council of Nicaea.

THE MEANING OF LORD AT THE TIME OF JESUS

Because the understanding of this title hinges upon the knowledge of it development from its Aramaic/Hebrew use to its usage in the Greek-speaking world, its meaning in Hebrew will first be examined, then the understanding of the term in Aramaic and finally in the language of the Hellenistic Jews which is the language of the New Testament, Greek.

LORD in Hebrew: ADON. Before the exile, Hebrew was the common tongue of the Jewish people; after the exile, when Aramaic was spoken, it remained as the language of the scriptures for the Aramaic speaking Jews of Palestine. It became, in a sense, the *liturgical* language.

The term ADON is somewhat equivalent to Mister or Sir or the British expression, m'lord. As Sir or m'lord, it denotes someone who exercises power and authority, like the boss at work. In this sense, it is to be distinguished from BAAL which has the connotation of ownership and when used in the religious sense denotes a god to which one turns as owner either of a territory or a city.

However, in its special form — a plural of majesty — ADONAI, it is the most common substitute for the divine name YHWH. From what can be gathered, "even in the pre-Christian period there was a prohibition against uttering the tetragrammaton [i.e., word of four letters: YHWH], to insure that the second commandment (Ex 20:7; Dt 5:1) was followed as scrupulously as possible and to exclude any misuses of the divine name."[48] Many, therefore, were the circumlocutions (periphrases) used by the Jews to get around pronouncing this Name which is above every other name. Often the passive was used (e.g., "It was said to you of old," which means "YHWH said to you. . . .") or the "NAME," or the "PLACE," or the "BLESSED ONE" and the list goes on. However, the more commonly used substitute for the holy tetragrammaton was ADONAI. When in reading the scriptures the word YHWH was encountered, ADONAI (LORD) would be the ordinary substitute. In later centuries within the Christian era, to insure that the sacred name would never be pronounced, the vowels of ADONAI were placed with the consonants YHWH, to indicate that ADONAI and not YHWH was to be uttered. The result? The term Yahowah, or Jehovah. In reality this is not a word at all but only an indication that ADONAI, (LORD) is to be said and not the sacred name, YHWH. At the time of Jesus, ADONAI appears to be the common substitute for the divine name, used in prayer, in liturgy, in scriptural reading. It is the name of the *Thou* of Jesus, the name of his ABBA.

LORD in Aramaic: MAR. This term for Lord also has a wide range of connotation. Basically, it stresses respect, authority, much like Sir or m'lord. During the New Testament period it does not appear to play any decisive role as a description of God; ADONAI would be the predominant expression for God who is LORD.

LORD in Greek: KURIOS. Greek is the *lingua franca* of the New Testament period. Among the pagans, kurios also had a wide range of meanings, going from Mister, to Sir, to m'lord, to a title for some of the gods and goddesses who at times were called lords and ladies. As a title of authority, it would of course be applied to the Emperor, for he is THE Lord of the state. Nero, therefore, is called KURIOS in Acts 25:26. But when the notion of a type of divinity for emperors was imported from the east into the Graeco-roman world[49] around the first century B.C., the title, depending upon the context, also took on the connotation of the divine Caesar: *KAISAR KURIOS*. Expressed in cultic or liturgical atmosphere, KURIOS when applied to the emperor was not only an expression of His Lordship in the sense of authority, but also in the sense of "divinity." Whether the Romans actually believed in some type of divinity of their emperors can be disputed; nonetheless, KURIOS could be an obsequious way of equating the emperor with the gods.

For the Greek speaking Jews in Palestine and especially for the Jews living in the diaspora, KURIOS was, therefore, a title with a wide variety of meanings, both religious and secular. There would be no difficulty in calling the man next door Kurios Smith or addressing the boss at work as kurios; there would be no hesitancy in calling state officials, including the emperor — outside of the context of worship — KURIOS. But the monotheistic Jew abhorred the galaxy of gods revelling on Mount Olympus; in no way would the name KURIOS be applied to these idols except in ridicule.

If ADONAI was an ordinary substitute for the divine name in Hebrew, then KURIOS appears to become the Greek substitute for the unpronounceable name YHWH. Although it seems that the pre-Christian Greek manuscripts of the Old Testament retained the term YHWH in the text out of respect,[50] nonetheless, it would still be unpronounceable and the Greek-speaking Jew would, therefore, — so we can well presume — say KURIOS in the place of YHWH. In the liturgy, KURIOS is for the Greek-speaking Jew, the "Name which is above every other name."

POSSIBLE USE OF LORD BY JESUS

The question of the use of LORD by Jesus as a self-designation can be settled quite easily. Surely, there is no indication — no possibility — that Jesus would ever use the Hebrew ADONAI when speaking of himself. He clearly makes a distinction between himself and ABBA. Outside of a few rare exceptions where the term GOD is applied to Jesus (cf. Jn 1:18; 20:28; Heb 1:8,9; Titus 2:13; Rom 9:5), the Father, ABBA, is the only one called GOD in the New Testament.[51] And ABBA is ADONAI. Again, Jesus prays to ADONAI, to YHWH. In no way does he say that he is YHWH, that he is ADONAI.

It is not surprising that his disciples would at times accord Jesus the Aramaic title, MAR, SIR. It is the sign of respect and probably underlies expressions in the New Testament, like Master and at times *Lord*. However, this indicates very little concerning the character of Jesus. It is an ordinary title of honor and therefore would merely say that Jesus was held in respect by his followers. It is not, then, what is termed a CHRISTOLOGICAL title, i.e., a title which would denote the *uniqueness* of Jesus as the personal expression of God in this creation.

Jesus, as we saw, probably knew some expressions in Greek but it was not his conversational language. KURIOS, then, does not enter into the discussion concerning the use of LORD as a self-designation by Jesus.

We can, therefore, conclude that LORD as a self-designation by Jesus could only take place in Aramaic (MAR) where it would have the meaning of SIR, a title of respect. Some theologians would go one step further and say that there is in this title a note of authority, awe, mystery. Probably so, but it still does not really go beyond what can be comprised within the expression, *m'lord*. It is not a christological title for the historical Jesus.

THE DEVELOPMENT OF LORD WITHIN THE CHRISTIAN COMMUNITY

It is in the third step of our methodology — the development of the title within the Christian community — that LORD takes on awesome meaning. Its development from a simple Master or Sir to an expression of divine status is quite entangled and therefore a disputed point among theologians. To oversimplify in the hopes of clarifying the important steps, this complex development will be reduced to four stages: The first enhancement of the title LORD takes place in Palestinian Judaism[52] through the use of the Aramaic term MAR. Both in 1 Cor 16:22 and in the Didache 10:6,[53] one finds the expression MARANATHA probably in connection with the eucharistic liturgy. Although the Aramaic *maranatha* is open to several translations,[54] the more probable one is "Our Lord, come!" (cf. Rev.22:20 where basically the same expression is found in Greek). There is now a pronounced eschatological connotation in the term MAR as applied to Jesus. It means far more than SIR. Since Jesus is risen from the dead, the end time has come and the Reign of YHWH is considered imminent. Jesus as the triumphant Son of Man will soon appear in clouds of majesty. And so the Church prays, MARANATHA! — OUR LORD, COME! LORD therefore implies the resurrection for it is an urgent plea for the quick return of Jesus in glory so that he will be the LORD in power. The celebration of the eucharist is the foretaste of the eternal heavenly banquet of the MAR.

Again, this is the probable reason why LORD is not a Marcan term; his community awaits the imminent coming of the Son of Man when Jesus will be exalted. For Mark's community, the parousia is the exaltation of Jesus; it is then that he shall become the LORD, it is then that he shall reign and his lordly influence experienced. Although the Holy Spirit operates in this time of waiting (cf. MK 13:11), not so the risen Jesus, as far as the Marcan community has explained its theology in its written Gospel.[55] A second stage is reached — although perhaps chronologically concomitant with stage one — when the good news of Jesus is interpreted by Hellenistic Jews both within and outside of Palestine. With the delay in the parousia, the eschatological note begins to recede and Jesus is considered to be NOW reigning as KURIOS, having been exalted at the right hand of the Father at his death/resurrection. (Luke, for example, never uses LORD for Jesus in his parousia.) Psalm 110:1: "The Lord said to my Lord, sit at my right hand until I make thy enemies the footstool of thy feet" becomes a favorite tool of the Greek-speaking Jewish Christians in expressing the meaning of LORD. Jesus is now at the right hand of the Father, reigning with the Father during this interim period, the time of the Church[56] as we await the parousia. LORD now means the reigning, active Jesus in heaven, the Lord of the cosmos. We are, therefore, in the time of the church, when Jesus' influence is experienced by the community of his followers as they await his return in glory. A more radical step is taken by the Hellenistic Jews in their attempt to express their understanding of Jesus through the term KURIOS. KURIOS, the Greek substitute for the tetragrammaton, YHWH, is now given consciously to Jesus for the Christ is the anointed of YHWH, his EMISSARY in bringing about the definitive, final reign of YHWH. Intentionally, therefore, the Greek speaking Jewish Christians apply the identical Name above all other names (KURIOS) to YHWH *and* to Jesus.

It should be noted that this fundamental development in christological thought occurs first among Hellenistic JEWS who were followers of the Risen Lord. The earliest decades of christianity are dominated by Jewish-Christian thought (both Aramaic speaking Jews and also Greek speaking Jews of Israel and of the diaspora). In other words, the basic christological thrust does not come from *Gentile* christianity but from *Jewish* thought. True, Hellenism definitely influenced the development of christology but it was, in the formative stages, through Greek speaking *Jews*. (There were several Hellenistic synagogues in Jerusalem itself.) When the Gentile mission was seriously undertaken almost two decades after the

Resurrection, the essential foundations of christology were already in place.[57] To speak, therefore, of pagan Greek myths at the source of christology does not tally with reality.

HOWEVER, this is not the first time in Judaism that others shared the name of YHWH, LORD. God's emissaries have been granted his name, as is written in the book of Exodus 23:20–23: "Behold I send my messenger before you . . . my name is in him."

Other messengers from God, like Moses, Enoch, are also called Lord. Enoch even acquires the seventy names of God.[58] In no way does this clash with the monotheism of Judaism for these emissaries function in God's name and as SPOKESMEN of God they share his name. Jesus, therefore, as the emissary of God, as the end-time, final word of God, is also given the title KURIOS and in a supereminent manner for he alone is the final, unsurpassable expression of YHWH. He, more than any other person "sent by the Father," truly functions in the name of God (commonly called "functional Christology") and is granted the name of YHWH, KURIOS. However, the early Jewish Christians apply the title *Lord* to Jesus in an absolute sense, denoting that he not only functions in the name of YHWH but that he is also equal to YHWH.[59] Jesus is risen from the dead; he is exalted and now reigns at God's right hand. Enoch, Ezra, Moses, although granted the title Lord are characters of the past who may — some thought — return at the end-time but who definitely are not here now. But the RISEN Jesus is vindicated by the Father, he is the inbreaking of the end-time, the very life of YHWH *for us*. The *WHO* of Jesus becomes clarified in and through the resurrection (to be seen in detail in subsequent chapters). He is the *RISEN* LORD dynamically present in the power of the Spirit in and through his followers. In him the final and ultimate victory of God has broken through. These characters of the past serve only as a tool or model which, in the mind of early Christians, Jesus far surpasses.

How can this "greater than Moses" be expressed? How can it be shown that Jesus shares in the NAME of YHWH — KURIOS — in a manner and degree unexpected by Judaism and never before realized? One of the chief tools at hand is the Wisdom Literature[60] especially the Books of Wisdom, Proverbs, Sirach. For is not Jesus the "Wisdom of God" (1 Cor 1:24)? Is he not greater than Solomon, the author of wisdom-sayings (cf. Mt 12:42)? Are not "all the treasures of wisdom and knowledge" hidden in him (Col 2:3)? Aspects of Wisdom literature of the Old Testament are, therefore, christologized by the early Christians as they search for means to express their belief in the fulness of Lordship found in Jesus. For example, texts like the following are applied to Jesus-Lord:

— "The Lord created me at the beginning . . . from of old I was poured forth, at first before the earth was created" (Prov 8:22–23).

— "For she (Wisdom) is a breath of the power of God, and a pure emanation of the glory of the Almighty; . . . she is a reflection of eternal light, a spotless mirror of the working of God, and an image of his goodness" (Wis 7:25–26).

— "With thee (O God) is wisdom, who knows thy works and was present when thou didst make the world" (Wis 9:9).

The early Jewish Christians find in these texts — and in others similar — the clarification of their mysterious encounter with God in their encounter with Jesus, a spelling-out of their belief that in the Risen Jesus, *God Himself has established in principle his Lordship in love*. Therefore the Christians can proclaim that Jesus is: "the image of the invisible God, the first-born of all creation for in him all things were created in heaven and on earth, visible and invisible, . . . all things were created through him and for him . . . in him all things hold together . . . for in him all the fulness of God was pleased to dwell and through him to reconcile to himself all things whether on earth or in heaven, making peace by the blood of his cross" (Col 1:15–20).

Jesus' very existence is an existence and activity from God. He is LORD in a unique way, for in him "the whole fulness of deity dwells bodily" (Col 2:9). All of this presupposes a belief in what is termed the *pre-existence* of Jesus, i.e., that as Word, Wisdom of the Father, he is from all eternity. At a moment in time the Wisdom of God is personally manifested, revealed, in and through the Virgin Mary. This incarnation ("enfleshment") of Eternal Wisdom is this man Jesus. He "functions" as Lord because he IS the Lord: it is not a question of either functional *or* ontological (i.e., the Word's very *being*; Greek *ontos* = being) christology. Precisely because he "functions" in such a unique way as the presence of the Father for us, Christians conclude that he is ontologically one with the Father. "To ask whether Christology should be functional or ontological is to pose false alternatives," as the International Theological Commission taught in its 1983 session.[61]

Even this clarification of pre-existence has its roots in Judaism, not only in the Wisdom literature, but also in sayings of rabbis which probably reflect early traditions. For example, reference was made to Gen 1:2: "and the spirit of God hovered" to prove the existence of the messiah before creation because this phrase meant — so they taught — the spirit of the messiah.[62]

Jesus, God's ultimate self-disclosure to all peoples, shares, as Wisdom literature provides the model, in the authority of God over creation itself which is God's domain. This was then a scandal to the Jews, for Christians were claiming that God's Wisdom is no longer to be communicated by a venerable body of laws which Moses received on Sinai but by a seducer of the people who endured the curse of the scriptures themselves by hanging upon the tree of the cross (cf. Dt 21:22–23). The scandal is intensified because this christology — worked out primarily by Greek-speaking Jews — is fed from Jewish sources. All of this John applies to Jesus by the use of the term *Word* for not only is *Wisdom* feminine (Greek: *sophia*) but there was a possibility of a misunderstanding by some of the wisdom cults of the Greek world.

The early hymn found in the *Letter to the Phillipians* 2:6–11,[63] stresses that Jesus being in the form of God, empties himself of glory (i.e., the external manifestation of divinity) taking upon himself our humanity. Living human destiny, he is obedient to the Father even to death upon the cross, as this song proclaims. He is, therefore, exalted, the hymn continues, and has the divine name LORD. This canticle of the early Church triumphantly concludes: "At the name of Jesus every knee should bow, in heaven and on earth and under the earth and every tongue confess that Jesus Christ is Lord, to the glory of God the Father" (2:10–11).

Thus the incarnation and its unfolding death/resurrection become an unsurpassable expression of divine love. Neither Graeco-roman nor Jewish tradition knew of such a "myth." In Jesus, God himself comes to us in love. He is a God *for people*, a God *for us*. This bold or "high Christology" expressed in one of the earliest New Testament works is not presented at first in the form of speculative prose but in hymns (cf. 1 Cor 14:26; Col 3:16, Eph 5:19, Rev. 5:9, etc.). The result is inescapable: texts of the Old Testament which are applied to God alone, are now applied to Jesus: e.g., Joel 3:5: "Everyone who calls upon the name of the Lord will be saved" (cf. Rom 10:13, Acts 2:21), Rom 10:11: "No one who believes in him will be put to shame" (cf. Is 18:16).

In the final analysis, LORD becomes the vehicle for the early Christians — before any contact with the pagan Greek world but from within Judaism itself — to express their belief that God is definitively, personally expressed in this man Jesus.[64]

THE COUNCIL OF NICAEA

When at the beginning of the fourth century, Arius of Alexandria speaks of the Word of God as a type of *demi-god created by the Father*, the first ecumenical Council, Nicaea (325 A.D.), will dogmatically reply that the Word is "one in being" (Greek: *homoousios*) with the Father. The Council insisted thereby that the "divine status" of the Word/Wisdom of the Father (and therefore of the *Incarnate* Word also) is definitely *ontological*: Jesus not only *functions* as an emissary of the Father, he is *in his very being* ONE with the Father.[65] Arius had declared that there was a time when the Word was not; to predicate *God* of the Word is, therefore, purely honorific.[66] In the eyes of the the great Fathers of the church, the redemptive incarnation was thereby annulled for it could not — according to Arius' teaching — truly be said that *God became man so that man might become God* through the sharing in divine life through grace (cf. 2 Pet 1:4). The Council of Nicaea, under the theological leadership of the great St. Athanasius and confirmed by the Second Ecumenical Council, Constantinople (381 A.D.), proclaimed that the Word is "one in being with the Father," thereby declaring that the Word Incarnate truly IS Lord. The First Council of Constantinople also expressed the clear experience of the church that contrary to the thought of the influential theologian, Apollinaris, Jesus truly possessed a human soul. The divinity, Lordship in the absolute sense, is predicated of Jesus *as well as* full humanity. Although this teaching of the Church will be refined at the Councils of Ephesus (431 A.D.) and Chalcedon (451 A.D.), it is already evident that BOTH the divinity and humanity of Jesus are definitively taught by the Body of Christ at the first two Ecumenical Councils. As all creation mirrors its Creator (cf. Gen 1:26, Rom 1:20) — in varying degrees and manners — so Jesus also "reflects the glory of God" (Heb 1:3). However, from the first moment of his conception, Jesus is the summit, the climactic point of God's self-disclosure in this cosmos. He is that point of creation where creation itself is the personal expression of God; it is not just a difference of degree but a difference in the *kind* of manifestation of God. Rather than diminish the humanity of Jesus, this enfleshment of the Word enhances and perfects this human personality of Jesus, for grace (i.e., sharing God's life) and freedom grow in direct, not inverse, proportion to each other.[67] There is, therefore, no one more fully human than Jesus the LORD, the personal, climactic expression of the infinite God in and through the finitude of creation.

While the christological titles of the New Testament, like *Lord* "primarily tell us what role or function he plays" in relation to humankind, that "God was present to them in Jesus,"[68] the Church — the "pillar and Ground of truth" (1 Tim 3:15) — insists at the Council of Nicaea that the Word of God is "homoousios" with the Father and therefore that this human being Jesus is personally our God; God is personally this human being, Jesus. The Church has come to a deeper clarity — although of course not exhaustive — of the "excess of meaning" found in the proclamation: Jesus Christ is LORD.

LORD becomes then for Christians the means to proclaim the divine status of Jesus. To proclaim that Jesus is Lord, is to declare that he "reflects the glory of God and bears the very stamp of his nature upholding the universe by his word of power" (Heb 1:3).

Summary

The title Jesus is LORD, expresses:

— his future coming in glory.

— his present status as the climactic point of all creation, as Lord of All.

— his status as THE emissary of the Father to bring about the Kingdom.

— his divine status: in a mysterious way he is the ultimate, final, personal epiphany of the Father's eternal Wisdom.

The Christian therefore belongs to Christ and Christ belongs to God: "You are Christ's; and Christ is God's" (1 Cor 3:23). All "await our blessed hope, the appearing of the glory of our great God and Savior Jesus Christ" (Titus 2:13).

CHAPTER ELEVEN

THE DISCLOSURE TITLE: SON OF GOD

The Gospel portraits depict Jesus as the *Son*, the *Beloved Son*, the *Only Son*, the *Son of God*.[69] The first impulse is to interpret these terms in the light of present day culture. However, to do so carries with it the danger of distorting the portraits of Jesus and of misunderstanding the beauty of the faith which the early followers of Jesus wanted to transmit.

As with the title *Lord*, the various authors of the New Testament accentuate different aspects of the title *Son of God*. No portrait of Jesus is so founded upon the proclamation of Jesus *The Son of God* as the Gospel of JOHN. No other writing of the New Testament can compare with John's insistence that Jesus is THE Son; in fact in the fourth Gospel, no one else is *Son* for the title is reserved for Jesus alone. Ten times in his Gospel John will refer to Jesus as the *Son of God*, and four of these times they are the Johannine Jesus' own words. For the community of John, Jesus is *Son of God* from all eternity (cf. 3:17, etc.).

PAUL employs the term only fifteen times as against the approximately 150 instances of Lord; nonetheless the title is used at critical places in his epistles (e.g., Rom 1:3, 4, 9; 8:3, 29, 32; 1 Cor 1:9; 15:28). In fact, the *Acts of the Apostles* summarizes the first preaching of Paul as: "He (Jesus) is the Son of God" (9:20). This "Apostle to the Gentiles" declares in the opening lines of the *Epistle to the Romans* that Jesus is "designated Son of God in power . . . by his resurrection from the dead" (cf Rom 1:3–4).

LUKE and MATTHEW will bring out this unique relationship of Jesus to God by proclaiming the virginal conception, which is not found in any of the other portraits. MARK stresses that Jesus is *Son of God* at his Baptism by John the Baptizer; Mark and Matthew have the centurion at the Cross — a Gentile — proclaim: "Truly, this was the *Son of God*" (Mt 27:54; cf. Mk 15:39) and Matthew purposefully places this profession of faith just a few verses after the Jews deride Jesus as the one who called himself the *Son of God* (cf. Mt 27:43). There is, therefore, a stress on Jesus as *Son of God* at the incarnation in Luke and Matthew, at the baptism in Mark, a stress on the eternal sonship of Jesus in John (and in the *Letter to the Hebrews*) while Paul in the beginning of the Romans, seems to opt for "sonship in power" through the resurrection.

Again, we notice that there are various christologies of the New Testament. Identical titles are used in different ways by the early Christian communities to express their own experience of the encounter with Jesus. Only later on, as the church continues its dialogue with the word of God, do we find a levelling off, a sort of common denominator meaning for the titles of Jesus. But in the New Testament era, not precisely so.

In spite of the various stresses, the different nuances given to the title *Son of God*, there is no doubt that it is a climactic profession of the Christian faith. The centrality of the expression *Son of God* is summarized in the ancient marginal note (called a *gloss*) which a scribe placed in the eighth chapter of the *Acts of the Apostles* and which later crept into the text itself. When the servant of the Queen of the Ethiopians asked Philip the deacon to baptize him, we read the comment of the copyist (which has become Acts 8:37), probably taken from an early baptismal liturgy:

"And Philip said: 'If you believe with all your heart, you may.' And he replied, 'I believe that Jesus Christ is the Son of God.' ' "

What is the meaning of this confession of faith, "Jesus is the Son of God?" As with the title Lord, an understanding of *Son of God* at the time of Jesus demands a knowledge of its meaning both in the Jewish and also in the Hellenistic world.

THE MEANING OF SON OF GOD

The term *Son, Son of* . . . is often used in a biological sense (55 times in the Gospel of John alone). For example, we read in Mark 6:3 "Is not this the carpenter, the son of Mary?" This would coincide with the ordinary understanding of the term in today's culture.

However, the term *Son(s) of* . . . is also often used in an extended sense, meaning a child, or a group of children, or the members of a club. This usage is also common today, e.g., *The Sons of Italy, The B'nai Berith (Sons of the Covenant), The Daughters of the American Revolution*, are designations of fraternal organizations. And it is not extraordinary for an older man to address a younger person as *son* even though there is no biological relationship whatsoever.

There is, however, a semitic manner of using the term Son of . . . which is quite alien to our way of speaking. The expression means that someone has a special relationship to the noun that follows.[70] For example, two of Jesus' disciples had a low threshold and so he called them *Sons of thunder* (Mk 3:17) possibly indicating that they would rumble at the least aggravation. *Sons of darkness* and *Sons of light* are common expressions in the Essene literature,[71] indicating the evil and the good. Judas is a "son of perdition" (Jn 17:12). The term is also used in the feminine sense, e.g., Isaiah speaks of the haughty *Daughters of Zion* (Is 3:16) connoting the women of the capital city. *Daughter of* . . . is also applied, so it would appear, to a village or suburb attached to a nearby town, as *Daughter of Zion* possibly first referred to a section of Jerusalem, whose principal hill is Zion (cf. Mic 4:8).[72]

When, therefore, we find the expression *Son of God* in Hebrew literature, it can ONLY refer to this figurative understanding of the term. For the Jews it is an horrendous abomination to believe that the transcendent YHWH biologically generates a child. YHWH is not a creature and the anthropomorphisms (i.e., applying human characteristics to God) attributed to him indicate the forcefulness of his personality and not any *human* emotion. So insistent is the monotheism of Israel upon this point that no images whatsoever could be made of the God who reigns above the firmament.

Son of God, therefore, indicates a community or a person who possesses a special relationship to God. There are overtones of call/response, mandate/obedience in this relationship. It is understandable that the term would be referred primarily to Israel as a whole (cf. Ex 4:22; Hos 2:1). Since YHWH entered into a covenant with the Jewish people, they believed themselves to be the chosen people, or to put it another way, the *Sons and Daughters of God*. Angels, united to YHWH as his messengers, are his *sons* (cf. Gen 6:2, Ps 29:1, 89:7, Jb 1:6). In the late Wisdom literature, the persecuted Jew in the diaspora is especially called a *Son of God* (cf. Wis 2:18, 5:5). Kings are also the *sons of God* since they are (or should be) in a unique relationship of obedience with him (cf. Ps 2:7; 89:28).

In the culture of Jesus' world, therefore, *Son of God* would generally denote the Jewish people as the prophet Hosea declares in speaking of the exodus event: "Out of Egypt I have called my son" (11:1). To designate a group or an individual as a *Son* of God is in NO WAY to speak of physical generation. It designates a relationship with YHWH, a relationship with overtones of loving obedience to the God who constantly calls. The title is not, therefore, christological at the time of Jesus for it refers to all Jews, not only to Jesus. It is, in fact, a "weak" title denoting Jesus as a member of the chosen people. If we move from strictly Jewish thought into the Hellenistic culture of Jesus' time, it is probable that two examples of the Greek concept of divine sonship would be encountered: "Sons of God" and "Divine Men." Some scholars believe it likely that the title *Son of God* as applied to Jesus was a transfer of pagan hellenistic thought to the earliest interpretations of the Risen Christ,[73] especially since Hellenism had penetrated into the land of Israel. The theory is contradicted, however, by the fact that Greek influence upon the definitive direction of christology was via hellenistic JEWS; pagan Hellenistic thought at times helped shape the later form in which Son of God christology was presented as is seen in the format of some of the miracle stories but this was after the content had been already clearly formulated.

Anyone familiar with Homer's *Iliad* and the *Odyssey* or with Vergil's *Aeneid*, is somewhat taken aback by the prolific Zeus! Countless divine, semi-divine and even mere mortal offspring trace their origins to the escapades of this frolicking god. A Jew — so steeped in monotheism — could never take these stories seriously (did the Greeks?) and even more so, no such blasphemous pagan stories could ever seep *as such* into Jewish religious thought. There is no link here between the ONE transcendent God and the ONE Son sent by the Father to redeem the world.

The Stoics considered everyone as *sons of God* because all share in various degrees in the *logos* or universal reason of God (to be distinguished from the Johannine Logos as the divine WORD of God).[74] Even disregarding the pantheism involved (although some early christian theologians like Justin the Martyr will attempt to baptize stoicism as a tool to describe Jesus)[75] such a system in itself has no place for a *Son of God* as mediator and redeemer. There is no link here between the ONE transcendent God and the ONE Son sent by the Father to redeem the world.

The pagan mystery religions of the time narrate the tales of dying and rising gods which some would declare to be the raw material for the resurrection of Jesus.[76] However, none of these dying vegetation deities ever died for others to bring salvation; they were personifications of the seasons, more specifically of the dying and rising of the crops in autumn and spring. Moreover, in the traditional stories they had their origins on this earth; any notion of pre-existence and the decisive theme of *sending by the Father*, intrinsic to the sonship of Jesus, is absent. There is no link here between the ONE transcendent God and the One Son sent by the Father to redeem the world. To declare that Son of God as applied to Jesus has its roots in pagan myth demands such violent contortions of history, religion, culture, that it can be declared untenable.

There is another aspect of Greek thought which some would declare had an influence on calling Jesus *The Son of God*. It appears that mythical heroes, famous men like Apollonius of Tyana, Plato, Pythagoras, and most especially healers of all sorts were at times called *divine men* (divine man in Greek = *theios aner*). The term "divine" appears to have been understood quite broadly and the concept of *theios aner* is being strongly questioned, therefore, by contemporary scholarship.[77] H. C. Kee summarizes modern thought on this issue: "It is almost surely too much to claim that there was a fixed type, the *theios aner*, to which Mark conformed the image of Jesus. This notion . . . has been repeated so often that it has come to be accepted as a fact. But in truth, except for a widespread fondness for apotheosis of great men, there is no set type or model of the *theios aner*."[78] Jesus as *Son of God* is not a variation on this pagan theme. And even granted a "strict" *divine man* belief in the pagan world, many of the reasons given above can be applied to a rebuttal of this theory also.

Moreover, Jesus never does anything in his own right but only as *sent by the Father*; he does not perform miraculous feats for show or money or renown. Jesus never sets up a tent for any miracle-service where he is to show-off extraordinary powers. His miracles are the inbreaking of God's kingdom. He does not fit into the category of the Hellenistic apotheosis of a wonder-worker.

Q, which contains only two miracles, (cf. Lk 7:2–3, 6–10; 11; 14:20) also has the detailed temptation narrative which is not consonant with any notion of pagan counterparts to *son of God*. Mark's Gospel, which in its *format* of some of the miracle stories may have been influenced by similar actions of the roving wonder-workers of the times, strenuously and repeatedly proclaims that Jesus is the suffering *Son of Man* who is to die, that his power is in his powerlessness, in his total cry of emptiness to the Father. We are not talking about Jesus as ANY TYPE of *theios aner*. So strongly does Mark — and the other portraits to some extent — battle against a glorious "wonder-worker" christology, that it very well may have posed a danger to an authentic understanding of Jesus when he was first proclaimed among the Gentiles.

The meaning of *Son of God*, then, is not to be sought in any pagan, polytheistic culture. It is a Jewish term, referring to an intimate, loving, obedient relationship to YHWH who sends the son on mission.

DOES JESUS DESIGNATE HIMSELF AS SON OF GOD?

Since the title *son of God* primarily connotes the Jewish people, it would not be surprising — nor of any moment — if Jesus so designated himself. Examining the portraits, the title *Son of God* is quite rare although it is found in the primary sources, *Mark* and *Q*. If we glance at Mark's Gospel, there are — in addition to the response to Caiaphas at the trial scene which was examined in the chapter on Jesus the messiah — two episodes where it at first appears that Jesus does use this title as a self-designation.

THE FIRST deals with the famous parable in Mark 12, where Jesus, using terms taken from Isaiah 5:1–7, speaks of Israel as a vineyard. Often, so the parable narrates, the owner (YHWH) sent his servants into the vineyard to get some of the fruit. All were beaten or killed: the reference is clearly to the prophets. Finally, the parable declares, the owner sent the only servant he had left, his *son*, who was also killed. Is the expression "the son" (together with the parable itself) from the lips of Jesus or an interpretation by the early church of salvation history? And if it is from the lips of Jesus, the final servant, called not extraordinarily, *son*, would appear to be more specifically a self-designation of Jesus as son in the sense of the final prophet. Limiting ourselves to this parable alone, there would be no indication of the title taking on a *christological* dimension, indicating Jesus to be the *incarnate* son of the Father.

THE SECOND episode (Mk 13:32) is found in the apocalyptic chapter of Mark. Here Jesus attributes ignorance to himself, declaring that even he does not know when those final days will come. It appears embarrassing for the early church to attribute ignorance to Jesus and therefore some declare that this text must be part of the ipsissima verba.[79] However, it could possibly be a desperate interpretation by the Marcan community to give some reason why the end has not yet arrived: Jesus himself did not know the date. Nonetheless, even in this hypothesis, the Marcan

Inexhaustible Presence

community had to have some foundation in the life of Jesus to call him the *son*. But in the apocalyptic context of Mk 13, *son* probably has the meaning not of *Son of God* but of *Son of Man* who is according to Daniel 7 an apocalyptic character. (It is best, in analyzing the titles of Jesus to attempt to treat each title separately.) We are on uncertain grounds, therefore, if we say that in Mark 13 Jesus clearly refers to himself specifically as the *son of God* in a unique and extraordinary sense.

When we examine *Q*, we are faced with the famous text of Mt 11:25–27 (Lk 10:21–22):

"I thank thee, Father, Lord of Heaven and earth that thou hast hidden these things from the wise and understanding and revealed them to babes; yea, Father, for such was thy gracious will. All things have been delivered to me by my Father; and no one knows the Son except the Father and no one knows the Father except the Son and anyone to whom the Son wishes to reveal him."

For years, this text has been stuck with the label: "the thunderbolt from the Johannine sky,"[80] since it does resemble a stress of John's Gospel (cf. 10:15; 17:2) but does not (supposedly) fit in with the synoptic view of Jesus. However, the text is clearly *Q*, of early origin, and pictures Jesus as the Wisdom of the Father (cf. Wis 6:12–9:18) who ALONE transmits to us the knowledge (in the Jewish sense, i.e., a lived-out relationship, not just facts and figures) of the Father. It would appear to be, *at least in its present clarity*, a formulation of the early *Q* community but based upon the attitudes, actions, words of Jesus which surely gave rise to the experience of the followers of Jesus that he is in a *unique, intimate* relationship with the Father. It discloses who Jesus is in terms easily understood by the *Q* community.

OUR CONCLUSION is, therefore, that *Son of God* is not a *title* used by Jesus as a christological self-identification. Jesus, so it appears, never spoke of himself precisely as THE *Son of God* or THE *Son*. These are, rather, clarifications on the part of the early Christian communities. Nonetheless, the *Q* statement does speak of an intimate, unique oneness of Jesus with the Father which *far* transcends the normal use of *son of God* at the time of Jesus. The development of *son of God* from a "weak" title to one indicating a high christology is taking place within the Gospels themselves. And this high christology is found not only in John but in one of the earliest of the Gospel strata, *Q*. In fact, the general reaction to any reading of the Gospels is that Jesus considers himself to be in an unheard of, shockingly (for some, blasphemous, cf. Jn 5:18) intimate union with YHWH. And this not only because of the *Q* statement cited above. Presuming the authenticity of the scriptural portraits and also that Jesus was not deluded, we have the basic raw material for the early Christians' *christological* designation of Jesus as the unique *Son of God*.

It can be said, therefore, that the behavior of Jesus as depicted throughout the Gospels — his being/actions/words — disclose a person who is the very intimacy of YHWH, who expresses God's healing love and power within a world estranged from its Ground, from its true self, from mutual love. He inaugurates, as we will see, the Reign of YHWH. Although *Son of God* would not appear to be in these precise terms a self-designation of Jesus, his lived-out commitments proclaim in an excess of meaning the fundamental content of a christological *Son of God*: a unique, obedient intimacy with God who in an hitherto unheard degree, dynamically shares his being with this man Jesus.

Moreover, not only in the Johannine portrait but also in the synoptics, there is the overriding conviction of Jesus that he is, in a mysteriously unique manner, *sent* by the Father (cf. Mk 9:37, 12:6; Mt 10:40, 15:24, 21:37; Lk 4:18, 4:43, 9:48, 10:16; Acts 3:26, 28:28; about 18 times in John) which is another scriptural way of indicating a special loving, obedient "familial" union with God: the raw material of the *christological* title *Son of God*.

However, there is here also a "greater than." According to the overall Gospel portraits, Jesus experiences an intimacy with the Father which is his very being; he is "the one sent" (Jn 9:7). While all may be *sons of God* (Mt 5:9,45) Jesus' exclusive use of *my Father* (a term out of the ordinary yet found in all strata of tradition) again substantiates the early Christians' belief that Jesus is uniquely THE Son who enables us to deepen our own oneness with the Father and, therefore, our oneness with this universe, our oneness with each other.

THE CONCLUSION concerning the question whether or not Jesus identified himself as *Son of God* is that, as far as we can tell, he never does so in these precise terms. However, the basic warp and woof of the Gospel portraits is made up of the conviction of Jesus that he is *uniquely* one with the Father, *uniquely* the one sent on mission by the Father to proclaim the kingdom *for us*, a command which he lovingly obeys: which is the content (and like all the titles, "more than" the content) of the christological *Son of God*. It is the Christian community which, in the light of the resurrection, brings the title itself, *Son of God*, to its explicit *christological* full flowering.

DEVELOPMENT OF SON OF GOD WITHIN THE EARLY CHRISTIAN COMMUNITY

The clearly christological title *Son of God* as applied to Jesus is, as we have seen, probably a creation of the early christian community basing itself on the actions, words, attitudes of Jesus. Though not found in the early speeches of Peter as elaborated in the *Acts of the Apostles*, although used with reticence by Mark especially and although apparently not a title used commonly by all the early churches (we do not find the title at all in the Pastoral Epistles — *Timothy, Titus* — nor in *James*, nor in *1 Peter*, only once in *Revelation* and twice in the *Acts of the Apostles*) it can still be said that it becomes a privileged creedal statement of the Church. A reason for its reticence may be that the title *Son of God* IN ITSELF does not adequately imply that mysterious uniqueness about Jesus and also, until it is explained, there was a danger that Gentile Christians could misunderstand it because of their polytheistic and hero-man culture. However, once the title is clarified with its full christian meaning, it became as it is today, a primary statement concerning Jesus Christ.

That it is a central proclamation of early Christian faith is evident from many texts in the New Testament. To quote a few: Mt 16:17: Matthew adds editorially to Peter's confession of faith "You are the Christ" (cf Mk 8:29), the proclamation, "the Son of the Living God."

Acts 8:37: Although as we have seen, a gloss, it does depict the early profession of faith needed to enter the christian community: "I believe that Jesus Christ is the Son of God."

Rom 1:3 ff: Paul inserts at the beginning of his letter to the Romans an early Christian confession (style, vocabulary, demonstrate that it is not pauline, at least in its basic statement): "Who was descended from the seed of David according to the flesh and designated Son of God in power according to the Spirit of holiness by his resurrection from the dead." Paul is not denying an intimate union of Jesus with the Father before the resurrection (cf. Phil 2:6–11) but with the early church seeing in his resurrection his exaltation in power.

Gal 4:4: "But when the time had fully come, God sent forth his Son, born of a woman, born under the law, to redeem those who were under the law, so that we might receive adoption as sons."

Rom 8:32: "If God is for us, who is against us? He who did not spare his own Son but gave him up for us all, will he not also give us all things with him?"

Gal 2:20: "The life I now live in the flesh I live by faith in the Son of God who loved me and gave himself for me." Notice that *Son of God* appears to be used by the early church as the climax of a proclamation of faith, faith in the intimate bond between Jesus and God and between Jesus and humankind.

The Virginal Conception: Both Matthew and Luke proclaim Jesus as *Son of God* at his conception. "Conceived of the Holy Spirit" says Matthew in 1:20; the explicit term "Son of God" is used by Luke 1:35 in narrating the conception: "therefore the child to be born will be called holy, the Son of God." Again, the stress is on oneness with the Father; Jesus the total gift of God who comes "to save his people from their sins" (Mt 1:21). *Son of God* was for Jewish Christians a tool of their own culture to express Jesus' intimacy with the Father. It is, as we can see from most of the quotes above a *soteriological* statement, i.e., Jesus as SAVIOR (*soter* in Greek). For evidently one with us, he is the intimacy of the Father, for us. He is the one sent by the Father, for us. Experiencing the estrangement of his brothers and sisters from their God, from their true selves, from all creation, Jesus the point of creation in unique harmony with the Father, heals this brokenness. Moreover, in christologizing the Old Testament the Christians found numerous texts dealing with sonship which they applied in a climactic sense to Jesus, e.g., Heb 1:5 quotes Ps 2:7: "You are my son, today I have begotten you" (originally a royal psalm); Is 42:1, from the first *Servant Song of Isaiah*: "Behold my servant whom I uphold, my chosen, in whom my soul delights" (since the word for servant [Greek: *pais*] could also be translated as *son*, it is this text which we find at the Baptism [Mk 1:11] and Transfiguration [Mk 9:7] episodes in the synoptics); 2 Sam 7:12–14, the ancient oracle given by Nathan to David: "I will raise up your seed after you . . . I will be his father and he shall be my son" (cf. Acts 2:30). Texts like these became vehicles for the early Christians to proclaim their belief that Jesus is truly the *Son of God*.

FINALLY, and more importantly, what precisely did the early church express in these creedal proclamations that "Jesus is the *Son of God*?" As employed by the early church, the term appears to take on a two pronged meaning: the Father's dynamic sending of his Life to be enfleshed for us, and Jesus' loving, obedient, dynamic response, for us. Again, its primary meaning is soteriological: Jesus is the Word sent by the Father to bring about the rejoicing of the Kingdom. It is, in a certain sense, a summary of the faith: another reason why its use is not found on every page of the New Testament, since it already demands a knowledge of the christian faith which it verbalizes.

However, following closely the development of the title LORD studied in the last chapter, the Old Testament (especially the Wisdom literature) supplies a tool for expressing the depth of the intimacy of this man Jesus with the Father and of his obedience to the Father's will:

"In the beginning was the Word and the Word was with God and the Word was God. He was in the beginning with God, all things were made through him and without him was not anything made that was made . . . and the Word became flesh and dwelt among us . . . no one has ever seen God; the only Son (or as important manuscripts read, "God the only Son") who is in the bosom of the Father, he has made him known" (Jn 1:1–18).

Throughout the Gospel of John we have a repetition of the theme that Jesus the

Son of God is, in some manner, equal to but distinct from YHWH. Nowhere is this more clearly stated than in the famous combination of texts (which must be read in total context) spoken by the Johannine Christ: "The Father and I are one" (Jn 10:30), clarified by the corresponding expression "The Father is greater than I" (Jn 14:28) indicating not any metaphysical subordinationism (i.e., the Word of God is not equal to the Father but in some sense subordinate to him)[81] but that Jesus is *sent* by the Father. There is, therefore, in the Johannine title *Son of God* a stress on pre-existence: this human being Jesus is God's existence, God's Love, God's Wisdom *for us*. ". . . *existence for others* means Jesus cannot be separated from his relationship and intimate communion with the Father and must for that very reason be rooted in his eternal Sonship. This pro-existence of Jesus Christ, in which God communicates himself to man, presupposes pre-existence. Otherwise the proclamation of Jesus Christ as Saviour would be merely a fiction and an illusion. . ."[82] As we have seen when studying the title *Lord*, Jesus does not merely "function" in the name of the Father; he is one with the Father. Since Jesus' *entire existence* as clearly portrayed in the Gospels is "for us," we cannot make a dichotomy between "functional" and "ontological" christology. It is not a question of either/or. It is BOTH. Jesus functions as the unique personal envoy of the Father for us in a manner which is "greater than" that of Moses, or Solomon or the prophets, precisely because he is *one* with the Father. We can, therefore, agree with the 1983 report of the International Theological Commission when it states: "To ask whether christology should be functional or ontological is to pose false alternatives."[83]

THE COUNCILS OF EPHESUS AND CHALCEDON

Although the Word of God was dogmatically declared *one in being* with the Father at Nicaea and First Constantinople with the implied conclusion that the *incarnate* Word, Jesus, is ontologically the Son of God, the church at the beginning of the fifth century experienced a traumatic discussion concerning the content of *Son of God* as applied to Jesus. The term implies a oneness with the Father and a oneness with us for *from the beginning* with the Father, he has been sent by the Father to us, for us. Nicaea and First Constantinople had dogmatically taught that the Word of God is NOT some sort of "second god," but *one in being* with the Father himself. The divinity of Jesus, the Word enfleshed — Jesus as *Kurios* in the absolute sense — was therefore firmly declared the authentic experience of the Body of Christ.

Yet another christological problem of the early church now surfaced: are we talking about TWO people when we speak about Jesus, one human and another divine? And if Jesus is ONE person, how can the Son of God at the same time be both one with the Father and also one with us, i.e., truly divine AND truly human. The disputes, which took place principally in the East,[84] led to the Third and Fourth Ecumenical Councils, Ephesus (431 A.D.) and the greatest christological Council of all times, Chalcedon (451 A.D.).

Unlike contemporary western christianity, the eastern church in the early part of the fifth century was leaning toward *monophysitism* (Greek: *monos* = single, alone, and *physis* = nature, or set of characteristics) which meant that the humanity of Jesus was at least downplayed if not considered to be "absorbed" by the divinity. The stress, unlike contemporary thought, was on the DIVINITY of Jesus often to the detriment of his HUMANITY.[85] The methodology associated with the school of thought of Alexandria was a "descending" christology (also called "from above") which emphasizes the Word's oneness in being with the Father and being sent by the Father into creation; contemporary thought — anticipated somewhat by the ancient christological school of Antioch — stresses an "ascending" christology (also called "from below") which begins christology with Jesus' oneness in being with us, yet insisting that he is the summit of creation for he is the personal epiphany of God. A balanced christology is not EITHER Antiochene OR Alexandrian but a combination of BOTH. For an adequate understanding of Jesus, both methodologies must be intertwined. The christology from below represents the "way Jesus *presented himself to his contemporaries and was able to be understood by them*" while the christology from above represents the "way those who came to believe in Jesus understood his life and his person *after the manifestations of him as one raised from the dead.*"[86] When the priest Nestorius was sent from Antioch to be the Patriarch of Constantinople (428 A.D.) the difficulty of reconciling the two natures — sets of characteristics — in ONE person, Jesus, became a public dispute. Nestorius was entrenched in Antioch's insistence that Jesus is ONE person BUT in TWO sets of characteristics, human and divine. Constantinople was in the Alexandrian camp stressing the ONENESS of his person. True to his Antiochene background, Patriarch Nestorius settled a theological dispute concerning Our Lady by requesting that preachers in his jurisdiction cease calling Mary simply *Theotokos* (Greek for "God-Bearer," "Mother of God") since he claimed the term was of doubtful propriety. Mary bore the "man" Jesus but not God, was Nestorius' thought. Classical Nestorianism (probably not the teachings of Nestorius himself)[87] gives, therefore, a simple answer to the question how Jesus could be truly the Son of God and yet one with us: he is, in reality, *two* Sons, joined by a moral or loving union.[88] The term, *Theotokos* was of long standing within the church[89] and in no way did it teach that Mary gave birth to the Godhead. Scripture itself calls Mary the Mother of the *Lord* twice in a context where *Lord* clearly refers to God, YHWH (Lk 1:43;2:11). "Mother of God" affirms that Mary is the Mother of this person Jesus who is our God in a fully human way: the Word of God, one with the Father from all eternity, at a moment in our time, took flesh of the Virgin Mary.

From Alexandria came the uproar of its fiery Patriarch, Cyril, against Nestorius and against the school of Antioch and its Patriarch, John. The matter was referred to a Third Ecumenical Council held at Ephesus in 431.[90] Amidst bitter charges and countercharges — Cyril called Nestorius a "new Judas" — the Council upheld the oneness of person in Jesus. He is one *Son of God*. The basic affirmation of this Council, so characterized by intrigue, politics, one-upmanship, is that the *union* between the eternal Word of the Father and this man Jesus is *personal*: Jesus is truly ONE person. Two years later, in a rare show of unity, both John of Antioch and Cyril of Alexandria issued a conciliatory statement of agreement, called the "Creed of Ephesus."[91] Nonetheless, neither Antioch nor Alexandria was truly content with the document. Without the clarification of terms (especially *hypostasis, physis, prosopon,* which were being used in a variety of ways to mean diverse concepts like "person" or "individual" or "nature" or "being") it raised additional questions concerning HOW this ONE PERSON could be truly God and truly human. Alexandria insisted on the ONENESS of the Person, Antioch on the DUALITY of the natures (i.e., human AND divine characteristics). The problem was heightened by a revered elderly monk of Constantinople, Eutyches, who "historically counts as the founder of an extreme and virtually Docetic form of monophysitism, teaching that the Lord's humanity was totally absorbed by his divinity."[92] After the disgraceful debacle of the *Robber Council of Ephesus* which attempted to uphold the monophysite doctrine of which Eutyches was the rallying-point,[93] a new Council was called to resolve the disputes: the Fourth Ecumenical Council, Chalcedon, which met in 451. It is at this greatest of christological Councils that the Church gave definitive guidelines for an understanding of Jesus Christ, the Son of God. The Council of Chalcedon not only clarified ambiguous terms but also stated in its Creed[94] that Jesus is ONE Person in two natures, human and divine, which are "undivided" and "unmixed." The following Ecumenical Council (Constantinople II, 553 A.D.) explicitly stated that the ONE Person of the Incarnate Word is the Son of God, one of the Persons of the Trinity.[95]

Contemporary christology has given the formula of Chalcedon bad press, claiming that the theology of Chalcedon is too abstract, not soteriological, abstruse in terminology, too philosophical and not sufficiently scriptural.[96] However, we should not forget that Chalcedon was dealing with the particular problems of its own day, using terminology employed by the opposing schools of Antioch and Alexandria. Moreover, Chalcedon's purpose was ultimately soteriological, teaching — implicitly, it is true — that we are redeemed precisely because the Son, while remaining one in being with the Father, is also one in being with us. He is, therefore, in his very person, our redemption. It also must be remembered that Chalcedon's definition, like all infallible statements of the church, was never intended to be the final word but a definitive direction.[97]

Chalcedon's contribution to christology was, in a sense, negative. It supplied no clear answers but it did give the boundary lines for authentic christology. As elucidated by following Councils, Chalcedon tells us that Jesus is one Divine Person, the Logos, in two natures which are unmixed and undivided; the human nature is not a person in its own right but is a person *in the person* of the Eternal Logos.[98] Since there are two natures in Jesus, we must speak of *two* intellects and *two* wills (the *one* will theory, called monothelitism, was explicitly condemned by the Third Council of Constantinople, 680–681 A.D.). If it be possible to decipher this theological code language of fifteen hundred years ago, its meaning would appear to be this: Jesus is ONE Person, the Eternal Word of God in a fully human way. "Person" applied to beings gifted with intelligence and will means the core center of unity, individuality: the "individual" Jesus is the Word of God expressed in and through Jesus' human personality (i.e., complete humanity): the eternal Word, the Second Person of the Trinity, takes to himself a full humanity thanks to Mary's faith-filled consent to be his Mother. The result is JESUS, the INCARNATE Son of God.

Nature, on the other hand, is the principle of operation of the individual, through which this "individual" thinks, wills, is conscious of self. Since Jesus is the God-Man, there are two principles of operation (therefore two intellects, two wills) which cannot be separated in Jesus and which also remain unmixed: Jesus is not a monstrous mixture of God and Man. The divine nature remains fully divine, the human nature remains fully human. The infinite divine nature expresses itself in and through the finite human nature. Jesus remains one person since the pre-existent Person of the Logos is the one "bearer" of both human and divine characteristics (natures). Simply put, Jesus is our God *in a fully human way*, with all the consequences mentioned above. It is within these parameters outlined by Chalcedon that christology seeks a clearer understanding of Jesus. The teaching is an authentic flowering of the scriptures. It is couched in what the Biblical Commission calls "auxiliary" language, in contrast to the "referential" language of the inspired writers; the "referential" language is not "less accurate" or "less suited to setting forth a doctrine in well defined terms."[99] The auxiliary language of Chalcedon was called for by the disputes of the age.

The question which contemporary christology wrestles with is how the formula of Chalcedon can be expressed in terms which are "new, beautiful, original, and comprehensible."[100] Often *verbal* fidelity to an ancient theological formula —

without studies on the historical, political, philosophical, theological thought-patterns which produced them — can lead to a betrayal of the teaching proclaimed through the formula.[101]

One of the primary reasons for the present chaotic situation in interpreting Chalcedon is — like one of the problems which occasioned Chalcedon — confusion in terminology. For one group of theologians, "person" retains its scholastic[102] meaning of an "individual," the core-center of unity; it is not the source of willing, thinking, self-consciousness. These "acts" flow from the "nature" of the individual. On the other hand, many theologians today think of "person" in a psychological sense, almost the equivalent of what the medievalists thought of "nature" — the source of self-consciousness, willing, freedom, thinking. Some use the term "personality" as synonymous with "personhood," others in the sense of "nature." The 1983 Pontifical Biblical Commission's Report attempts to clarify terms when it states: "But would it not be better to speak of his 'human personality,' in the sense in which the scholastics used to speak of his 'individual' and 'singular human nature'?"[103]

When we use the same expression like "nature," "person," and predicate it both of the Word of God AND of a created being, the term is used "analogically," i.e., God is more unlike "nature," "person," as found in human beings than he is like it. We are not, therefore, working with two *identical* natures when we speak of the infinite nature of the Word of God and the human nature, nor are we talking about two *identical bricks* when we speak of the Divine Intelligence and the finite intellect. Retaining the expression "personality" for "set of characteristics" we must say that Jesus enjoys a fully human personality. This fully human personality is actually created precisely by the manifestation of the Word of God into this creation; it is the fully human vehicle, the means whereby the Word of God expresses himself in and through this creation, becoming one with us in order to redeem us. The "person" of Jesus is then the *Word of God as expressed, enfleshed, manifested* in and through this man Jesus. There is no "mixture" of the human and divine but there is "involvement," for the divine while remaining divine, manifests itself in and through the human. While nothing finite can be the total expression of the Infinite, Jesus is the climactic point of God's self-manifestation, a self-disclosure which in Jesus is truly "personal."[104]

When we speak of Jesus' two intellects, two wills, therefore, we are in no way talking of "two identical bricks" placed side by side. We are declaring that Infinite Intelligence is expressed in and through this human intellect with all of its essential limitations and finitudes. The *Logos* thinks, understands, reasons in a fully human way. When the Third Council of Constantinople dogmatically condemned monothelistism, it was in no way declaring that two identical wills exist side by side which would be nothing more than classical nestorianism. Rather, it was stating that Infinite Love is now part of this creation, personally working, manifesting itself in and through the created will of this man Jesus. The Second Vatican Council sums it up beautifully: "He who is the 'image of the invisible God' (Col 1:15) is himself the perfect man who has restored in the children of Adam that likeness to God which had been disfigured ever since the first sin. Human nature, by the very fact that it was assumed, not absorbed in him, has been raised in us also to a dignity beyond compare. For by his incarnation, he, the Son of God, has in a certain way united himself with each human being. He worked with human hands, he thought with a human mind. He acted with a human will, and with a human heart he loved. Born of the Virgin Mary, he has truly been made one of us, like to us in all things except sin."[105]

Jesus is then, in his person, *incarnate* "pure gratitude, eternal eucharist, pure obedient response to the word and will of the Father."[106] Formed by the overshadowing of the Holy Spirit, the ecstasy of Love in the Godhead,[107] Jesus is the Son of God in a fully human way. Does Jesus always "know" *who* he is? The answer is best given by a question: "Do human beings always know *who* they are?" The child Jesus experiences God as ABBA much like a child experiences his/her own father. This knowledge is at first "intuitive" and becomes clarified and more clearly verbalized as Jesus, much like any human being, "increased in wisdom" (Lk 2:52). The term "much like" is used, since it is impossible for us to know *precisely* what it means to be the personal epiphany of God in this creation. Every human being is a mystery; so too, and even more so, Jesus.

The enfleshed Word of God is, therefore, truly our brother. The ramifications of this truth for an understanding of humankind, of our destiny, of the entire history of this cosmos, of the interrelatedness of all things especially all peoples, are immeasurable. Moreover, the incarnation is the pattern by which we come to a better understanding of how God discloses himself: it is always through this creation. The entire cosmos is a *sacrament* of God in the sense that it is in varying degrees and ways a manifestation of the Creator; loving, sharing, human communities are privileged places of this expression of God; the christian community, the church, is the the Body of Christ suffused with the Holy Spirit; Jesus is the climactic, *personal sacrament* of God's Word. In him, we see and hear and touch the Word Itself (cf. 1 Jn 1:1–2).

Summary

SON OF GOD: The Eternal Love of the Father is personally sent to us — he is one with us — so that we may become one with the Father. God has assumed our full humanity for "what has not been assumed has not been healed," as Saint Gregory Nazianzen stated so many centuries ago.[108] This is the christian belief expressed through the title, *Son of God*. No better summary of this rather complicated chapter could be given than the famous text of the *Letter to the Hebrews* 1:1–8, which may be the clearest expression of what Christians mean when they call Jesus *Son of God*:

"In many and various ways God spoke of old to our fathers by the prophets; but in these last days he has spoken to us by a Son whom he appointed the heir of all things through whom also he created the world. He reflects the glory of God and bears the very stamp of his nature upholding the universe by his word of power . . . For to what angel did God ever say, 'Thou art my Son, today I have begotten thee'? Or again, 'I will be to him a father and he shall be to me a son'? . . . Of the Son he says, 'Thy throne, O God, is for ever and ever.' "

CHAPTER TWELVE

THE DISCLOSURE TITLE: SON OF MAN

Although impossible in this overview to study all of the titles which the Gospels apply to Jesus, there is one which cannot be overlooked: the enigmatic *son of man*.[109] If there be any title which Jesus may have used as a self-designation, it is *Son of Man*. It is likely that all other christological labels given to Jesus are embellishments of the early Church (implicit christology); *Son of Man*, however, appears to be from the lips of Jesus himself, and perhaps in a christological sense (explicit christology).

Whether or not Jesus actually called himself *Son of Man* (and in a christological sense), nonetheless it is this title which the synoptics ordinarily use to qualify Jesus as the *Christ*. When Peter answers Jesus' question "Who do you say that I am?" with "You are the Christ," Jesus quickly retorts, "the son of man must suffer" (cf. Mk 8:29–31); when Caiaphas demands a response from Jesus to the interrogation: "Are you the Christ, the Son of the Blessed One?," Jesus modifies his "I am" with "And you will see the son of man. . ." (cf. Mk 14:61–62). In other words, the favorite title of Jesus is, at least according to the Gospel portraits — and that goes for ALL of them — *son of man*.

The Gospels never have anyone call Jesus the *son of man*; it is solely a self-designation. (Possible exceptions would be if the expression of Mk 2:10: "But that you may know that the son of man has authority on earth to forgive sins" does not represent the words of Jesus but those of the evangelist and if we understand John 12:34, "How can you say that the son of man must be lifted up?" as an address to Jesus as the Son of Man.) Moreover, outside of the Gospels the title is given to Jesus only by the dying protomartyr Stephen (Acts 7:56), twice in the *Book of Revelation* (1:13; 14:14) and in Heb 2:5–7 the author quotes in relationship to Jesus Psalm 8:4 which has a reference to "son of man." Never used by Paul, never used by any of the sermons of Peter in the Acts, never used in any other books of the New Testament, yet the Gospels are saturated with it. It is an expression found repeatedly on the lips of Jesus in the Gospels (over 80 times) yet it apparently dies out quite early as a popular designation for Jesus. And it has remained dead; when is the last time Christian liturgy offered a prayer "in the name of Jesus, the *son of man*?" If there be any title of Jesus which should be examined, it is *son of man*.

In order to try to make some headway through the incredible maze of conflicting opinions concerning this enigmatic title, the three basic steps of the methodology will be followed:

— The meaning of the title at the time of Jesus.
— Did Jesus accept/reject the title.
— The development of the title within the early Christian community.

THE MEANING OF THE TITLE SON OF MAN AT THE TIME OF JESUS

The nub of the enigma: what does this title mean? Today, people use it as a synonym for humanity as they use Son of God for divinity. But that is not the point. What did it mean AT THE TIME OF JESUS? HOW WOULD HE HAVE UNDERSTOOD IT?

First of all, we will ignore the lengthy and erudite studies done to prove that this expression is ultimately from Persian/Egyptian/Babylonian mythology. No matter its ultimate provenance, there is no doubt that it has been assimilated into Jewish thought and it is in Jewish thought that we must try to discover its meaning for Jesus. There are basically three sources in Jewish culture which should be examined in order to try to discover the meaning of *son of man* in "late Judaism" (the second and first centuries before Christ):

THE EXPRESSION ITSELF. As we saw when studying *Son of God*, the term "*Son of. . .*" is a semitism denoting a relationship to the noun which follows. *Son of man* would mean, therefore, a human being. The Greek expression for *son of man* (*ho huios tou anthropou*) is barbaric; it surely is a semitic and not a Greek phrase. Its root would probably be the Aramaic *bar nasha*. In some pre-Christian texts, this phrase has been found and is used, as Fitzmyer explains, "either in a generic sense (=a human being, a mortal) or in an indefinite sense (=someone [or if in a negation, no one])."[110] The first possible meaning of the term *son of man* would be, therefore, a human being. So far, the phrase has never been found in literature of Jesus' time as a direct substitute for the personal pronoun "I," or in the vocative ("O Man").[111] Now if this is the full significance of *son of man*, and presuming Jesus did use the expression, the meaning is simple: Jesus designates himself as a human being. The early Christians, faithful to Jesus' usage did, however — according to this theory — develop the term into a *title* with varying overlays of nuances.

ANOTHER possible source for *son of man* would be — indirectly — from the *Book of Ezechiel*. About 90 times, the prophet is addressed as *Son of Man* (Hebrew: *ben adam*) which would indicate "O mortal man," or even more strongly, "O You weak human being," for *adam* in Hebrew refers to the red clay of the earth. Ezechiel can only be an indirect source at best since its usage in that prophetical book is limited to the vocative ("O Man"), which is not its use at the time of Jesus as far as can be ascertained. Some modern English translations of *Ezechiel* use the expression *Man*, or the inclusive *Human Being* instead of *son of man* which although literally correct, regrettably lose the semitic atmosphere of the original text.

Even though the two uses — the Greek (ultimately Aramaic) title *son of man* as found in the Gospels and the Hebrew vocative, *O son of man*, as found in Ezechiel — are distinct, nonetheless, for the ordinary Jew of Jesus' time, the possibility of a connection to the prophet cannot be entirely ruled out. *Son of man* would take on, therefore, not only the meaning of human, weak, but possibly also the connotations of a "prophet like Ezechiel."

THE THIRD possible source for *son of man* is Daniel 7:13–14:

"I saw in the night visions and behold with the clouds of heaven there came one like a son of man, and he came to the Ancient of Days and was presented before him. And to him was given dominion and glory and kingdom, that all peoples, nations, and languages should serve him; his dominion is an everlasting dominion, which shall not pass away, and his kingdom one that shall not be destroyed."

The context is important. First of all, the text is situated in apocalyptic literature with all its strange imagery and cryptic expressions to proclaim the final victory over evil. In chapter seven, the enemies of Israel are described as horrible beasts (e.g., "another, like a leopard, with four wings of a bird on its back; and the beast had four heads and dominion was given to it" [Dan 7:6]). The "one like a *son of man*" who "came to the Ancient of Days" (YHWH) is the personification, as verse 18 tells us, of "the saints of the Most High," i.e., the devout of Israel. The *son of man* is the heavenly symbol of the holy ones of Israel who will surely conquer the beasts, their enemies. *Son of man* in Daniel is, then, a collectivity, the saints of Israel.[112]

HOWEVER, the four beasts of chapter seven can also be considered as the four individual kings who represent their empires. This is called *corporate personality*: an individual summarizes, epitomizes, personifies a *corpus*, a body of people. A president, for example, is in a certain sense a corporate personality: an enemy attack upon him is an attack upon the country itself. The notion of corporate personality was much stronger in ancient times than it is in the democratic age in which we live; the patriarch surely was the summary of the clan and the king of his people. It is a legitimate presumption, then to see in the *son of man* of Daniel not only a collectivity but also a *symbolic* individual who summarizes in himself the holy ones of Israel. As far as the original meaning of *son of man* in Daniel, there is little need for dispute. The problem lies in the development of the expression in the intertestamental period.

The apocryphal *Book of Enoch* (at least part of which was written sometime before the Roman conquest of 63 B.C. and which seems to be a flowering of the Danielic *son of man*) speaks clearly of the *son of man* as an individual, an eschatological figure:

"And at that hour the son of man was named in the presence of the Lord of Spirits, and his name before the head of Days. Before the sun and the signs were created, before the stars of the heaven were made, His name was named before the Lord of Spirits . . . And he shall be the Light of the Gentiles . . . For from the beginning the son of man was hidden. And the Most High preserved him in the presence of His might, and revealed him to the elect . . . And all the kings and the mighty and the exalted ones and those that rule the earth shall fall before him on their faces, and worship and set their hope upon that son of man and petition him and supplicate for mercy at his hands . . . And with that son of man shall they (i.e., the chosen) eat and lie down and rise up for ever and ever . . . for that Son of Man has appeared, and has seated himself on the throne of his glory, and all evil shall pass away before his face, and the word of that son of man shall go forth. . ."[113]

The sections of the *Book of Enoch* which so describe the *Son of Man* have not been found at Qumran and many believe them to be of a much later date within the christian era; nonetheless, they are so Jewish in tone that they would appear to represent Jewish apocalyptic tradition which is definitely pre-christian. In this *Book of Enoch*, the *son of man* is, as Reginald Fuller notes, "a pre-existent divine being . . . he is hidden in the presence of God from before all creation . . . He is revealed 'on that day', i.e., at the End. He appears in order to deliver the elect from persecution . . . he presides over the elect as a redeemed community in eternity . . . note especially the allusion to the Messianic banquet (69:29;62:14)."[114]

Another — and definitely post-70 A.D. work — which elaborates the title son of man of Daniel is the apocryphal *Fourth Ezra* which interprets this figure as the messiah, the servant/son of YHWH (cf. 13:1–3, 25–26). This represents an inter-twining of the original apocalyptic tradition of *son of man* with a variety of other elements from the Old Testament. These would be the three possible sources for our present day insight into the meaning of *son of man* at the time of Jesus. Compositely, they are more than an enigma; they form a bag of apparent contradictions:

— The phrase means lowly, human, weak; it also means the exalted, powerful, divine agent of judgment and salvation.

— The phrase denotes the nation of Israel; but also an individual who summarizes the people.

— And we can perhaps add another apparent contradiction: the victorious *son of man* is also, at least by implication in Daniel, and explicitly in later writings, the servant, the son of YHWH (in the sense explained in the previous chapter). Would not the very notion of the *Son of Man* as servant, as an agent of salvation, as intimately united to the *Ancient of Days* in delivering the just from persecution, imply for many the thought of suffering (cf. Dan 11:33 ff; Wis 2:12–20, 5:1–5)? And is not this notion of suffering an intrinsic element of *prophet* (presuming some indirect connection with Ezechiel) and also of *human* so stressed by the etymology of the term itself? However, to claim that Jesus himself fused *Son of Man* with that of *Suffering Servant* is a pure hypothesis as will be seen in the chapter on *Suffering Servant.*

It would appear that in various Jewish circles, at various stages, different aspects of *son of man* were accentuated. There is no doubt that the concept *son of man* at the time of Jesus is elusive, complex.

Son of man is, therefore, a semitic term which seems to reflect two contrary poles concerning a human being: strength and weakness.[115] Ezechiel, through whose weakness the Mighty God works wonders, is a *ben adam* (*adam* denotes, as we have seen, the slime of the earth). The *Son of Man* of *Daniel* is in the Aramaic section of the book and appears as *bar nasha*, an apparent derivative of the Hebrew, *ben enosh,* which has a connotation of strength. Is it not probable that considering its variety of uses — connoting both strength and weakness — both in the Gospels and in pre-Christian texts[116] that the term at the time of Jesus encompassed both "strength" (Daniel) and "weakness" (human, mortal)?

It does not appear that we can go any further in our attempt to understand the meaning of the term *at the time of Jesus*. It is an elusive, complex, open-ended expression, open on both ends of the spectrum: such weakness, such strength. On balance, the power of the *son of man* would appear to be the more predominant connotation at the time of Jesus, considering its connection with the *son of man* of Daniel who will be served by all peoples, all nations.

DID JESUS ACCEPT THE TITLE SON OF MAN?

This is the outer core of the enigma. In an attempt to clarify the question, scholars usually divide the *son of man* sayings found in the Gospels into three kinds. First of all, the future use of the phrase, e.g., "And then they will see the *son of man* coming in clouds with great power and glory" (Mk 13:26). Secondly, the present *son of man* sayings, e.g., "The foxes have lairs, the birds in the sky have nests, but the son of man has nowhere to lay his head" (Mt 8:20). Finally, the suffering *son of man*, e.g., "And he began to teach them that the son of man must suffer many things and be rejected by the scribes and be killed, and after three days, rise again" (Mk 8:31).

As can well be imagined, the variety of opinions concerning the derivation of these three types of *son of man* statements is vast.[117] Basically, there are theologians who hold that NONE of these statements are expressions of the historical Jesus, and other scholars who hold that at least some are. To clarify:

— None of the *son of man* statements originate with the historical Jesus.

Son of man is considered in this opinion as a christological title and therefore could only have been, so it is claimed, the creation of the early Christian community after the experience of the death/resurrection when hopes for the "day of the Lord," the Parousia, the coming of the *son of man*, were so intense.[118] The identification of Jesus with the Danielic *son of man* presupposes, so this opinion goes, the Easter experience. Moreover, the varied and imaginative ways in which *son of man* is employed in the Gospels would appear to point to a creation by the early church rather than to a self-designation of Jesus. Norman Perrin declares: "I am of the considered opinion that every single *Son of Man* saying is a product of the theologizing of the early church."[119]

— Some of the *son of man* statements originate with Jesus.

No scholar would hold that each and every instance of the more than 80 times *son of man* is used in the Gospels is part of the ipsissima verba. Those who hold that this phrase is a self-designation would also say that the early church apparently felt free to multiply its use; it is, nonetheless, an ipsissima vox. There are, however, some interesting sub-divisions of this general stance:

That Jesus referred to SOMEONE ELSE as *son of man* is one of the opinions which attempts to solve the riddle of *son of man*.[120] According to this thought, Jesus' sayings concerning the *son of man* were limited to the coming of a future judge (Dan 7). Jesus, a man of his times, shared in this common apocalyptic expectation and he looked to the coming of this *son of man* to vindicate his own mission. This opinion is based upon especially the *Q* saying found in Luke 12:8: "I tell you, whoever acknowledges me before men, the son of man will acknowledge him before the angels of God." The text presumes, so they say, a distinction between Jesus and the *son of man*. However, the parallel in Mt 10:32 declares: "Whoever acknowledges me before men, I will acknowledge before my Father in heaven," which this opinion takes as an adaptation of the "more original" Lucan phrase. Moreover, Jesus' statement in Mark 10:23, "You will not have gone through all the towns of Israel before the son of man comes," again seems to point to Jesus' belief in a coming judge, other than himself. Now with the delay in the Parousia, this opinion declares, these sayings about a future *son of man* became more and more assigned by the early church to Jesus himself and then extended by early Christian preachers to his ministry and also to his status as the suffering messiah.

The preceding opinion is denied by those who would say that Jesus employed the phrase *son of man* not as a christological title for himself or for anyone else, but only to denote nothing more than a human being, since that is the only use we find of this phrase in contemporary Aramaic literature.[121] During the tunnel period it did assume a titular sense, and that is why we find the barbaric Greek expression (*ho huios tou anthropou*) for the Aramaic *bar nasha, son of man*.

That Jesus referred to SOMEONE ELSE when he spoke of *son of man* is also opposed by those who insist that Jesus understood himself as the FINAL emissary of the Father (cf. Mk 12) in a unique and never to be surpassed oneness with God. That someone else, "still to come" — even if it be only as a "rubber stamp" (R. H. Fuller's phrase) — contradicts the tenor of the Gospels as will be seen explicitly when "End-Time Prophet" is examined. Moreover, such an opinion does not adequately explain the fact that for all practical purposes the title is found only on the lips of Jesus and also so quickly fades away. It appears to be a too facile attempt of our age to try to bring some order into the chaos of opinions concerning *son of man*. W. Kasper, while upholding the authenticity of the present and future *son of man* sayings, suggests that: "The *son of man* [in its future sense] is hardly more than a symbol for the eschatological, definitive importance of the sayings and work of Jesus and of the decision of faith . . . To claim a personal identity of Jesus with the coming *son of man* may not be justified, but there is certainly a functional identity."[122] Jesus, therefore, speaks of himself as the future *son of man* but only to indicate that the function attributed to the Danielic symbol — exercising dominion over all peoples — is his.

Other theologians hold that *son of man* is from the lips of Jesus as a *titular* christological self-designation.[123] To declare that Jesus identified himself by the title *son of man* is tantamount to accepting its usage in a christological sense considering its predominant Danielic roots reflected in the apocalyptic understanding of the title in the literature of the times. This does presuppose, however, not only that Jesus himself used the expression in the Danielic sense but also that Daniel 7 was accepted by Jesus to refer to a divine individual. The "if's" are many.

The principal reasons for upholding that *son of man* is a titular self-designation of Jesus are that the Gospels are permeated with this title for Jesus which never becomes part of a Christian "confession of faith" and also the fact that this title is, for all practical purposes, solely a Gospel designation of Jesus. If it were totally a creation of the early church, it would be expected that the Gospel authors (who are proclaiming the faith of the early church) would have someone — be it the evangelist, or Peter, James, or some disciple — call Jesus *son of man*, as is done for the christological usage of the titles Messiah, Lord, Son of God. Finally, the title is such a barbarism in Greek that its inclusion in the Gospels — all written in Greek — implies a fidelity to an expression of Jesus himself.

After considering the reasons for upholding that *son of man* is a titular self-designation of Jesus, Bruce Vawter concludes: "Hence it is that some scholars continue to find it more likely that Jesus not only used the title but used it of himself and for this reason it was remembered, even as the Gospels profess."[124]

All these reasons, taken cumulatively, militate against an elaborate and complicated theory of church invention (to be then quickly dropped by the church) and point to its use by Jesus as a titular self-designation not only in present and suffering sayings but also as the *son of man* of Daniel. It would appear extremely difficult for Jesus to employ *son of man* and abstract from Daniel 7. Presuming he did use the title, it would include some reference to the Danielic figure. However, that Jesus thought of the *son of man* of Daniel only in a figurative or symbolic sense is a possibility, as Kasper upholds. Moreover, it is by no means certain that Jesus himself would have attributed a *christological* meaning to this expression.

WE CAN CONCLUDE, therefore, that this expression comes from the lips of Jesus. However, what *precisely* he meant by it, will never be known. The importance of the title would, therefore, reside in the fact that Jesus identifies himself through an expression which is mysterious, open-ended, insinuating both divine power and utter weakness. The power of God is expressed in and through weakness: is this Jesus' self-designation? Quite possibly. The future *son of man* sayings accentuate strength; the suffering sayings, weakness; the present sayings, either weakness ("The son of man has no where to lay his head. . .") or both elements (e.g., "The son of man has the power to forgive sins. . ." i.e., this human being is the manifestation of God's forgiveness).

In fact, it is precisely this mystery of strength expressed in weakness that appears to substantiate the use of the title as a self-designation by Jesus, for it so resembles the "foundations" for the title, *Son of God* discussed in the previous chapter. (No wonder that *son of man* in John's Gospel appears at times to be interchangeable with *Son of God*.) As *son of man*, Jesus expresses that double polarity intrinsic to *Son of God*: intimacy with the Father, a sharing in his omnipotence, the eschatological messenger who is, therefore, in his person the judgment on this world (*Son of Man* as power, in the Danielic sense) and also "sent" in deepest intimacy with us in our creatureliness (*son of man* as weakness). As W. Kasper puts it: "The mysterious phrase 'son of man' allowed Jesus to express the tension which ran through his whole message: The eschatological fulness of time becomes reality in and through a miserable, despised, persecuted and finally executed wandering preacher. The pattern of humiliation and exaltation which was to become so important for later christology is already present in outline here."[125]

Moreover, the fact that the title is elusive (i.e., open-ended as far as strength and weakness are concerned), that it could not box Jesus in with any defined boundaries would appear to make it appealing to Jesus as he tries to express in the alienation of language his deep experience of oneness with the Father and oneness with us.

All things considered, the more probable opinion is that this is the one title with which Jesus felt comfortable, a title which could, more than any other, express the mystery of his being. It could be considered an ideal semitic expression of a deep experience of Jesus: the *Son of Man* as described in Daniel denoting oneness with the Ancient of Days; the *son of man* as so human, a notion intrinsic to the phrase itself.

It does, therefore, appear that Jesus did use the title *son of man* as a self-designation. Its meaning as expressed in this chapter must remain, however, in the realm of opinion. No one can speak with certainty about the precise meaning of the title as it appears on the lips of Jesus.

DEVELOPMENT OF SON OF MAN IN THE EARLY CHRISTIAN COMMUNITY

If we follow the theory that Jesus did use *son of man* as a self-designation there is no development of this title by the early church except for extending its use to additional episodes in the Gospel accounts. The expression never takes on a confessional stance (no one ever says Jesus is the *son of man* as one of the summaries of the Christian faith) and its use quickly fades away.

The motives for the elimination of this title are yet to be fully understood. Possible reasons for its disappearance are, first of all, its thoroughly Jewish spirit which made it a difficult tool of evangelization in the Gentile world (not to speak of its barbarism as a Greek phrase); secondly, the elusiveness of the title itself made it inept for proclaiming the Gospel in the Graeco-roman world. If the Christian missionary responded to the question "Who is Jesus?" with "He is the *son of man*," little if anything would be accomplished. Lurking somewhere in the hidden corners of history yet to be discovered must be some other reasons. Or are we complicating what is, in reality, a quite simple process: the expression *Son of Man*, retained in the Gospels out of fidelity to Jesus, was not an easily understood title especially in the Hellenistic world and was, therefore, dropped.

Summary

Presuming *son of man* to be from the lips of Jesus, there is the real possibility that it is the only christological title which he used as a self-designation. However such an assertion needs to be strictly qualified primarily because the precise meaning of the title at the time of Jesus is unknown. To declare that Jesus did use this title to express his identity is one assertion; it is another to declare what Jesus would mean by such a self-disclosure.

Such contrary emphases appear to be embraced within this one title that it is truly the enigma of christology. Rather than claim that Jesus clearly grasped the full meaning of *son of man*, we should perhaps see in it a self-disclosure of the mystery which he himself experienced. Mystery in the theological sense: the loving plan of the Father, beyond comprehension. The mystery who is Jesus is strongly experienced by his followers and not only after Easter. It is one of the basic ingredients of their awe and wonder as they hear him speak, see him act. The title *son of man* with its implications of BOTH human weakness and divine strength heightens that sense of mystery. It makes us understand that Jesus is beyond our grasp not only because of the literary genre *Gospel* but far more so because of his person. The more christology gives us glimpses of Jesus, the more we understand that he is truly accessible only through faith.

CHAPTER THIRTEEN

THE DISCLOSURE TITLE:
SUFFERING SERVANT OF YHWH

That Jesus is God's Servant is perhaps the Christian community's earliest interpretation of the person of Jesus. Although Peter's sermon in the third chapter of the Acts is a Lucan elaboration, nonetheless it does portray an ancient christology and Jesus is twice described there as the servant: "The God of Abraham, and of Isaac and of Jacob, the God of our fathers, glorified his servant Jesus. . ." (3:13); "God having raised up his servant, sent him to you first" (3:26). ("Raised up" here does not refer to the resurrection but is synonymous with "having given to to us.")

Servant in itself has a wide, general meaning. The Hebrew root is *ebed* (slave) which often underlies the Greek *pais* which can be translated as child, son, servant. (As previously mentioned, the expression "This is my beloved son" spoken at the Transfiguration and the Baptism of Jesus probably is a reference to Is 42:1: "Behold my servant whom I uphold, my chosen, in whom my soul delights.") The term originally expresses the submission of the slave to its master, or of an official to the king; in a transferred sense, it refers to loving obedience to YHWH who has given a person a special mission. The Old Testament will easily, therefore, apply this title *Servant of God* to prophets (cf. 1 Kgs 18:36, etc.), to kings (cf. Ps 89:4, etc.), and especially to Moses (cf. Ex 14:31, etc.)

At this stage of our study it is, therefore, of no great import that Jesus would be called *servant*. For if he is the *son of God* as explained earlier, then surely he would consider himself as *Servant of God*, although there is no reference in the portraits that he ever used the title itself as a self-designation. Even if he thought of himself as uniquely the servant of God, it actually says no more than what was already discovered in the title *Son of God*.

However, the subject of this chapter is not Jesus as *servant*. The title is a SPECIFIC one, differing from the general phrase servant of God. We are asking if Jesus actually considered himself to be that specific *Suffering Servant* described so vividly in the second part of the book of Isaiah and even more precisely, whether Jesus thought of himself in the terms of a *servant* whose death is redemptive for all, as Isaiah describes in chapter 53.[126] If by examining the portraits we could even come to a probability that Jesus did so, we have a profound insight into his self-understanding, especially concerning his interpretation of impending execution. Did he believe that he was dying for others? Did Jesus actually consider his death redemptive, in atonement for the sins of the world? The question is surely central in any study of Jesus whom Christians call *The Savior* who died upon a cross "for us and for our salvation." In order to probe these aspects of the personhood of Jesus, we will critically examine whether or not Jesus identified with the *Suffering Servant*. The question, which has such serious ramifications for christianity itself will be studied following the three step methodology we have been using throughout this section:

— The Meaning of SUFFERING SERVANT at the time of Jesus.
— Did Jesus accept/reject the title.
— The development of the title in the early Christian community.

THE MEANING OF SUFFERING SERVANT AT THE TIME OF JESUS

The book of Isaiah is a collection of collections of prophecies by various servants of God. The first section (1–39) is, for the most part, due to a rather cryptic and pompous prophet called Isaiah (and his followers) who proclaims God's word from about 742 to 701 B.C. The second part of the book (40–55) is ascribed to an anonymous prophet who ecstatically hails the return of the exiles from Babylonian captivity. This section is called Second (Greek: *deuteros*) Isaiah. The generally somber final part of the book (56–66) — often called Trito-Isaiah — contains preachings of various prophets after the return from the exile. These divisions were unknown at the time of Jesus.[127]

Interspersed within Second Isaiah are four beautiful poems about a servant of YHWH which many scholars, at least from the end of the last century, believe to have been originally one unit: 42:1–4; 49:1–6; 50:4–9; 52:13–53:12. Some add a verse or two to one or another of the poems but that is immaterial to our study.[128]

Although even in the second poem the servant experiences opposition to his mission, it is the fourth poem which so vividly and poignantly describes the incredible vicarious suffering of this innocent — and ultimately vindicated — servant on behalf of sinners. The precise question to be asked, then, is whether or not Jesus identifies with this specific character of Second Isaiah, and more precisely, with this fourth poem, often called Isaiah 53, or THE "suffering servant" poem:

"He had no form or comeliness that we should look at him and no beauty that we should desire him. He was despised and rejected by men; a man of sorrows and acquainted with grief; and as one from whom men hide their faces he was despised and we esteemed him not. Surely he has borne our griefs and carried our sorrows; yet we esteemed him stricken, smitten by God, and afflicted. But he was wounded for our transgressions, he was bruised for our iniquities; upon him was the chastisement that made us whole and with his stripes we are healed. All we like sheep have gone astray; we have turned every one to his own way; and the Lord has laid on him the iniquity of us all . . . Yet it was the will of the Lord to bruise him; he has put him to grief; when he makes himself an offering for sin, he shall see his offspring, he shall prolong his days; the will of the Lord shall prosper in his hand; he shall see the fruit of the travail of his soul and be satisfied; by his knowledge shall the righteous one, my servant, make many to be accounted righteous. . . ."

With the Ethiopian eunuch, we ask: "About whom, pray, does the prophet say this, about himself or about some one else?" (Acts 8:34). Before we accept the early Christians' answer that Deutero-Isaiah is foretelling Jesus, we must ask a first question: how was this text concerning the *Suffering Servant* understood at the time of Jesus for only then can we know if it were even likely for Jesus to identify with it.

And here is the difficulty. First of all, it does not appear that in Jesus' time the four poems were even considered as a unit, and secondly, the nineteen times the word servant is mentioned in these poems, a variety of interpretations are given: ISRAEL (49:3 explicitly calls the servant Israel); a GROUP WITHIN THE NATION like the pious ones (Hebrew: *hasidim*), an HISTORICAL FIGURE like an Old Testament king (David?) or prophet (Jeremiah?), or Moses, or the prophet Isaiah himself, or perhaps a FUTURE IDEAL CHARACTER.

In searching for the identity of this suffering servant, it should be noted that although the notion of vicarious atoning suffering (though perhaps not "for all") was quite widespread in first century Judaism, Isaiah 53 is never — as far as we can ascertain — explicitly adduced in support of it. Atoning power of vicarious suffering of the messiah is not found in contemporary literature. In fact, according to Cullmann, there is even a definite tendency to strip the servant as found in Is 53 of all suffering and transfer it to the enemies of Israel.[129]

At the time of Jesus, the suffering servant songs of Deutero-Isaiah were, so it would seem, subject to a rather confused, piecemeal exegesis, even to a point of ignoring the sufferings of the servant as outlined in the final poem. "Late Judaism" appears to avoid references to Is 53 in statements about expiation. Who is this servant of Second Isaiah? In the culture of Jesus' people, the servant could be a collectivity, it could be an individual; there is no clear determination in contemporary literature.

DID JESUS ACCEPT/REJECT THE TITLE SUFFERING SERVANT

There is no indication in the portraits that Jesus ever explicitly identified himself as the servant of Deutero-Isaiah. As a man of his culture Jesus probably accepted the indecisive understanding of the day (as he would the then current understanding of Jonah living for three days in the belly of the big fish) and therefore did not see in the *Servant* the concept of vicarious suffering for all people. For such was, as far as we can tell, the state of the exegesis of the text at the time.

Yet, is it not possible that Jesus himself went beyond the thought pattern of his day and in reading these words of the prophet experienced a mysterious identification with the servant as described in chapter 53? Jesus would come to a deeper realization of his mission, a deeper understanding of the meaning of his approaching execution through a meditative reading of this word of his Father. Such an opinion is, of course, possible. But can it be substantiated in any way? THE QUESTION is founded upon a far more basic one which must be first considered: Did Jesus understand his execution as redemptive, as a death "for all?" (The technical term for this is, as we have seen, *soteriological*, i.e., saving, redeeming.) The following reasons (taken collectively) are the basis for the opinion — difficult to deny — that Jesus did understand his death as soteriological, although ultimately it can only be accepted in faith.

FIRST OF ALL, two reasons often adduced to demonstrate that Jesus understood his death as soteriological should be rejected:

— Dismissed as irrelevant to the precise question is the fact that Jesus does consider himself a prophet (as will be seen in the next chapter) and therefore, like all prophets, expected opposition, even death (cf. Neh 9:26; Ezra 9:10–11). The precise point being considered must be addressed: does Jesus see his execution as "redemptive for all," as vicarious suffering and death in the name of and for sinners.

NONETHELESS it should be noted here: Jesus would have to be declared totally incompetent if it would be maintained that he did not understand that his life-style was bringing him to condemnation by the authorities. He was considered a blasphemer (Mk 2:7), a breaker of the Sabbath and many regulations of the Pharisees (Lk 13:14–15, etc.): the penalty (judging from Stephen's death in Acts 7) is stoning. Herod had already done away with John the Baptizer and Jesus was considered to be a John *redivivus*, i.e, come back to life (Mk 6:14): the penalty would be, as it was for John who was not as radical as Jesus, beheading (cf. Lk 13:32–33, considered "biographical" material,[130] where Jesus speaks of Herod: "Go and tell that fox, 'Behold, I cast out demons and perform cures today and tomorrow and on the third day I finish my course'. Nevertheless I must go on my way today and tomorrow and the following day; for it cannot be that a prophet should perish away from Jerusalem"). And Rome was extremely sensitive to any one disturbing the peace, who would appear to be a leader of opposition to Rome; the penalty could be crucifixion.[131]

Jesus well knew that his preaching of the imminent reign of YHWH, his authoritative interpretations of the Torah (which included in the eyes of the religious leaders, the breaking of the Law) were stirring up violent opposition from the authorities. Condemnation could not take him by surprise. As is often noted, Jesus did not die of natural causes, he did not die at home in bed. He faced death willingly as the mysterious outcome of his obedience to the Father; there is a divine MUST (Greek: *dei*) about his suffering and death which flows from his status as the enfleshed obedient Son in the midst of the disobedience of humankind. As the Word of God *in a fully human way*, he must experience death, and in that climactic moment of his life, cry out in love to his ABBA in the name of all of us, his brothers and sisters.

Historians generally agree that sometime in the course of his public ministry, Jesus finally became convinced of his impending execution. This could very well have been about the time of his decision to leave Galilee (where he had experienced failure coupled with fierce opposition) and to preach in Jerusalem where the antagonism would be even greater. The fact that Jesus could eventually foresee his condemnation because of his fidelity to his prophetic end-time mission does not in itself demonstrate that he considered his death redemptive for the sins of the world. We must try to decipher the portrait to see if it can give us even an inkling into how Jesus understood his impending condemnation.

— SECONDLY, we cannot automatically appeal to Isaiah 53. Often it is mentioned that the soteriological understanding of his death is due to Jesus' recognition that he is that *Suffering Servant* described in such clear terms in Deutero-Isaiah. As mentioned above, from what we know of the interpretation of this text at the time of Jesus, it is an unsubstantiated statement to declare that Jesus read Isaiah 53 as did the post-easter Christians who saw in these words the reality of the Lord's life.

Having excluded the above "solutions," the following reasons may be proposed in order to uphold that Jesus did indeed consider his death as soteriological:

Jesus is the SERVANT OF ALL

Even a cursory reading of the Gospels demonstrates that according to the general background of all the portraits, existing "for others" is an essential element of the *WHO* of Jesus. Against this horizon, there are texts if not from Jesus, are the authentic interpretations of his words, deeds, behavior by those who knew him which strongly accentuate this life of service (Greek: *diakonia*):

Mark 10:45: "For the Son of Man has come not to be served but to serve and to give his life as a ransom for many."

Lk 22:27: "For which is the greater, one who sits at table, or one who serves? Is it not the one who sits at table? But I am among you as one who serves."

Lk 12:37: "Blessed are those servants whom the master finds awake when he comes; truly I say to you, he will gird himself and have them sit at table and he will come and serve them."

Jn 13:2–5: "And during supper when the devil had already put it into the heart of Judas Iscariot, Simon's son, to betray him, Jesus, knowing that the Father had given all things into his hands and that he had come from God and was going to God, rose from supper, laid aside his garments, and girded himself with a towel. Then he poured water into a basin and began to wash the disciples feet and to wipe them with the towel with which he was girded."

Joined to these texts are the many instances where Jesus demands of those who follow him, a life of service (Mk 9:35; Mk 10:28; Mk 8:34–35).

Possibly all of these texts have some point of origin in the recollection of the Last Supper tradition.[132] Keeping in mind the culture of the times, like all the fellowship meals of Jesus with the poor, the outcast, the despised, the Last Supper especially is an effective sign of a covenant with Jesus, a demonstration of Jesus' acceptance of the unaccepted in the name of God. ("For this day salvation has come to this house," the Lucan Jesus can say to Nicodemus the publican after spending the day as his guest, "for the Son of man came to seek and to save the lost" Lk 19:9–10.) Considering the basic tenor of the Gospels, can we not say that especially at the final meal of Jesus with his friends, like the prophets of the Old Testament he carries out a symbolic act (washing the feet of others, serving others) which demonstrates and brings about a reality: through this Son of God, the Father is for others; through this servant, the Father gives himself to his creatures, thereby sharing life with them; through the service of Jesus, the loving reign of YHWH is being brought about. Which is a description of redemption.

Now if this be the very essence of his life, then it is also the tenor of his death. He dies as a servant *for others*. To state otherwise would demand in Jesus a total breakdown at the end, a total rupture with the very conviction of his life; it would demand a new personality. Such an opinion, though theoretically possible, is a pure hypothesis and flouts the authenticity of the Gospel portraits which describe Jesus, even in the loneliness of betrayal, of desertion and rejection by his people, as one with the will of his Father. Death is not just a rupture, an ending from without but is a fulfillment from within: it embodies the result of what a person has made of him/herself during life.[133] Jesus, therefore, dies as he lives: *for others*. His death is the full realization of his being-for-others. Presuming this, K. Rahner expresses the consequence of the death of Jesus for others: "To the innermost reality of the world there belongs what we call Jesus Christ in his life and death, what was poured out over the cosmos at the moment when the vessel of his body was shattered in death and Christ actually became, even in his humanity, what he had always been by his dignity, the heart of the universe, the innermost center of all created reality."[134] Jesus' death is soteriological.

The Words of Jesus at the Last Supper

Taking into consideration all that has been said above, the eucharistic words at the Last Supper also are indicative of the belief of Jesus that his impending death is "for others." Although the actual words of institution as given in Lk 22:20; 1 Cor 11:25 (which form one tradition) and in Mk 14:24; Mt 26:26–28 (which are of another tradition) have been embellished by the liturgy of the early church, there is one expression which, never developed by the liturgy, forcefully represents the thought of Jesus at this final meal:[135] "Truly, I say to you, I shall not drink again of the fruit of the vine until that day when I drink it new in the kingdom of God" (Mk 14:25; cf. Lk 22:16–18). Facing certain death, Jesus still offers fellowship — the last cup — which is in anticipation (technically: *proleptic*) of the fulness of the kingdom. There is a connection here between Jesus' impending death and the kingdom of God, which is redemption. Despite his rejection by his people, he remains firm in his belief that through him (the sharing in the final cup) the Kingdom comes, as he now realizes, in and through the trials of his suffering and death.

It appears that Jesus now has been able to put together the pieces of his rejection by the people, and of his belief that he is THE servant through whom the Father brings about his Kingdom. Jesus now knows that his death, far from being an isolated event of his proclamation, forms an integral part of it. The power of the Father — his Love — will be revealed in weakness "even unto death, even death upon a cross" (cf. Phil 2:6–11). Facing death, he still offers the cup of sharing in the Kingdom. His death is soteriological.

No individual text in itself can be considered as evidence that Jesus understands his death "for many." It is within the entire context of the Gospels that the episodes mentioned must be studied. The conclusion is that the whole tenor of the portraits as accentuated especially by the Last Supper events disclose the understanding of Jesus — at least sometime before Calvary — that his dying is part of his being-for-others, an effective proclamation of the Reign of God.

The early church in its liturgy surely understands the Last Supper eucharistic words in this manner, for in both traditions, there is agreement on a critical point: Jesus declares that he sheds his blood "for many," a semitism for "all." It is significant that not agreeing in other respects, all four accounts understand that his death is soteriological.

Jesus Christ as Son of God and Son of Man

As explained in previous chapters, the early church, basing itself on the words and attitudes of Jesus, firmly believes that he is the Son of God and the Son of Man. To accept this belief is to accept that Jesus takes on death for all, that he recognizes in some manner that his sufferings and death are soteriological. For as Son of God and Son of Man Jesus is, in his person — to use later theological language — the eschatological, definitive, expression of God. He is the Wisdom of God personally expressed into our foolishness; the Love of God personally manifested in our estrangement; the Power of God personally revealed in our weakness. Jesus, as the climactic point of creation's union with God, is its corporate personality. As the final victorious Word of the Father, all creation derives its ultimate meaning from him. "All things were created in him and for him. He is before all things and in him all things hold together" (Col 1:16–17).

As was mentioned in a previous chapter, the early Greek Fathers of the Church put it succinctly: "What has not been assumed (by God), has not been healed."[136] But Jesus, as Son of God, Son of Man, is the fully human expression of God's healing Life. He is, therefore, IN HIS PERSON, healing, salvation, redemption of his "brothers and sisters" whose life he so fully shares. Every act of the Incarnate Wisdom of the Father is soteriological; to say otherwise is to make what is only an abstract distinction, a concrete one: his person and his work, Son of God/Son of Man and his effective proclamation of God's healing. *What* we do and *Who* we are, cannot be divided except in theory. Soteriology and christology are studied separately for pedagogical reasons. Jesus IS Savior. He IS redemption. He IS the loving surrender of this universe to the Father, and it is through that life-long cry of Love to ABBA that we are healed.

As the Angelic Doctor, Thomas Aquinas, wrote centuries ago, every act of Jesus, everything he experiences, is redemptive.[137] His life is soteriological for He is personally the healing Life of the Father within this world so distorted by humankind's sin. The incarnation is, therefore, redemptive; the death of Jesus is redemptive. His entire life, as the "acting out" (and not in a make-believe fashion!) of Who he is, is soteriological. Such is the faith-experience of the Church as it meditates upon the words/deeds of Jesus who appears to call himself explicitly the Son of Man and at least implicitly, the Son of God. His life is for others; it is soteriological.

Assuming all the provisos brought out above, Jesus does understand his death as soteriological. Although never identifying himself as the *Suffering Servant* of God as described in Second Isaiah, the possibility that he did identify with the servant of Isaiah 53 at least toward the end of his life when death appeared a certainty, does not appear as unfounded as it did earlier in this chapter. But whether he actually did so or not, we can never discover.

THE DEVELOPMENT OF THE TITLE SUFFERING SERVANT IN THE EARLY CHRISTIAN COMMUNITY.

It is common to declare that the texts of the New Testament which speak of Jesus as "dying for us according to the Scriptures" (cf. 1 Cor 15:3–5), as being a "ransom" for us (cf. Mk 10–45), "put to death for our sins" (cf. Rom 4:25), "who took on the form of a slave" (cf. Phil 2:6–11) all stem from Is 53. Some go further and would declare that the three prophecies of the passion and death found in Mk 8, 9, 10 must refer to Is 53, and even references to Jesus the "Servant" in the Acts must have their roots in the final servant song. However, there can be at best a probability that such references in the New Testament are elaborations of the Suffering Servant of Is 53.

That Jesus died for our sins according to the Scriptures is an early cry of faith of the primitive church, as we see in 1 Cor 15:3–5. Yet this belief in the soteriological aspect of Jesus' death was perhaps not rooted in any one explicit text of the scriptures but in the very dynamic of salvation history which, Christians believe, reaches its climax in Jesus through whom we are reconciled to God (cf. Eph 1:3–10). It could also be founded on the words and deeds of Jesus himself, which, as we have seen, do not necessarily refer to Is 53. The early church surely believes in Jesus as the savior who dies for us; but whether this is a paraphrase of Is 53 can only remain a probability at best. Surely, the title *Suffering Servant of God* could be applied to Jesus whether there had been Suffering Servant Songs or not.

Nonetheless, alongside modern skepticism concerning the broadly indiscriminate use of Is 53 by the early church, there is also the conviction that this section of Deutero-Isaiah was definitely christologized by early Christians. Perhaps the earliest (conclusive) application of Is 53 to Jesus was made by the author of 1 Peter 2:22–25:

"He (Jesus) committed no sin; no guile was found on his lips. When he reviled, he did not revile in return; when he suffered, he did not threaten; but he trusted to him who judges justly. He himself bore our sins in his body on the tree, that we might die to sin and live to righteousness. By his wounds you have been healed. For you were straying like sheep but have now returned to the Shepherd and Guardian of your souls."

To this reference may very well be added the eucharistic words of Jesus at the Last Supper which in their present form express the liturgy of the early church, most probably influenced by Is 53.

The reason for the scarcity of explicit references to this text of Isaiah[138] to describe Jesus as expiation for sin may be due not only to the fact that Is 53 was ambiguously understood at that time but most especially to the fact that there were other interpretations of Jesus' death which were also current within the early church. Jesus as the prophet-martyr (cf. Acts 4:10), Jesus as the "Yes" to Israel's "No" (cf. Acts 7:51–53), Jesus as the subject of God's mysterious plan of salvation (cf. Lk 17:25), Jesus as having to experience death in order to be glorified (cf. Mk 8:31), are all part of the early church's preaching concerning the death of the Lord.[139] They do not contradict the soteriological understanding of Good Friday; they again demonstrate the variety of christologies in the New Testament.

The title *Servant*, not common in the New Testament as compared with other titles like *Son of God, Son of Man, Lord, Christ*, does not become a favored instrument of evangelization. Perhaps its implicit inclusion in the title *Son of God*, the difficulty of explaining Jesus as *slave* of the Father and taking on the "form of a slave" for us, accounts for the fact that it becomes absorbed by other more practical titles.

Summary

A christology which strips suffering away from Jesus is an unrecognizable caricature of the Gospel portraits. Intrinsic to the good news is the clear stress on this divine *must* which calls Jesus to the cross. It is not that the Father is vindictive which is utterly blasphemous. Suffering is, rather, an essential element of the incarnation itself for to be truly human in this creation so mangled by sin is *ipso facto* to embrace the cross. Jesus accepts this with great anguish but also with great love. In the name of creation which he represents as its highest point, he cries out in love to the Father even when more than any other human being he experiences as THE Son, anguish, pain and the agony of death.

Suffering in itself is an evil. But when caught up in this effect of the world's sin (which is not just a byproduct of an early stage of evolution, cf. Rom 5), Jesus still surrenders to the Father's love, suffering becomes redemptive. To cry out in love, even when everything prompts us to curse, is the height of fidelity. It is love which makes the suffering of Jesus soteriological (cf. Heb 10:5–10). That anguished shout of love from Calvary echoes eternally throughout the universe. It is a cry from within the discordance of death and yet in total harmony with the Ground of All Being, God, thereby restoring harmony to this out-of-tune universe. In and through the distortion human beings have created, a human being will restore the human race by his love. The *Letter to the Hebrews* beautifully summarizes this in one sentence: "And by that will [Christ's love] we have been sanctified through the offering of the body of Jesus Christ once for all" (10:10).

Although it is the role of the reader to enter into dialogue with the text, there is one practical aspect of *Suffering Servant* which it may be helpful to explicitly surface, for many have seen it "in between the lines." If Jesus is the servant *for us*, then this qualifies the meaning of "Christ the King." Jesus is a King who serves. Strangely, Christians often proclaim Jesus as King, acclaim Him as King, but rarely "claim" him as King. To claim the Kingship of Jesus is to recognize that He is "for us." The King awaits our command: "Ask and it will be given you; seek, and you will find; knock and it will be opened to you" (Lk 11:9; cf. Mt 7:7–8). Jesus is the King we are called upon to command. And the Lord will always answer, in fact he will respond with that "excess of meaning" so characteristic of his person. Even more than we ask he shall give to us, if we ask with loving boldness, with firm faith. Although so often hidden from our eyes, the answer of Jesus goes "beyond" our hopes and expectations. In total surrender to the King of Infinite Love for us, we "ask" knowing that we shall always "receive" — not precisely what we may ask for, but far more. Such is the mystery of Infinite Love.

CHAPTER FOURTEEN

THE DISCLOSURE TITLE: ESCHATOLOGICAL PROPHET

Perhaps the most fundamental, basic title which can be given to Jesus (and not by Christians only as we know from the Qu'ran) is the designation *prophet*.[140] It is, in a sense, the first rung on the ladder of christology.

When Jesus' friends and neighbors heard his words and observed his actions, some thought that he was "beside himself" (Mk 3:21); the scribes thought he was possessed by the prince of demons (Mk 3:22). But many, as we know from the response to Jesus' query "Who do men say that I am?," saw in him "John the Baptist [considered a prophet] . . . Elijah . . . one of the prophets" (Mk 8:28).

For his countrymen who were attracted to him, the first thought that entered their mind was that "a great prophet has risen among us" (Lk 7:16). Matthew undoubtedly refers to an historical situation when he declares that at first the leaders hesitated to arrest Jesus for "the multitudes . . . held him to be a prophet" (21:46). Some would never proceed any further in their understanding of Jesus. Others would eventually go on to declare: *THE prophet* . . . the *end-time prophet* . . . the *Suffering Servant*, the *Christ*, the *Lord*, the *Son of God*, the *Son of Man*.

Rabbi, Master, Teacher, Sir — yes; but those titles are given to so many at the time of Jesus. A new twist, a new direction is reached when the people take that radical stance: "(Jesus) is a prophet" (Mk 6:15). Each evangelist will have his own nuances, his own coloring but the first decisive stroke of the brush for all the Gospel portraits of Jesus is: the *prophet*. To return to an earlier analogy, it is the first rung, true. But in a certain sense also the highest for Jesus not only speaks God's word which would characterize any prophet. He *is* the Word made flesh (cf. Jn 1:14).

In order to clarify what appears to be so simple a title, the three step methodology followed throughout this section will again prove useful:

— The Meaning of PROPHET at the time of Jesus.
— Did Jesus accept or reject the title?
— The Development of the title within the early christian community.

THE MEANING OF PROPHET AT THE TIME OF JESUS

Before declaring Jesus to be a specific type of prophet, i.e., *eschatological*, a more basic question must be asked: "What is a prophet?" Only then can the more precise point be raised: what is the meaning of ESCHATOLOGICAL PROPHET at the time of Jesus?

PROPHET:[141] The term conjures up palm-readers, soothsayers, gazers into a crystal ball, interpreters of lines on the hand and bumps on the head. Or more disastrous still, it is applied to those who claim to predict the future with unerring accuracy either through the crisscrossing of stars or through a misguided interpretation of the books of Daniel and Revelation. Soothsayers, fortune-tellers, frenzied ecstatics existed in the Old Testament period (cf. 1 Sam 28:7, ff; Is 2:6; 2 Kg 17:17; 1 Sam 19:20–24) however, divination was severely condemned by YHWH (cf. Lv 19:31; Dt 18:10–11).

Hebrew classical prophecy is of a far different sort. The etymology of the word *prophet* gives us a clue to its meaning: one who speaks before (or for) others. Moses, for example, is given his brother Aaron as his "prophet" (Ex 7:1) since Moses himself complains that "I am slow of speech and of tongue" (Ex 4:10). Strictly speaking, the charism proper to classical Old Testament prophecy is to proclaim the word of YHWH through the gift of a transforming experience of God's presence; there is also the concomitant insight into the ultimately victorious will of God as it relates to the present situation. "Thus says the Lord. . ." is the standard beginning of a prophet's words which often end with the expression, "the oracle of YHWH." The prophets' symbolic actions (Is 20:1 ff; Jer 13:1–11, etc.) are extensions, dramatizations of the prophetic word. Deluded or "false" prophets are present in Israel's history (cf. Is 28:7, Jer 23:5 ff). To distinguish the "true" from the "false" prophet was no easy matter. The criteria given in Dt 13:1–7 appear to declare that "anyone who really knows God will recognize his true prophet and discern him from the false, for the prophecy must conform to God's nature as he has revealed it."[142]

Jeremiah, Isaiah, Ezechiel, Amos, Hosea, etc. are truly great classical prophets of the Old Testament, whose proclamations concerning the situations of their day (with the intrinsic implications for the future) are recognized by Jew and Christian alike as inspired by God.

Prophecy begins to die out in the post-exilic era. As Judaism becomes more rigorously structured and institutionalized, there is little room for a charismatic prophetic voice within the community. The prophet Malachi (dated around 450 B.C.) is considered the last of the official classical prophets. Although presumably there were some authentic prophecies in the "late" period of Judaism, nonetheless, the prophet was replaced by the BOOK (the Scriptures) and the words of the prophet by the scribal studies and interpretative commentaries (*midrash*) of the BOOK, through *halakah* (an explanation of the scriptural laws, deriving norms for present-day conduct) and *haggadah* (an explanation of scriptural narratives for a wide variety of edifying purposes).[143]

ESCHATOLOGICAL PROPHET: In "late Judaism" hopes flared for the return of the prophet (cf. 1 Mac 4:46; 9:27; 14:1.) In this period of yearning for deliverance by YHWH who would bring about his kingdom — the end-time — it is not surprising that a current of thought stressed that "the coming one" would be a prophet. When true prophecy returns, it is a sign of God's coming intervention, a sign of the end-time. As Zechariah's canticle in Luke proclaims of John the Baptizer: "And you, child, will be called the prophet of the Most High; for you will go before the Lord to prepare his ways" (Lk 1:76). The Essenes living at Qumran during the time of Jesus awaited not only a double messiah, as we have seen, but also an end-time prophet.[144]

To disentangle the complexity of the traditions of "the coming prophet" is impossible. Yet, the situation is clarified when it noted that the expectation of the end-time prophet was influenced by two principal texts, which gave rise to two different types of prophet-to-come. The first was based on an interpretation of Malachi 3:1; 4:5: "Behold I send my messenger to prepare the way before me . . . Behold I will send you Elijah the prophet before the great and terrible day of the Lord comes. . . ." Since Elijah was "taken up in a chariot" (cf. 2 Kgs 2:1 ff) it was believed that he would come again at the end-time. The eschatological prophet would, in this opinion, be like the fiery and bombastic Elijah of the Old Testament, announcing the day of judgment, restoring the twelve tribes of Israel (cf. Sirach 48:10) and preparing the way for God Himself. Although there is no room for a messiah figure in such an opinion, nonetheless, this strand of tradition became associated with the political end-time hopes of the nation and this "new Elijah" became the forerunner of the messiah who would restore the kingdom to Israel. The

Elijah type eschatological prophet has two sides: the fiery, screaming reformer who calls down fire from heaven and the Elijah who consoles, who heals even foreigners, who raises the dead to life (cf. 1 Kgs 17:23).

The second type of prophet-to-come finds its roots in Dt 18:15–18: "The Lord your God will raise up for you a prophet like me (i.e., Moses) from among you, from your brethren — him you shall heed . . . And the Lord said to me . . . I will raise up for them a prophet like you (i.e., Moses) from among the brethren and I will put my words in his mouth and he shall speak to them all that I command him."

In this opinion, the eschatological prophet will be in the mould of THE prophet, Moses, who is far more than a classical prophet because of his unique intimacy with God. Acts 3:22 and 7:37 apply Dt 18:15–18 to Jesus, presuming that a prophet like Moses was expected at the end-time. The Moses-like-prophet is another type from the Elijah-like-prophet. With great signs and wonders, Moses leads the people of God from Egypt to the promised land, he is the great lawgiver, the one who clarifies for his people the mysteries of YHWH, the instrument in the covenant which YHWH makes with the escaped slaves creating the chosen people, Israel. The Samaritans themselves had strong hopes for this new Moses who would authentically teach the Torah and reveal the final mysteries of God. As with the Elijah end-time prophet, this strand of hope also became intertwined with a coming messiah.

That a prophet would come — perhaps Moses and/or Elijah personally (*redivivus*) or at least someone with their spirit — seems to be the general understanding of the people, but his/their characteristics were often melded into those of messiah, and the two types of eschatological prophet — Moses/Elijah — were often intertwined.

If it be possible to list some of the characteristics of this eschatological Moses/ Elijah prophet, the following would appear to be the more important:

— He will proclaim the final word of God with great authority.
— He will restore the Torah with great signs and wonders.
— He will reveal the final mysteries: a "new Torah."
— He will restore Israel religiously and as a nation.
— He will issue the final call to repentance.
— He will be the forerunner of God who establishes the end-time kingdom.

DID JESUS ACCEPT THE TITLE OF END-TIME PROPHET?

If the question were to be limited to *prophet*, there is no doubt that Jesus was recognized as such by many and that he thought of himself as a prophet (cf. Mk 6:4; Jn 6:14; Lk 12:49).

The topic to be probed, however, is more specific: is Jesus THE end-time prophet, THE eschatological prophet. Since in some manner THE end-time prophet is instrumental in ushering in the final, eternal Kingdom, in effect this would mean that Jesus is the final, definitive word of God: strictly speaking, the LAST prophet. And so christians believe.[145] To be the *final* word of YHWH does not necessarily imply the *incarnate Word*. The title, therefore, is not of itself christological.

None of the portraits ever have Jesus declare: "I am the eschatological prophet"; not only because his Jewish mindset would not think in the technical language of later Greek theology but also because he does not fulfill the characteristics of the end-time Elijah/Moses prophet. He transcends them. Can this be substantiated? Again, the ultimate response to the question of the decisive disclosure of God in Jesus as the FINAL Word of the Father can only be given in faith. It is, however, clearly the teaching of the word of God: "There is no other NAME under heaven given among men by which we must be saved" (Acts 4:12).

Presuming all that has been studied thus far, the task is to show whether these characteristics of end-time prophet are fulfilled/transcended in Jesus as far as can be determined by a scrutiny of the portraits. Each of the above characteristics will be briefly examined, taking into account the preceding chapters, to determine if it does apply to Jesus.

— Proclaim the final word of God with great authority. We will develop this point at some length, since it is practically a summary of eschatological prophet.

Jesus considers himself to be the final messenger sent by the Father, as we read in Mk 12, the parable of the vineyard of Israel. If the expression "a beloved Son" (12:6) is not from the lips of Jesus (the point can be disputed since it does appear as a possible allegorizing of the early church), nonetheless, it is evident that there is a last messenger who is "finally sent" by the Father. There can be little doubt that the Marcan Jesus was clearly referring to himself, as his hearers apparently understood (cf. 12:12). He is the final messenger, the final prophet sent by the Father.

Mark also summarizes in his own words, Jesus' understanding of the ultimate reason for his preaching and entire ministry: "Jesus came into Galilee, preaching the Gospel of God, and saying 'The time is fulfilled and the kingdom of God is at hand, repent and believe in the Gospel.' " (Mk 1:14–15). In the light of Is 40:9; 52:7; 61:1, this good news signified that the time of waiting was over and God's reign had now appeared. By declaring that the TIME (Greek: *kairos*) is fulfilled, Mark is using an expression which is difficult for the "time is money" western mentality to grasp. We regard time as quantity in the sense that it is the succession of one second to the next; however, in another sense, *kairos* is rather a quality of this clock-time. Every passing tick of the clock is also a *kairos* for it is a moment in which God's saving offer of himself is present, an offer which demands response. This present *kairos* summarizes the past of salvation history and effectively promises — contains — its future fullness. We are speaking, then, of God's time, i.e., God's decisive moment of saving action of which Jesus is the fulfillment. Jesus is the *kairos* of the Father, his time of salvation, his decisive, climactic, saving act historically offered to man in love, calling forth a response. In Jesus we are "in the last kairos" (cf. 1 Pet 1:5). In Jesus, we experience the quality (*kairos*) of every second: God's offer of Himself in and through his incarnate Word. In Jesus, salvation history is fulfilled; there is no more *kairos* left for God's eternal plan of redemption is fulfilled in him. He is the last prophet.

The imperative used by Jesus: "Follow me!" (Mk 1:17) indicates within context, that he demands allegiance to himself for entry into the final Kingdom. Although adapted by the early church, the teaching of the Lord is expressed in sayings like: "If any man would come after me . . . let him follow me. For whoever would save his life will lose it and whoever loses his life for my sake . . . will save it" (Mk 8:34); "Whoever is ashamed of me and my words . . . of him will the Son of Man also be ashamed" (Mk 8:38). The eschatological choice — implied in these sayings — is presented in the appearance and preaching of Jesus. It is in relation to him that we make the choice about refusing or accepting God's reign of Love. Jesus is the final messenger, He is the fulfillment of the destiny of this universe.

This attitude is seen also in Jesus' typical manner of speaking: never like a prophet does he declare: "Thus says the Lord. . ." Although the rabbis of the time would also employ the expression "but I say to you," they always remain *within* the Torah. Jesus goes beyond, and with the circumlocution for the divine name, "it was said to you of old. . . ," he makes a claim to say God's last word, a word which brings the Old Testament to fulfillment. "What is this," say his contemporaries, "a new teaching and one proclaimed with authority" (Mk 1:27). He believes himself to be God's word in person.

Finally, if he is THE Son as we saw in a previous chapter, he is the decisive expression of God in this creation. In this sense, he is the Father's vocabulary, there is no other word to speak, no other word to pronounce into what is outside of Himself; there is no one else to send, for the life of the Father is definitively manifested in Jesus. And as Son of Man, he is the judge of all (cf. Mt 25:31 ff). Ultimate destiny is decided on the basis of our response to Jesus, for it is at the same time our response to God (cf. Lk 12:9). As Son of man, as we have seen, Jesus is THE representative of God's kingdom and also the representative of humankind. The relationship between God and creation is decided in him and through him. As noted previously, acceptance of the Lord may only be possible for many through an implicit desire expressed in accepting one's own humanity. If this is one's sincere and only possible response in the circumstances, it is an acceptance of Jesus as the Son of Man/Son of God.

— He restores the Torah, using signs and wonders. Again, the expression is too limiting according to what the portraits depict as the authentic Jesus. Of signs and wonders, there can be no doubt as will be seen explicitly when the miracles of Jesus are studied. That he restores the Torah is not precise for in a certain sense he goes beyond it and assumes an authority beyond that of Moses, beyond that surely of the rabbis of his day, to the extent that he regards himself as God's mouth, God's voice in determining the Torah. His countrymen apparently understood this quite well, even in rejecting it.

— He will reveal the final mysteries, a new torah. In the Q statement of the mutual knowledge of Jesus and the Father, it is seen that only Jesus "knows," i.e., truly experiences, lives the Father's Life. He is in himself the final mystery, he is in himself the "new Torah" of Love the Father gives to people. Only Jesus knows the mystery of the Father; his life is the sharing of that mystery, Infinite Love, with us and for us. Again, nothing about the coming Moses/Elijah ever encompassed such concepts.

— He will renew Israel, religiously, as a nation. Jesus fulfills this but in an entirely new manner. He is not a davidic messiah as we have already seen. He restores Israel not by expelling the Romans but by liberating humankind from its estrangement which it encounters on every level, cosmic, social, personal. He reestablishes humankind's loving relationship to the Father, he brings freedom to humankind caught in the cosmic prison of death and the personal prison of sin. Again, the concepts of eschatological prophet in no way embrace the restoration of Israel as accomplished by Jesus, for he does not renew Israel in a worldly manner; he frees the world by restoring harmony with the Ground of All, the Father.

— He will issue the final call to repentance. Unlike the Baptizer, Jesus proclaims *Good News* (the root meaning of *evangelize, Gospel*). In implementing the Good News of God's healing love, there is the call to faith, an aspect of Jesus' ministry seen throughout the portraits. Faith is the correlative of repentance, for repentance, (Greek: *metanoia*) does not mean simple self-denial on one point or another but a complete turn-about accomplished through the power of God's grace. Faith implies, therefore, a wrenching on every level of personality from everything which is not the Lord's and a turning around to God, seeing in Him and in Him alone the ultimate meaning of life. Linking, as he does, surrender to God's Love with following him (as we saw above), then it can be said that Jesus is in his person the eschatological, effective call to turn to the Lord (faith) which also means to turn away from everything which is not of God (repentance).

— He will be the forerunner of God who establishes the Kingdom. It is here especially that there is confusion in the Gospel portraits. Did Jesus consider himself like Moses or like Elijah? Neither one nor the other, would appear to be the answer.

As will be seen more in detail in the next section, Jesus inaugurates the kingdom; he is not its forerunner. As Risen Lord who is the future of this universe, He is the Kingdom; he does not merely point to it. This latter task Jesus has attributed to John the Baptizer (cf. Mk 9:13) or at least his attitude toward the Baptizer has led the christian community to describe John as the Elijah to come, as the forerunner. As Malachi sees the Elijah-returned as preparing the way for God's reign, so the early church will see the Baptizer — the new Elijah — as the forerunner of Jesus himself. Again, this characteristic of the eschatological prophet is transcended by Jesus.

Jesus, therefore, breaks the mold of the eschatological prophet. He goes beyond the characteristics which appear to have been prevalent at the time about the coming prophet. There is in Jesus the experience of such intimacy with the Father, such a call/response which is constitutive of his very person, that there is the "more than" — the excess of meaning — implied in Jesus' words and deeds. And this "more" has an eschatological quality in the sense that Jesus does not identify himself as one of the prophets but THE eschatological one in a manner far transcending the hopes of Israel. He is God's final word, his definitive will. In the thought of the age, this Spirit had died out after the time of the prophets; God is silent. Not until the last times is the Spirit expected again. Jesus is filled with the Spirit of God (Mk 3:28–29; Mt 12:28); the prophetic voice of God is heard again in Israel. In Jesus, God has broken his silence. As St. Augustine so beautifully expresses it: "You have shouted and you have shattered my deafness."[146] The only word the Father "shouts" into this creation is his Word, his Wisdom, Jesus the Lord. Spoken in silence from all eternity, the Word is spoken out loud at the incarnation; we are deaf no longer, for we now hear our God.

THE DEVELOPMENT OF THE TITLE IN THE EARLY CHURCH

Jesus' actions, words, led many to look upon him as the end-time prophet. His resurrection confirmed for his small group of followers that he is the new age, that the eschaton (the end, the goal) has broken into ongoing time in Jesus. One of the ways to express this was in terms of the Elijah/Moses typology which is developed in various ways in the redaction of the Gospels always with the connotation, which has its roots in the life of the historical Jesus and not only in his resurrection, that Jesus is "more than. . ."

In order to understand the early Church's use of this title, it is well to recall that there are distinct traces in the early writings of the church of difficulties between the followers of the Baptizer and those of Jesus. Perhaps some of the followers of John believed him to be the messiah (cf. Jn 1:19–28) or, at least, John was considered by his followers to be greater than Jesus for was not Jesus baptized by John? The theme of the eschatological prophet is used, therefore, not only to underline the role of Jesus, but also to clarify the relationship between the Baptizer, the withdrawn reformer ascetic who may have at one time been a member of the Qumran group, and Jesus who proclaims the good news of God's love to the poor by word and deed.

Mark at least implicitly classifies John the Baptizer as the Elijah to come: "But I tell you," the Marcan Jesus declares, "that Elijah has come and they did to him whatever they pleased as it is written of him" (Mk 9:13). Already the early church is attempting to resolve the conflict between the followers of John and those of Jesus: John is Elijah, the forerunner of the anointed with the Spirit, Jesus, who inaugurates the kingdom.

Nonetheless, Mark's Jesus does appear to have Moses-like-prophet overtones as we can see in the following episodes: Jesus' forty day stay in the wilderness (as Moses was in the desert for forty years); the miracles of Jesus (as Moses [and Elijah also] performed miracles); the miraculous feeding (similar to Moses' feeding the crowd with manna from heaven); the Transfiguration scene where Jesus appears between Moses and Elijah as their fulfillment; the voice from the overshadowing cloud (the sign of God's presence in Scriptural terms) proclaims "listen to him," which appears to be taken from Deut 18:15. Nonetheless, compared to the other Gospels, the Marcan community does not stress Jesus as a Moses/Elijah *redivivus*.

Luke goes a step beyond Mark. In the *Acts of the Apostles*, this role of a Moses-like prophet is explicitly given to Jesus in Peter's temple speech (Acts 3:22–23) and in the stylized speech of Stephen (Acts 7:37) where again, Deut 18:15 is cited. The role of the Elijah-to-come is attributed to Jesus by the Baptizer (Lk 3:16; 7:19). Strangely enough, Jesus then identifies the Baptizer as fulfilling this role (7:27) and at least implicitly rejects a similarity to Elijah when he refuses to act like Elijah and call down fire from heaven on those villages which did not receive him (9:54–55; cf. 1 Kgs 18:36–38; 2 Kgs 1:9–14). To complicate matters, Luke also portrays Jesus in the role of Elijah after Jesus identifies himself in the Nazareth synagogue scene with Is 61:1–2 (Lk 4:16–27).

The resemblance of Jesus to Elijah — and also to Elisha — is not in the prophet's role as a fiery social reformer, but as the healer of the poor and foreigners (cf. Lk 4:25–28). The role of Elijah as the ascetic reformer who prepares the way for the Lord is given by Luke to the Baptizer. In the post-resurrection scene of the disciples on the road to Emmaus (Lk 24:19), Luke has the disciples acknowledge that Jesus is not simply a prophet but the eschatological prophet: "who was the one to redeem Israel." However, the principal point that Luke is trying to get across is that Jesus, penetrated with the Spirit, is now God's instrument in the pouring forth of the Spirit in these "last days" (cf. Acts 2:17,33). As in Mark, Jesus is always something "more."

In the *Q* narrative (Mt 11:2–15, Lk 7:18–35) the question of whether Jesus is "the one who is to come" is posed explicitly to Jesus by the followers of John the Baptizer. It would appear that the ambiguous "one who is to come" is understood by the followers of John as someone who would continue the work of this Elijah-like fiery reformer. If this is what is meant, Jesus rejects such a concept and identifies himself through Is 61 (as done in the Lucan description of the Nazareth synagogue episode in chapter four). The notion of the end-time prophet is modified by Jesus' acceptance of the role of healer, of the proclaimer of joy which for Isaiah 61 is characteristic of the last times. Perhaps it is Jesus' way of telling John's disciples that he does not continue the work of the Baptizer but takes on an entirely new role as expressed in Is 61.

Matthew in the very structure of his Gospel appears to allude to Jesus as a prophet-like-Moses. As there are five books of the Torah given by Moses from a mountain, so the Matthean Jesus gives the Torah of the new covenant from a mountain (the Sermon on the Mount) and divides his Gospel into basically five sections. Comparisons with Moses are also seen in the nativity scene where the childhood of Jesus is made analogous with the childhood of Moses (Mt 2:13–23). Presuming that Matthew is writing his Gospel for a predominantly Jewish-christian community, it is not surprising that such a stress would be put on Jesus as the new Moses, or rather, as Jesus surpassing Moses.

John's Gospel appears to represent a time within the christian community when the dispute between the followers of Jesus and those of John the Baptizer was particularly intense. The Baptizer, after having been definitely excluded as the LIGHT in John's prologue (1:6–8), openly and firmly proclaims that he is not the Christ, not Elijah, not "the prophet" (apparently alluding to the prophet-like-Moses). The Baptizer in John's Gospel is a voice crying out in the wilderness, pointing the way to Jesus (1:23 cf. 3:25 ff).

The allusions, however, to Jesus as the prophet-like-Moses are intertwined throughout John's Gospel with the notion of "more than. . ." For example, Jn 1:17 states "For the law was given though Moses; grace and truth came through Jesus Christ"; this is to be compared with Ex 34:6 where YHWH reveals his name to Moses: "YHWH . . . full of grace and truth."[147] Moses made a bronze serpent, raised it up and set it on a pole so that everyone bitten by a snake who gazed at it would live (Num 21:4–9); yet Jesus is greater than Moses for "And as Moses lifted up the serpent in the wilderness so must the Son of Man be lifted up" (Jn 3:14): through Jesus himself we are to be healed. In Exodus 16, we read of the feeding of the crowd with manna from heaven by Moses; in the discourse on the bread of life (Jn 6), a direct reference is made to this power of Moses: "I say to you it was not Moses who gave you the bread from heaven: my Father gives you the true bread from heaven" (6:32) and Jesus then describes himself as the bread come down from heaven (vv. 35 ff). Finally, Jesus is surely more than Moses, for Jesus alone is the Son of God, Jesus alone is the Word of God enfleshed (1:14).

Summary

The title end-time prophet applies to the historical Jesus but in its fullest sense is developed in the light of the Resurrection. The title easily becomes entwined with many others — servant, Son of God. Its use is limited in the early church, for in its truly christological connotation as the Word enfleshed, as the Son who is sent to bring about the Kingdom, other titles appear more apt: Son of God, Lord.

The fact that Christians recognize Jesus as the final Word of God, His eternal Word enfleshed in our estranged world, distinguishes them as followers of the Christ. It is this precise point — Jesus is the end-time prophet and even "more than" the final word of God — which separated church from synagogue and later still, mosque from church. For christians firmly believe that Jesus is "the Way, the Truth and the Life" (Jn 14:16) and, therefore, everything is to be seen, measured, judged in the power of the Spirit, through THE Incarnate Word of the Father, Jesus. This does not imply that Jesus is limited to one cultural mindset, that he can only be understood by western metaphysical theologizing.[148] God does disclose himself through daily events, through creation itself, through non-christian religions, etc.[149] Nonetheless, even these disclosure situations are implicitly and unconsciously revelatory of Jesus.[150] There is no such thing as a "grace of God" but all is a "grace of Christ," i.e., any participation in the Life of the Father — whether we are speaking of angels, or of a supralapsarian (i.e., Adam and Eve before the Fall) state or of any persons in outer galaxies — is due to the redemptive incarnation. All creation derives its meaning from its climactic point where it is the personal disclosure of God. It is through the incarnate Word that, in the power of the Spirit, creation enters the Father's Life; it is through the incarnate Word that in the power of the Spirit, the Father shares Life with us.[151] Yet as has been often stated, this "way to the Father" is not limited to those who are christians; provided that one seeks the Father according to the best means possible in one's circumstances, according to one's informed conscience, that person is on the road to the Father through Jesus, even without realizing it. Karl Rahner words this beautifully and concisely: ". . . if someone who is still far from any explicit and verbally formulated revelation accepts his . . . humanity, . . . he is saying Yes to Jesus Christ even if he does not realize it . . . If someone lets go and jumps, he falls into the depth which is actually there, not merely the depth he has measured . . . (he) has accepted the Son of Man because in him God accepted man."[152] There is then no call for "christian triumphalism" which would change authentic biblical christocentricity into christomonism or *Jesuology* which ignores the Trinity and demands that there be a *formal* acceptance of Jesus as one's personal Savior in order to enter the Kingdom.[153]

SECTION FOUR

THE DISCLOSURE THEME: THE REIGN OF YHWH

Some of the more important titles attributed to Jesus in the Gospels — *Messiah, Lord, Son of God, Son of Man, Suffering Servant, Eschatological Prophet* — disclose in a limited fashion his lived out commitments which reveal his "character."

However, there is another manner of clarifying the Gospel portraits. Even a superficial reading of the synoptic Gospels reveals that the basic theme of Jesus' message is the Reign of YHWH; everything is subordinated to this proclamation.[1] The expression itself is found 31 times in Luke, 14 times in Mk, 35 times in Matthew (31 of these under the more semitic form *The Kingdom of Heaven* or literally, *the kingdom of the heavens*). Although John's Gospel uses the explicit term only twice (3:3,5) nonetheless the equivalent is stated in John's symbolic use of *light, life*.

"And Jesus went about all the cities and villages, teaching in their synagogues and preaching the Gospel of the kingdom" (Mt 9:35). *The Kingdom of God* — or more correctly, *The Reign of God*[2] — is the central issue for Jesus. He is consumed with the call to proclaim the Kingdom. " 'I must preach the Good News of the Kingdom of God to the other cities also; for I was sent for this purpose' " (Lk 4:43). This is the Good News, the Gospel which He announces in his behavior, his deeds and words. Its importance and centrality in christology is difficult to exaggerate, for it is clearly THE message of the Lord, a message which cannot be separated from his person. "The herald is already being presented as the one heralded."[3] The Kingdom is identified with a poor, itinerant preacher; he is the proclamation of the Reign. "Jesus is the Kingdom of God in the form of concealment, lowliness and poverty. In him the meaning of his message is made visible and tangible; in him is made manifest what God's kingdom is . . . Person and 'cause' cannot be separated in Jesus. He is cause in person. He is the physical embodiment and personal form of the coming of the Kingdom of God."[4] Nothing can better clarify the portraits of Jesus, nothing can give a deeper insight into his work and his person than a study of the all pervasive theme of Jesus' life: *The Reign of God*. It is a deep, personal commitment founded upon his unique relationship with YHWH and his relationship with us.

This section will be divided into the following chapters:

1. The God Who Reigns
2. The Miracles of the Reign of God
3. The Time of the Reign of God
4. The Inheritors of the Reign of God
5. The Parables of the Reign of God

CHAPTER FIFTEEN

THE REIGN OF GOD: THE GOD WHO REIGNS

Since the Reign of God is letting who God is permeate all creation, letting God be God, there is no better way of trying to grasp its meaning than by reflecting on the *God who reigns*. In order to clarify the New Testament understanding of the God Who rules by sharing Life, the Gospels must be placed in their proper context, the Old Testament. The notion of the reign of YHWH-King in the Old Testament[5] will first be briefly outlined before considering the further developments given to us in the New Testament.

THE REIGN OF YHWH-KING IN THE OLD TESTAMENT

Because of the experience of God's loving kindness (Hebrew: *hesed*) which so mysteriously and continually guided and protected the people especially in the Exodus event, Israel acclaims YHWH as King. An exemplary king in the Middle East of ancient times showed favoritism to the poor, to the weak, fulfilling justice by surpassing it through mercy.[6] God has, so the escapees from Egypt believed, freely become their king, freely initiating a special covenant with them, the weak, and not with the Egyptians, the strong. As the bylaws of the covenant — the Ten Commandments — declare, YHWH is their Lord, they are his people and are to render him total loving obedience (cf. Ex 20, Dt 5:6–27). After the miraculous escape from Egypt, the people chant: "The Lord will reign forever and ever" (Ex 15:18). In the book of Numbers, Balaam describes the Israelites: "The Lord their God is with them and the shout of a king is among them" (23:21).

This sovereignty of YHWH must, so the Israelites conclude, extend backwards and also forwards. *Backwards*: He is always the King, always the Lord, therefore he is the source of all, the Ruler of creation, the creator. *Forwards*: He will always be king, his dominion will be without end.[7] The notion of kingship is then a dynamic one, including the confident hopes for the future. God's rule embraces not only Israel but all peoples, all nations, the entire cosmos. However, his rule is not accepted by all, not even in Israel. Intrinsic then to the understanding of "YHWH is King" is the eschatological dimension — the future glorious reign of YHWH — which especially in the post-exilic period becomes highly pronounced.[8]

The psalms are filled with the cries of YHWH the king who will come in glorious triumph. The theme of psalms 47,93,96,97,98,99 is the acclamation: "YHWH malak," i.e., YHWH reigns! All nations, all creation must acknowledge the reign of God: "Say among the nations, 'The Lord reigns!' . . . Let the heavens be glad and let the earth rejoice, let the sea roar and all that fills it, let the field exult and everything in it! Then shall all the trees of the wood sing for joy before the Lord, for he comes, for he comes to judge the earth" (Ps 95:10–13). The psalmist not only considers the present rule of God but knows that YHWH's reign is forever, from creation to its fullness of royal glory in the future when the entire world shall be freed by his saving power. The hope of Israel is not in the future in itself but in their God who now, tomorrow and forever reigns as Ruler and therefore as Judge over all. His reign embraces all of history. Nonetheless, the future holds the assured promise of his complete reign of justice and peace, of healing and salvation for all who accept his loving rule. No matter the present difficulties, God is reigning and will bring the evil to judgment, the good to their reward, in some future order.

After the exile, a horrible dilemma faced the Jewish people. They had returned to their God, they had become again his faithful people, they had separated themselves from any alliances with their pagan neighbors, many had even died because of heroic devotion to the Law (cf. 2 Mac 5–7). Yet the kingdom of God did not come. Rather, they were ruled by the persecuting kingdom of the Greeks, of the Seleucids (one of the groups which inherited the empire after the death of Alexander the Great), and then in 63 B.C. the sovereignty of Israel was crushed by the Roman armies under Pompey. The king who reigned was the despicable Roman emperor. Yet Israel believed itself faithful to YHWH the King.

The situation was beyond their comprehension. More than ever, Israel believed, there must be an intervention in history by God to rescue them and assert his sovereignty over the nations. Israel awaited this "Day of the Lord."[9]

These times of persecution, of occupation by foreign forces who desecrated the Temple with the hated Roman standard, gave rise to an apocalyptic understanding of YHWH's reign. Writings, both canonical and non-canonical, stressed an apocalyptic view of the kingdom, especially during the years 200 B.C. to 100 A.D.[10] As seen in a previous chapter, apocalyptic literature is marked by the literary device of weird cosmic symbols, strange dreams, visions, angelic guides who reveal the *why* of suffering, of persecution, of the absence of God's saving kingdom. The usually anonymous authors of these works make believe that they are in the distant past and then foretell the future thereby re-interpreting history so that some explanation could be given for the horrors of the present.

However, these apocalyptic "stage-props" often were employed to teach a world view where there is no gray, only evil vs. good. The strict apocalyptic world view uses these strange literary forms to convey, first of all, rather clear divisions between the "good" and the "evil," or to use the semitic terms, *the sons of light* and the *sons of darkness*. This clear division can also be seen in the understanding of good spirits and evil spirits (both under the one God of Israel) and the evil in the world attributed to the evil spirits and satan. Within creation itself is a power hostile to the just, to Israel; God must come and assert his royal power over this creation. The division was also pronounced in the separation of history into "this age" and "the age to come" or a "this age" and "a new heaven and a new earth."

However the most important aspect of the strict apocalyptic world view is that — so upset by the experience of God's absence in spite of their fidelity — the apocalyptic authors paid little attention to God acting NOW in the history of the people; rather, he is the God who WILL COME after fixed, pre-determined periods which are coming to a close. It is no longer "God reigns" which the suffering apocalyptist cries, but "God WILL reign" at the cataclysmic end of history to deliver his people who are now being unjustly persecuted by forces over which they seem to have no control, no responsibility.[11]

On the other hand, the prophetic view or the simple eschatological vision, although using some of the same apocalyptic "stage-props," sees the present in the light of the ultimate assured victory of God the King; he reigns NOW and will reign fully in the FUTURE. God's present reign shall ultimately overcome all evil beginning a new and transformed order.[12] According to this understanding, it is not only "God will reign" which is to be chanted, but also "God NOW reigns," even if it be in an incomplete manner.[13]

The Reign to be initiated by God is interpreted in highly different ways at the time of Jesus. The more religious would look upon it as the fulfillment of the Torah, the more politically minded would consider it more of a theocracy which would be initiated by God but implemented through the force of arms. However such views were usually transcended by the apocalyptists who looked forward to that new aeon, that new heaven and new earth.

It is this varied understanding of God as King or to use the almost unknown phrase in Jewish literature, of the kingdom of God,[14] which is prevalent at the time of Jesus. No doubt, YHWH-King is a merciful, forgiving monarch. However, his awesome transcendence is accentuated in a somewhat legalistic framework of reward/ punishment which the deuteronomic editing of many Old Testament books brought to the fore.

Whether the stress be prophetic or apocalyptic, it is eschatological, looking FORWARD to the coming in power of God over all forces of evil which will take place "on that day," i.e., the day of judgment for the evil which will also be the day of the full reign of YHWH with his just. That *Day of the Lord* was not thought to be far off.

THE REIGN OF YHWH-KING IN THE NEW TESTAMENT

Jesus speaks repeatedly about the the Reign of YHWH, using the expression, *Kingdom of God*; Jeremias considers this phrase a "characteristic of Jesus' speech to which there is no analogy in contemporary literature."[15] Yet no where does Jesus clearly define it, at least according to the Gospels. Why no explanation? It could correctly be replied that the Reign is a mystery, i.e., the unfolding salvific plan of the Father's free choice which is revealed in and through human events lived in the light of faith. It is a dynamic concept which cannot, then, be put into a neat formula. However it is not precisely correct to say that Jesus does not explain the Reign. True, nowhere does he give the etymological or real definition of the term. His explanations are found especially in his understanding of the GOD who reigns.

Nothing so clarifies the notion of the Reign of God as Jesus' understanding of the Father.[16] For the Reign means principally the reign of God as God. To proclaim that "the kingdom is at hand" is, therefore, to proclaim that God himself is at hand. The reign of God announces the day of his pervading salvific presence in all creation, the day of his rule when the universe recognizes its Lord and is a joyful cry: "The Lord is King."

Does Jesus give any understanding of WHO the King is? If so, we have an insight into the meaning of his reign. Against the background of the entire New Testament, a few texts will be considered which accentuate WHO the King — YHWH — is.

— The Sermon on the Mount (Mt 5–7). For Jesus, God is near, he is close, he is for humankind. The Sermon on the Mount discloses a God who is neither distant, nor to be encountered only through the Torah. The teaching of Jesus is heard through the mouth of the Matthean Christ:

"Look at the birds of the air: they neither sow nor reap nor gather into barns and yet your heavenly Father feeds them. Are you not of more value than they? . . . Consider the lilies of the field, how they grow; they neither toil nor spin yet I tell you even Solomon in all his glory was not arrayed like one of these. But if God so clothes the grass of the field . . . will he not much more clothe you, O men of little faith . . . Seek first his kingdom and his righteousness. . ." (Mt 6:25–33). God is close, disclosing his loving care in the *today* of ordinary events. The reign of YHWH is the reign of love.

— For Jesus, God is ABBA. As seen in previous chapters, this bold, unheard of address of the mighty God gives us a deep insight into WHO God is. He is tender strength, loving power. God-ABBA dynamically shares his life — Love — with this universe in and through his Son. This does not mean that the kingdom consists in some vague notion of the "Fatherhood of God and the Brotherhood of Man" as 19th century liberalism taught. A radical change of heart, a new vision of reality is demanded of those who like children enter the kingdom of ABBA (cf. Mt 18:3).

Moreover, ABBA stresses the infinite difference and yet the dynamic, personal intimacy of God. The more we experience the intimacy of his life through grace, the more we experience distance. The "closer" we are to ABBA, the more we grasp how awesome is the difference between Creator and creature. *Love unites but also perfects the other as other*. This gives us an insight into the Reign of God. Sharing his divine life with us, he does not destroy us in our humanity, he does not obliterate our self-consciousness, our individuality. Rather, his love perfects us as humans and as fully human, i.e., in harmony with the Ground of all Being, in harmony with ourselves, in harmony with creation, in harmony with one another. As ABBA — the God of Love — we have a new insight into WHO reigns; we understand a little more clearly the meaning of the Reign of God.

— The miracles of Jesus also reveal WHO God is, for Jesus performs these signs with the finger of God (cf. Lk 11:20), indicating that the Reign of God has come upon us.

The miracles are signs of the inbreaking of the reign, of the healing of the primordial rupture between a person and his/her real self, between people and God, between one person and others, between humankind and this creation. The miracles are, then, revelatory of God himself: he is the loving, healing God who restores life, concerned with the well-being of the entire person, body/soul, who wipes away the tears of suffering and death. "On that day," that day of YHWH's glorious reign, the blind see, the deaf hear, the cripple walk (cf. Is 61). These kingdom signs, Jesus works. The evil powers which he drives out with authority (no matter how a modern-day scientist may want to explain these actions) are expressive of Jesus' firm belief that God is a God who cares, who yearns for us more than we can ever long for Him. Not the abstract unmoved mover but YHWH is Love itself who in Jesus bends low over the sick and the outcast, who accepts the unaccepted (cf. the parables of the prodigal son, the lost coin, the lost sheep), who shares covenant meal with the so-called sinners of his day. "To be in Christ," says Saint Paul, "means being a completely new creature. Everything of the old is gone, now everything is made anew" (2 Cor 5:17). The Reign of God, omnipotent love, creates all things new.

Summary

The fundamental insight into the meaning of the mysterious reign of God is an understanding of the God WHO reigns. He IS Love. Therefore, the reign of God is the full-flowering of his omnipotent love throughout the cosmos. It calls for an openness to this omnipotent Love. He as dynamic Love takes the initiative: "We love because he first loved us" (1 Jn 4:19; cf. Rom 5:8). Through faith, we share in that empowering life of God (grace) and become his transforming presence in a distorted world, hastening the day of that victorious reign.

The Reign of God is therefore characterized by a loving harmony among peoples no matter the differences of race or barriers of culture. For a Christian, that power is not in a far-distant future; it is poured forth into our hearts through the Spirit of Love, the Spirit of the Risen Jesus. As we will see, the Reign in its total sense is eschatological but it is also a contemporary happening inasmuch as the Spirit of the Lord is empowering us to be responsible instruments in bringing about the fulness of His reign. Accepting the realities of a world which is not yet fully open to the Reign, the Christian armed with the the love of God — the Spirit — is an effective instrument in the transforming of this world into the new creation. Not through violence, not through a do-nothing attitude but through that dynamic sharing in the life of the God who reigns, the kingdom becomes more intensely present. "The news of the coming of the Reign of God is therefore a promise about everything that is done in the world out of love. It says that, against all appearances, what is done out of love will endure for ever; that it is the only thing which lasts for ever."[17]

WHAT is the Reign of God? It is the dynamic sovereignty of God's healing, forgiving Life. It is the new beginning, the new start, the inbreaking of the victorious loving, omnipotent saving power of our God bringing about *shalom*, joy, freedom, for the "whole person." Far from being just an "inward attitude," it is the transformation of all things through the acceptance of God as God, through the acknowledgment of the God of Love as King. It is the reign of God as God so that this creation will truly become his realm.

The acceptance of this Gospel teaching concerning the Reign creates a new vision of reality.

CHAPTER SIXTEEN

THE REIGN OF GOD: THE MIRACLES OF THE REIGN

For Jesus, miracles are the effective instrument of the inbreaking of God's Reign.[18] For modern men and women, they are an impregnable barrier or at least a difficult hurdle in accepting the person of Jesus.

For Jesus' cures, contemporary medicine substitutes the *empirical* evidence of the healing accomplished by modern health care. For Jesus' miracles of nature like the stilling the storm, contemporary science substitutes the visible wonders of space shuttles and telecommunications satellites. And for the resurrection, some find a substitute in genetic engineering which they hope will one day cure death. The primitive and fairytale miracles of the Gospel, so it is claimed, have no place in the scientific world of today.

In order to respond to contemporary skepticism concerning the miracles of Jesus, a basic question should be answered: What is the point of all these wonders in the Gospels? Only when we clarify the *role of miracles* in the proclamation of Jesus should we venture into the field of a possible explanation.[19] The chapter will, then, be divided into three sections:

— The Role of Miracles in Jesus' Proclamation of the Reign of YHWH.
— An Overall Assessment of the Gospel Miracles.
— A "Scientific" Explanation?

THE ROLE OF MIRACLES IN JESUS' PROCLAMATION OF THE REIGN

To speak of a Jesus of History without miracles and a Christ of Faith with miracles, is an absurdity. As far as history is capable of demonstrating, the words of Peter refer to fact: "Jesus of Nazareth, a man attested to you by God with mighty works and wonders and signs which God did through him in your midst as you yourselves know" (Acts 2:22). But precisely *why* these "signs and wonders?" Would it not make Jesus more "acceptable" to the contemporary world if we could only divest him of all this folklore? Bultmann, in fact, does precisely that. Starting with the conviction that miracles as such are impossible, Bultmann must reach his demythologizing conclusion that the miracles were invented by Jesus' early followers especially by those adept in story-telling. How else could Christianity compete in a world where miracles of wonder-workers were so commonplace?[20] Jesus, Bultmann would maintain, did "certain things which in his eyes and the eyes of his contemporaries were real miracles — acts, that is of which God must be accounted the author . . . (but) Christian faith has nothing to gain, on the contrary has everything to lose, by trying to prove the possibility and the reality of Jesus' miracles as objective facts."[21]

Bultmann did bring to the fore the undeniable evidence that the miracles of Jesus — like all the Gospel material — have been interpreted, with adaptations and embellishments taking place. However, Bultmann was working with a rather antiquated understanding of miracles still popular at his time ("an exception to the laws of nature such as *Mirakel* claims to be")[22] and also primarily stressing the probative or apologetic aspect of Jesus' miracles. Concerning the "nature" of a miracle, we will examine that point in the final section of this chapter. However,

Bultmann is incorrect in stressing that the miracles of Jesus — which he insists as a whole are "legendary" — "sprang from the conviction that Jesus was the Messiah and from the desire to spread this conviction by making it seem credible."[23]

The miracles of Jesus are *not* primarily apologetic. Bultmann was no exception to the general run of theologians in classifying miracles both as contrary to laws of nature and as — to a certain degree — grounding faith in Jesus. However, a study of the Gospels shows that "Jesus' miracles were not only or primarily external confirmations of his message; rather the miracle was the vehicle of his message. Side by side, word and miraculous deed gave expression to the entrance of God's kingly power into time . . . miracle (is) an intrinsic part of revelation, rather than merely an extrinsic criterion."[24]

Jesus' miracles — found in *every strata of tradition concerning Jesus* — are not for "display" as is so often the case in the wonder workers of the age.[25] To stress the miraculous without seeking the reason for these deeds is to miss the point of the Gospel message. What is the purpose, the significance of the miracles of Jesus: their theological import? The most significant would appear to be the following:

THE KINGDOM OF GOD INVOLVES ALL CREATION. The miracles condemn any dualism which claims that the spirit is good but matter is evil, for the wonders wrought by Jesus are done through creation and for creation. If Jesus heals the body, it is because the body is good; if he is uses clay made of dirt and spittle to heal blindness, it is because this creation is good. All creation — even every particle of matter in outer space — is to share in the glory of our Tripersonal God. The body, the entire cosmos is to be respected for it is destined to be transformed through Jesus, in the power of the Spirit, into the realm of the Father. The extraordinary acts of Jesus are dynamic proclamations and one of their primary lessons is a repetition of the words of the first book of the Bible which so simply and repeatedly describe God's one reaction to his creation: "And God saw that it was good" (Gen 1:12, 18, 21, 25, 31).

MIRACLES ARE A CALL TO FAITH. Involved in the miracles of Jesus is faith, either of the individual, "Do not fear, only believe" (Mk 5:36) or of the community, "And when Jesus saw their faith, he said to the paralytic. . ." (Mk 2:5). It would appear that "faith" in this context is synonymous with "trust," "confidence," not in Jesus as a wonder worker but as the means by which God's healing love reaches out to humankind. It is not yet that full flowering of christological faith which the Easter Christians profess in the Lord as revelation itself. Miracles then presuppose this personal or communitarian "trust" but are even more so a call to a new life centered on the Father through Jesus in the power of the Spirit (which is the meaning of "christocentrism"). They are the challenge of God to see in this extraordinary event his loving action thereby accepting a new vision of reality founded on his loving, healing care. The purpose of the miracle is not to bring out the "ooh's" and the "aah's" of the crowd (Jesus is not a circus magician) but to lead us to the loving Father.

THE WONDER OF THE KINGDOM. If a description of the Kingdom eludes human words, Jesus' miracles supply what "no eye has seen nor ear heard, nor the heart of man conceived, what God has prepared for those who love him" (1 Cor 2:9). The signs of the beauty of the kingdom are expressed in the blind receiving their sight, the deaf hearing the words of God's love, the cripple leaping for joy. The miracles become a faint taste now of the beauty and the power which will be fully revealed when God's rule will penetrate every element of creation. The mute whose voice is restored is to sing the praises of God, the deaf to listen to his word, and the suffering are to radiate his strength and love. These wonders are eloquent although necessarily feeble explanations of the wonders of the Reign of YHWH.

THE INBREAKING OF THE KINGDOM. The miracles of Jesus are not only signs of the coming Kingdom; they are *bringing it about*. In and through Jesus, the Father is transforming this world into his realm. In healing the sick, in driving out demons, Jesus is actually *implementing the kingdom*. The miracles of Jesus are an *effective proclamation* that the Reign of God is here in Jesus: "But if it is by the finger of God that I cast out demons, then the kingdom of God has come upon you" (Lk 11:20). They are, therefore, *effective* signs of the God who cares, who is closer to us than we are to ourselves. The primary emphasis of the miracles of Jesus is NOT apologetic but "establishing God's reign."[26]

JESUS THE FULFILLMENT OF SALVATION HISTORY. Finally, the miracles of Jesus are proclamations that the yearnings of the prophets have come in Jesus. The signs of the Kingdom as given by Isaiah are now seen in Jesus: "Go and tell John what you hear and see: the blind receive their sight and the lame walk, lepers are cleansed and the deaf hear and the dead are raised up and the poor have Good News preached to them. And blessed is he who takes no offense at me" (Mt 11:4–6; cf. Is 35:5–6; 61:1). In the context of salvation history as described in the Old Testament, it is impossible to speak about the end-time, the Kingdom, without miracles.

Gospel miracles are, therefore, neither magical feats nor convincing proof that Jesus is the divine messenger of the Father. In the final analysis, they are the inbreaking of the victorious Reign of YHWH through Jesus and in him.

AN OVERALL ASSESSMENT OF THE GOSPEL MIRACLES

Theological speculation cannot take place in a vacuum and still survive in a world of such intense interdisciplinary activity. Taking into consideration the findings of historians, students of religion, sociologists, literary experts, theology today can with a high degree of probability come to the following conclusions in assessing the miracles of Jesus.

JESUS DEFINITELY PERFORMED MIRACLES. It would be anti-historical to conclude that there are NO miracles of Jesus. As the Tubingen theologian, Walter Kasper, summarizes: "There can scarcely be a single serious exegete who does not believe in a basic stock of historically certain miracles of Jesus."[27] Just as historians accept certain words and expressions as historical, following the criteria mentioned in previous chapters, the same can be said of the miracles. All traditions about Jesus, whether Christian or Jewish, refer to the wonders accomplished by Jesus. The earliest Gospel, Mark, has formed the first part of his proclamation of the Good News almost exclusively around the miracles of Jesus. Precisely which are historical is debated. However, following the general norms for deciphering the precise words and deeds of Jesus, the historical core would include *especially* those which cannot be explained by any reference to Jewish or Greek literature or custom, e.g., the Sabbath healings which have such a non-Jewish ring to them. The exorcisms, the curing of various diseases are also to be included for they are found in multiple and diverse sources and are extraordinary actions which did amaze the people, friend and foe. That there is an historical core of Gospel miracles — without going into detail of time, place, manner — is an accepted scholarly conclusion.

THE GOSPELS EMBELLISH MIRACLE-STORIES. A tendency to intensify and to multiply miracles is evident in the formation of the Gospels. Some of the traditional examples: when Mark (1:34) says that Jesus healed many sick, the parallel passage in Matthew (8:16) says that he heals them all. Matthew — or his sources — using the typical semitic exaggeration to denote importance, often doubles miracles (as he does with the one blind man and the one possessed man of Mark's Gospel). When Mark says that the daughter of Jairus is at the point of death, Matthew says that she is dead (Matthew is probably expressing the semitic mind which would say that "to be at the point of death" is already to be "reckoned among those who go down into the Pit," as we read in psalm 88:3–4).

These embellishments come as no surprise, considering the nature of the literary form Gospel and the development of the oral traditions about Jesus before they were put into writing. The miracle-stories are not immune to these factors. They too are subject to adaptations and embellishments, taking on a rather stereotyped format.

SOME MIRACLES MAY BE POST-EASTER "PARABLES." Jesus' resurrection convinced the Christians that the end-time had come, that the Reign of God was truly here. Characteristic of the kingdom is this new age where death will be no more, where the dead will rise from their graves, where sickness and grief will be healed. In the admirable story-telling culture of Jesus' time, the basic truth of the power of the resurrection was proclaimed not only through the words of Jesus but also through his actions. There are some miracles, therefore, like the "resurrection" of the dead from their tombs at the death of Jesus (Mt 27:52–53)[28] which read like parables to explain this belief, embellishments in order to clarify the meaning of Easter-faith. As noted in previous chapters, the joyful, victorious experience of Easter has left its mark on every page of the Gospels.

It can, therefore, be said with historical certainty that Jesus performed outstanding wonders. It can also be said with equal certainty that the miracles have been embellished and adapted in the light of the Easter faith.

A "SCIENTIFIC" EXPLANATION?

Modern men and women look upon miracles as a medieval curiosity. What were classified as miracles years ago — and even today — are called the result of natural factors. For who knows the power of nature? Even a sudden remission of a malignant tumor can surely be ascribed to the powers — even if as yet hidden — of the human body. What then is the meaning of the statement: It is an historical certainty that Jesus performed miracles? Can miracles be scientifically explained?

When humankind lived in the world of fixed laws of nature (thanks to Roger Bacon et al.) miracles were thought to be acts which were above or against the powers of nature. They were considered, according to the culture of the age, as direct interventions of God which circumvented if not contradicted the laws of nature. Miracles were thought to be the startling exceptions done by God to these laws which he had fixed forever. This understanding of miracle lasted right up to modern times[29] and is still held by some christian fundamentalists.

Within such a scientific framework of determinism and closed causality, miracles were claimed whenever there was no natural explanation possible. However, such a procedure makes no sense today; in fact, following such a principle, there would definitely be NO miracles, since no citizen of this age, especially scientists, would dare say that we know all the laws of nature and especially how they operate in each and every possible situation. How then can it be said that miracles circumvent the laws of nature? "Laws of Nature" do not refer to the inexorable workings of the Great Machine once built by God, wound up and now merrily ticking away. A law of nature is best defined in terms of our own knowledge of an event; it is, in effect, a statement of statistical probability on the likelihood of the occurrence of an event under specifically and carefully stated conditions. There is considerable room for error, since any statement of scientific probability presumes that factors have been identified, labelled and accounted for. Yet how can one know for sure that elements have been labelled and accounted for unless one knows how many there are to begin with? The best that can be said is that we have accounted for all the elements we have *now* found or could *now* think of. The potential of God's majestic creation is beyond our comprehension; solve one mystery and five others are revealed. It is impossible for the most advanced of sciences to list all the factors involved in every single action. As never before, there is a sense of awe and mystery involved in modern science and citizens of a computerized world should be the first to acknowledge, not deny, this point. Science of itself cannot settle the question of miracles, one way or another. On the other hand, this is not to say that science can produce square circles, like a human-angel. Nor can men and women on their own power transform this world into the realm of the Father: God must take the initiative and empower us through his invitation.

A scientific framework, which insists that miracles are "done by God" who substitutes for the inexorable laws of nature, practically turns God into an idol, putting him on the plane of natural causality.[30] A divine intervention, i.e., a directly visible action of God which totally pushes aside created secondary causes is a theological contradiction.[31] Theology insists that the "unity of God and the world and the autonomy of creation are not inversely but directly proportional."[32] Which is to state something quite simple: God — Omnipotent Love — does not destroy but perfects. Holiness does not mean becoming dehumanized; sanctity does not entail becoming transformed into an angel. The intensity of our oneness with the Creator does not destroy freedom; rather it posits our freedom. The more we are in harmony with our God, then the more human we are, in the best sense of the term: the more approachable, the more loving and yearning to be loved, the more sensitive, the more simple, the more *in harmony* with our God, with creation and with ourselves and with one another. That is why christian theology will postulate that there is no one more human than Jesus, the victorious epiphany of the Word of God himself. Miracles do not circumvent God's mysterious creation.

It is the biblical understanding of miracles which helps us to grasp their meaning in today's scientific age. The common Gospel terms for miracles are *dunameis*: acts of power (more common in the synoptics), and *semeia*: signs (favored by John's Gospel). Even the Vulgate New Testament (the translation of the scriptures into Latin by Saint Jerome; the Gospels were completed in 382–383 A.D.) does not contain the word *miraculum* which signifies "the marvelous, something to be wondered at." The Greek term for miracle, wonder, *teras*, is never used alone in the gospels to describe what we call in English, a *miracle* of Jesus.[33]

These acts of power, these signs, indicate observable, extra-ordinary (the word purposely left vague) unexpected events which cause wonder, amazement. The biblical notion of miracle does not consider the laws of nature for that concept was unknown in the ancient world. Through these signs, contemporaries of Jesus penetrate into the mystery of life and sees the omnipotent love of God as ultimate meaning.

In a general sense, we can say that just about everything is a miracle *if* the event is interpreted as the loving presence of God. The smile of a child, the beauty of a

Inexhaustible Presence

sunset, the courage of the ill, all can in a broad sense be called miracles if we see through them to the loving face of God. However, it would be erroneous to omit the term extra-ordinary when speaking of the historical miracles of Jesus; it would be to misinterpret the Gospels to say that miracles are purely subjective, i.e., the sense of forgiveness, of being loved by Love Itself. As important as these insights are, they do not do justice to a critical examination of the Gospel portraits. A miracle is an *observable* event which is truly considered by ordinary people to be *extra-ordinary*, unexpected, prompting people to see the saving hand of God reaching out to them in love. The cure of someone with disfiguring skin disease, the healing of a blind man, the cure of a cripple are miracles, for they are extra-ordinary events and can be recognized as such.

A miracle, although extraordinary is an *ambiguous* event; it is seen as the act of God by faith. There is no happening — not even a return to life ("neither will they be convinced if some one should rise from the dead," Lk 16:31) — which in itself forces a person to cry: "miracle!"

The study of the miracles of Jesus, brings us ultimately to the question of the meaning of reality as expressed in this particular event we call extra-ordinary, miraculous. This is well explained by Kasper: "The question of the mode of reality to which miracles belong turns finally into the question of what the ultimate meaning of reality as a whole is. Is it pure chance, blind fate, a universal regularity which allows no . . . freedom, or an all-determining freedom which we call God? . . . is he . . . the God who in constantly original ways offers his love to human beings in and through the events of the world?"[34]

The pre-Easter Jesus performed extra-ordinary wonders during his ministry. Should it even cause surprise that he decisively called forth these miraculous events? In Jesus, *God is part of this creation*, infinite healing penetrating a distorted world. Accepting the understanding of Jesus as presented in the last section, it would be inexplicable if people open to his call did NOT experience a wholeness in his presence, if the universe were not being affected by Jesus, the human presence of God.

Considering the infinite Love of God working through his creation, culminating in the dynamic presence of the incarnate Word, extraordinary events are part of the history of this cosmos. Nonetheless, they are ambiguous and rather than force faith, are a call to faith. It is only faith which gives the insight to see in these extraordinary deeds the loving hand of the Father working in and through human causality and therefore to claim: "This is a miracle."

Summary

The miracles of Jesus appear to be rejected by modern men and women because of a so-called modern, scientific view of the world. Basically, it is a question of faith or the vision of reality. Do we live in such a tightly-closed system that the scientist knows all the "rules and regulations" of this creation? The scientist would be the first to say such a statement is absurd. Through creation, then, God expresses in novel ways his concern, his love, his power and purpose. At times the event must be declared extra-ordinary. But only through the gift of faith — to which the miracle effectively calls us — can we see the hand of God and praise him for his wondrous deeds. Miracles are not an option which a Christian can "take or leave." They are integral to the portraits and when correctly understood, clarify the power, the love and the mission of Jesus as the inbreaking of the Reign of YHWH.

CHAPTER SEVENTEEN

THE REIGN OF GOD: WHEN DOES IT ARRIVE?

One of the most difficult problems concerning the Reign of God is the apparent tension between present and future. Often Jesus speaks of the kingdom as present; at other times, it is in the future. Some have opted for what is called *realized* eschatology declaring that in Jesus the Reign of God has arrived; it is NOW.[35] Others support what is termed *consistent* eschatology which sees the Reign as a FUTURE event.[36] Still others uphold what may be called "eschatology being realized," declaring that the hour of fulfillment has arrived in Jesus but the consummation is not yet complete.[37]

A clear-cut distinction — either Jesus preached realized OR consistent eschatology — does not tally with the Gospel portraits. This present/future tension must be accepted as an historical element in Jesus' preaching, no matter the serious difficulties it entails. An examination of the parables of the kingdom, of the miracles, of Jesus' sermons, all contain this double polarity: the Reign is NOW, the Reign is FUTURE.

The question of the "time" of the Reign also brings up the thorny question of whether or not Jesus himself thought that the end of the world — with the full flowering of the Reign of God — would be imminent. If he did so, and yet the end did not arrive in his lifetime, does this error have any repercussions on who he is?

We will therefore divide this chapter into three main headings:

— Jesus preaches the Reign as a *present* reality.
— Jesus preaches the Reign as a *future* reality.
— Did Jesus Believe the End to be imminent?

JESUS PREACHES THE KINGDOM AS A PRESENT REALITY

Jesus himself led his hearers to believe that the Reign of God was present in and through him and yet that the Reign of God was still to come. This strange manner of speaking about the kingdom is interwoven throughout the portraits giving every reason to hold that this NOW/FUTURE was an integral element of his Reign preaching. Texts supporting the Reign NOW:

— Mk 1:15: "the time is fulfilled and the kingdom of God is at hand."

— Lk 4:18–21: When Jesus visits his hometown of Nazareth, Luke describes a scene which again portrays the kingdom as a present reality: "The Spirit of the Lord is upon me because he has anointed me to preach good news to the poor. He has sent me to proclaim release to the captives and recovering of sight to the blind, to set at liberty those who are oppressed, to proclaim the acceptable year of the Lord." The astounding part of this reference to Isaiah's description of the signs of the kingdom (cf. Is 61:1–2), is Jesus' comment: "Today, this scripture has been fulfilled in your hearing." There is no apocalyptic hope expressed here, no looking into the future for the liberation by YHWH. It is a happening. NOW.

— Lk 10:23–24 (Mt 13:16–17): "Blessed are the eyes which see what you see! For I tell you that many prophets and kings desired to see what you see and did not see it and to hear what you hear and did not hear it." Both Matthew and Luke associate this saying with the Reign of God; the hopes of all past generations have now been fulfilled. The Reign is here. NOW.

— Mt 11:4–5: When John's disciples ask Jesus if he is "the coming one," Jesus responds with Is 32:5–6; 61:1 which speak of the coming time of God's healing: "Go and tell John what you hear and see; the blind receive their sight and the lame walk, lepers are cleansed and the deaf hear and the dead are raised up and the poor have good news preached to them." The fulfillment is taking place. NOW.

— Mt 12:28 (cf. Lk 11:20): "But if it is by the Spirit of God that I cast out demons, then the kingdom of God has come upon you." Jesus, filled with the Spirit — a sign of the end-times — firmly declares in this episode that the Reign is NOW.

The Meaning of The Kingdom NOW

What is surprising in the Gospel portraits is that Jesus claims that the Reign is breaking into ongoing creation in him and through him. This is unheard of in Judaism; he is not just the eschatological prophet who precedes the Reign, he is the inbreaking of the Reign itself.[38] In his proclamations, in his healings, in his sharing life with the outcast, Jesus makes it known that the kingdom of God is here. Jesus is no apocalyptic even though he may at times use apocalyptic stage-props. The Reign of God is not only operative now but is also fulfilled now — no apocalyptist could accept such a stance. For them the kingdom is future and no explicit consideration is given to the fact that God NOW reigns. Fulfillment of the Reign in a simple, vagabond preacher from despised Galilee is not only abhorrent but, so they would probably claim, impossible.

At face value, these texts seem to involve a contradiction. Jesus is teaching that in his proclamation of the end-time Reign of YHWH, the end-time has begun. Although allowance must be made for adaptations of these texts on the part of the christian communities after the resurrection, nonetheless, for the reasons mentioned above, they still retain the inherent problem: in Jesus, the FUTURE is NOW. The hearers are baffled, and rightly so. Some, like the leaders of the ruling factions in Israel, could sit back and scoff. For the entire scene is ludicrous: an *unlettered* man from the hills of unknown Nazareth is preaching that God's eschatological promises are now fulfilled in his words and deeds.

It is difficult for us, two millennia later, to capture the apparent absurdity of the situation. Yet if Jesus is the Son of God, then in sharing life with him in meal, response, faith, the life of the Father is effectively encountered. Faith is a sharing-with; since Jesus' existence is the Father's intimacy, following Jesus is to share in the life — or to put in another way — in the *reign* of the Father. This is the astounding claim of Jesus. No wonder that Jesus could say: "And blessed is he who takes no offense at me" (Mt 11:6).

JESUS PREACHES THE REIGN AS A FUTURE REALITY

Running together with the proclamation that the kingdom is NOW, is the clear affirmation that the Reign is FUTURE. (Those sections of the portraits which speak of the kingdom as NOW are interpreted by the consistent eschatologists [the futurists] as referring to the imminence of the coming, not to its present realization.) Again, against the general background of the Gospel portraits a few texts can be cited manifesting this mind of the Lord that the Reign is future and then some attempt made to explain what Jesus means by apparently joining the NOW and the FUTURE together.

Texts Supporting the Reign as FUTURE

— Mk 10:30: Jesus in responding to Peter's statement that the disciples have left all to follow him, speaks of their rewards, culminating in the phrase "and in the age to come, eternal life." Eternal life is a reality of the Reign. Jesus states that it is FUTURE.

— Mt 6:10: In the one prayer Jesus taught his disciples, we are to beg the Father, "Thy kingdom come." Evidently the kingdom is FUTURE.

— Mk 9:47: "It is better for you to enter the kingdom of God with one eye than with two eyes to be thrown into hell." The judgment, intrinsic to the notion of the inbreaking of the kingdom, is FUTURE.

These texts reveal another dimension of the Reign: it is coming, it is future; which apparently means it is not NOW. Yet Jesus also stresses the NOW of the Reign of God.

Meaning of the FUTURE-NOW

Considering the portraits as a whole, it appears representative of Jesus' thought concerning the Reign of YHWH to say that it is NOW, it is FUTURE. It is not an either/or; it is BOTH. The fact that such apparently contradictory elements are found repeatedly makes us believe that this is truly the manner in which Jesus "preached the good news of the kingdom of God" (Lk 4:43; Mt 4:23).

Is there any way to decipher what Jesus meant by these statements? Or does it display the confusion which Jesus himself may have experienced concerning the meaning and the coming of the Reign? If it be a personal mixup on the part of Jesus it has far reaching effects, since the proclamation of the Reign is the central issue for Jesus. It would be legitimate to conclude that if Jesus shows such bafflement and confusion on this fundamental point, then this must have repercussions on his own self-understanding. Yet he speaks with authority, he acts decisively. There does not appear in the portraits any confusion or basic identity crisis of Jesus. To be consistent with the portraits as a whole, there must be some other solution than merely brushing the problem aside as a sign of Jesus' utter confusion concerning his identity. Such a solution offends the entire tenor of the Gospels. Yet what response can be given to the apparent contradiction of Jesus' preaching of the Reign NOW, the Reign FUTURE?

The problem is a difficult one especially for our scientific culture. Considering the semitic notion of time, it was probably not such a hurdle for Jesus' contemporaries and taking into account this Jewish mindset, shows no confusion on the part of Jesus. Even in the eschatological thought of the age (not precisely the apocalyptic strand) the kingdom of God is both a present and a future reality: God reigns NOW, and the universal fulfillment of his actual reigning will be in the FUTURE. This is not an invention of Jesus; it represents the thought pattern of his times. Jesus accepts this double polarity but then with calm conviction radically gives it new meaning: the present and the future are bound together IN HIM (there is the problem for Jesus' hearers!) as the *kairos* of the Father. The universal fulfillment is but the flowering of what is actually happening NOW in and through Jesus. This is the radically "new" of Jesus' proclamation: the eschatological kingdom of God is breaking into present history in and through a human being (and from Nazareth, no less). It is not precisely a question of realized, or consistent or "becoming" eschatology. Rather, speaking of the present *is speaking of the future*; speaking of the future *is speaking of the present*, for we are speaking of the one climactic *kairos* of the Father, the fulfillment of all history which occurs definitively in Jesus. Chronological future and present fuse together in the one definitive *kairos* of God, Jesus the Lord. The problem for Jesus' audience therefore is not reconciling the Reign as a NOW and as a FUTURE but how to understand that in Jesus the Reign is appearing.

Did Jesus Believe in an Imminent End of the World?[39]

Through the hindsight of the resurrection, the christian community could come to an acceptance of Jesus' proclamation of the Reign of YHWH as a NOW and as a FUTURE, in him and through him. However, the problem which persisted through the New Testament period was the question of the imminence of the universal Reign. For if the Risen Jesus is the coming of the kingdom in power, the end of this age and the beginning of the next, then the end of the world must be imminent so the christians seem to conclude. The resurrection — the great sign of the end-time — is not the destiny of one man alone, believe the Jewish people, but the restoration (no matter how it may be imagined) of the community, at least of the just. Matthew, in order to proclaim this truth embellishes the account of the first Good Friday: "The tombs also were opened, and many bodies of the saints who had fallen asleep were raised and coming out of the tombs after his resurrection they went into the holy city and appeared to many" (27:52–53). The purpose of the interpretation is clear: in Jesus the end of the world has broken into on-going history. The conclusion the christians apparently reached is: the end of the world is soon and we shall all share in the glory of the Lord.

And did not Jesus speak of an imminent coming? The issue is intensified by the fact that some aspects of the portraits clearly speak of the imminence of the kingdom, i.e., it is a near-future:

"But I tell you truly, there are some standing here who will not taste death before they see the kingdom of God" (Lk 9:27; cf. Mt 10:23).

"Truly I say to you, there are some standing here who will not taste death before they see the kingdom of God come with power" (Mk 9:1). Was he wrong in his expectations of an immediate flowering of the kingdom?

To complicate matters, the portraits also reveal a Jesus who apodictically declares that he does not know when this age will come, whether it be imminent or in the distant future; all he knows is that when it does come, it will come suddenly (cf. MK 13; Mt 24:36–44).[40] Evidently these sayings of Jesus concerning the imminence of the kingdom are not immune to the general rule of adaptation and embellishment. Is there any way to disentangle these diverse strands of tradition so that the thought of Jesus on this issue could be more clearly perceived? Attempts are made but considering the nature of the Gospels, the conclusions from scripture itself are at best probable. Basically, two solutions may be proposed:

Jesus Erred Concerning the Imminence of the Reign

To uphold that Jesus actually *taught error* concerning the central issue of his life — the kingdom of God — does not appear to cohere with the general outline of the

Gospel portraits or with theological speculation. However, to uphold *ignorance* of the time of the *Day of the Lord* appears to be consonant with scripture and theological interpretation of the word of God.[41] Is there any solution to the portrait's disclosure of Jesus as proclaiming an imminent reign which never came — and still has not arrived?

Several can be offered:

— The sayings of the Lord concerning the imminence of the parousia have been greatly adapted by the evangelists in light of the resurrection and the need of their audiences (often difficult if not impossible to reconstruct). A possible kernel of the teaching of Jesus in these texts would be the need for faith to bring about the kingdom in power.

God, the victorious King, offers Himself in love in and through Jesus; the offer is firm, forever. However, the Reign of God has another essential element: individuals are free and a choice must implement this offer. A gift becomes fully operative as gift only when it is accepted. Jesus appears to be stressing the need for accepting him in order to enter the kingdom, in order that the kingdom may come with power into one's life. God does not force his people endowed with free-will; rather, he enters into dialogue with those he has created to his own image and likeness. Accepting Jesus is to share in the realm. In this opinion, the proclamation of the imminence of the kingdom is — if we try to arrive at the teaching of Jesus and exclude the embellishments of the evangelists — a stress on the fact that his coming will be as soon as it is accepted in faith.

— On God's side, the reign comes in power through the damnation of the Cross with its subsequent glorification, the resurrection. If the saying of the imminence of the kingdom is from the lips of Jesus then it is possible that Jesus had by this time integrated his death and subsequent acceptance by the Father into the proclamation of the the reign of YHWH. It is then that the reign comes with power. In this sense, it is imminent.

— Similar to the above is the opinion that the passages which deal with the imminence of the reign of God would mean that some of those now living will see the power of the kingdom in Jesus' return to the Father through death and resurrection. Considered as a post-Easter embellishment, it may mean that some of those with Jesus during his preaching in lowliness also have the joy of being with him in the power of his Easter appearances.

— The statements are either of the Lord or a redaction of the evangelists which have as their principal source a reference to the scene of the Transfiguration when Jesus appears in glory.[42]

Summary

In trying to decipher the meaning of those texts which speak of the imminence of the Reign, it should be noted that it is more likely that the expectations of a soon-to-come parousia stem from the early christians' belief in the resurrection of the Lord than from Jesus himself. It is apparent that even the early church did not know exactly what to do with these awkward fragments of tradition concerning Jesus' parousia. Irrelevant chronological calculations do not appear to cohere with the portraits of Jesus and are in fact contradicted by certain texts where Jesus professes ignorance of the time of the coming of the Reign (cf. Mk 13:32; Acts 1:7). To declare, therefore, that Jesus taught the chronological imminence of the parousia is to be on tenuous grounds indeed.

Two points appear to have their source in Jesus: present and future are intertwined into the one *kairos*, and the power of the kingdom comes even now to those who surrender in faith. The question of the TIME of the full flowering of the kingdom does not appear to be part of Jesus' preaching on the Reign of God (cf. Acts 1:7). This is not to say that the pre-resurrection Jesus actually knew the precise time of the full-flowering of the Reign; he shares in our lack of knowledge of future times and dates (cf. Mk 13:32). This is not an error: it is the human condition in which Jesus truly shares.

However, in light of the Lord's resurrection the time of the kingdom does become a problem for early christians and so the delay of the parousia has left its mark on the New Testament, even in the chronologically last booklet, Second Peter (cf. 3:8–13).

CHAPTER EIGHTEEN

THE REIGN OF GOD:
THE INHERITORS OF THE KINGDOM

Who are those who will inherit the Reign of God?[43] This theme forms a predominant aspect of Jesus' kingdom preaching, of his kingdom miracles and of his kingdom parables. He appears to be insistent that this message be correctly understood: "Blessed are the poor in spirit, for theirs is the kingdom of heaven" (Mt 5:3). Yet there is also more than a penchant for proclaiming the reign to his own people, the Jews; he is sent to them, and to them only, firmly declares the Matthean Jesus (cf. Mt 15:24; 10:6). To whom, then belongs the Reign of YHWH? Who are those who share in the fulfillment of human hope by sharing in the the new age, the life of God? The response to the question not only has practical importance concerning the role of Jesus but also clarifies the meaning of the central theme of the historical Jesus, the Reign of God.

Three questions, then, have to be answered as best as possible in this chapter:

— The proclamation of the Kingdom to the Jews alone.
— The proclamation of the Kingdom to the poor.
— The theological implications of the evangelization of the poor.

THE PROCLAMATION OF THE KINGDOM TO THE JEWS ALONE

Jesus understood his proclamation of the Kingdom to be limited to the House of Israel, the Jews: "I was sent only to the lost sheep of the house of Israel" (Mt 15:24). Only rarely would he leave Jewish territory, and in fact, gives a mandate to his disciples: "Go nowhere among the Gentiles, and enter no town of the Samaritans, but go rather to the lost sheep of the house of Israel" (Mt 10:5–6). No matter what Jesus' precise words may have been on this point, there is little dispute that this is at least the conclusion the early Christians drew from his words and deeds.[44] Many Christians find this shocking. It appears so incredible that this aspect of Jesus is either ignored or through some weird exegesis the Lord is pitilessly wrenched from his own people and baptized into the Christian faith. "Well, at least he converted!" was the reply of one Christian when told that Jesus was an observant Jew. G. Beasley-Murray writes: "When I commenced theological studies it was difficult to name a leading New Testament scholar in England who believed that Jesus could have uttered Matthew 10:5–6 and 23 . . . I concluded that the British had forgotten that Jesus was a Jew . . . they had not contemplated what it meant to Jesus that he was a Jew, sent to proclaim to his own people the dawn of the fulfillment of the promise. . ."[45] This transformation of the historical Jesus into a Christian is even evident in John's Gospel, when the evangelist repeatedly speaks of Jesus responding to "the Jews," implying that he was not one of them.[46]

It is always from within his cherished Jewish faith that Jesus speaks and acts. And as a firm believer in his people as the "chosen race," the proclamation of the Reign of God is made to them. Not only is this the thought of Matthew, but Mark writes of Jesus speaking offensively — at least to modern western ears — to a Gentile woman who asks his assistance. "Let the children first be fed," Jesus tells her, speaking of the Jewish people, "for it is not right to take the children's bread and throw it to the dogs," meaning the non-Jews (Mk 7:27). So harsh do these words appear that some have even tried to translate "dogs" by "puppies" or "doggies."[47] Yet "dogs" was a rather common term used by the Jews of Jesus' time for the Gentiles. Jesus is a Jew and his thought patterns are Jewish; it should not be surprising that he speaks and acts like a Jew at that period of history. The more the portraits are examined, the clearer it becomes not only that Jesus is immersed in his own culture and religion but also that he shows favoritism to his own. His own people are those whom he calls to share in the reign of his ABBA.

This posed problems even for the Gospel authors. The evangelists writing at a time when the Gentile mission had already produced astounding results, interpret any clues of Jesus' kindness to non-Jews as an indication that his proclamation of the reign of YHWH is universal in scope. For example, he does respond favorably to the Gentile woman to whom he spoke in an apparently harsh manner (cf. Mk 7:28–29); he does cure the Roman centurion's servant and even praises his faith (cf. Mt 8:5–13; cf. also Mk 5:19). The evangelists do not hesitate to openly proclaim Jesus' universal mission (cf. Mt 28:19; 21:43; Mk 13:10; Lk 24:47).

Are the evangelists wrong in attributing a universal mission to Jesus? Are they in error when they speak of non-Jews being invited into the Kingdom of God? By no means. For if Jesus is truly an observant Jew, the universalism of the prophets is part of his heritage: "I am coming to gather all nations and tongues: and they shall come and shall see my glory . . . they shall declare my glory among the nations . . . and some of them I will take for priests and Levites, says the Lord" (Is 66:18–21). All this is to happen "on that day," the day of the inbreaking of the reign of YHWH, when "the mountain of the house of the Lord shall be established as the highest of the mountains and shall be raised above the hills and all the nations shall flow to it and many peoples shall come and say: 'Come, let us go up to the mountain of the Lord . . . He shall judge between the nations and shall decide for many peoples; and they shall beat their swords into plowshares and their spears into pruning hooks; nation shall not lift up sword against nation, neither shall they learn war any more' " (Is 2:2–4; cf. Is 60, 66:19 ff; Mic 4:1 ff; Zech 8:20 ff, etc.)

Through the people of God, the Jews, all will come to the Kingdom for as we read in John: "salvation is from the Jews" (4:22).

In proclaiming the kingdom to his people, Jesus is proclaiming the Reign of God to all for his purpose is not to destroy Judaism but to perfect it; not to contradict his Father's plan for Israel as the instrument for universal salvation but to bring it to fulfillment and thereby implement the world vision of the prophets. Rejected by his own, he trusts in God who will surely carry out this promise, even, as Jesus surely understands from the turn of events, through his death and ultimate vindication.

However, Jesus' appeal is not to the nation of Israel as such. Unlike a rabbi, Jesus chooses his disciples, demands from them a deep personal relationship which does not end; no one ever graduates or becomes a rabbi in his own right after a few years with Jesus. It is only through a living relationship with Jesus — demanding a total change of heart — that Israel will achieve its destiny. The kingdom is from the Jews, through the Jews; the kingdom is from Jesus, through Jesus for he personifies Israel. The new people of God are those who belong to Israel as the Reign of God, i.e., those who through faith, belong to Jesus. Paul therefore calls the Christian community, "the Israel of God" (Gal 6:16; cf. Phil 3:3; Rom 9:6) in contrast to "Israel according to the flesh" (1 Cor 10:18). The mystery of Israel as the chosen people and yet as a nation rejecting Jesus has posed a problem for theologians down through the ages, even from apostolic times (cf. Paul's grappling with the question in Romans 9–11).

THE PROCLAMATION OF THE KINGDOM TO THE POOR

This personal commitment (faith) demanded by Jesus for participation in the kingdom is equivalent to saying that the kingdom is for the poor. For faith is the living-out of the reality of our utter poverty. Poverty does not have wealth as its opposite in this context; rather its opposing concept is pride, haughtiness, self-righteousness. And Jesus makes it quite evident that he has not come for the righteous, for the haughty, but for those who are open to the good news of the kingdom because of their childlike simplicity: their poverty. "Truly, I say to you, unless you turn and become like children, you will never enter the kingdom of heaven. Whoever humbles himself like this child, he is the greatest in the kingdom of heaven" (Mt 18:3–4).

The Gospels stress this point by depicting Jesus as "proclaiming the Gospel" to the "poor" (cf. Mt 9:35; 11:5). The ABBA's Reign is for those who "labor and are heavy-laden" (Mt 11:28), for "tax-collectors and sinners" (Mt 11:19), for the sick, the lame, the deaf, the blind. All of these people suffer in this life because they are considered sinners outside the law; they are also led to believe that the reign of God is closed to them. They are people who no longer have the strength even to hope. These are the friends of Jesus; it is to these "sinners" that he proclaims the forgiveness of the kingdom. It is with these outcasts that he shares his life — the life of his ABBA — by eating and lodging with them (cf. Mk 2:15; Lk 15:2; 19:1–10) thereby entering into covenant with them. It is "the poor (who) have the good news preached to them" (Mt 11:6). The contribution of a balanced *Liberation Christology* is to make all aware of Jesus' *practical* concern for the poor, for those on the periphery of society, for the disenfranchised, for those who daily experience prejudice, for the oppressed. These are his friends. It is especially to these that he shares his liberating, healing presence. No wonder that "Liberation Theology's consuming passion (is) the reign of God."[48]

Jesus' stance is in sharp contrast to many of the leaders of Israel in his day, and in blatant contradiction to the thought of the Essene community at Qumran which declared that the time of fulfillment will be characterized by an exclusion of the sinners, of the sick: "No one who is afflicted with any human impurity may come into the assembly of God . . . anyone who is afflicted in his flesh, maimed in hand or foot, lame or blind or deaf or mute or with a visible mark on his flesh or who is a helpless old man who cannot stand upright in the assembly of the community, these may not enter to take their place in the midst of the community of the men of THE NAME, for the holy angels are in their community."[49] The Essenes wanted to form a holy remnant; Jesus opens his heart to all, especially those rejected. Small wonder that the people would sing a ditty as Jesus walked the street: "Behold a glutton and a drunkard, a friend of tax collectors and sinners" (Mt 11:19).

So insistent is Jesus that the Kingdom is only for the poor that he proclaims in the first beatitude which summarizes them all: "Blessed are you poor, for yours is the kingdom of God" (Lk 6:20; Mt 5:3). So insistent is Jesus on this point that he declares: "I came not to call the righteous but sinners" (Mk 2:17). His boldness seems to reach its climax in his response to the haughty of his time: "Truly I say to you, the tax collectors and the harlots go into the kingdom of God before you" (Mt 21:31). Jesus is not talking about an ecclesiastical procession led by tax collectors and harlots; rather his words can be taken in an exclusive sense: tax collectors and harlots will enter the kingdom, but NOT YOU. Yet he was talking to those who so strictly observed each of the 613 laws of the Torah and also the hundreds of other rules which formed a "hedge" so that the Torah itself would never be offended.

According to Jesus, those who are divorced from God are the righteous, the pious; not because they commit any of the nasty sins they find in "the people of the land" but they are condemned by their own self-righteous "piety." Jeremias points out that Jesus' words of judgment are almost always directed not against adulterers, liars, cheaters, but against those who condemned such people in this life and proudly excluded them from "the life to come."[50]

THEOLOGICAL IMPLICATIONS OF JESUS' CALL TO THE POOR

For these pious people, wealthy in their own self-righteousness, Jesus becomes a stumbling-block, an offense. The kingdom, however, is not earned. It is a gift, it is inherited (Mt 25:34; Lk 12:32). Only those who are childlike enough to see God as the loving ABBA, who do not believe that they deserve God's life because of their own work at it, can share in the reign of God. Not that Jesus is demanding a do-nothing attitude. He calls for an active faith with the radical demands of a change of heart. It is only through this dynamic lived-out faith with its prerequisite of a total self-emptying of all idols that the kingdom is inherited. His constant call empowers all to so respond.

Understandably, in the eyes of those who looked down on the "rabble," who thought it their highest duty to avoid all "sinners," who believed that they were earning entrance into that new age by their own hard work — these people considered Jesus as dangerous for it appeared that he was destroying all ethics, all morality. In a sense, they were correct for Jesus is proclaiming that the Kingdom of God is for those who turn worldly values upside-down.

There is no doubt that Jesus' words and deeds loudly proclaim that the kingdom is only for these poor. In modern jargon, we would speak about an existential poverty, a lived-out conviction that of ourselves we can do nothing, that we are being dynamically gifted by the Ground of All Being with existence itself, that we are the Lord's. Poverty is ultimately *WHO* we are, not *WHAT* we have. Material wealth can make it *exceedingly* difficult to recognize our existential poverty (cf. Mk 10:23) but in itself it is not condemned by the Lord. Haughtiness is.

Only when we accept this existential reality and shed the unreal self which asserts its own power and goodness, can we share in the reign. For only then are we speaking of faith. And faith is entrance into the kingdom. Faith denotes this total acceptance of the reality of our nothingness so that we may share in the omnipotence of God.[51] The need for faith with its concomitant radical *metanoia* is another way of saying that only the poor share in the kingdom. The gift of faith empowers the believer to freely and responsibly — and in this sense, meritoriously — live the radical demands of the Gospel in spite of the pervading thought-patterns of the day. An arduous task. As has often been stated, faith may be free but it is not cheap.

Summary

The inheritors of the kingdom: Jesus calls his own people and through them all nations. But citizenship in the kingdom is only through a total surrender to his call, even for his Mother, the first disciple.[52] This message of Jesus — so bold, so strong, so opposed by the haughty of his world — has profound effects on those who today would call themselves Christians. It gives a deeper insight into the meaning of faith which is needed to accept the gift of the kingdom and thereby render it a dynamic reality in one's life. It demands that the Christian reach out with the love of Christ to the poor, the lonely, the sinner, the despised of this world. Measured by the standards of the world, it is the Christian who is counter-culture.

CHAPTER NINETEEN

THE REIGN OF GOD:
THE PARABLES OF THE REIGN

Through his deeds, Jesus brings about the Reign of his Father. His miracles, his "scandalous" table-fellowship with sinners and outcasts, his zeal in proclaiming this Good News, his perseverance in this evangelization even through death upon the cross are means of transforming this world into the life of God. However, through his performative words, Jesus also proclaims — brings about — the reign. His sermons, pithy statements, his riddles all form an essential element of the inbreaking of the kingdom. But his favored instrument of proclaiming the Good News is neither through "academic" classes nor through imparting an accumulation of facts and figures. He proclaims the Reign of YHWH through *story-telling*. A special type of story, so foreign to the western scientific mind: parables.[53] The parables become a favored instrument of Jesus in effectively proclaiming — not just talking about — the Reign of God.

Our scientific age is not adept at story-telling, especially in the manner of parables. In order to appreciate this simple yet powerful tool of Jesus in proclaiming the Reign, this chapter will scan the following points:

— The meaning of PARABLE.
— The teachings of the PARABLES.
— The PARABLES as Concealment of the Reign of God.

THE MEANING OF PARABLE

Parables are defined by the dictionary as "a short story designed to convey a truth or moral lesson." Simple enough. Yet western culture is not comfortable with parables. Story-telling is considered for children; clear, scientific computer-readouts are the sign of intellectual maturity. A sad situation. For through the *story* we are challenged on an existential level, we are called to make a decision, we are forced to make a choice even if it be only to ignore its call. The means Jesus took to explain the reign was through story-telling, through parables. "We are standing right before Jesus when reading his parables."[54]

The term parable is derived from the Greek *parabole*, i.e., placing things next to each other in order to compare them. In the Greek world it becomes a technical oratorical expression meaning a "figure of speech." However a parable is a special type of "figure of speech." More precisely it is an extended *simile* (one thing is LIKE another) made up of an artificial story based upon true to life events and characters. When each point of the story is clearly identified we no longer are speaking of a parable strictly so called: it has been transformed into an extended *metaphor* (one thing is IDENTIFIED with another) called an *allegory*. At times allegorical elements may be intertwined with what is basically a parable.

A form of parable can be found in the Old Testament, e.g., the story of the ewe-lamb narrated by the prophet Nathan to David (2 Sam 12:1–4), Isaiah's story of the vineyard (5:1–7; cf. other parable-like stories in the O.T.: 2 Sam 14:1–11; Ez 17:3–10; 19:10–14). Rabbinic literature — after the time of Jesus — is said to contain about two thousand parables,[55] ordinarily given as a response to a question of a student. Their purpose was pedagogical: to illuminate, to instruct. For Jesus, the principal aim was *to proclaim*, to bring about the reign of YHWH.

As narrated by this itinerant preacher, parables clearly have a two-level construction: first, the story itself taken from real life situations; secondly, the *unexplained* comparison of this real life situation to the point to be clarified, e.g., the reign of God. This can be illustrated by the simple parable found in Mk 4:30–32: "With what can we compare the reign of God or what parable shall we use for it? It is like a grain of mustard seed which, when sown upon the ground is the smallest of all the seeds on earth; yet when it is sown it grows up and becomes the greatest of all shrubs and puts forth large branches so that the birds of the air can make nests in its shade." The "real life story" is the growth of the mustard seed ("it is LIKE" refers to the entire situation, not just to the word which follows "like") and the unexplained, undeveloped point to be clarified by this story is the reign of God.

A story can be explained, i.e., allegorized in multiple ways. As a general rule it can be said that Jesus does not allegorize, he does not identify the details of the story. Yet the Church often does as it applies the parable to the *sitz im leben* (i.e., the specific life context) of its hearers. This is evident in the parable of the sower (Mk 2:3–8) which is allegorized by the christian community, applying the story to its specific context (Mk 2:14–20). A parable is a challenging question; the hearer must supply the answer.

THE TEACHINGS OF THE PARABLES

By not allegorizing the parable, Jesus heightens its power, for each individual can apply the story to his or her own situation; it challenges each individual where the person is. Moreover, the parables of Jesus are for the most part, made up of a topsy-turvy story: a shepherd who leaves ninety-nine sheep to go in search of one which is lost; a woman who throws a celebration because she has found a lost coin; a father who welcomes home a prodigal son while ignoring another son who stayed at home with him; laborers who worked from one hour to all day, yet everyone paid the same wage; a Samaritan (whom the Jews grouped among the sinners) who is "Good";[56] invited guests who do not show up for a wedding and are replaced by anyone off the street; a neighbor who keeps banging at the door even when told to go home since everyone is in bed, etc. There is a jolting, shock-effect intended by Jesus in these stories. "Life-like," yes — in the sense that the "material" of the story is taken from well-known things or events; but also "unreal," "agitating" in many respects. Again, the parable is a challenging question, making the listener discover the response in his/her own life situation.

The allegorizing of the parable gives an answer; it appears that Jesus ordinarily posed only a puzzling question to shake up his hearers, to let them experience the radical newness of the reign of God. His parables, then are not only a teaching tool; *they are an integral part of Jesus' proclamation of the reign.* Just as the story is often impossible (a *Good* Samaritan) so the hearers are experiencing the overturning of their value-system, their judgments, which is a necessary requirement to accept the reign of God. In these topsy-turvy stories, the inbreaking of the reign of Yahweh is being shared with the hearer as empowering call. Only those who accept this *new age*, this *kairos* of the Father with its new vision of reality in Jesus, truly inherit the kingdom of heaven.

The explicit *Kingdom Parables* are found principally in Matthew: six in chapter thirteen, and one each in chapters 18, 20, 22, 25. Luke and Mark have two (cf. Mk 4 and Lk 13). The theme of the reign is implicit in many of the approximately forty parables found in the synoptics. The parables disclose much about the Kingdom: its newness, its radical demands for repentance and faith, its character as unmerited gift (so difficult for the religious leaders of Jesus' time to grasp), its presence in Jesus, its coming into our hearts through the simple events of life, its challenge to surrender to this inbreaking of God's Love. Yet to explain what the parables say is to allegorize them! The parables are not to be *read*. Rather, we are to *dialogue* with them as challenging questions within the context of our own situation. The true allegorizing can only be done by each person as the topsy-turvy story is applied to the specifics of one's own life. And then respond.

THE PARABLES AS CONCEALMENT OF THE REIGN

The parables of Jesus may be considered both a disclosure and a concealment of the reign. As a call to the new life of the reign with its value system so opposed to the value system of the world, and even shocking to the *earn-your-own-way* religious mentality of the times, it is a disclosure of the reign; but it demands such a "turnabout" (*metanoia*), such a new life that it is incomprehensible to those who refuse the call. It is only by responding to this new life, which turns worldly values on their head, that the parables are understood.

Jesus does not purposefully conceal in order to make sure that his hearers will not understand. Some do uphold this opinion basing themselves on Mk 4:11–12 (cf. Mt 10:13–15; Lk 8:9–10): "for those outside everything is in parables; so that they may indeed see but not perceive and may indeed hear but not understand, lest they should turn again and be forgiven." This text is a paraphrase of Is 6:9–10 and points up the theological question of the rejection of Jesus by his own people. ". . . human beings will be charmed by the simplicity of the parable-preaching of Jesus and yet fail to understand what it should mean to them."[57] As applied to Jesus' use of parables, it appears more consonant with the portraits of Jesus and also with the semitic mind which made no grammatical distinction between PURPOSE and the RESULT foreseen by God, to declare that Mark is speaking about the RESULT, not the PURPOSE of Jesus' preaching in parables. Mark himself states: "In many such parables he spoke the word to them according as they were able to understand it" (4:33). If the parables blinded people's eyes and hardened their hearts, it is primarily because they did not accept the challenge inherent in the parables, not that the parables were intellectually beyond their grasp. "He who has ears to hear, let him hear" (Mk 4:9).

Summary

As simple as the stories of Jesus may appear they represent a middle-east mindset and are not easily grasped by a culture which gives high grades for clarity. At times Jesus did have to explain some of them because he was describing a reign so unlike the one to be inaugurated by a *davidic* messiah. Even the early Christians gradually explained them more and more and therefore much of the jolting effect has now been lost. Extreme care is needed in trying to interpret these challenging stories where the conclusion is *ours* to decipher and apply to *our own situation*. Seen in their true light, they become conquering instruments of the reign, for they crack humankind's set ways of viewing God, self, neighbor. The parables are indicators that the reign comes through the simple and ordinary events of life: the baking of bread, the sowing of a field, a difficult job situation, etc. However the genius of the parable is in using something so ordinary to produce a questioning shock effect which makes us hang for a moment: it tears away at our view of reality and forces us to respond. The parables exemplify primarily the mysterious aspect of the reign: they constantly challenge us and we never appear to be able to grasp the full meaning. To brush aside a parable as the dictionary does and just call it a "short story" is to totally misinterpret its unique character. Especially as used by Jesus, a recognized master in story-telling, parables become challenging calls to enter the inexhaustible mystery of the reign of God.

SECTION FIVE

THE DISCLOSURE OF JESUS: THE RESURRECTION

"If we look at this life of ours, it is of itself not of such a nature that one would like to go on forever here; of itself it strives towards a conclusion to its present mode of existence. Time becomes madness if it cannot reach fulfillment. To be able to go on forever would be the hell of empty meaninglessness."[1]

To be doomed to this existence forever is not the will of God nor is it truly the deepest yearning of the human heart. Without any definite future, without any goal, with endless tomorrows: it would be eventually a living hell. Even those indescribable glimpses of perfection in fleeting moments of deepest love and peace, heighten the yearning for a new age, an eternity of fulfillment. Yet such a goal is not within the power of finite human beings. In spite of some utopian claims, no advances in science can ever transform this universe into that perfect harmony for which the heart was made. Often modern progress heightens our frustration, like the planet shattering bombs, the impersonalism of modern medicine, the sophisticated, faceless machines which so coldly drag on the agony of dying in the antiseptic loneliness of a hospital unit. Caught up in the anger and fear of the contemporary situation, many turn to quiet resignation, if not despair. Yet there is another way which cannot be suppressed: HOPE.

Only those whose hearts still hope in spite of the tears — only *those* are open to the good news: "He is Risen, He is not here, behold the place where they laid him." It is often said that only those who love can understand resurrection and eternal life; with equal truth it must be stated that the question of resurrection can only have relevance to those who have drunk deeply of finitude, of limitedness, of death, of one's personal weakness and of the sin of the world. It is in this context of an existential yearning for the eternal fulness of peace and love that we must situate our study of the resurrection.[2]

The resurrection of Jesus is not only central for him; it is central for us. It is not an abstract truth to be memorized in a catechism class but one which must be experienced now in the context of the finitude, of the mortality of human existence. For only in the power of the resurrection can this world be transformed. It is the Father's will that through Jesus in the power of the Spirit, the face of the earth be renewed through us and with us. And at a time we know not when, this universe will be empowered by the Spirit of the Risen Lord to take that ultimate leap forward and truly become what it so yearns to be: new, eternal life in the Victorious Christ, the Reign of God.

But is the resurrection of Jesus, the source of christian hope, REAL? Are the preceding paragraphs just wild rantings? Who ever heard of someone returning from the dead? O'Collins reminds us that the English philosopher Hume declared that even if he were to read in all the histories of England that Elizabeth I died and then returned to the palace, he would scoff at the lunacy of the chroniclers of the empire.[3] Yet the serious claim has been constantly made for two thousand years that Jesus — who summarizes and speaks for all creation — is risen to that new life of eternal, dynamic love and peace. And it is that life for which we all yearn no matter how much we may try to stifle its demand by saturating ourselves with the finite goods of this creation.

The study of the resurrection of Jesus will be divided into the following sections:

1. The meaning of Resurrection at the time of Jesus.
2. The New Testament accounts of the Resurrection.
   — The Creedal Affirmations of the Resurrection.
   — The Gospel Accounts of the Easter Appearances.
3. The Theological Implications of the Resurrection.

CHAPTER TWENTY

THE MEANING OF THE RESURRECTION
AT THE TIME OF JESUS

Although central to Christianity, the Easter event is misunderstood by many followers of Christ. For too many it means that Jesus returned to this life after his death upon the cross, spent forty days with his disciples and then, rocket-like, ascended to the Father. Our time-bound situation makes it difficult to express an event which is meta-historical: beyond time and space categories.[4] Easter is a new creation, a new age, the coming of the reign of God in power, in and through this man Jesus. Better to grasp the mind-boggling cry of the early christians: "The Lord has risen indeed" (Lk 24:34), this chapter will examine the understanding of resurrection in the Old Testament[5] in order to discover the meaning of resurrection at the time of Jesus.

THE RESURRECTION IN THE OLD TESTAMENT

The sources for the christian understanding of the resurrection of Jesus are to be sought in Jewish history, not in the pagan myths of the dying and rising gods, which as already seen, bear little if any resemblance to the christian proclamation (*kerygma*).[6] Even if Persia be the instrument providing Israel with some of the basic raw-material for the belief in resurrection, the concepts were thoroughly transformed and made part of the strictly monotheistic religion of the people of God. Our task is to examine the development of the theme within Israel, regardless of its ultimate provenance.

At first sight, the resurrection does not appear to be a "theme" of Old Testament history. Rather, in seeming anticipation of modern thought, the early books of the Bible limit human life to this world. There is, however, a radical difference between biblical and modern fatalism and it is founded upon the predominant Old Testament explanation of the constitution of a human being.[7] So immersed is the western mind in the Greek division of body and soul, that it is not easy to conceive of a culture which sees the human person as a unity, a totality, a "psycho-physical being whose life can manifest itself by extension or concentration in all parts of the body."[8] In this framework, "without a body there is no real life."[9] A human being in Old Testament thought is "monistic" (Greek: *monos* = alone, single), the existing totality of an animated body and not a composite of spirit, soul, body as the Greeks believed.[10]

The Old Testament citizens would not say that a person ceases to exist at death. Rather, God withdraws his Spirit by which "man became a living soul" (cf. Gen 2:7) and the individual continues a strange type of existence — if it should even be so called — in the "underworld," She'ol. However, this land of the *shades* can hardly be called a place of life: the earth is the "land of the living" (Is 38:11). Psalm 88 dramatically describes this strange afterlife:

"like the slain that lie in the grave, like those whom thou dost remember no more for they are cut off from thy hand. Thou has put me in the depths of the Pit, in the regions dark and deep . . . Dost thou work wonders for the dead? Do the shades rise up to praise thee? Is thy steadfast love declared in the grave or thy faithfulness in Abaddon (i.e., perdition: a name for the region of the dead)? Are thy wonders known in the darkness or thy saving help in the land of forgetfulness?" (cf. 115:17; 49:15).

She'ol is where God is not. For he no longer remembers the dead nor do they, him. There is, therefore, no praise of God in She'ol, the nadir of the universe. The *shades* who dwell there are not separated souls; rather, they are ghost-like shadows of the entire being (cf. 1 Sam 28:14; Is 14:9). She'ol "is no more than a vast tomb where the bodies of the dead lie inert (Jb 10:21; 17:13–16)."[11] The evil they experience is not the pain of fire described in later literature, but their very existence as separated from God.

Two points have to be underlined here: She'ol is the destiny of all, good and evil alike. Secondly, She'ol is forever. When the psalmist speak of being "ransomed from She'ol" (cf. Ps 49:15; 1 Sam 2:6) it appears to be the thanksgiving of someone "deathly-sick" but now cured by God, rescued, ransomed from She'ol (cf. 2 Kgs 5:7). There is therefore the yearning for a "multitude of days," for "long life" and then "full of years" to "go the way of all flesh" (1 Kgs 2:22). "Man cannot abide in his pomp, he is like the beasts that perish" (Ps 49:12). This basic concept can be found even in post-exilic books like Job (cf. Jb 3:17–19).

It is within this rather somber context that the first signs of hope appear. Ezechiel may be the first to imply that God will one day (an eschatological hope) "raise the dead" for he uses this concept — as a metaphor — to speak of the restoration of a defeated, "dead" nation in his vision of the dry bones (cf. Ez 37:1–14). Hosea speaks in similar terms of the healing of a sick people: "Come, let us return to the Lord; for he has torn that he may heal us; he has stricken and he will bind us up. After two days he will revive us; on the third day he will raise us up, that we may live before him" (Hos 6:1–2).

In the apocalypse of First-Isaiah, composed probably around the third century B.C., the hope of resurrection becomes clearer, although still centered on the nation: "Thy dead shall live, their bodies shall rise. O dwellers in the dust, awake and sing for joy! For thy dew is a dew of light and on the land of the shades thou wilt let it fall" (26:19). This hope looks forward to the end-time redemption of the whole people; therefore even the shades in She'ol must come forth to join in this community restoration. A resurrection is then eschatological, an end-time event and it encompasses all the people, at least all the just of Israel. ". . . the Israelite conception of human nature and of human life . . . knows of no principle that could survive death. When the hope is finally expressed, it takes the only possible form that it can take in Israelite thought: the resurrection of the body . . . Resurrection is not, like the Egyptian form of survival, merely a resumption of terrestrial existence; it involves an eschatological life in a new world."[12]

As history unfolds and approaches the time of Christ, a significant step is taken concerning belief in the resurrection. During the war with the Greeks (the Maccabean period), the author of Daniel writes: "Many of those who sleep in the dust of the earth shall awake, some to everlasting life, and some to shame and everlasting contempt" (12:12). The resurrection is ascribed to all people, for all are to be judged by God. Daniel in typical apocalyptic fashion is giving a solution to the fate of the many Jews who were slain in the Maccabean revolts against the Greek domination. It was inconceivable that their destiny would be identical to that of the enemies of YHWH. During this same period however, the first book of Maccabees is strangely silent on a return from She'ol, while the highly embellished second book of Maccabees repeats the theme of Daniel: "The King of the world will raise us up who die for his Laws in the resurrection of eternal life" (7:9 ff).

In the period of "late Judaism," the resurrection of the dead becomes the more common teaching of Israel, but not without its opponents. The Saducees especially see it as not only foolishness but also as an affront to Jewish belief, for it is not mentioned in the Torah (cf. Acts 23:8). Even among those who hold to the resurrection, like the Pharisees, there appears to be a wide spectrum of belief concerning the *who and the how*. Do all rise (cf. Ethiopian Enoch 22:1) or only the just of Israel (cf. 2 Mac 7:14)? How do they rise? As transformed bodies, or as reassembled bodies (cf. 2 Mac 7:11)? Moreover, under the influence of the Hellenistic Jews, the Greek notion of death as separation of body and soul was introduced and the immortality of the soul — with no explicit reference to the resurrection of the body — is taught in Wisdom 1:15 ff; 15:1 ff. Apocryphal literature of the time, like the *Psalms of Solomon, Ethiopian Enoch, Fourth Esdras* reflect the fundamental belief in the resurrection with differences concerning the details.[13]

At the dawn of the New Testament period, amidst the variety of opinions concerning "resurrection," what appears to be the more accepted belief of Israel[14] encompasses three points:

— Resurrection entails that the WHOLE human being will one day share in the salvation of the world to come.
— Resurrection of the dead is an eschatological event, occurring on the DAY OF THE LORD when YHWH shall reign over all peoples.
— This eschatological resurrection entails a personal and individual resurrection, bringing all the dead together with those still alive "on that day" to form the new community of Israel under the rule of YHWH.

Discussion may take place concerning who is to be raised, some extending the resurrection even to the non-Jew, and even to the sinners although the latter are raised only to be judged by the Living God. Discussion may also take place concerning the precise manner of resurrection, some apparently upholding a return of the earthly body, others stressing a transformed body. Nonetheless, at the time of Jesus the fact of the resurrection of the dead was well-established within Israel. The chief opponents to the teaching were the Saducees who were to disappear as a party in Israel at the destruction of Jerusalem in 70 A.D. when the re-organization of the Jews would be in the hands of the Pharisees.

A basic, fundamental insight into resurrection is already found at the time of Jesus: this raising from the dead is NOT a return to this life. It is not a resuscitation, no matter how crassly it may be imagined. It is the great event of the end-time and thereby beyond the limitedness of our space/time-bound world. It a new creation, a new age, and earthly categories can only faintly describe its reality. It is not being claimed, to borrow Hume's example of Elizabeth I, that the dead shall return to their homes and lead "ordinary" lives once again, only now it will be forever. That would not be heaven; it would be hell. It is to turn resurrection into a curse if it be defined as a coming back to an endless living of *this* life without ever reaching our goal, seeing our God face to face.

No matter how one may want to understand the historicity of the Lazarus story, it does not entail a resurrection; it is a resuscitation. Lazarus comes back to this life. He is once again subject to all the finitudes of this existence. And one day he will die. Resurrection is not a *Lazarus-event*. The biblical notion of resurrection is intrinsically tied up with the eschaton when death will be no more, when in the totality of our being, the fulfillment of dynamic life with YHWH will be ours: the Reign of God.

JESUS' UNDERSTANDING OF THE RESURRECTION

During his ministry, Jesus raised people from the dead (the daughter of Jairus Mk 5:21 par.; the son of the widow of Naim, Lk 7:11–17; Lazarus, Jn 11:1–44). These are primarily signs that Jesus in giving *physical* life, is the inbreaking of *eternal* life for us.[15] But how did Jesus understand resurrection itself? Did he know that he would "rise from the dead?"

The *locus classicus* for an insight into Jesus' position concerning resurrection is found in his dispute with the Saducees who, as we know not only from the New Testament but also from Josephus[16] had no use for the doctrine. After listening to their story about a man who had seven wives, (a good biblical number) they ask Jesus: "In the resurrection, therefore, whose wife will the woman be? For the seven had her as wife" (Lk 20:33 par.) The response of Jesus, as interpreted by Luke is to the point:

"The sons of this age marry and are given in marriage; but those who are accounted worthy to attain to that age and to the resurrection from the dead neither marry nor are given in marriage for they cannot die any more because they are equal to angels and are sons of God, being sons of the resurrection. But that the dead are raised, even Moses showed, in the passage about the bush where he calls the Lord the God of Abraham and the God of Isaac and the God of Jacob. Now he is not God of the dead but of the living, for all live to him" (Lk 20:34–37).

Jesus affirms with the Pharisees: there is definitely a resurrection of the dead. He responds to the Saducees hidden agenda — the resurrection is not found in the Torah — by declaring that in the Torah God said to Moses that He is the God of Abraham, Isaac and Jacob who are dead. The thought of the Maccabees appears to be repeated here: those who die as friends of God are not doomed to the forgetfulness of She'ol but will have eternal life. Jesus also stresses that the resurrection is an eschatological event, a new age where death will be no more and therefore marriage itself, the begetting of children, will be no more. Here Jesus runs counter to the crass symbols of resurrection bliss given by some Pharisees as if eternal life were merely this life "writ large."

For Jesus, as with the majority of the Palestinian Jews of his day, the resurrection is an eschatological event entailing a radical transformation of all those who will rise from She'ol *on that day.*[17] If it can be said with sufficient probability that Jesus himself believed in the resurrection as a "Kingdom" event (the eschatological age of sharing in the eternal life of YHWH), the question must be asked before the Easter narratives are examined whether or not Jesus gave any indication of believing in his own resurrection?

The answer is in the affirmative, for if Jesus claims a resurrection for all the friends of God at the inbreaking of the Reign, it must be said that he surely would include himself in that category, for he believes himself to be in a unique, intimate sharing of life with YHWH. Moreover, if he does believe himself to be the inbreaking of YHWH's wisdom and power, the effective instrument, proclaimer of the Reign, he must see himself as one day fully sharing — even in his humanity — in the eternal life of YHWH. He must, then, see himself as definitely participating in the resurrection since for Jesus, a Palestinian Aramaic-speaking Jew, there is no life where there is no body. In some way — perhaps not *precisely* ever verbalized — Jesus would look forward to a resurrection, a return to his ABBA. For Jesus this means his whole person.

Although the words of Gabriel Marcel have been used at times in a maudlin way, there is no reason to deny their truth: "To love someone is to say: 'You will not die.' "[18] We bestow a type of immortality on those we love — through our loving memory of them, by a lived-out gratitude for the support they gave us, etc. But infinite love is creative. In granting eternal life, the Father does not destroy the incarnate Son by assimilating him into his person, thereby destroying the personhood of the Son. Kasper therefore joins to these words of Marcel the famous phrase of Hegel: "Love . . . is the discernment and the cancellation of difference."[19] Love does not destroy, it perfects us in who we are. Jesus knows that his ABBA will say to him — the ABBA's UNIQUELY beloved — at his death: "You will not die." For God IS love and Jesus is the "Son" through a dynamic call of ABBA and Jesus' loving response of acceptance; a response of Jesus which makes that Love operative, which accepts that constantly offered gift of the Father's Life. The incarnation is not a static reality; it is a "state" because it is a dynamic, never-ending giving/ acceptance, call/response. In that surrender of love on the Cross in his name and in the name of the entire human race which Jesus summarizes, the Father responds with the gift of eternal life.

Mark contains three announcements made by Jesus of his death and resurrection (8:31; 9:31; 10:32 ff; Mt and Lk retain Mark's threefold prediction). When studying Jesus as *Suffering Servant*, it was seen that Jesus could easily have foreseen the certainty of his death considering the life he was leading. The question that faces us here is a more difficult one. Did Jesus, as Mark narrates, actually foretell his resurrection? Some accept these three predictions at face value, while many others consider them *vaticinia ex eventu*, i.e., foretellings after the fact or in other words, constructs of the early church.

That these predictions have been adapted by the early church would be difficult to deny. Especially the third one contains such details of the passion narrative that it surely appears to have been composed after the event. The question is not, therefore, the number of predictions, not the preciseness of the predictions but simply: did Jesus in some way foresee his resurrection and share this belief with his disciples. If that be so, it is also easily admitted that the early church clothed this historical core with details culled from what actually transpired in Jesus' passion.

That Jesus did foresee his resurrection in some fashion has already been shown as highly probable. Did Jesus share this with his disciples? All that can be said is that it would appear to be a a likely element of his instructions to them concerning the kingdom (without going into any detail about words used, time, place, etc. which will always remain unknown). But at least in some manner — not clearly grasped apparently by his disciples, and understandably so — Jesus most likely did speak about his impending execution and his faith in a loving response by the Father. This knowledge on the part of Jesus of some manner of resurrection following his proclamation of the kingdom in his death does not destroy his freedom nor take away the suffering. Christians die with the conviction of entering into eternal life and this faith in no way destroys their freedom nor does it take away the physical suffering involved in dying.

The expression "after three days" found in these predictions, would appear to indicate a post-Easter embellishment since it is so clear, so precise. Yet the expression can mean "after death" since it was commonly held that the spirit hovered around the body for three days, or it more probably would refer to the eschatological times which is indicated by the formula "on the third day" (cf. Hos 6:2). Basing himself on the Septuagint translation of Hos 6:2 (". . . on the third day we shall be raised and we shall live before him") and on the Aramaic paraphrase of the text which also contains a clear reference to resurrection ("he shall raise us up and we shall live before him"), Grelot concludes that "the application of Hos 6, 2 to the eschatological resurrection had taken place in current Jewish tradition, not only before the time of the apostles, but before that of Jesus."[20] Jesus would not be using the expression — presuming that these are his words — in any chronological sense but to indicate "that day," the inbreaking of the kingdom with power. The use of the term "three days" does not, therefore, necessarily indicate that these predictions are a whole-cloth production of the early church. On the contrary, considering Jesus' conviction of a coming execution which the mysterious ways of his ABBA is permitting, Jesus is assured even in the midst of his fear and anguish that the love of ABBA will never abandon him in death but will gift him with resurrection.

Summary

In Jesus that Rule of God, characterized by eternal life, love, a new creation, has broken into our history. The Gospel portraits indicate Jesus' firm belief in resurrection for the just. There appears to be no reason that he would exclude himself from this future which he held as so certain. As he began to see that his death — in loneliness, betrayal, in an expression of the weakness and emptiness of humankind — would be the supreme proclamation of the power of the Reign, his faith in his own resurrection would become even more predominant in his thought. That he shared this faith in some way with his disciples can hardly be doubted.

CHAPTER TWENTY-ONE

THE RESURRECTION OF JESUS:
THE KERYGMATIC PROCLAMATIONS

It is one thing to admit that Jesus believed in the resurrection and held firmly to the belief in his own resurrection. It is quite another topic to say that Jesus is actually risen from the dead. Moreover, since the resurrection is an eschatological event, it cannot be considered historical since it is beyond time/space categories. It is not empirical. If the term *historical* is used in connection with the resurrection it can only be employed to indicate the continuity between the Jesus who dies and the Jesus who is raised, and that the risen Jesus "made himself to be seen" — and still is experienced[21] — by people of faith bound within the horizons of *this* world. Since the resurrection is therefore, *meta-historical*, an eschatological event, how can it be proven?

Moreover, it is possible for someone to hope for vindication and yet not be vindicated; it is possible for someone to hope for release from prison yet never receive the governor's pardon. No matter how confident of the future, no matter how certain that "things will turn out this way," cannot the future actually hold no more than despair, disillusion? Could not Jesus have been deluded in his sure hope of the resurrection?

True, the resurrection, as an eschatological event, can only be accepted in faith. Yet the scriptures themselves say: "Always be prepared to make a defense to any one who calls you to account for the hope that is in you, yet do it with gentleness and reverence" (1 Pet 3:15). What defense can a Christian give for the belief in the resurrection of Jesus? An examination of the sources is necessary. After briefly stressing the centrality of the resurrection in Christian belief, this chapter will examine the early creedal proclamations of the resurrection. Subsequent chapters will deal with the Gospel accounts of the Easter appearances and the theological conclusions deduced from the resurrection.

THE CENTRALITY OF THE RESURRECTION

Were it not for belief in the resurrection, there would never be such an enduring phenomenon as Christianity. The splinter group of Judaism made up of the followers of the Nazarene would have faded away at his ignominious execution on a cross. The core group of the disciples themselves including the Apostle John[22] — if our interpretation of the scriptures is correct — had fled back to Galilee after Jesus' arrest and had returned to their former way of living. There was shock, dismay (cf. Mk 16:14; Mt 28:17; Lk 24:37; Jn 20:24–29). Yet there was also the tough realism of the simple, unsophisticated countryfolk: they needed a job, they had to make a living. At least according to one tradition, they lost no time returning to their work as fishermen (Jn 21:2–3). To remain around Jerusalem had its dangers of arrest for being part of the sedition instigated by Jesus the so-called "King of the Jews."

Without the resurrection-faith, there would be no christianity. The story of Jesus would by this time be tucked away in a footnote of history as a rather exceptional example of the many deluded *messiahs* who finally provoked Rome to send Titus and Vespasian to level Jerusalem in 70 A.D.

Christians themselves recognize this fact. The Jewish-Christian, Paul, clearly insists that were it not for the resurrection of Jesus, the entire cause of Jesus would be in vain: "If Christ has not been raised, then our preaching is in vain and your faith is in vain . . . If Christ has not been raised your faith is futile and you are still in your sins . . . If for this life only we have hoped in Christ, we are of all men most to be pitied" (1 Cor 15:14–19). All that is left is to follow the thought of the pagans of the time: "Eat, drink and be merry, for tomorrow we die" (1 Cor 15:32). And rightly so. For the resurrection is considered by the early Christians as an essential element of the faith, not just an postscript to the crucifixion: "raised for our justification" says Paul (Rom 4:25). Christianity — and therefore christology — rises or falls on the teaching concerning Jesus' resurrection. If there be no Easter, there is no possibility of faith in the *Lord*, there is no redemption.

The apologetic dimension of Easter is not much in vogue today, i.e., using the resurrection as a proof for christianity and especially for the divinity of Jesus. Certainly the apologetic angle was misused in times past. Christology hardly considered the resurrection as a *fides quae* (an object of faith); it was rather a *fides qua* (a motive of faith). Which means that the resurrection was considered as a "proof for faith" and not so much as the central mystery of faith.[23] The stress on apologetics was a response to the narrow question of opponents who were denying that the resurrection was an historical fact. Instead of pointing out the inadequacy of the question, the church's theologians met the opponents on their own ground and attempted to *prove* the resurrection (through the empty tomb, through the spread of the church, through a rebuttal of arguments put forward, etc.) rather than stressing the theological content of the resurrection. The resurrection itself became a side issue in theology, a proof-prop that Jesus is really divine.

It is not that the apologetic dimension is to be disregarded. However, the resurrection must be considered primarily as a part of christology, in fact, its central core. It is not that the resurrection itself is verifiable. As a meta-historical event it eludes historical probing. The Risen Lord is accessible to academic study only through his manifestations (the empty tomb, the appearances, the faith expressions of the witnesses). It is this data which must be examined to understand the resurrection more clearly.

CREEDAL PROCLAMATIONS THAT JESUS IS RISEN

The earliest testimonies of faith in the resurrection are not the detailed appearance stories as found in the Gospels but rather the short creedal affirmations (*kerygmatic* statements) sprinkled throughout the New Testament. After briefly reviewing the most important of these "shouts of joy," a brief study will be made of the most important creedal proclamation, 1 Cor 15:3–8.[24] Examples of Easter Proclamations are found in all the portraits: "The Lord has risen indeed and has appeared to Simon!" (Lk 24:34). "God raised him on the third day and made him manifest; not to all the people but to us who were chosen by God as witnesses who ate and drank with him after he rose from the dead. And he commanded us to preach to the people . . ." (Acts 10:40).

> "He was manifested in the flesh,
> vindicated in the Spirit
> seen by angels,
> preached among the nations,
> believed on in the world,
> taken up in glory" (1 Tim 3:16).

"Descended from David according to the flesh and designated Son of God in power according to the Spirit of holiness by his resurrection from the dead, Jesus Christ Our Lord" (Rom 1:3–4).

"This Jesus God raised up and of that we are all witnesses" (Acts 2:23).

"If you confess with your lips that Jesus is Lord and believe in your heart that God raised him from the dead, you will be saved" (Rom 10:9).

"to wait for His Son from heaven whom he raised from the dead, Jesus who delivers us from the wrath to come" (1 Thes 1:10).

"Why do you seek the living among the dead? He is not here but has risen" (Lk 24:5).

"He has risen, he is not here, see the place where they laid him" (Mk 16:6).

It is not a question of adding up the words used in these kerygmatic statements and in the appearance narratives, then to compare them to the greater number of words employed for the other Gospel episodes (this is especially true for Mark). These Easter kerygmatic statements are the climax of the Gospels which could never have been written were it not for the resurrection of Jesus; Paul's epistles would never have been composed if there were no resurrection because there never would have been Paul the Christian. The New Testament is founded upon this basic proclamation: *Jesus is risen*. Without that belief there would be no possibility of stating that "the Word became flesh" (Jn 1:14).

OF ALL the kerygmatic statements concerning the resurrection the most important is 1 Cor 15:3–8:

"For I delivered to you as of first importance what I also received, that Christ died for our sins in accordance with the scriptures, that he was buried, that he was raised on the third day in accordance with the scriptures, and that he appeared to Cephas, then to the twelve. The he appeared to more than five hundred brethren at one time, most of whom are still alive although some have fallen asleep. Then he appeared to James, then to all the apostles. Last of all, as to one untimely born, he appeared also to me."

No other proclamation of the Easter event carries as much weight as this excerpt from one of Paul's letters. A study of its contents clarifies the meaning of resurrection.

This statement, which at least up to verse 5 ("the twelve") is pre-Pauline as vocabulary (e.g., "the twelve," "sins," are not considered pauline terms) and strophic style indicate,[25] is probably the earliest proclamation of the resurrection. Paul tells us that he *received* this formula. Perhaps he is referring to his instructions in the faith at Damascus after his conversion experience, or during his first visit to Jerusalem (Gal 1:18 ff). Rather than quibble over the precise date and place where Paul first memorized these lines, let it be said it is recognized as the most primitive account of the Easter faith, reflecting the early proclamation of the Christian community only a few years after the death/resurrection of Jesus.

And it contains some surprises. There is no explicit mention of the empty tomb (although implied, for it does state that he was buried and was raised), there are no times and places of the appearances, there are no words attributed to the risen Lord, there is no account of an ascension, no descriptions of any encounters with the Risen Christ. This earliest account is basically stark. Its core contains four "that" clauses: *that* Jesus died, *that* he was buried, *that* he was raised, *that* he appeared to certain witnesses. These points are what the early church believed to be of primary importance and handed down in a fixed formula.

— *That* Jesus died is commonly accepted. Novels which describe Jesus as only fainting on the cross and then being revived by the coolness of the tomb are definitely not published to advance scholarship. Moreover, even if *per absurdum* such were the case, there is no question of "resurrection" as understood by the early Christians: a kingdom life entailing a new creation beyond death, corruption, time, space. That his death was "for our sins, according to the scriptures" not only demonstrates the belief in the soteriological aspect of Jesus' death but also that it fulfills the plan of God.

— *That* Jesus was buried is also commonly accepted; the fact that both the Johannine and synoptic traditions speak of a stranger, Joseph of Aramithea, taking charge of the burial is an embarrassing situation which probably implies an historical fact. However, the essential point is that Jesus truly died, was therefore buried, with the implication that his burial was witnessed. The problems revolve around the final *that's*: raised, appeared.

— *That* he was raised: There are two basic teachings which flow from this term "raised." First, it is the work of the Father. The verb used by this early confession of faith is in the passive, denoting an implicit "by God." That this is so Paul makes clear throughout his epistles: "God the Father who raised him from the dead" (Gal 1:1); "God raised the Lord" (1 Cor 6:14; cf. Rom 10:9; 8:11; 1 Cor 6:14). When Paul does write in his first letter to the Christians of Thessalonika: "We believe that Jesus died and rose again" (4:14), the entire context makes it clear that the raising of Jesus is the work of the Father. Even when the Johannine Jesus says: "I lay down my life that I may take it again. No one takes it from me but I lay it down of my own accord. I have power to take it up again" (10:17–18; cf. 2:19), it is because, proclaims Jesus, "this charge I have received from my Father" (10:18). In John's christology it is never stated that it is Jesus ALONE who would be the cause of the resurrection but always Jesus — as John understands him — the Son of the Father. The resurrection is belief in an extraordinary act of the Father transferring Jesus into the sphere of the "new age."

Raised by the Father has important connotations. The expression reveals who the Father is. He has power over life and death, he is creative love, he is enduring faithfulness. Moreover, by firmly stating that Jesus is raised by the Father, the early Christians express their conviction that the resurrection is not something which has its origins in the imagination or delusions of the disciples. It is the Father's doing. Finally, the phrase "raised by the Father" accentuates an important theological insight into the person of Jesus. The Father effects something in Jesus: there is a "becoming" in Jesus. This becoming is to be applied not only to his resurrection but is a characteristic of his entire life.[26]

The scriptures themselves allude to this becoming: "And Jesus increased in wisdom and in stature and in favor with God and man" (Lk 2:51). "Although he was a Son, he learned obedience through what he suffered" (Heb 5:8). It can be said that he must learn who he is in this sense: through the instruments of the Spirit, e.g., the scriptures, daily events, his mother, he deepens and verbalizes that intuitive experience of oneness with his ABBA which was ALWAYS his as enfleshed Word of the Father. "What he learned about himself, he discovered only gradually. And what he taught he had first to learn."[27]

John is perhaps the clearest on this becoming in the historical Jesus when he declares: "As yet the Spirit had not been given because Jesus was not yet glorified" (7:39); "Father glorify thou me in thy own presence with the glory which I had with thee before the world was made" (17:5). Since Jesus truly shares in our nature (cf. Heb 2:14), emptying himself of the external manifestation of divinity (cf. Phil 2:6– 11), he lives within the confines of our creatureliness. His entire life is therefore a "growing," a "becoming"; the final becoming is the resurrection when in his transformed, glorified being with the Father he becomes the sender of the Spirit.

There is, therefore, not only a becoming in the realm of knowledge, but also as climactic expression or sacrament of the Wisdom of the Father. Having taken on the opaqueness of this humanity — in revolt against God from the beginning — this man Jesus must experience a constant transformation by the Spirit so that he will become more and more TRANSPARENT of who he is from the first moment of his conception; the personal epiphany of the Wisdom of God. His resurrection is the permeating of his entire being by the Spirit and in the Spirit. Not that Jesus divests himself of his creatureliness in his resurrection. Though transformed and glorified in this ultimate becoming, he remains one of us, our brother. However in his redemptive resurrection he becomes fully the New Adam, the "pioneer of salvation" (Heb 2:10), the first-born of the dead, the Way to eternal life.

The second conclusion drawn from the term "raised" is that Jesus is raised to *eschatological* life. The scripture writers use two Greek terms to denote "raise": one is the literal word for "rising from sleep" (*egeiro*),[28] the other, "standing up on one's feet" (*anistemi*).[29] They are used symbolically to express what human words cannot bear: someone is "raised," transformed into the realm of YHWH beyond time, space categories. The term, employed in an end-time context as it is in this early confession of faith, denotes not any return to life, but a getting up, a rising into the new creation through the Spirit of the Father. Precisely what does this mean? Paul attempts an explanation in subsequent verses of chapter fifteen:

"So it is with the resurrection of the dead. What is sown is perishable, what is raised is imperishable. It is sown in dishonor, it is raised in glory. It is sown in weakness, it is raised in power. It is sown a physical body, it is raised a spiritual body. If there is a physical body there is also a spiritual body. Thus it is written, 'The first man Adam became a living being'; the last Adam became a life giving spirit . . . I tell you this, brethren, flesh and blood cannot inherit the kingdom of God, nor does the perishable inherit the imperishable . . . For this perishable nature must put on the imperishable and this mortal nature must put on immortality . . . then shall come to pass the saying that is written: 'O death, where is thy victory? O death, where is thy sting?' . . . Thanks be to God who gives us the victory through Our Lord Jesus Christ" (1 Cor 15:35–57).

Through metaphors, symbolic language, Paul is trying to express the transformation in continuity which marks the resurrection. Jesus is raised: the same Jesus who hung upon a cross, but radically transformed into a spiritual body. Flooded by the very Spirit of God, the change is so radical that Paul will even call the risen Christ a "life-giving spirit" while in no way denying the reality of Jesus himself. Paul shares in the Jewish conception that life demands a body; the resurrection of Jesus is somatic (the Greek *soma* = body).[30] The Risen One is more open to this universe and interacting far more intensely with it for he is not bound by the limitations of this body as we know it. In and through this risen body, suffused with the Spirit, the Easter Lord is more dynamically active and present in this cosmos "for us and for our salvation." Resurrection does not, therefore, mean to "withdraw from us."

Rather, it is to be inserted in and through the power of the Spirit into the ordinary day-to-day events of our personal life (cf. Jn 14–16). Beyond this we cannot fathom. Speculations on what a risen body "looks like," whether it would be formed as the physical body with limbs and organs, etc., are pointless and useless for they automatically drag the resurrection back into this empirical world of time/space.

The proclamation includes the reference to "the third day." The statement may refer to the finding of the empty tomb "on the third day." However, presuming that "on the third day" is also qualified by the expression "according to the scriptures," then it is difficult to brush aside the theological aspect: "on the third day" refers to the day of YHWH, the day of the eschatological raising of the dead implied in Hosea: "After two days he will revive us; on the third day he will raise us up, that we may live before him" (Hos 6:2). Although this text of Hosea is not found explicitly in the early preaching of the church, nonetheless, it may very well play a role in the constant stress on "the third day" as was seen in a previous chapter concerning Jesus' saying that he would rise "on the third day."

— *That* he appeared. The Greek term the early Christians employ for the Easter appearances in this confession of faith is *ophthe*,[31] the Greek root for many English words dealing with sight, like "ophthalmology." The verb is open to several translations. However the expression which seems to correspond best to the tenor of the context is: "he made himself to be seen." For *ophthe* connotes basically two concepts: something which is invisible now is seen in some fashion. For example, the angel at the burning bush *ophthe* (LXX), i.e., made himself to be seen by Moses (cf. Ex 3:2). The second concept transmitted by this Greek verb is that the initiative does *not* come from the person seeing but from what is "making itself to be seen." It is the angel of the Lord who intrudes, who initiates the encounter with Moses. But intrinsic to this second element is also the openness of the person who is seeing, i.e., he must accept this intrusion, this initiative, this showing of self, and be open to assimilate the "sight."

As applied to the resurrection, the early Christians are, first of all, clearly making a distinction between these appearances, and the visions which can originate within the mind of a person. In some way, the Risen Lord himself is "making himself to be seen." The scriptures themselves distinguish between "visions" and Easter appearances. Paul will claim that he experienced an appearance of the Easter Lord on the road to Damascus, a unique event in his life. Yet he does admit to having visions of the Lord (cf. 2 Cor 12). Secondly, the term will underline that the Easter appearances are not psychosomatic: the initiative is with the Risen One. He who is now somatically in the realm of the Father "makes himself to be seen" to people who are willing to see: an indication that the *ophthe* is a call to faith.

The creedal formula of 1 Cor 15 concludes with an enumeration of the witnesses of the Risen Lord, thereby stressing the reality of the Easter appearances. Peter (Cephas) is listed first for he, as the one whose faith (cf. Mt 16:18) is to strengthen the brethren (Lk 22:32; Jn 21:15–17) is the primary witness to all that Jesus is Lord. Even James, presumably the relative of the Lord who does not appear to be a follower of the pre-Easter Jesus, has seen the Lord. Paul adds to this early confession of faith that Jesus also appeared to a group of more than 500, some of whom, he says, are still alive. And finally, the Risen Christ himself, Paul says, appeared even to him. As we know from the Acts and the Epistles, the Lord transformed this hunter of Christians into the *Apostle of the Gentiles*. Paul, open to the workings of the Spirit, accepted the empowering call of that *ophthe* and surrendered in faith to the Lordship of Christ.

Summary

The earliest proclamations of the Easter event are given in these joyful, kerygmatic exclamations. The first formula of faith in the resurrection appears to be the few phrases which Paul received at his conversion and which he includes in his Second Letter to the Christians at Corinth. Its simplicity can fool us. In strong terms, the early church declares its firm belief that Jesus truly died, was buried, was raised and appeared. This is the core of the Easter faith, perhaps the most important summary of the Christian faith. All these kerygmatic proclamations join together in one basic theme: in Jesus, the end-time has come, the new age has begun, the longed-for victory of YHWH is ours. The liturgy of the church will intersperse its repeated ALLELUIA (*Praise YHWH!*) with these scriptural exclamations, to show its inexpressible joy and thanksgiving that God has in Jesus given us the sure hope of eternal Life.

CHAPTER TWENTY-TWO

THE RESURRECTION:
THE GOSPEL EASTER APPEARANCES

When we leave the pithy kerygmatic confessions of Easter faith and enter into the Gospel descriptions of the appearances of the Lord, it is immediately apparent that theologizing embellishments have taken place. While the earliest creedal proclamations are devoid of time and place categories, stripped of all narration of an appearance-event, the Gospel accounts elaborate these encounters between the Risen One and the disciples. Never, however, do the canonical Gospels picture the resurrection itself, so convinced that this eschatological act of the Father is indescribable.[32]

The Easter appearance accounts deal with two distinct traditions which eventually become intertwined: appearance stories[33] themselves, and the finding of the empty tomb.[34] This chapter will, therefore, consider both points and conclude with a response to the often asked question: Does the evidence prove the resurrection of Jesus?

THE EASTER APPEARANCE STORIES

There are actually six Gospel accounts of the Easter event plus another in the first chapter of the Acts of the Apostles. If it appears strange that four Gospels contain six Easter narrations, it is because the final chapter of John's Gospel (21) is from another hand and the ending of Mark's Gospel (16:9–20) is a later addition. This is not to deny their canonical status but to indicate that they are of a different source than the body of the Gospels and must be studied as such.

The number of appearances, the places of the appearances and the people to whom Jesus appeared are not identical in all Gospel accounts: The ORIGINAL ENDING OF MARK has no appearances, merely the announcement of the fact that the Risen Christ "is going before you into Galilee; there you will see him, as he told you" (16:7). The ADDED MARCAN CONCLUSION contains three appearances: to Mary Magdalene (probably taken from John), to two disciples along the road (probably taken from Luke) and one to the eleven (taken either from Matthew or Luke). MATTHEW reports two appearances: one to women near the empty tomb and another in Galilee to the eleven (28:9–10; 16–20). LUKE narrates an appearance to two disciples on the road to Emmaus, another to the eleven and their companions in Jerusalem (24:13–25; 36–53). JOHN tells of three appearances: at the tomb to Mary Magdalene, in Jerusalem to the disciples without Thomas and then with Thomas (20:14–18; 19–23: 24–29). THE FINAL CHAPTER OF JOHN describes an appearance in Galilee (21:1–22). THE ACTS OF THE APOSTLES speaks of Jesus appearing to the apostles "during forty days" (1:3) and then recounts the final appearance, in Jerusalem, where he was "staying with them" (1:4–11). A cursory reading of the various easter texts gives the indelible impression that there is no academically honest manner of harmonizing them. Contradictions abound. For example, the number and locations of the appearances; the names of the women going to the tomb and the purpose of the visit; the reaction of the women (amazement, fear, joy, silence, talking); the description of the angel — or angels — or young men — at the tomb or in the tomb and the message they delivered, etc.

These differences cannot be wished away by crude harmonization or by any spiritualizing exegesis.

To declare that these evident contradictions are indicative of the joyful confusion which reigned when Jesus made himself to be seen after his death and therefore portray the historical situation is a difficult thesis to uphold indeed. Rather, it appears that these stories, edited as a *literary* piece *many years* after that first easter, are filled with theologizing embellishments, each author interpreting the basic event according to his purpose and to the needs of his hearers. In other words, *the Gospel easter appearances are theological commentaries on the resurrection event.* There is common agreement on the source of all the interpretations: the Risen Lord made himself to be seen by "chosen witnesses."

At face value, the Gospel resurrection/appearance accounts seem to contradict other references in the New Testament where the resurrection itself is apparently bypassed and Jesus is described not explicitly as risen from the dead but as exalted.[35] The model employed to explain what happened to Jesus is taken from the story of Elijah (2 Kgs 2:1–13) — and also Enoch and Moses — who are *exalted*, i.e., they were taken on high but not risen from the dead. Many Jews, therefore, believed in a return of these exalted heroes of the Scriptures.

The early hymn which Paul included in his letter to the Philipians (2:6–11), the letter to the Hebrews (with only one reference to resurrection (13:20) but many to exaltation (e.g., 4:14; 6:19–20; 2:9) lay little stress on the resurrection. In John's Gospel, there is also an exaltation theme (e.g., 3:14; 6:62, etc.) alongside a resurrection theme. Taking these texts in context, and especially in relationship with the earliest creedal formulations, it seems that some of the christian churches did stress the exaltation of Jesus the crucified but *as a consequence of his resurrection*. The exaltation or glorification theme must be understood within the context of the somatic resurrection itself and not in opposition to it. It does underline important aspects of the resurrection as will be seen in the following chapter.

There is, however, an inherent danger in not explicitly referring to the resurrection of Jesus from the dead. To pull the exaltation/glorification theme out of context could lead to a type of docetism (from the Greek *dokein*: to seem) which would deny the reality of the somatic resurrection of Jesus and influence some — especially the Greeks — into believing that Jesus "left behind" the "prison of the body" (some even thought it unbecoming if not impossible for the Word of God to be manifested in this *evil* matter)[36] — and now in some ghostlike form is with the Father. Docetism hounds the christology of the early church, and its condemnation is the reason for some of the embellishments of the easter appearances.

The easter apparitions can be divided into several categories:

— Appearances which stress the continuity of Jesus and those which express discontinuity.
— Appearances which are are apologetic in character.
— Appearances as mandate.
— Appearances in Jerusalem and appearances in Galilee.

Each of these types of appearances will be briefly considered in order to come to a deeper understanding of the early church's teaching concerning the resurrection.

Appearances Stressing Continuity/Discontinuity

The inability of the evangelists to express the reality of the resurrection — an impossibility due to the nature of this eschatological event — is manifest in the descriptions of the Risen Christ. In order to combat any docetic tendencies, the appearance narratives at times stress the *physical* reality of the risen Lord. He invites Thomas to touch his hands and side (Jn 20:27), he shares meals with the disciples (Lk 24:41 ff; Jn 21:13–15), he speaks with them (Jn 21:15 ff). The early Christians go to extremes to demonstrate that it is truly the identical Jesus who shared life with the disciples before the crucifixion who now is risen from the dead; it is the same Jesus and not some ghost.

Luke and John especially stress this physical reality of the risen Lord because of the needs of their hearers who are apparently tempted to think of the Risen Christ as only a disembodied spirit. The church almost overstates its case that such an opinion is not the faith of the church: "See my hands and my feet that it is I myself; handle me, and see; for a spirit has not flesh and bones as you see that I have" (Lk 24:39). This is a far cry from Paul's statement that "flesh and blood cannot inherit the kingdom of God" (1 Cor 15:44). Especially Luke and John embellish to clarify the continuity inherent in the resurrection.

On the other hand, the evangelists do recognize that in so depicting the risen Christ some may go to the other extreme and think of the resurrection as a Lazarus-event, a return to *this* life. There is, therefore, alongside the "earthly flesh and bones reality" stories, events which stress the discontinuity inherent in the resurrection: the disciples on the road to Emmaus do not even recognize Jesus until he breaks bread with them (Lk 24:31); Jesus makes himself to be seen "out of nowhere," so to speak, for the doors are locked and yet offer no barrier to him (Jn 20:19; 20:26). In the final chapter of John, Jesus is first thought to be a stranger standing on the shore of the lake and it takes some time for the apostles to identify him (21:4 ff). The addition to Mark will even say that the risen Lord appeared in "another form" (16:12). These narratives stress the *otherness* of the Risen Christ; in language understandable to their hearers, the insistence is on the transformation which is essential to the notion of resurrection.

These appearance stories are theological narratives attempting to explain in time/ space language what is beyond our empirical world. The basic truth conveyed through these literary tools is that Jesus in the *totality of his being* is now in the realm of YHWH. Some would want to postulate a special act of God whereby the Risen Christ — beyond *earthly* physical flesh and bones reality which characterize this side of the eschaton — is seen at times by the disciples as if he possessed limbs, organs, features of someone not risen, so that there could be no doubt that this is the same Jesus who hung upon the cross. Such an opinion is possible,[37] but it is fruitless to argue the point. The insistence must be on the somatic resurrection of Jesus who made himself to be seen in some manner by his disciples. To dispute precisely how Jesus appeared goes beyond what is necessary for faith, and also beyond what can ever be known.

The Apologetic Character of the Easter Appearances

At the time of the writing of the Gospels, opponents to Christianity were spreading false rumors to discredit the resurrection (never denying some type of visions or the empty tomb). The preaching of the early Christians, the Matthean community especially, had to respond to these erroneous stories: this is termed the apologetic character of the easter appearances. To scotch the rumor that the apostles had stolen the body (Mt 28:15), the Christian community responds (in the typical fashion of the day) with a counter-story about the guards who were posted at the tomb and who even knew on Good Friday that Jesus was to rise on the third day (Mt

27:62:66) although Luke tells us that the disciples did not even know that much (Lk 24:20 ff). This account is *apologetic*, i.e., a response to the arguments put forward against the truth of the resurrection. It is possible that Jn 20:13–15 reflects the opposition of Christians to the rather far-fetched story that a gardener removed the body of Jesus since the visitors to the tomb were trampling on his cabbage patch. Luke's almost vehement insistence on the reality of the risen Lord probably springs, as we have seen, from stories of Gentiles that the disciples saw not Jesus but some ghost. In keeping with the nature of the literary form *Gospel*, these appear to be embellishments of the early church in order to preserve the fundamental truth of the resurrection.

The Appearances as Mandate

A characteristic of the appearance narratives is a commission to deliver a message, e.g., "go to my brethren and say to them. . ." (Jn 20:17) or to proclaim the good news to the world, e.g., "Go into all the world and preach the Gospel to the whole creation. . ." (Mk 16:15). Even the disciples at Emmaus, although not explicitly told to do so, hurry back to Jerusalem to announce the Good News to the disciples gathered there (Lk 24:33); some, like the apostles and especially Peter are given a special mandate ("Feed my lambs . . . Feed my sheep" Jn 21:15–19). It seems to be an intrinsic element of these narratives that those who "see the Lord" are not only witnesses of the Risen Christ but are are also mandated, at least implicitly, to proclaim the good news of salvation.

Yet only gradually is the conviction formed that this Good News is for *all* people (cf. Acts 11, 13:44–48) as they see Gentiles accepting the Lord and their own people often rejecting him. The early church understands that the source of their mandate to proclaim the inbreaking of the Kingdom is the resurrection of Jesus; the power of the Spirit of Christ which so fills them is itself the command to be apostles to the world. The appearance narratives are also, therefore, a clarification of the source of the *Great Mandate* (Mt 28:18–20) to preach and baptize all people, as Matthew explicitly states (using the later baptismal formula in the name of the Trinity and not as it seems to have been at first, in the name of Jesus, with its implicit trinitarian dimension). There is, in the mind of the early Christians, an intrinsic connection between "seeing" the Lord and spreading the good news. It is for this reason that the successor of Judas had to be someone who was with the Lord from his baptism until his ascension (Acts 1:21) and Paul will say to his opponents: "Am I not an apostle? Have I not seen Jesus our Lord?" (1 Cor 9:1).

Appearances in Jerusalem vs. Appearances in Galilee

It is evident that the early Christians were interested in the Risen Lord and not precisely where or when he encountered the disciples. Differences in time and place should not be forced into some logical order, for chronology and topography were not a paramount concern for the early preachers of Jesus. When we do find, therefore, an insistence on Jerusalem (Luke) or Galilee (Matthew) the suspicion is that it is for some theological and not historical reason. Considering Luke's overall plan, it is only natural that the Ascension — the farewell of Jesus to his disciples — should take place in Jerusalem, the center of God's revelation. Matthew, however who is disappointed if not downright antagonistic because of the refusal of the Jerusalem authorities to accept Jesus, will show Jesus as separating himself from the unbelieving city; it is in Galilee of of the Gentiles that the ascension with its *Great*

Mandate is located. Contradiction? Yes, surely, if the Gospels are being read as chronological history; not at all, if the Gospels are read according to their specific literary genre.

Nowhere in the Gospel portraits is there such a heavy overlay of embellishments as in the easter appearance narratives. And understandably so. For nowhere else in the Gospels are the evangelists faced with the insurmountable difficulty of describing in human language what is "beyond history." The fundamental model they chose to teach this truth is personal encounter. Truly risen, Jesus enters into the lives of his disciples and in that exchange, the disciples are themselves transformed into apostles of courage, boldness and joy. All of the embellishments would appear to have their ultimate purpose in explaining the new, deeper mutual relationship between the Lord who is truly Risen and his followers. They search for words to express this unexpected, loving, salvific encounter with the Risen Lord which enables them to freely open up to a new level of union with God. In the story-telling culture of their time, this is best expressed by "sharing a meal," "proclaiming peace," "seeing," "hearing," being incorporated into the very mission of the Lord. These accounts are important theological teachings, inspired by God. But it would be a pity to dispute over the *where* and the *when* and the *how*, and to overlook the truth conveyed: the Father, through an extraordinary act of Love has raised Jesus who now enters into a new depth of life with those who turn to him in faith.

THE EMPTY TOMB

In addition to the appearance tradition, the early Christians proclaimed that women were witnesses of the empty tomb. A few clarifications:

An empty tomb is not a proof of a resurrection. As the saying goes, "An empty tomb leads to an empty faith." That the tomb of Jesus is found empty no one at the time denies, whether they be Jews or Christians. But an empty tomb is an ambiguous fact. To conclude from an empty tomb to a resurrection is a clear *non-sequitur*.

It could be stated that according to a philosophical understanding of death, there is no need of an empty tomb to uphold the concept of resurrection. As a human spirit, the soul can never be divorced from its expression, "body," except in the abstract. At death, the soul must and does express itself in creation in a new and more universal way, not through the cadaver which rots away in the earth.[38] The conclusion of this theory is that a resurrection may take place which does not involve the entombed cadaver; the remains of Jesus may, therefore, be somewhere in the earth of Jerusalem. As possible as this theory may be philosophically, it cannot be accepted theologically concerning the resurrection of Jesus. While Jesus at his death does effectively manifest himself victoriously in and through the cosmos ("he descended into hell"),[39] the Christian community has always insisted that it is the specific body of Jesus which hung upon the Cross and was laid in the tomb which shares in his radically transformed, glorified, spirit-penetrated expression.[40] Admitting the typical embellishments of the age — the interpreting angel, the earthquake, the stupefaction of the guards, etc. — we are still faced with solid reasons to admit the empty tomb as part of the core historicity. Why would women be named as witnesses of the empty tomb? "Women, barred from bearing testimony considered valid in a Jewish forum, were nevertheless remembered as being the first to witness to the fact (of the empty tomb) . . . (this) is an important factor in considering its historical likelihood."[41]

Moreover, the question does not concern modern day practices or beliefs or philosophies; the ancient empty tomb story must be situated in its own context.

According to the common belief of the Palestinian Jews, there is no resurrection without the body. In no way could the disciples have preached the resurrection if the corpse of Jesus were still lying in death.[42] And even in the height of Jewish-Christian dispute, no opponent of the followers of the Risen Christ ever denied the empty tomb. Other explanations were given for it — the apostles stole it, the gardener moved it, Mary Magdalene had it transferred to another plot, etc., etc. The fact remains: the tomb is empty and the strained explanations of those who say the body was snatched away do more to disprove their theory than substantiate it.[43] Raymond Brown strongly affirms: "we think it biblically irresponsible to claim that Christian faith in the resurrection is independent of the question of whether or not Jesus lies buried in Palestine — Christian faith in the resurrection is in continuity with apostolic faith in the resurrection, and there is no evidence that the first witnesses took such a stance of indifference toward the body in the tomb."[44]

The statement that the women found the tomb empty "on the third day" probably refers to an historical reality that the women went to the tomb at dawn on the third day and surprisingly found it empty. As mentioned in previous chapters, "on the third day" also has "end-time" overtones which cannot be ignored, for as Schillebeeckx states: "The third day is not, therefore, a focal point of time but of salvation."[45]

The value of the empty tomb is not as a proof, but only as a sign, and an ambiguous one at that. It is only the easter appearances which give meaning to the empty tomb and it is therefore not surprising that even in Mark's Gospel the two traditions, probably originally distinct, were already intertwined. The empty tomb is explained by the proclamation: "The Lord has risen indeed and has appeared to Peter."

DO FACTS PROVE THE RESURRECTION?

The western mentality easily transfers scientific methodology to all facets of study. The question, therefore, is often asked both by Christian and non-Christian: "Can you prove the resurrection of Jesus?"

The question is not specifically theological. Proof in the scientific sense deals with objects; the only manner in which the notion of scientific proof can be applied to persons is to treat them as objects for some type of scientific analysis. However, that does not explain an individual's uniqueness, personhood. For a person to disclose his/her inner reality to another, he or she must take the risk of revealing the commitments, lived-out relationships, which constitute this person specifically as this person. Moreover, there must be some type of reciprocity: there is no disclosure if there is no one to respond and take a risk of disclosing him/herself by responding. In other words, personal relationships cannot be subject to scientific, mathematical or laboratory-type proof. Real personal knowledge of another is only brought about through the mutual risk of self-disclosure. Is love scientifically demonstrable? Can fidelity be measured? It is a tragic mistake to transpose scientific methodology into interpersonal relationships and for example, demand that love be proven before love be given. Contrary to much of modern thought, the demonstration methods of what are called the "exact natural sciences" touch on only a very limited section of life.

The reason why we do not speak of proving the resurrection is not only because it is a meta-historical reality, but because the Risen Christ is a personal reality (and because risen, in the fullest sense of the term) and in the realm of the personal there is no proof. On Jesus' part, there is the openness, the disclosure, through the ordinary events of day, especially through the Christian community and its Spirit-filled actions, its preaching, and its supremely dramatized preaching, the sacraments, most especially the eucharist. However, "to know" that the Lord is truly revealing himself to us, we must be open to this encounter, to take that risk of letting life — in all its dimensions — be qualified by this person, Jesus, who through the Spirit is inserting himself with power into our history. There is a technical word for this mutual openness: faith. The Risen Christ cannot be proven anymore than any personal interrelationship can be proven. No one learns to swim without jumping into the water; easter becomes known by bathing in the Pool of Siloam (cf. Jn 9:7), i.e., through the "leap" of faith. Even the witnesses of the Risen Lord were not forced by these appearances as glorious and inexpressible as they were. They had to take a risk, they had, in other words, to be open in faith.

It is for this reason that the easter event is not transmitted to another by proofs in our modern sense of the term; the only method that can be used is testimony and proclamation. This is not a weakness of theology, in fact it is not something negative. It is found wherever a person is to be known.

However, this does not mean that clarifications are not to be sought, that the historical circumstances surrounding the resurrection are unimportant (as was generally stated in the *No Quest* period of the *Quest of the Historical Jesus*). In fact, Wolfart Pannenberg declares, "If the appearance tradition and the grave tradition came into existence independently, then by their mutually complementing each other they let the assertion of the reality of Jesus' resurrection . . . appear as historically very probable and that always means in historical inquiry that it is to be presupposed until contrary evidence appears."[46]

Some may think that Pannenberg has overstated the case. However, there is one aspect of the culture of the times of Jesus which is often overlooked and yet is of extreme importance in clarifying — not proving — the resurrection. Easter is an end-time event. It is the common belief that the resurrection from the dead, the great act of the eschaton, brings together the new community of Israel. There are, therefore, two points to be taken into account: resurrection is a sign of the end of the world, and resurrection is a community event. Now what the apostles preach is that the end of the world has occurred in ONE person as history still CONTINUES. The Pentecost event with its concomitant preaching of the Risen Lord naturally brings out the reaction: " 'What does this mean?' But others mocking said, 'They are filled with new wine' " (Acts 2:12–13).

How can the end-time be proclaimed as history — with its lame, its poor, its calamities — still ticks away? How can the end-time be proclaimed as occurring in one person? The raw material for such a proclamation is at hand but not the way the pieces are put together. The end of the world has broken into ongoing history in Jesus. This is not according to the mindset of the day, this is not according to the culture of the apostles. (It should be clearer now why the early Christians awaited the end of the world, considered it as imminent, for the *end* has occurred in the resurrection of Jesus. The surprising delay of the end of the world cannot be long, was their conclusion.)

What is being stated is that the resurrection of Christ crucified is such foolishness to the eyes of the world (cf. 1 Cor 1:22 ff), the event so startling,[47] that it is difficult to find another explanation for the preaching of the disciples of the Lord than that the resurrection actually did take place. But this is not proving the easter faith. It may clear the air, it may show the sincerity of the apostles but it cannot force anyone to take that risk of being open to the encounter with the Risen Lord. The risk of faith is the only way to meet Jesus, risen from the dead.

Summary

The Gospel narratives of the easter appearances are basically theological commentaries on the reality of Jesus' somatic resurrection. They proclaim that the risen Christ is the same Jesus who lived, preached and died but now totally transformed into the realm of the Father. They also powerfully dramatize that the resurrection calls for a personal response, that Jesus is risen for us, to meet us and share risen life with us. All this is beyond proof even though the circumstances surrounding the resurrection would appear to render highly improbable any psychological invention of the resurrection by the followers of Christ. But even this does not prove faith. The Risen Lord can only be known through the risk of integrating the proclamation into one's own life as any person is only known in that risk of mutual self-disclosure.

CHAPTER TWENTY-THREE

THE THEOLOGICAL CONSEQUENCES
OF THE RESURRECTION

In the context of yearning for infinite *shalom* (peace, fulness of life), men and women encounter through faith a fulfillment which goes even beyond hope, the Easter mystery: light in the midst of darkness, life in the midst of death, love in the midst of estrangement. The Risen Lord calls with the power to share his risen life with us. But that call only becomes truly effective when it is accepted in faith. Flowers never become truly *gift* until they are accepted as such from the giver. No matter how convinced someone may be that Jesus is risen from the dead, that the eschaton has broken into ongoing history, nothing more has been accomplished than accumulating a fund of knowledge if Easter is not accepted, integrated into practical living. Presuming such an integration, what is the result? What are the theological consequences — the practical relevance — of the resurrection? The question needs a double response: its relevance for Jesus and its relevance for us. In reality the two are intrinsically bound together since who he is, he is for us. Nonetheless, for the sake of clarity, with some evident and inevitable overlapping, this chapter will be divided into two sections:

— The Implications of the Resurrection for Jesus.
— The Implications of the Resurrection for us.

IMPLICATIONS OF THE RESURRECTION FOR JESUS

What is the resurrection's meaning for Jesus?[48] The consequences presume not only a belief in the resurrection but an acceptance of the humanness of this citizen of Nazareth.

As the personal expression of the Father's Word there is no one more human than Jesus. Union with God — sanctity — does not transpose human beings into another order of creation; it rather perfects us in what we are: human. There is, therefore, no one who is more entangled with the joys and anguish of this world than this man of Nazareth. Anyone who denies the reality of the humanness of Jesus can never appreciate the "christological dimensions" of the easter event. Docetists really need no easter for they consider Jesus' life a mere charade: a divine person who makes believe that he is human.

But the Gospels describe him quite differently. Jesus is the Word made *flesh* (cf. Jn 1:14). He is a vagabond proclaimer of the Reign of his ABBA experiencing homelessness, loneliness, the frustrations of daily life. He cries at the death of a friend, weeps over the unbelief of the holy city, Jerusalem, cries out in trembling fear as he sees the police approaching to arrest him and condemn him to the torture of the Cross. Yet he enjoys friendship, get-togethers, yearns to share for he is so simple, so approachable, so sensitive, so loving, so yearning to be loved. And in the midst of the alienation of this world from its God, he remains *truly* human: obedient to his ABBA, in harmony with his brothers and sisters, in harmony with his true self, in harmony with the universe.

Only in the context of the true humanity of the incarnate Wisdom can the following consequences of the resurrection be understood.

THE DISCLOSURE OF THE FATHER. Throughout his life, Jesus experiences God as his ABBA in a unique way which encompasses his very existence. Even when tempted to disregard the Father's will (cf. Lk 4:1–13) he remained faithful. Easter is the Father's ultimate self-disclosure, his faithful response to this obedience of Jesus even in death upon a cross (cf. Philip 2:6–11). The resurrection is for Jesus primarily the full self-revelation of the Father. Only in the new life of the resurrection can Jesus know the depths of his Father's faithfulness and love. The *hesed* of the Father takes on a meaning which is only possible when Jesus enters in the totality of his being, through the resurrection, into the dimension of the Father.

THE PERFECTION OF JESUS AS HUMAN. In this new depth of oneness with ABBA, there is also the perfection of Jesus precisely as distinct from the Father. The resurrection does not absorb Jesus into the Father in the sense that he no longer exists in his subjective consciousness[49] or no longer exists as human. That would be the equivalent of denying that God is Love for it would denote the destruction of the beloved as a person, as an individual. The resurrection rather perfects Jesus in who he is: our brother, an individual. The Easter event is the fullest and most novel exemplification of the dictum that love not only cancels division but also constitutes the person loved precisely as another.

NEW DEPTH OF UNION WITH THE SPIRIT. There is for the Risen Christ a depth of union with the Spirit which was never possible when caught up in the limitedness and the distortion of this life.[50] The resurrection is the suffusion of the body/soul unity of Jesus with the Spirit; it is the Spirit which renders him a "spiritual body" as Paul puts it (1 Cor 15:44–46), a body totally penetrated with the Spirit of love. This is, as we have seen, the very resurrection itself: the Trinity so sharing the Spirit with the totality of this man Jesus in that absolute, loving surrender of death that Jesus is now in the realm of YHWH.

AVAILABILITY FOR ALL PEOPLES. Beyond time/space categories, the Risen One has not gone away from us. He is risen so that he may now insert himself with power into the life of all people. The somatic resurrection proclaims that Jesus is still interrelated with this universe as one of us and for us. In fact, as the risen one he is more deeply enmeshed with this world than was ever possible when bound by the strict limitations of this life.[51] Outside of time, he embraces all time. Not in an *ophthe* experience, but in a true encounter nonetheless, the Risen One meets each person in and through the Spirit.

THE "APPROVAL" OF JESUS. The resurrection is a vindication of his words and deeds, of his claims and attitudes. To believe in the resurrection is to accept the Lord as the truth; he is not deluded. His claims to a unique oneness with the Father, his authority to interpret the word of God cannot be doubted by those who know his resurrection. It is the Father's manifest approval of his *Son*. The Easter event is therefore an epiphany: Jesus is clearly manifested to the world precisely as THE beloved, as THE final prophet, as THE beginning of the eschaton.

THE EXALTATION OF JESUS. Jesus truly shares the glory and power of the Father (cf. Phil 3:21; 2 Cor 4:4) for us (cf. Rom 1:3 ff; 2 Cor 12:9; Phil 3:10; 1 Pet 3:22): "he sits at the right hand of Father." Not only will "he come again in glory" but he is now reigning as the Lord in power precisely because he is now the eschaton, he is now the fulfillment, he is now the power of the future.

The exaltation of Jesus must be seen in the context of the cross: he is risen "from the dead." Exaltation, therefore, comes through the total weakness of death.[52]

Through the Cross God reaches out to us in a definitive way and only through the Cross can we go to the Father. Exaltation cannot be considered as something which happens after the Cross; it is what happens in and through the total bodily surrender of Christ crucified.

The title the early Christians use to express this exaltation is "the LORD." All things are subject to him (cf. 1 Cor 15:27–28; Heb 2:8) for as the exalted apex of the cosmos, all meaning, all power, all Life is derived from the Father through him in the power of the Spirit.

THE CONSTITUTION OF THE REIGN OF YHWH. In the Resurrection of Jesus the Kingdom has come with power. The reign of YHWH has fully broken into this world through the transforming eschatological event of the resurrection. In Jesus the forces of evil are now destroyed *in principle* through his cross and the response of the Father in raising the Crucified to his Kingdom. Jesus does not "go to heaven"; rather heaven is the Risen Lord. Accomplished in principle through the life, death and resurrection of Jesus, the Reign has to be implemented through the dynamic Spirit-filled faith of men and women. From our "time" point of view, therefore, we can "look forward" to the parousia when this entire universe will be an eternal cry of praise to the Father through the Son in the power of the Spirit. Jesus as the fulfillment of the Kingdom, as summarizing in himself all creation, is the future of all peoples and of all creation: from the very start, all things were made dependent on the Risen Lord (cf. Col 1:15–20). But we are to pray daily "thy kingdom come," that eschatological prayer for the inevitable victory of this universe in and through the risen Lord who encapsulates in Himself the outcome of the world. "Here on earth the kingdom is mysteriously present; when the Lord comes it will enter into its perfection." [53]

JESUS THE CENTER OF THE UNIVERSE. As the brother of the human race who is now exalted with the Father, Jesus, Risen Lord, is at the center of creation. The fulfillment of salvation history will come about when all peoples, all matter will come to the Center and be one in Christ Jesus to the eternal praise of the Father. [54] To be in harmony with the Center of all is to advance the evolution of this universe toward total harmony with its God. Summarizing in himself all creation as its climax and Risen Lord, he is the goal ahead, the "Alpha and the Omega" (cf. Rev 22:13), the heart of the cosmos. John can summarize Jesus as the center of all by describing the Risen Lord as "The Way, and the Truth and the Life" (Jn 14:6).

THE IMPLICATIONS OF THE RESURRECTION FOR US

Resurrection has not only meaning for Jesus; it also has profound significance *for us*. [55] One of the reasons for a lethargy in Christianity is a widespread misunderstanding of the Easter event among the followers of Christ. To speak about the resurrection's implications for us demands a faith acceptance of Jesus not as returned to *this* life but as the New Adam, the beginning of a new creation, transformed into the glory of the Father. By taking the literary forms of the Easter narratives in a fundamentalistic sense, Christians destroy the very center of the faith. For to believe that Jesus got up from the sepulcher slab and returned to life with his disciples is definitely not resurrection faith. The implications of the resurrection demand then a faith/knowledge in Christ Risen, as described in the Gospels through its embellished narratives and not as depicted by the majority of religious art, no matter their aesthetic value.

AN UNDERSTANDING OF HISTORY. As revelation is a slow, progressive "lifting of the veil," the Easter event is the final, decisive act to which all events in history tend and from which they ultimately derive their meaning. As in a play, the climactic scene renders everything that went before it intelligible, so too in history, its climactic moment — the resurrection of Jesus — is the fundamental insight into the meaning of this universe and its history. The very beginnings of creation contain as in a seed this unfolding of God's plan of salvation history: all things reach their *kairos* in the death/resurrection of Jesus (cf. Eph 1:3–10). The end, the goal, of all history is anticipated for us in the Easter event. Scriptures view history as not unfolding upon itself, but unfolding toward its author ground and goal, God. The past, the present and future are to be understood in the light of the summit experience of all history: the end time event which has pierced on-going history, the resurrection of the incarnate Wisdom of the Father.

AN UNDERSTANDING OF GOD. It is only in the resurrection that humankind comes to the full self-disclosure of God. In the resurrection, then, God supremely reveals himself; the peak experience of creation is nothing less than the peak self-disclosure of the Ground of all Being, God. The Christian concept of God as omnipotent, dynamic Love, rises or falls with the resurrection. For it is only in the light of the resurrection that the New Testament speaks of God's redemption of humankind, that the divinity of God is so powerfully disclosed. He is a God who from all eternity is *for us*, *with us*, who reaches out to us in victorious Love. In the *ophthe* experience of the disciples, it is ultimately God who is disclosing himself and it is this event which will be ours in the parousia. We know God the Father in the resurrection of his Son.

A NEW VISION OF REALITY. Faith in the resurrection radically determines a person's view of the world and of self since the final outcome of all creation is revealed and *in place* through the resurrection of Jesus. The purpose of history can only be found in its goal and the goal of history has come in the eschatological victory of Jesus Christ. Humankind's purpose then does not come from within history; its goal is in the Risen Lord. The victory is won in the Easter cry: "The Lord has risen indeed!" Jesus, risen from the dead, is our sure hope.

The Christian is then a person of hope. A hope which springs not from idle speculation, not from a tentative analysis of history not from a study of the human psyche: rather, a sure hope which is centered on the known victory of creation in its summit, the Lord. This assurance leads to what the scriptures call "boldness" (cf. Acts 4:13,4:29,4:31; Eph 3:12): the ability to risk all in that trust in God's victory in Christ Jesus. The easter faith accepts realistically however, God's mysterious ways in present history which cannot be logically explained.

This hope has backfired in the course of the history of the christianity. Some, as even the *Second Letter to Timothy* declares (2:17–18), were acting as if *our* resurrection had already taken place. The consequences of such a stance are disastrous, for they may lead to an amoral life and/or a total disregard for the realities of life, living in the dream world of an actual personal easter transformation. Or it shows its head in theories which claim that the world — because of its assured goal — is always on an *upward* evolutionary spiral. Present events, with the possibility of atomic holocausts contradict such misinterpretations of the easter founded hope. This realistic christian hope understands that it also springs from the cross and that all is never "Joy, Joy, Joy!" The implementation of the victory must come as it did for Jesus: there is no short cut to the empty tomb, the only path is over Calvary's hill.

Moreover, such unrealistic hope encloses God within our human plans, forgetting how "inscrutable his ways" (Rom 11:33).

Hope does not give anyone the right to determine how the goal will be implemented. Although the war has been won, many battles may be lost. Although the final chapter has been published, preceding chapters are still being written. And that is the challenge of the easter faith: to remain people of hope in spite of and because of the daily dyings with Christ (cf. 2 Cor 4:8–10).

A new definition of our quest for freedom is also given in the resurrection of Jesus. The liberty which is intrinsic to the victory of easter is a freedom like that of the Risen Christ: *for others*, a freedom to serve and in that service to find fulfillment. To speak of freedom as selfishly "doing one's thing," disregarding the essential interrelatedness of creation, is a contradiction and can only lead to anarchy on a personal and community level. Paul describes both the misunderstanding of christian freedom (1 Cor 6:12; 10:23; Gal 5:1–13) and its correct interpretation: a freedom from sin, death and the law (Rom 6–8). Freedom from sin is the life in the Spirit of the Risen Lord which empowers men and women to place their trust not in the idols of power, prestige, wealth, or to be controlled by over-anxiety, over-concern, or even that "determination" to be a saint, but to totally and freely trust in the Lord. As the victorious risen Lord, he is the Lord of each individual and the freedom which is ours (Gal 5:1,13) is founded upon that conviction of his loving Lordship. This entails obedience to the Lord which is always the necessary ingredient for freedom for only in the obedience of faith can the power of the risen Lord be shared. (cf. the Sermon on the Mount, Mt 5–7).

Freedom also means a freedom from death. Not that a Christian does not die! Yet in a certain sense, there is no death for those who share the Easter faith: "I am the Resurrection and the Life. He who believes in me . . . shall never die." says the Johannine Christ (Jn 11:25–26). Death takes on a meaning through the light of easter: a fuller, eternal sharing in the Father's life through the Risen Lord in the power of the Spirit. The hope of the resurrection transforms the fear of death: "O death, where is thy victory? O death, where is thy sting? The sting of death is sin and the power of sin is the law. But thanks be to God who gives us the victory through our Lord Jesus Christ" (1 Cor 15:54–56).

Yet, like the Lord, death has its existential ambiguities, doubts and pains; again, victory is through the cross. Sharing in his sufferings, the Christian knows he will rise with Christ; our resurrection is assured in the resurrection of the Lord. The Second Vatican Council puts this beautifully: "It is, therefore, through Christ and in Christ that light is thrown on the riddle of suffering and death which, separated from his Gospel, overwhelms us. Christ has risen again, destroying death by his death and has given life abundantly to us so that becoming sons in the Son, we may cry out in the Spirit: Abba, Father."[56]

The freedom granted to us through Easter is also, Paul firmly maintains, a freedom from the law. Pushing aside any discussions concerning the validity of the Torah's regulations for the new Christians (a problem for the early church and for Paul in particular), freedom from the law can be considered from a broader view. The Christian, living in the Spirit of the Risen Christ, is not constrained by the law: Christians accomplish the demands of the Gospel through love, not through servile fear nor self-interest nor self-glorification. It is not a disregard for law; it is a freedom from legalism: obeying the rule just for the sake of the rule or to accomplish a difficult deed or to appear righteous before others. The law is obeyed out of love (cf. Gal 5:13): love for the Lord who is its author, love for the Body of Christ, the church, which is His instrument. Laws which would contradict the law of God cannot be obeyed.[57]

LOVE FOR THE WORLD. Before the ecological movement ever began, Paul could speak of the creation awaiting with eager longing for its fulfillment, because "creation itself will be set free from its bondage to decay and obtain the glorious liberty of the children of God" (Rom 8:19–21). All creation, every molecule of matter is drawn by the Risen Christ to its ultimate fulfillment. The earth is to be respected, held in awe as the handiwork of God destined in some way to share in the glory of Christ. Yet love for the world which typifies the Easter vision, extends especially to its history, its anguish, its yearnings: to all who are citizens of the world. Again, the Second Vatican Council sums up this Christian love for the world which is so intense because of Christ's resurrection on its behalf: "The joy and hope, the grief and anguish of the men of our time, especially of those who are poor and afflicted in any way, are the joy, the hope, the grief and anguish of the followers of Christ as well. Nothing that is genuinely human fails to find an echo in their hearts. For theirs is a community of men, who, united in Christ and guided by the Holy Spirit, press onwards towards the Kingdom of the Father and are bearers of a message of salvation intended for all men. That is why Christians cherish a feeling of deep solidarity with the human race and its history."[58]

When Paul tells us not to be conformed to this age (Rom 12:2), when John speaks of the Christian as not being "of the world" (15:19), the term is used as denoting this world *as not yet turned to its goal*. It is rather the challenge for Christians to be involved with this world to transform it by the love of the Risen Christ. If disengagement from the world and its problems were the motive for the life of the hermit or the monk, it would not be christian; it would be a selfish escape. The Christian must be immersed in the world. The monk or nun must see in the cloistered life an even more intense involvement with the anguish and problems of this world as they immerses themselves more deeply into the center of all, the Risen Lord. The yearning for true political freedom, the cry of the outcast, the disenfranchised, the prejudiced, the poor must all resonate within the heart of a Christian who sees reality in the light of the victory of Christ.

A COMMUNITY OF BELIEVERS. All those who share through faith in the life of the Risen Lord form one Body: "we, though many, are one body in Christ" (Rom 12:5; cf.1 Cor 10:17; 12:12–28). A dynamic "communioning" in the Spirit of the Risen Lord marks the believers in the new life of Christ. This new community is intrinsic to the understanding of the resurrection of Christ with its sharing of one life by all who believe in him. Just as it was in the community meals, especially in the Last Supper that Jesus shared his life, as it was through his words and deeds that reconciliation, healing and peace were proclaimed, so too through the sharing among believers the life of the Risen Lord is effectively proclaimed. This "communioning" — the Church — is then the privileged *locus* of encounters with the Risen Lord. We hear his word through those who have been designated for this office; we share his life in eucharistic meal; we share in the reconciliation brought by the Risen Christ to his disciples who had deserted him, as we enter into the life of the community which is the Body of Christ. The sacraments of the Church, therefore, need no "official" words of institution[59] for they are the actions of the community of Christ, the actions when the church exercises itself to the fullest as the Body of Christ. These supremely efficacious proclamations of the community are the words of the Risen Lord who shares life in community. They are our analogous *ophthe* experiences in this interim period as we await the final and full *ophthe* when he comes again in glory as the fulfillment of the destiny of all creation.

The faith-experience in the Risen Lord is the source of the Church's apostolate. Although recognizing the mysterious ways of God, the followers of the Lord are to proclaim by example and word the eschatological victory which is ours in Christ Jesus. However the Christian must always remember that "since Christ died for all and since all men are in fact called to one and the same destiny which is divine, we must hold that the Holy Spirit offers to all the possibilities of being made partners, in a way known to God, in the paschal mystery."[60]

Summary

No better summary of the theological implications of the resurrection faith, no better conclusion of our study could be given than by quoting Paul:

"So we do not lose heart. Though our outer nature is wasting away, our inner nature is being renewed every day. For this slight momentary affliction is preparing for us an eternal weight of glory beyond all comparison because we look not to the things that are seen but to the things that are unseen; for the things that are seen are transient but the things that are unseen are eternal. For we know that if the earthly tent we live in is destroyed, we have a building from God, a house not made with hands, eternal in the heavens. Here indeed, we groan and long to put on our heavenly dwelling so that by putting it on we may not be found naked. For while we are still in this tent, we sigh with anxiety; not that we would be unclothed but that we should be further clothed so that what is mortal may be swallowed up by life. He who has prepared us for this very thing is God, who has given us the Spirit as a guarantee. So we are always of good courage . . ." (2 Cor 4:16–5:6).

ABBREVIATIONS

JBC   R. E. Brown, J. A. Fitzmyer, and R. E. Murphy (eds.), *The Jerome Biblical Commentary.* Englewood Cliffs, NJ: Prentice Hall, 1968.

APOT   R. H. Charles, *The Apocrypha and Pseudigrapha of the Old Testament in English.* 2 vols. Oxford: Clarendon Press, 1913.

Vatican II A. P. Flannery, ed., *The Documents of Vatican II*, New York: Pillar Books, 1975.

DB   J. L. McKenzie, *Dictionary of the Bible.* New York: Macmillan Publishing Co., 1965.

TD   *Theology Digest*, Bernhard. A. Asen, ed., Saint Louis University.

DBT   X. Leon-Dufour, ed., *Dictionary of Biblical Theology.* New York: Seabury Press, 1973.

TDNT   G. Kittel and G. Friedrich, eds., *Theological Dictionary of the New Testament.* 10 vols. Grand Rapids: Wm. B. Eerdmans, 1964–1976. Word study reference listed alphabetically by Greek words. Although often difficult reading, it contains a mine of information. The *Index*, Vol. X, gives a listing in English of where topics may be found.

SM   K. Rahner, ed., *Encyclopedia of Theology: The Concise Sacramentum Mundi.* New York: Seabury Press, 1975.

TI   K. Rahner, *Theological Investigations,* vols 1–20. Baltimore: Helicon Press, 1961–1981.

FOOTNOTES

INTRODUCTION

[1]Karl Rahner. "Theology," *SM*, p. 1689. The entire article by Rahner on the nature of theology is an important introduction to the study of christology. Much of what is said here concerning *theology* is taken from Rahner; see also K. Rahner, "Theology and Magisterium: Self-Appraisals," *TD*, 29:3, pp. 257–261.

[2]cf. R . E. Brown, *Biblical Exegesis & Church Doctrine* (New York: Paulist Press, 1985), pp. 26–53, where Brown explains the development of dogma. My difference with Brown's excellent presentation is with the terminology, "the right of the church to move *beyond* the Scriptures" (p. 29, italics added). Brown makes it eminently clear that *beyond* does not mean that the church is exempt from the scriptural norm. Nonetheless, the term *beyond*, taken out of context (as is so often done) can imply just the opposite of what Brown intends.

[3]Karl Rahner, "Theology," *SM*, p. 1689.

SECTION ONE: INTRODUCTION TO GOSPEL PORTRAITS

[1]The question of the existence of Jesus is hardly treated by theologians. W. Kasper's comment on the topic is typical: "In the early years of this century, various theses were propounded which all assert that Jesus never lived, and that the story of Jesus is a myth or legend. These claims have long since been exposed as historical nonsense." W. Kasper, *Jesus the Christ* (New York: Paulist Press, 1976), p. 65. R. Bultmann who states categorically that the personality of Jesus "has no particular significance," also sharply says: "Of course the doubt as to whether Jesus really existed is unfounded and not worth refutation. No sane person can doubt that Jesus stands as founder behind the historical movement whose first distinct stage is represented by the oldest Palestinian community." *Jesus and the Word* (New York: Charles Scribner's Sons, 1958), pp. 13–14. Nonetheless, the topic was one of the more debated questions among the many hundreds of "telecomputer students" of this christology course as it is for those beginning christology especially college undergrads. The question concerning the existence of Jesus appears to be a topic of interest to a great number of people, perhaps because they have been exposed to the "historical nonsense" of books like J. M. Allegro, *The Sacred Mushroom and the Cross* (Garden City, N.Y.: Doubleday, 1970). Even G. A. Wells who specializes in trying to demonstrate that Jesus is most likely a mythical character, speaks of the "obvious extravagance" of Allegro's work: *The Historical Evidence for Jesus* (Buffalo, N.Y.: Prometheus Books, 1982), p. 218.

[2]For studies dealing with this question, see G. Wells, *The Historical Evidence for Jesus*.

[3]W. B. Smith, *The Birth of the Gospel: A Study of the Origin and Purport of the Primitive Allegory of the Jews*, ed. A. Gulick (New York: Philosophical Library, 1957), p. 142; G. Wells, *The Historical Evidence*, attempts an erudite study of the comments of Christian scholars in order to come to the conclusion that ". . . critical theologians themselves provide(s) a basis for taking more seriously the hypothesis that Christianity did not begin with a Jesus who lived on earth" (p. 218). Wells not only stresses the works of the right and left wing theologians but more seriously, never seems to grasp the nature of the literary genre "Gospel," with its embellishments and adaptations. To conclude from the divergences in the Scriptures to the non-historicity of Jesus requires an impossible logical leap.

[4]For a list of the New Testament booklets with the more probable dates of composition, see R. E. Brown, "Canonicity," *JBC*, 67:57. Brown follows the common opinion that Paul's letters to the Christians at Thessalonika are the earliest New Testament writings, dating from the early 50's, and 2 Peter is the chronologically last booklet written around 125 A.D. J. A. T. Robinson, *The Redating of the New Testament* (Philadelphia: Westminster Press, 1976) claims that the *entire* New Testament was composed before the destruction of Jerusalem, 70 A.D. His thesis has not met with general acceptance; see the review of Robinson's thesis by J. Fitzmyer, *Interpretation* 32 (1978), pp. 309–313.

[5]For a study of the differences between John and the Synoptics, see R. E. Brown, *The Gospel According to John (i–xii)* (Garden City, N.Y.: Doubleday & Company, 1966) pp. XLII–LI.

[6]G. Wells, *The Historical Evidence*, p. ix.

[7]Pliny, *Letters*, 10.96, 7.; see A. Sherwin-White, *Fifty Letters of Pliny* (New York: Oxford University Press, 1967).

[8]Suetonius, *Lives of the Twelve Caesars* (New York: Modern Library, 1959), 25.4, p. 226.

[9]Tacitus, *Annals*, 15.44 (Cambridge: Harvard University Press, 1931), Vol. IV.

[10]H. C. Kee, *Jesus in History: An Approach to the Study of the Gospels* (New York: Harcourt Brace Jovanovich, Inc, 1977), pp. 47–48. For an opposing view, see G. Wells, *The Historical Evidence*, pp. 16–17.

[11]The complete works of Josephus which include *The Jewish Wars, The Antiquities of the Jews, Against Apion* and a short biography can be found in the one volume *The Works of Josephus* (Peabody, Mass: Hendrickson Publishers, 1985), translated by W. Whiston (+ 1752).

[12]Josephus, *Antiquities*, 18.3.3.

[13]This appears to be the view of Whiston given in his wordy *Dissertation I* of the *Appendix* to *The Works of Josephus*, pp. 639–647.

[14]J. Fitzmyer, *A Christological Catechism: New Testament Answers* (New York: Paulist Press, 1982), p. 11, summarizes his conclusions concerning this longer quote: ". . . that testimony is widely suspected of being at least partly interpolated by Christian glossators of manuscripts of Josephus, if not wholly so."

[15]Josephus, *Antiquities*, 20.9.1.

[16]H. C. Kee, *Jesus in History*, p. 46.

[17]*The Mishnah*, translated by H. Danby (London: Oxford University Press, 1933).

[18]J. Klausner, *Jesus of Nazareth* (New York: Macmillan, 1925; Boston: Beacon Press, 1964), p. 46.

[19]The use of the terms "historical," "historic," varies in theological writings. The distinction between the two terms stems from the German, *Historie* and *Geschichte*. In the Pontifical Biblical Commission's April 1983 report on *Bible and Christology*, the term *Historie* is used to mean "the truth of this fact can be proved by historical investigation." J. Fitzmyer, *Scripture & Christology: A Statement of the Biblical Commission with a Commentary* (New York: Paulist Press, 1986), p. 11 (paragraph 1.1.6.2. of the Statement of the Biblical Commission). Fitzmyer comments on the usage of *Historie* and *Geschichte*, pp. 73–74. Fitzmyer's translation of the Biblical Commission's text and his commentary originally appeared in *Theological Studies* 46 (1985) 407–479.

[20]Practically G. Wells' entire book, *The Historical Existence for Jesus* is devoted to demonstrating that the New Testament is NOT reliable.

[21]This opinion was held by a number of theologians of the *Quest of the Historical Jesus* as will be seen in the following chapters.

[22]See the critique found in the Biblical Commission's 1983 Report concerning the "postulating the integral 'historical' truth of everything, even the most minute details found in the Gospel texts." 1.1.3.1. cf. J. Fitzmyer, *Scripture & Christology*, p. 6, and Fitzmyer's commentary, pp. 63–65. The Biblical Commission cites some of what were the more popular books dealing with "The Life of Christ" as examples of this view, e.g., F. Prat, *Jesus Christ: His Life, His Teaching and His Work* (2 vols.; Milwaukee: Bruce, 1950); G. Ricciotti, *The Life of Christ* (Milwaukee: Bruce, 1947). (References supplied by Fitzmyer, p. 64, note 147.) Fitzmyer rightly declares that it was the attitude of the early Biblical Commission which "cast a dark cloud of fear over Catholic biblical studies in the first part of this century and induced a mentality of suspicion about any kind of critical or historical study of the Gospels and the NT . . ." (p. 64). A *Life of Christ* was often required reading in seminaries right up to recent times and exercised great influence in forming a conservative if not fundamentalistic understanding of the Gospels among those in ministry. The pendulum has swung to the opposite extreme — which should be expected — in many of the "younger generation" and has, therefore, even more deeply entrenched the ultraconservatives in their views.

[23]On the validity of the typical sense of Scripture and also of the accommodation of scripture to a variety of circumstances, see R. E. Brown, "Hermeneutics," *JBC*, 71:71–81.

[24]For a description of these difficulties in the early Church, see J. N. D. Kelly, *Early Christian Doctrines* (New York: Harper & Row, 1978) pp. 64–78.

[25]Like many of the Founding Fathers of the United States, Deists look for a natural religion which can be agreed upon by all, regardless of the positive historical and theological differences among the various faiths; cf. J. Livingston, *Modern Christian Thought: From the Enlightenment to Vatican II* (New York: The Macmillan Company, 1971), pp. 12–37.

[26]For a brief but excellent study of Reimarus and Lessing, see Livingston, *Modern Christian Thought*, pp. 30–35; for excerpts of Reimarus' writings, see C. Talbert, ed., *Reimarus: Fragments* (Philadelphia: Fortress Press, 1970).

[27]The classic work on this topic is A. Schweitzer, *The Quest of the Historical Jesus* (New York: Macmillan, 1964). cf. J. Kselman, "Modern New Testament Criticism," *JBC*, 41:1–13; for a summary and critique of the Jesus-quests based upon the insights of David Tracy, see W. Thompson, *The Jesus Debate: A Survey & Synthesis* (New York: Paulist Press, 1985), pp. 90–107.

[28]For an overview of *Q* see H. C. Kee, *Jesus in History*, pp. 76–119 and R. Worden, "Redaction Criticism of Q: A Survey," *Journal of Biblical Literature* 94 (1975), pp. 532–546.

[29]For an overview of F. Schleiermacher's contribution to christology, see D. Duling, *Jesus Christ Through History* (New York: Harcourt Brace Jovanovich, 1979), pp. 159–163; a more detailed study of Schleiermacher is found in J. Livingston, *Modern Christian Thought*, pp. 96–114. cf. also R. Niebuhr, *Schleiermacher on Christ and Religion* (New York: Charles Scribner's Sons, 1964).

[30]D. Strauss, *The Life of Jesus Critically Examined*, ed. P. Hodgson (Philadelphia: Fortress Press, 1972). Perhaps the best insight into D. Strauss' thought is found in A. Schweizer, *Quest of the Historical Jesus*, pp. 68–120. cf. also J. Livingston, *Modern Christian Thought*, pp. 173–180.

[31]cf. J. Livingston, *Modern Christian Thought*, pp. 180–187.

[32]E. Renan, *The Life of Jesus* (New York: Modern Library, 1955). For a summary of Renan's work, see D. Duling, *Jesus Christ*, pp. 190–196.

[33]cf. A. Harnack, *What is Christianity* (New York: Harper & Row, 1957); J. Livingston, *Modern Christian Thought*, pp. 257–262; J. Kselman, "Modern New Testament Criticism," *JBC*, 41:13.

[34] R. Bultmann, *Jesus Christ and Mythology* (New York: Charles Scribner's Sons, 1958), p. 13.

[35] A. Schweitzer, *The Quest of the Historical Jesus;* D. Duling, *Jesus Christ,* pp. 228–233.

[36] G. Tyrell, *Christianity At the Crossroads* (London, 1963) p. 49.

[37] cf. D. Tracy, *The Analogical Imagination: Christian Theology and the Culture of Pluralism* (New York: Crossroad, 1981) pp. 249, 254–259.

[38] For an overview of *myth* in the Scriptures, see N. Perrin, D. Duling, *The New Testament: An Introduction*, 2nd ed. (New York: Harcourt Brace Jovanovich, 1982), pp. 47–60; W. Kasper, *Jesus the Christ*, pp. 43–48; J. McKenzie, "Aspects of Old Testament Thought," in *JBC*, 77:23–31; H. Fries, "Myth," *SM*, pp. 1011–1016.

[39] Among the major works of Bultmann are the following: *The History of the Synoptic Tradition* (New York: Harper & Row, 1968, from the second German edition, 1931); *The Theology of the New Testament* (New York: Charles Scribner's Sons, 1955, first published in German in 1949, 1951); *Jesus and the Word* (New York: Charles Scribner's Sons, 1958, first published in German in 1926); *Jesus Christ and Mythology* (New York: Charles Scribner's Sons, 1958), a compilation of lectures given at various institutions in the United States. Commentaries on the works of Bultmann abound, e.g., G. Bornkamm, "The Theology of Rudolf Bultmann," in *The Theology of Rudolf Bultmann*, ed. C. Kegley (New York: Harper & Row, 1966), pp. 3–20; W. Schmithals, *An Introduction to the Theology of Rudolf Bultmann* (Minneapolis: Augusburg Publishing House, 1968); A. Malet *The Thought of Rudolf Bultmann* (Garden City, N.Y.: Doubleday & Company, 1971); M. Ashcraft, *Rudolf Bultmann* (Waco, Texas: Word Books, 1972); T. O'Meara & D. Weisser, eds., *Rudolf Bultmann in Catholic Thought* (New York: Herder and Herder, 1968).

[40] Bultmann belongs to the existentialist school of thought, an umbrella title which covers thinkers like Kierkegaard, Heidegger, Buber, Marcel, Sartre, Camus. The existentialist never starts with an abstract concept, e.g., faith, and then attempts to squeeze one's experience into it. Rather if *faith* does "exist" it is found *through* my experience and through my participation in the experience of others. This personal experience also entails that truth is only fully possessed when a person "makes it his/her own" by integrating it in one's life. The Existentialists accept — without morbidity — the fact that human beings are finite, limited, that anxiety (*Angst*, which is a quality of human existence and has no direct object as fear does), doubt, guilt, death are inescapable even though inexplicable realities. Authentic existence gives our lives meaning, a significance, a freedom while being-in-the-world. The christian existentialist theologian sees faith in Jesus Christ as "setting us free from the bondage" of unauthentic existence and bestowing on us the authentic existence of the freedom of the children of God. Other existentialists like Satre, Camus have sought for that authentic existence within the framework of atheism. cf. J. Livingston, *Modern Christian Thought*, pp. 345–384.

[41] cf. R. Bultmann, *Jesus and the Word*, pp. 13–14.

[42] R. Bultmann, *Jesus and the Word*, p. 11.

[43] R. Marle, "Demythologization," *SM*, p. 337.

[44] cf. C. Anderson, *The Historical Jesus: A Continuing Quest* (Grand Rapids: Wm. B. Eerdmans Publishing Co., 1972). Anderson, a conservative Protestant scholar, while strongly upholding *sola fide* sharply criticizes Bultmann for his understanding of the phrase, pp. 66–67, 154, 175–176.

[45] cf. R. E. Brown, P. J. Cahill, *Biblical Tendencies Today: An Introduction to the Post-Bultmannians* (Washington, D.C.: Corpus, 1969); D. Duling, *Jesus Christ*, pp. 281–283.

[46] E. Kasemann, "The Problem of the Historical Jesus," in *Essays on New Testament Themes* (London: SCM Press, 1964), pp. 15-47. For a bibliography on the post-Bultmannians, see R. E. Brown, P. J. Cahill, *Biblical Tendencies Today.*

[47] E. Fuchs, "The Quest of the Historical Jesus," in *Studies of the Historical Jesus* (London: SCM Press, 1964), pp. 11–31.

[48] G. Bornkamm, *Jesus of Nazareth* (New York: Harper & Row, 1960).

[49] cf. J. M. Robinson, *A New Quest of the Historical Jesus and other essays* (Philadelphia: Fortress Press, 1983), especially pp. 66–72. For an anthology of essays on aspects of the new quest and related topics, see H. K. McArthur, ed., *In Search of the Historical Jesus* (New York: Charles Scribner's Sons, 1969).

[50] G. Ebeling, "The Question of the Historical Jesus and the Problem of Christology," in *Word and Faith* (Philadelphia: Fortress Press, 1960), pp. 288–304, *The Nature of Faith* (Philadelphia: Fortress Press, 1961).

[51] cf. N. Perrin, *Rediscovering the Teaching of Jesus* (New York: Haper & Row, 1967), pp. 39–47; R. H. Fuller, *A Critical Introduction to the New Testament* (London: Duckworth, 1966), pp. 94–98; M. Cook, *The Jesus of Faith: A Study in Christology* (New York: Paulist Press, 1981) pp. 31–34.

[52] J. Jeremias, *New Testament*, p. 37.

[53] cf. J. M. Robinson, J. B. Cobb, Jr., *The New Hermeneutic* (New York: Harper & Row, 1964); P. Achtemeier, *An Introduction to the New Hermeneutic* (Philadelphia: Westminster Press, 1969); A. C. Thiselton, "The New Hermeneutic" in I. H. Marshall, ed., *New Testament Interpretation: Essays on Principles and Methods* (Grand Rapids: Wm. B. Eerdmans Publishing Co., 1977), pp. 308–333.

[54] The term has its roots in *Hermes (Mercury)*, the god who delivers messages from the gods and interprets them for the recipients. See Acts 14:12 where Barnabas and Paul are called Zeus and

Hermes: "Barnabas they called Zeus, and Paul, because he was the chief speaker, they called Hermes."

[55]cf. S. Kistemaker, *The Gospels in Current Study* (Grand Rapids: Baker Book House, 1972), pp. 73–75. Kistemaker outlines and criticizes the New Hermeneutic from a conservative, evangelical point of view.

[56]cf. W. Wink, *The Bible in Human Transformation: Towards a New Paradigm for Biblical Study* (Philadelphia: Fortress Press, 1973). Wink is highly critical of New Testament scholars who intentionally suspend any personal involvement in their studies and as a result, the outcome of biblical studies in academia is "a trained incapacity to deal with real problems of actual living persons in their daily lives" (p. 6). Wink berates scholars who raise not the questions proposed by the scriptures, but those which will help them attain a place within the professional group of academicians. A summary of Wink's thought may be found in D. Duling, *Jesus Christ Through History*, pp. 304–308. For a response to similar complaints against contemporary scripture scholars, see R. E. Brown, *Biblical Exegesis & Church Doctrine*, pp. 19–20.

[57]A. Thiselton, "The New Hermeneutic," p. 317. For an insight into the philosophical underpinnings of the post-Bultmannian school, see J. M. Robinson, J. Cobb, eds., *The Later Heidegger and Theology* (New York: Harper & Row, 1963).

[58]cf. J. Reese, *Experiencing the Good News: The New Testament as Communication* (Wilmington: Michael Glazier, Inc., 1984), pp. 47–48.

[59]R. Bultmann, "The Primitive Christian Kerygma and the Historical Jesus," in C. Bratten, R. Harrisville, eds., *The Historical Jesus and the Kerygmatic Christ* (Nashville: Abingdon Press, 1964), pp. 15–42.

[60]J. M. Robinson, *A New Quest of the Historical Jesus*, pp. 5–6.

[61]J. Jeremias, *New Testament Theology* (London: SCM Press, 1971), Vol. I, p. 2.

[62]J. Jeremias, *New Testament Theology*, p. 37; cf. C. Colpe, *TDNT*, Vol. VIII, pp. 432, 434 ff.

[63]G. Ebeling, "Time and Word," in J. M. Robinson, ed., *The Future of our Religious Past: Essays in Honor of Rudolf Bultmann* (London, 1971), p. 265, as quoted by A. Thiselton, "The New Hermeneutic," p. 309.

[64]Considering that for the most part, even these precise words/deeds of Jesus have lost their original context, the ipsissima verba et facta are few indeed.

[65]R. E. Brown, *Biblical Exegesis*, p. 16.

[66]R. F. Smith, "Inspiration and Inerrancy," *JBC*, 66:85. Richard Smith is quoting the *Constitution on Divine Revelation*, n. 11, Vatican II.

[67]A. Thiselton, "The New Hermeneutic," p. 328, italics added.

[68]cf. A. Thiselton, "The New Hermeneutic," p. 325.

[69]cf. K. Lehmann, "Hermeneutics," in *SM*, pp. 611–615.

[70]D. Duling, *Jesus Christ Through History* (New York: Harcourt Brace Jovanovich, 1979)

[71]W. Thompson *The Jesus Debate*, p. 107. cf. D. Tracy, *The Analogical Imagination: Christian Theology and the Culture of Pluralism* (New York: Crossroad Publishing Company, 1981), pp. 258–259: "When we look down the famous "well of history" to search for the real Jesus we may, . . . see only the reflection of our own face (the good liberal Jesus, the revolutionary Jesus, the priestly Jesus, the monastic Jesus, etc.). But as all later classic christological interpretations of the event of Jesus Christ remind us, we may also see, . . . dimly but really, the real Jesus in this Christ."

[72]For a survey of the variety of paths taken by contemporary christology, cf. W. May, *Christ in Contemporary Thought* (Dayton: Pflaum, 1970); W. Thompson, *The Jesus Debate*, pp. 45–89; D. Duling, *Jesus Christ*, pp. 288–312; W. Kasper, "Orientations in Current Christology," *TD*, 32:2, pp. 107–111; an overview and critique of modern approaches to christology is given in the 1983 Pontifical Biblical commission Report on *Bible and Christology*, found in J. Fitzmyer, *Scripture & Christology*, pp. 3–32.

[73]This is presumed in all the recent documents from the Biblical Commission and the International Theological Commission: International Theological Commission, *Select Questions on Christology* (Washington: USCC, 1980), *Theology Christology Anthropology* (Washington: USCC, 1983); Pontifical Biblical Commission, *Bible and Christology* (1983) found in J. Fitzmyer, *Scripture & Christology*, pp. 3–53. Pope Paul VI in speaking about devotion to Mary lists the Bible as the first guideline for the right ordering of devotion to the Mother of God; the same holds true of course for an understanding of Jesus. cf. Pope Paul VI, *Devotion to the Blessed Virgin Mary* (Washington: USCC, 1974); the Second Vatican Council gave a strong impetus to a renewed study of the Scriptures, especially in its *Constitution on Divine Revelation*, stating in no. 24: "Sacred theology relies on the written Word of God taken together with sacred Tradition as on a permanent foundation. By this Word it is most firmly strengthened and constantly rejuvenated, as it searches out, under the light of faith, the full truth stored up in the mystery of Christ. Therefore the 'study of the sacred page' should be the very soul of theology."

[74]cf. K. Rahner, "Magisterium," *SM*, pp. 871–880; H. Fries, J. Finsterholzl, "Infallibility," *SM*, pp. 711–717.

[75]cf. R. E. Brown, *Biblical Exegesis*, pp. 26–53.

[76]See the critique of the Pontifical Biblical Commission (1983 Report) on the approach of classical theology and a clarification of this critique by Fitzmyer, in J. Fitzmyer, *Scripture & Christology*, pp. 19–20, 58–60.

[77]For the theory of "orality" see W. Ong, *Orality and Literacy: The Technologizing of the Word* (New York: Methuen, 1982). For its practical application to the Scriptures, see W. Kelber, *The Oral and the Written Gospel: The Hermeneutics of Speaking and Writing in the Synoptic Tradition, Mark, Paul, and Q* (Philadelphia: Fortress Press, 1983).

[78]cf. W. Kelber, *The Oral and Written Gospel*, pp. 16–22.

[79]"To the extent that the gospel draws on oral voices, it has rendered them voiceless. The voice prints of once-spoken words have been muted . . . language has fallen silent; the ground of Jesus' speech and that of his earliest followers is abandoned. Sayings and stories are rescued, but at the price of their transportation into and . . . transformation by a foreign medium." W. Kelber, *The Oral and Written Gospel*, p. 91.

[80]W. Kelber, *the Oral and Written Gospel*, pp. 102–105.

[81]cf. e.g., Paul Ricoeur, *Interpretation Theory: Discourse and the Surplus of Meaning* (Fort Worth: Texas Christian University, 1976). David Tracy's writings show the strong influence of Ricoeur, e.g., D. Tracy, *Blessed Rage for Order: The New Plualism in Theology* (New York: Seabury Press, 1975) and more recently, *The Analogical Imagination*.

[82]The notion of the "actual" Jesus is studied by D. Tracy, *The Analogical Imagination*, pp. 248 ff.

[83]See Bernard C. Lategan, William S. Vorster, *Text and Reality: Aspects of Reference in Biblical Texts* (Philadelphia: Fortress Press, 1985); Edgar McKnight, *The Bible and The Reader: Introduction to Literary Criticism* (Philadelphia: Fortress Press, 1985); Terrence Keegan, *Interpreting the Bible: A Popular Introduction to Biblical Hermeneutics* (New York: Paulist Press, 1985).

[84]"Neither language nor human self-awareness conceals any reference to things as they are . . . philosophers should not be so pretentious as to maintain they are writing "about" anything . . . The referent of a word, i.e., that which is signified by a token of language, consists primarily in an intransitive jump from sign to sign . . ." Carl Raschke "The Deconstruction of God" in *Deconstruction and Theology* (New York: Crossroad, 1982) pp. 1–32, as found in J. S. O'Leary, *Questioning Back: The Overcoming of Metaphysics in Christian Tradition* (Minneapolis: Winston Press, 1985), pp. 37–38.

[85]J. Fitzmyer, *A Christological Catechism*, p. 121, note 38, speaks of "the more recent fads and trends in interpretation, such as structuralism, or those in hermeneutics, such as the recommendation that what is important is not the intended meaning of the author but what the text, having acquired an autonomy of its own — so it is alleged — may mean to readers today." On the other hand, A. Thiselton, "Semantics and New Testament Interpretation," in I. H. Marshall, ed., *New Testament Interpretation*, p. 100, declares that the interpreter of the New Testament in so far as he is concerned with language and meanings, "can ignore their method [i.e., those involved in language studies] only at his own peril."

[86]See Lynn M. Poland, *Literary Criticism and Biblical Hermeneutics: A Critique of Formalist Approaches* (Decatur, GA.: Scholars Press, 1985).

[87]cf. J. O'Leary, *Questioning Back*, p. 1: "Metaphysics has been normative for Western thinking for two and a half millennia, the governing Logos of our culture, identical with the force of reason itself. Yet it has increasingly become a fact that we are no longer at home in metaphysics, that it no longer chimes with reality as it used to. Metaphysics has become questionable in a radical sense . . ."

[88]cf. W. Thompson, *The Jesus Debate*, pp. 15–42; Vatican Council II, *Pastoral Constitution on the Church in the Modern World*, no. 1, which sets the tone for the entire *Constitution*: "The joy and hope, the grief and anguish of the people of our time, especially of those who are poor and afflicted in any way, are the joy and hope, the grief and anguish of the followers of Christ as well. Nothing that is genuinely human fails to find an echo in their hearts."

[89]Many have claimed that the Shroud of Turin provides us with an exact picture of Jesus. Whether it does or not is not of particular interest to the theologian for such items are irrelevant to christology. For a study of the extreme difficulties in identifying the Shroud of Turin as that of Jesus, see R. E. Brown, *Biblical Exegesis*, pp. 147–155.

[90]Apocryphal Gospels are non-canonical books as will be seen in more detail. Concerning these apocryphal Gospels, like the famous *Protoevangelium of James*, R. E. Brown comments: " . . . it may be said almost without exception that such attempts to fill in blank spots in the life of Jesus do not preserve real historical memories." R. E. Brown, "Apocrypha," *JBC*, 68:54. These so-called Gospels were rejected by the Christian communities since they did not in their eyes faithfully reflect the faith of the early Christians.

[91]Private revelations are directed to an individual(s) but not directly to the Church at large; they appear to be "within the framework of the charismatic element in the Church" and "must stay within the general revelation given to the Church, although this does not mean that the private revelation may not contain an imperative with a ''new' direction." K. Rahner, "Private Revelation," *SM*, pp. 1471–1473. Since any approved private revelation is within the framework of the general revelation given to the

Church and to be judged by public revelation (and not vice-versa), if they are included in a theology course it is only as an explicitation of a truth already known.

[92]J. M. Robinson, *A New Quest*, p. 68.

[93]E. Schillebeeckx, *Jesus: An Experiment in Christology* (New York: Seabury Press, 1979), p. 259 (italics added: in his behaviour).

[94]J. Fitzmyer, *Scripture & Christology*, p. 45.

[95]cf. R. E. Brown, *The Community of the Beloved Disciple: The Life, Loves, and Hates of an Individual Church in New Testament Times* (New York: Paulist Press, 1979), p. 29.

[96]J. Fitzmyer, *A Christological Catechism*, p. 111, note 27 uses this expression in his commentary on the Biblical Commission's 1964 *Instruction* on the historical truth of the Gospels. The Biblical Commission repudiated those who "make light of the authority of the apostles as witnesses to Christ, and of their task and influence in the primitive community, extolling rather the creative power of that community." (Text as found in J. Fitzmyer, *A Christological Catechism*, p. 133.) Fitzmyer, therefore, recommends that instead of using the term "creation" by the early christian community of a story about Jesus, that the word "formation" be employed so that people will not think that the story is a "fabrication out of whole cloth."

[97]*Dogmatic Constitution on Divine Revelation*, no. 19., Vatican II (italics added).

[98]cf. J. Fitzmyer's commentary on this specific point of the Pontifical Biblical Commission's 1964 *Instruction* on the historical truth of the Gospels, *A Christological Catechism*, pp. 128–129; X. Leon-Dufour, *The Gospels and the Jesus of History* (Garden City: Image Books, 1970), "The Reliability of Traditions about Jesus," pp. 209–214; V. Taylor, "The Historical Value of the Gospel Tradition," *In Search of the Historical Jesus*, pp. 74–81.

[99]See R. E. Brown, *The Birth of the Messiah: A Commentary on the Infancy Narratives in Matthew and Luke* (Garden City: Doubleday & Company, 1977), pp. 547–556.

[100]F. Bruce, *The New Testament Documents: Are They Reliable?* (Grand Rapids: Wm. B. Eerdmans Publishing, 1960), p. 15.

[101]S. Smalley, "Redaction Criticism," *New Testament Interpretation: Essays on Principles and Methods*, I. H. Marshall, ed. (Grand Rapids: Wm. B. Eerdmans Publishing, 1977), pp. 188–189.

[102]cf. W. Kelber, *The Oral and Written Gospel*, pp. 16–19.

[103]W. Ong, *Orality and Literacy*, p. 46.

[104]W. Ong, *Orality and Literacy*, p. 41.

[105]G. O'Collins, *Interpreting Jesus* (Ramsey: Paulist Press, 1983), pp 43–45.

[106]W. Kelber, *The Oral and Written Gospel*, p. 11; for an excellent summary and critique of Gerhardsson's thesis, see Kelber, pp. 8–14. An excerpt of B. Gerhardsson's thesis of a *professional* transmission of traditions about Jesus is found in H. K. MacArthur, ed., *In Search of the Historical Jesus*, pp. 33–40.

[107]cf. D. Harrington, *Interpreting the New Testament: A Practical Guide* (Wilmington: Michael Glazier, 1979). pp. 1–15.

[108]cf. I. H. Marshall, "Historical Criticism," *New Testament Interpretation*, pp. 126–138; D. Harrington, *Interpreting the New Testament*, pp. 85–95.

[109]R. E. Brown, *The Birth of the Messiah: A Commentary on the Infancy Narratives in Matthew and Luke* (Garden City: Doubleday & Company, 1977).

[110]cf. F. Gast, "Synoptic Problem," *JBC*, 40: 1–25; N. Perrin, D. Duling, *The New Testament: An Introduction*, second edition (New York: Harcourt Brace Jovanovich, 1982), pp. 66–69; D. Harrington, *Interpreting the New Testament*, pp. 56–69; D. Wenham, "Source Criticism," *New Testament Interpretation*, pp. 139–152.

[111]cf. R. Pesch, "Form Criticism," *SM*, pp. 525–528; S. Travis, "Form Criticism," *New Testament Interpretation*," pp. 153–164; E. V. McKnight, *What is Form Criticism?* (Philadelphia: Fortress Press, 1969); A. Wikenhauser, "Assessment of Form Criticism," *In Search of the Historical Jesus*, pp. 68–73.

[112]The tunnel period stretches from about 30 A.D. to at least 50 A.D. if we end the tunnel at Q or Paul's writings; to 67 A.D. if we would think that the tunnel should end with the chronologically first Gospel, Mark.

[113]J. Fitzmyer speaks of Cardinal Bea using a version of this important phrase in his 1935 edition of a book on inspiration; see J. Fitzmyer, *A Christological Catechism: New Testament Answers*, p. 118, note 34.

[114]INSPIRATION is the special assistance given by God to the human author so what is written will express the mind of God. Early christians came to the conclusion that certain letters, booklets, were inspired because the writings so powerfully and authentically mirrored the faith.

[115]cf. N. Perrin, *What is Redaction Criticism?* (Philadelphia: Fortress Press, 1971); D. Harrington, *Interpreting the New Testament*, pp. 96–107; S. Smalley, "Redaction Criticism," *New Testament Interpretation*, pp. 181-192.

[116]S. Smalley, "Redaction Criticism," pp. 191-192.

[117]For a highly critical view of these tools from a strongly conservative writer, see S. Kistemaker, *The Gospels in Current Study*, pp. 35–61.

[118]The *Text* and a *Commentary* are found in J. Fitzmyer, *A Christological Catechism*, pp. 97–140.

[119]*Dogmatic Constitution on Divine Revelation*, Vatican Council II, no. 19.

[120]J. Fitzmyer, *A Christological Catechism*, p. 115.

[121]For Catholics, there can be no doubt that the church approves and encourages the analyses of Scripture mentioned in this chapter. It is strange, therefore, to still hear some members of the Church disparaging the historical-critical study of the word of God and accusing some of the most faithful scripture scholars of infidelity to the magisterium of the Church.

SECTION TWO: THE DISCLOSURE WORDS

[1]cf. 1983 *Report* of the Pontifical Biblical Commission, *Bible and Christology*, in J. Fitzmyer, *Scripture & Christology*, pp. 24–25.

[2]C. Pozo, *The Credo of the People of God: A Theological Commentary* (Chicago: Franciscan Herald Press, 1980), p. 211, which is reprinted from the *Allocutio* of Paul VI on July 3, 1968, published in *L'Osservatore Romano*, July 4, 1968. Most of the published copies of the *Credo of the People of God* omit this important commentary by Paul VI.

[3]J. Fitzmyer, *Scripture & Christology*, p. 25 for the *Text* of the Commission, p. 75 for the *Commentary* on this section.

[4]A covenant is a treaty, a pact to bring about peace. Applied to the Jewish people, it denotes the unique love of YHWH for them which they experienced especially in the Exodus from Egypt and which they interpreted as a covenant which God initiated with them.

[5]cf. *Dogmatic Constitution on Divine Revelation*, n. 10, Vatican Council II.

[6]"Statements of historical personalities can so embody their feelings and a consciousness (or conviction) as to their own significance, even if only at a particular point in their lives, that we today can know something of their feelings and sense something of that consciousness through these same statements." J. D. G. Dunn, *Christology in the Making: A New Testament Inquiry into the Origins of the Doctrine of the Incarnation* (Philadelphia: Westminster Press, 1980), pp. 25–26.

[7]J. Jeremias, *New Testament Theology*, p. 67. For other studies on the term ABBA see, e.g., J. Jeremias, *The Prayers of Jesus* (London: SCM Press, 1967), pp. 11–65, *New Testament Theology*, pp. 61–68, *The Central Message of the New Testament* (London: SCM Press, 1965), pp. 9–30; M. Cook, *The Jesus of Faith: A Study in Christology* (New York: Paulist Press, 1981), 47–51; E. Schillebeeckx, *Jesus*, pp. 256–271; J. D. G. Dunn, *Christology in the Making*, pp. 26–28.

[8]cf. G. Schrenk, *TDNT*, Vol. V, p. 985.

[9]G. Screnk, *TDNT*, Vol V, p. 985, discussing ABBA, says: "This basic word tells us that God is not a distant Ruler in transcendence but One who is intimately close."

[10]Protocanonical books are recognized by all Christians as part of the Old Testament. Deuterocanonical books of the Old Testament are recognized as canonical by Catholics, the Orthodox Churches, and some Anglicans — with some variations on the number of the books accepted. Protestants list the deuterocanonical books as the *Apocrypha*. The books involved are 1 & 2 Esdras (at times referred to as 3 & 4 Esdras since the Book of Ezra used to be called 1 Esdras and the Book of Nehemiah, 2 Esdras), Tobit, Judith, Wisdom, Sirach (Ecclesiasticus), Baruch with the Letter of Jeremiah, 1 and 2 Maccabees, Additions to the books of Daniel and Esther and the Prayer of Manasseh; among these books called "apocryphal" by Protestants, Catholics recognize all as canonical except 1 & 2 Esdras and the Prayer of Manasseh. The non-canonical books of the Old Testament which are called "apocryphal" by Catholics are classified as the the "pseudepigrapha" by Protestants. They include 1 & 2 Esdras, 3 & 4 Maccabees, Book of Jubilees, Books of Adam and Eve, the Martyrdom of Isaiah, Psalms of Solomon, Books of Enoch, the Sibylline Oracles, Books of Baruch, the Assumption of Moses. For a concise study of the question and a summary of the books involved, see *DB*, pp. 42–46.

[11]After examining the objections of G. Vermes (*Jesus the Jew: An Historian's Reading of the Gospels* [New York: Macmillan, 1973], pp. 210 ff.) to Jeremias' statement that ABBA as a term for God is not found in Judaism, J. D. G. Dunn, *Christology in the Making*, p. 27, concludes: "the evidence points consistently and clearly to the conclusion that Jesus' regular use of 'abba' in addressing God distinguished Jesus in a significant degree from his contemporaries." For a response to objections that ABBA need not denote an intimate relationship and moreover, that Jesus did not reserve the usage to himself, see I. H. Marshall, *The Origin of New Testament Christology* (Downers Grove: InterVarsity Press, 1976), p. 59 note 11.

[12]Aramaic was the language of the Jews at the time of Jesus (it had supplanted Hebrew — a cognate tongue — during the Babylonian Exile). When the Scriptures were read in Hebrew, it was customary to have someone give an Aramaic paraphrase (TARGUM) in order that the people could understand the sacred text. Since Jesus, an observant Jew, apparently rarely had any dealings with people outside of his little enclave and never travelled outside of the general area of Palestine, it is not likely that he was *fluent* in Greek, the *lingua franca* of the times. Surely he knew the Greek phrases which had crept into the ordinary language of the Palestine of his age or which he may have easily learned as a child

since Galilee had some well settled Greek cities. In fact, the town of Sepphoris, with its gymnasium, its hippodrome and other elements of the typical Greek city of the age, was only four miles from Jesus' childhood home at Nazareth. See J. Fitzmyer, "The Languages of Palestine in the First Century A.D.," *Catholic Biblical Quarterly*, 32, 1970, pp. 501–531.

[13]"This word (i.e., Abba) is always the original of "Father" in the prayers of the Gospels. " G. Schrenk, *TDNT*, Vol. V, p. 985. (The original quote has "Father" written in Greek.)

[14]cf. E. Schillebeeckx, *Jesus*, p. 261.

[15]E. Schillebeeckx, *Jesus*, p. 269. Schillebeeckx is, however, overcautious about the use of ABBA in christological thought, for while admitting that Jesus stands out "in a historico-religious context, purely on the ground of his addressing God as *Abba*, there can be no question, *per se*" (p. 260) he also declares "That Jesus should say *Abba* to God — apart from the great solemnity, holding God at a distance from men, with which people in Jesus' time used to pray to him — makes no essential difference." (p. 259); true, as Schillebeeckx mentions, one cannot logically deduce the Trinity from Jesus' use of ABBA! However, the misuse of ABBA by some theologians seems to have made him too hesitant to explain the full consequences of the mysterious use of ABBA by Jesus.

[16]"Angelus Message," September 10, 1978, in *The Message of John Paul I* (Boston: St. Paul Editions, 1978), p. 100.

[17]cf. W. Kasper *Jesus the Christ*, p. 79.

[18]cf. J. Jeremias, *New Testament Theology*, pp. 178–203, where Jeremias explains Jesus' teaching "on being a child."

[19]E. Schillebeeckx, *Jesus*, p. 270.

[20]H. Schlier, *TDNT* Vol. I, p. 338. The entire article of Schlier on *Amen* should be read: pp. 335-338.

[21]Christian prayer has a privileged place for the "GREAT AMEN" in the eucharistic liturgy, whereby the congregation freely participates in the action, acclaiming it to be true and binding; by freely responding/accepting, the eucharist truly becomes operative in the life of the community and of each individual.

[22]J. Fitzmyer, *Luke I-IX*, p. 536.

[23]R. F. Fuller, *Foundations*, pp. 104–105

[24]R. F. Fuller, *Foundations*, p. 105.

[25]N. Perrin, D. Duling, *The New Testament*, pp. 123–124. For an explanation of *apocalyptic*, see N. Perrin, D. Duling, *The New Testament*, pp. 96–99, 112–123, 237–239, 431–432; *DB*, 41–42; H. C. Kee, *Jesus in History*, pp. 26–27.

[26]J. Jeremias, *New Testament Theology*, p. 36.

[27]"The critical Gk text reads *talitha kum. . .* ; the received text *talitha cumi* is grammatically accurate but represents an editorial correction." *DB*, p. 866.

[28]Quoted by R. Patai, *The Messiah Texts* (Detroit: Wayne State University Press, 1979), p. 199.

[29]cf. D. E. Nineham, *The Gospel of Saint Mark* (New York: Penguin Books, 1963), p. 162.

[30]G. Kittel, *TDNT*, Vol. IV, p. 107; cf. A. Oepke, *TDNT*, Vol. III, p. 210.

[31]D. E. Nineham, *Saint Mark*, p. 428.

SECTION THREE: THE DISCLOSURE TITLES

[1]Some of the works dealing with a study of the titles of Jesus are: R. Fuller, *The Foundations of New Testament Christology*, (New York: Charles Scribner's Sons, 1965); O. Cullmann, *The Christology of the New Testament*, (Philadelphia: The Westminster Press, 1957); F. Hahn, *The Titles of Jesus in Christology: Their History in Early Christianity*, (New York: World Publishing Company, 1969); L. Sabourin, *The Names and Titles of Jesus* (New York: The Macmillian Company, 1967); V. Taylor, *The Names of Jesus* (London: Macmillan & Co Ltd, 1962); D. Stanley, "Titles of Christ," *JBC*, 78:1–61.

[2]V. Taylor, *The Names of Jesus*, p. 1; cf. J. Fitzmyer, *A Christological Catechism, New Testament Answers* (New York: Paulist Press, 1981) p. 84.

[3]D. Stanley, "Titles of Christ," *JBC*, 78:3.

[4]Studies concerning the title *Messiah* are found in the bibliography on the titles of Jesus given above. cf. also W. Grundmann, F. Hesse, H. de Jonge, A. van der Woude, *TDNT*, Vol. IX, pp. 493–580; P. Bonnard, P. Grelot, "Messiah," *DBT*, pp. 312–315; S. Mowinckel, *He That Cometh: The Messiah Concept in the Old Testament and Later Judaism* (Nashville: Abingdon Press, 1956).

[5]cf. S. Mowinckel, *He That Cometh;* J. Becker, *Messianic Expectation in the Old Testament* (Philadelphia: Fortress Press, 1980); "Messiah," in *DBT*, pp. 312–313.

[6]The so-called messianic prophecy is found in the Fourth Eclogue. A translation of the poem and a commentary may be found in R. E. Brown, *Birth*, Appendix IX, pp. 564–570.

[7]The Hellenistic world recognized charismatic elderly women whose "oracles" were held to be from the gods. These women were termed "Sibyls" after a Greek prophetess named Sibyl. The prophecies of these women — and others imitated by Jews and Christians — were composed as *Sybilline Oracles*

and contain a reference to the coming messiah. Excerpts of these *Oracles* may be found in *APOT*, Vol. II, 368–406.

[8]J. Becker, *Messianic Expectation*, p. 87.

[9]On the significance of olive oil in the Old Testament, cf. C. Lesquivit & M. Lacan, "Oil," *DBT*, p. 353.

[10]There is an anti-monarchic strain which runs through Israel's history, for primarily sociological and not so much for religious reasons; monarchy as such was not easily merged with the seminomadic lifestyle of the Israelites, who even after settling in the land of Canaan, retained the tribal, clan structure. cf. R. de Vaux, *Ancient Israel* Vol. I (New York: McGraw-Hill, 1961), pp. 3–15. For literature concerning priestly duties undertaken by the monarchy, cf. R. de Vaux, *Ancient Israel* Vol. II (New York: McGraw-Hill, 1961), pp. 376–377; J. Becker, *Messianic Expectation*, p. 42 is quite forceful: "The kings seem in truth to have been 'priests forever according to the order of Melchizidek' (Ps. 110: 4)."

[11]cf. G. von Rad, *Old Testament Theology*, Vol. I, pp. 334–347.

[12]cf. D. McCarthy, "II Samuel 7 and the Structure of the Deuteronomic History," in *Journal of Biblical Literature*, 84 (1965), pp. 131–138.

[13]cf. J. Becker, *Messianic Expectations*, p. 87.

[14]The Essenes were a strict Jewish sect of "late Judaism," lasting through the time of Jesus up until the the destruction of Judaea by Titus and Vespasian around 70 A.D., with holdouts against the Romans continuing until the beginning of the following century. So disillusioned were they with the political/ religious state of affairs that the members — especially those at their 'monastery' at Qumran near the Dead Sea — totally separated themselves from the ordinary affairs of Israel.

[15]cf. A. van der Woude, *TWNT*, Vol. IX, p. 517, where references to the Qumran Documents may also be found.

[16]A compilation of eighteen Psalms probably composed in the first century B.C. Psalms 17 and 18 yearn for a Davidic messiah. They may be found in *APOT*, Vol. II, pp. 625–652.

[17]Concerning Enoch literature, cf. R. E. Brown, "Apocrypha," *JBC*, 68: 7–15; concerning Esdras literature, cf. R. E. Brown, "Apocrypha," *JBC*, 68:38–41.

[18]Jerome translated this into Latin as 'she', with all of its consequences in mariology; the Hebrew has the neuter 'it', agreeing with 'seed'; the Greek translation of the Old Testament — called the Septuagint [LXX] uses the masculine since 'seed' of a woman is a manner of saying her child.

[19]The original sense of Gen 3:15 is well described by Charles Miller: "It seems clear that Vatican II's mariological reference to Gn 3:15 in LG (*Lumen Gentium, The Constitution on the Church*) is really more an appeal to Tradition than to a proof-text from the Old Testament. Literally, the text says nothing about the woman sharing in the victory of her seed over the serpent, if indeed there be such a victory. Even the patristic tradition itself, furthermore, is not unanimous on the mariological significance of the passage." Charles Miller, *"As it is Written," The Use of Old Testament References in the Documents of Vatican Council II*, St Louis, 1973, p. 56.

[20]A prophet is someone who speaks for another. Prophets speak in the name of God; to foretell is not an essential element of prophecy, even though it erroneously becomes its exclusive meaning in today's parlance.

[21]Deriving the meaning of a text is called *exegesis*; often we impose our preconceptions into the text: *eisegesis*.

[22]cf. R. E. Brown, *Birth,* Appendix IV, pp. 517–531 which also contains an excellent bibliography on the subject; R. E. Brown, *The Virginal Conception and Bodily Resurrection of Jesus* (New York: Paulist Press, 1973); R. E. Brown, *Biblical Exegesis*, especially pp. 35–37; J. McHugh, *The Mother of Jesus in The New Testament* (Garden City, New York: Doubleday & Company Inc., 1975) pp. 269–342.

[23]For a detailed study of the various texts of Is 7:14, see R. E. Brown, *Birth*, pp. 143–149.

[24]There is no doubt as Raymond Brown so firmly maintains (cf. references above) that the Catholic church considers the historical virginal conception a dogma, at least from the ordinary magisterium of the Church.

[25]cf. Vatican II, *The Constitution on The Church*, n. 56: The books of the Old Testament describe the history of salvation by which the coming of Christ into the world was slowly prepared. The earliest documents, as they are read in the Church and are understood in the light of a further and full revelation, bring the figure of a woman, the Mother of the Redeemer, into a gradually clearer light. Considered in this light, she is already prophetically foreshadowed . . ."

[26]Israel was an occupied country at the time of Jesus and hopes were high that the Roman overlords who had even desecrated the Temple would be expelled. Many of the Jews believed that God would intervene to restore Israel to its former glory. cf. Josephus, *Wars of the Jews*, Book II, for a narration of the increasing number of rebellions against Rome from the death of Herod until Vespasian.

[27]J. Becker, *Messianic Expectation*, pp. 93–96.

[28]cf. D. E. Nineham, *Saint Mark* (New York: Penguin Books, 1969) pp. 223–232; Hahn, *Titles*, Excursus III, pp. 223–238; Cullmann, *Christology*, pp. 1232–124; Fuller, *Foundations*, pp. 109–111.

[29]Matthew, typically, enlarges this simple response of Mark to: "You are the Christ, the Son of the living God" (Mt 16:16).

[30]The question "Who do you say that I am?" is the most fundamental in christianity. It is not a "catechism question" to be answered by rote or only when the specific topic arises. Every moment is the question; every moment carries our response. As the clock ticks away, each second bears with it — through the ordinary events of the day — this question of Jesus. And the way one lives, speaks, judges, plans, is the answer being given to the question. This dynamic call-response, question-answer is the quality of every moment of life.

[31]cf. W. Wrede, *The Messianic Secret* (Greenwood, S. C.: Attic Press, 1971).

[32]Matthew's typical enhancement of the situation including the praise of Peter's faith, reflects a post-resurrection embellishment.

[33]cf. J. Fitzmyer, *The Gospel According to Luke I–IX* (Garden City: Doubleday, 1981), pp. 506–520.

[34]G. B. Caird, *Saint Luke* (Baltimore: Penguin Books, 1963), pp. 79–80.

[35]J. Fitzmyer, *Luke I–IX*, p. 512

[36]cf. D. Lane, *The Reality of Jesus* (New York: Paulist Press, 1975), p. 123.

[37]cf. J. Fitzmyer, *Luke X–XXIV* (Garden City: Doubleday, 1985) pp. 1359 ff; G. Sloyan, *Jesus on Trial: The Development of the Passion Narratives and Their Historical and Ecumenical Implications* (Philadelphia: Fortress Press, 1973); P. Benoit *Jesus and the Gospel* (New York: Herder and Herder, 1973), Vol. I, chapters 7 and 8, "The Trial of Jesus" and "Jesus Before the Sanhedrin," pp. 123–166.

[38]cf. D. Nineham, *Saint Mark*, pp. 400–405.

[39]The "I am" response which the Marcan Jesus gives to the double question of the High Priest does not appear identical with the usage of "I AM" in the Gospel of John where it is an expression of Jesus' divinity. cf. R. E. Brown *The Gospel According to John I–XII* (Garden City, New York: Doubleday, 1966) pp. 533–538. This Johannine manner of depicting Jesus' divine status cannot be automatically transferred to the synoptics. The response should be taken as a blunt affirmative answer to Caiaphas' question, quickly modified by *Son of Man*. Jean Galot is overreacting to some modern christological opinions when he makes the broad statement: "In the Johannine Gospel, the transcendent meaning of the *ego eimi* (I AM) is accentuated, with allusion to the name of Yahweh in Exodus (Jn 8: 58;cf. Ex 3: 14). This meaning equally appears in the same formula reported by the synoptics, especially in the response to the question of the High Priest (Mk 14:62; Lk 22:70) and in the definitive promise of the covenant (Mt 28:20)." J. Galot, *Le probleme christologique actuel* (C. L. D., esprit et vie, 1979) p. 31. Galot's stance is especially strange since the expression *ego eimi* is not even found in Lk 22:70 and its usage in Mt 28:20 does not correspond to the Johannine manner of employing the expression.

[40]Could it be that Mark hesitates to put an ambiguous reply on Jesus' lips (as is done by Luke and Matthew) because the people of his community were undergoing trial for their faith and needed encouragement to be firm in their reply to their judges?

[41]Matthew 21:1–11 typically enhances the scene, stressing far more the kingship of Jesus.

[42]cf. B. Vawter *This Man Jesus* (Garden City, New York: Image Books, 1975), pp. 100–103.

[43]D. Hagner states: "It is quite remarkable that the majority of modern Jewish scholars conclude that Jesus believed himself to be the Messiah. Without exception, of course, it is held that on this point Jesus was deluded." *The Jewish Reclamation of Jesus* (Grand Rapids: Academie Books, 1984), p. 243.

[44]cf. O. Cullmann, *Christology*, pp. 195–237; F. Hahn, *Titles*, 68–128; R. Fuller, *Foundations*, pp 50, 67ff, 87–93, 119, 156–158, 184– 186, 230 ff; G. Quell and W. Foerster, *TDNT* Vol. III, pp. 1039–1095; V. Taylor, *Names*, pp. 38–51; J. Fitzmyer, *Luke I–IX*, pp. 200–204.

[45]cf. E. Schillebeeckx, *Jesus*, pp. 417–423.

[46]These two books come from the same pen; the Acts is the continuation of the Gospel, showing how the Christian community carries on the work of the Lord.

[47]cf. J. Alfaro, "Faith," in *SM*, pp. 508–509.

[48]J. Jeremias, *New Testament Theology*, p. 9. Jeremias quotes G. Dalman's work, *The Words of Jesus* (Edinburgh: Clark, 1909) in support of his statement.

[49]cf. O. Cullmann, *Christology*, p. 198.

[50]cf. J. Fitzmyer, *Luke I–IX*, p. 201. Fitzmyer advances the theory that the practice of referring to YHWH as KURIOS in the Greek translations of the Old Testament "is said to be found only in Christian copies . . . dating from the fourth century A.D. on . . ." (p. 201); L. Sabourin, *Christology: Basic Texts in Focus* (New York: Alba House, 1984) refers to Fitzmyer's "opinion" and comments: "Very few known manuscripts, however, testify to this usage, which can be discounted for our purpose" (p. 214, note 5). Fitzmyer's statement in *Luke I–IX* is substantiated by examples; Sabourin's rebuttal is undocumented.

[51]cf. K. Rahner, "Theos in the New Testament," *TI* Vol. 1, pp. 79–148; R. E. Brown, *Jesus God and Man: Modern Biblical Reflections* (Milwaukee: Bruce, 1967), pp. 1–38. Brown considers the certain uses of *God* for Jesus in Jn 1:1, 20:28; Heb 1:8–9. Fitzmyer (*Luke I–IX*, p. 219) writes: ". . . by the time Luke wrote his Gospel and Acts it would not have been impossible for a Christian author to refer to Jesus as God."

The Mystery of Jesus

[52]The theory of a *Hellenistic* origin of the Christian title *Kurios* is strongly propounded by W. Bousset, *Kyrios Christos* (Nashville: Abingdon Press, 1970 [written in German in 1913]). The book represents the *history-of-religions* school and was strongly supported by Bultmann. Its basic thesis, however, has been denied by many theologians, e. g. O. Cullmann, *Christology*, pp. 213 ff. ; J. Fitzmyer, *JBC*, 79:59–63.

[53]DIDACHE: The term is Greek, meaning "Teaching." The full title of this early non-canonical christian book (c. 100 A.D.) is *The Teaching of the Twelve Apostles*. The first part is a collection of moral precepts based on rabbinical teachings, the second contains directives for the celebration of baptism and the eucharist, and the third contains directions for bishops and deacons.

[54]cf. O. Cullmann, *Christology*, p. 209.

[55]The Gospel of Mark ends at 16:8; the last few verses — although recognized by the church as canonical — are a rather bizarre addition trying to bring Mark's Gospel into greater conformity with later developments within the Christian communities as expressed by Mathew and Luke.

[56]This corresponds to Conzelman's threefold period of Lucan salvation-history: The time of the Law and the Prophets, the Period of Jesus, and the time of the "Church under stress." cf. H. Conzelman, *The Theology of St Luke* (New York: Harper, 1960), pp. 12–17 as modified by J. Fitzmyer, *Luke I–IX*, pp. 181–187.

[57]"The basic trends in Christianity were touched off by Jews and were firmly established long before non-Jewish, Gentile–Christian influences had started to operate." E. Schillebeeckx, *Jesus*, p. 32. cf. also p. 19.

[58]cf. E. Schillebeeckx, *Jesus*, p. 491, basing himself on K. Berger, "Zum traditionsgeschichtlichen Hintergrund christologischer Hoheitstitel," in *New Testament Studies*, 17 (1970–71), pp. 414–416.

[59]cf. J. Fitzmyer, *JBC*, p. 812, no. 65.

[60]cf. R. Wilken ed., *Aspects of Wisdom in Judaism and Early Christianity* (Notre Dame, Indiana: Notre Dame University Press, 1975), especially the article by J. M. Robinson, "Jesus as Sophos and Sophia: Wisdom Tradition and the Gospels"; E. Schillebeeckx, *Jesus*, pp. 429–432.

[61]International Theological Commission, *Theology, Christology, Anthropology*, p. 9.

[62]"R. Shim'on ben Laqish explained: '*and the spirit of God hovered over the face of the water*' — this is the spirit of King Messiah, as it is written, *And the spirit of the Lord will rest upon him* (Is 11: 2)" Gen. Rab. 2: 4 as quoted in R. Patai, *The Messiah Texts* (Detroit: Wayne State University Press, 1979), p. 19.

[63]Commentary on this early christian hymn may be found in J. Fitzmyer, *JBC*, 50:17–19; R. Fuller, P. Perkins, *Who Is This Christ: Gospel Christology and Contemporary Faith* (Philadelphia: Fortress Press, 1983), pp. 58–60; J. Sanders, *The New Testament Christological Hymns: Their Historical Religious Background* (New York: Cambridge University Press, 1971); R. Fuller, *Foundations*, pp. 204–214. The traditional interpretation of this hymn is challenged by J. Murphy-O'Connor, "Christological Anthropology in Phil. II, 6–11." in *Revue Biblique*, 83 (1976), pp. 25–50.

[64]"The New Testament does not intend to convey mere historical information concerning Jesus. It seeks above all to hand down the witness which ecclesial faith bears concerning Jesus, and to present him in the fulness of his significance as "Christ" (Messiah) and as "Lord" (*Kyrios*, God.) International Theological Commission (1980), *Select Questions on Christology*, p. 2.

[65]For a study of the early christological teachings and the first four Ecumenical Councils, see A. Grillmeier, *Christ in Christian Tradition* (Atlanta: John Knox Press, 1975), Vol. I; a short pamphlet on the subject is R. Barr, *Main Currents in Early Christian Thought* (New York: Paulist Press, 1966); a brief survey of the Councils may be found in H. Jedin, *Ecumenical Councils of the Catholic Church: An Historical Outline* (New York: Herder and Herder, 1960); J. N. D. Kelly, *Early Christian Doctrines* (San Francisco: Harper & Row, 1976, Fifth Edition), pp. 223–309.

[66]For a brief summary of Arius' teachings, see J. N. D. Kelly, *Early Christian Doctrines*, pp. 226–231. The Creed of Nicaea-Constantinople is proclaimed during major liturgical celebrations in many christian churches.

[67]cf. D. Lane, *The Reality of Jesus* (New York: Paulist Press, 1975) p. 132; W. Kasper, *Jesus the Christ*, p. 95.

[68]D. Stanley, R. E. Brown, "Aspects of New Testament Thought," *JBC*, 78:61.

[69]Studies on the title *Son of God* may be found in: O. Cullmann, *Christology*, pp. 270–305; F. Hahn, *Titles*, pp. 279–346; V. Taylor, *Names*, pp. 52–65; M. Hengel, *The Son of God* (Philadelphia: Fortress Press, 1976); D. Stanley, "Aspects of New Testament Thought," *JBC*, 78:20, 35, 50; R. Fuller, *Foundations*, pp. 31–33, 65, 68–72, 114–115, 164–167, 192–197, 231–232; E. Schweizer and E. Lohse, *TDNT*, Vol. VIII, pp. 347–392; W. Kasper, *The God of Jesus Christ* (New York: Crossroad, 1984), pp. 158–197.

[70]This usage is found today among the names of some religious orders, e.g., *Sons of the Immaculate Heart of Mary*, *Sons of Divine Providence*, *Daughters of Charity*, *Daughters of Wisdom*, etc.

[71]cf. E. Lohse, *TDNT*, Vol. VIII, p. 359.

[72]For a detailed possible explanation of the term *Daughter of Zion* and its use in mariology, cf. E. McHugh, *The Mother of Jesus*, pp. 438–444.

[73]This appears to be the general theme of W. Bousset, *Kyrios Christos*, p. 207: "It appears as if Paul could make a connection, in the milieu surrounding him, not only with the general vague and general concept of sons of gods but also with the more definite idea of a son deity." Bousset traces the Johannine deification of the christian as "children of God" through the Son, to pagan cults which gazed upon an image of a deity (cf. pp. 222–228).

[74]For a discussion of this subject, see R. E. Brown, *Gospel According to John, I–XII*, pp. 519–524.

[75]Justin upholds the superiority of Christianity because "the rational principle in its entirety [greek: *to logikon to holon*] became the Christ Who appeared because of us, body and Logos and soul" (J. N. D. Kelly, *Early Christian Doctrines*, p. 146).

[76]For a study of this opinion, see P. Grelot, "The Resurrection of Jesus: Its Biblical and Jewish Background" in P. Surgy, ed., *The Resurrection and Modern Biblical Thought* (New York: Corpus Books, 1970), pp. 1–6; W. Bousset, *Kyrios Christos*, upholds the theory of the influence of the dying and rising gods and of the Primal Man myth upon Paul's doctrine of dying and rising with Christ, pp. 189–200.

[77]D. Tiede, *The Charismatic Figure as Miracle Worker* (Missoula: Scholars Press, 1972) ably demonstrates the imprecision in the term *theios aner*. Perhaps the best critical study of *theios aner* is found in C. Holladay, *Theios Aner in Hellenistic-Judaism: A Critique of the Use of This Category in New Testament Christology* (Missoula: Scholars Press, 1977).

[78]H. C. Kee, *Jesus in History*, p. 152.

[79]See the discussion on this point in D. Nineham, *Saint Mark*, pp. 360–361.

[80]cf. J. Fitzmyer, *Luke X–XXIV*, p. 866; O. Cullmann, *Christology*, pp. 287–288.

[81]Traces of subordinationism are found in the great and influential theologian, Origen (c. 185–c. 254) and it becomes clearly enunciated in the teaching of Arius. "Arius had carried (Origen's) subordinationism to radical lengths, reducing the Son to creaturely status. In doing so, he was following, despite his consciously Biblical starting point, a path inevitably traced for him by the Middle Platonist preconception he had inherited." J. N. D. Kelly, *Early Christian Doctrines*, p. 231.

[82]International Theological Commission, *Theology Christology Anthropology*, p. 9.

[83]International Theolological Commission, *Theology Christology Anthropology*, p. 9.

[84]For the western contribution to the development of christology, cf. A. Grillmeier, *Christ and Christian Tradition*, pp. 392–413; 464–472. A monk of Gaul, Leporius, taught essentially the same doctrine as Nestorius in the east. However, Nestorius met with the fiery, public condemnations of Cyril of Alexandria. Leporius met with Augustine who resolved the problem peacefully through dialogue. Would there have been such an uproar in the east if Nestorius had met someone like Augustine and not the hot-tempered Cyril?

[85]An extreme of this thought is apollinarianism which denied a human soul to Jesus; cf. A. Grillmeier, *Christ in Christian Tradition*, pp. 329–360.

[86]Pontifical Biblical Commission, *Bible and Christology*, in J. Fitzmyer, *Scripture & Christology*, p. 17.

[87]cf. A. Grillmeier, *Christ in Christian Tradition*, pp. 448–463.

[88]It is often forgotten that Nestorius himself did not begin the controversy over the use of the term *Theotokos*. As Nestorius himself writes: "When I cam here, I found a dispute among the members of the church, some of whom were calling the Blessed Virgin Mother of God while others were calling her Mother of the man. Gathering both parties together, I suggested that she should be called Mother of Christ, a term which represented both God and man, as it is used in the Gospels." Quoted by A. Grillmeier, *Christ in Christian Tradition*, p. 451.

[89]The term is included in the prayer "Sub Tuum" ("We fly to thy patronage") which has been found on an ancient papyrus dating probably back to the third century. See Michael O'Carroll, *Theotokos: A Theological Encyclopedia of the Blessed Virgin Mary* (Wilmington: Glazier, 1982), p. 336.

[90]The description of this Council can be read in H. Jedin, *Ecumenical Councils*, pp. 28–36; A. Grillmeier, *Christ in Christian Tradition*, pp. 451–487; J. N. D. Kelly, *Early Christian Doctrines*, pp. 310–330.

[91]The Creed of Ephesus reads as follows: "We confess therefore, Our Lord Jesus Christ, the only begotten Son of God, perfect God and perfect man composed of rational soul and a body, begotten before the ages from His Father in respect to His divinity, but likewise in these last days for us and for our salvation from the Virgin Mary in respect to His manhood. For a union of two natures has been accomplished. Hence we confess one Christ, one Son, one Lord. In virtue of this conception of a union without confusion we confess the holy Virgin as *Theotokos* because the divine Word became flesh and was made man and from the very conception united to Himself the temple taken from her. As for the evangelical and apostolic statements about the Lord, we recognize that theologians employ some indifferently in view of the unity of person but distinguish others in view of the duality of natures, applying the Godlike ones to Christ's divinity and the humble ones to His humanity." The official Greek and Latin text of the Creed of Ephesus ("The Formula of Union") is found in J. Alberigo et al. ed., *Conciliorum Oecumenicorum Decreta*, (Bologna: Istituto per le Scienze Religiose, MCMLXXIII), pp. 69–70.

[92]J. N. D. Kelly, *Early Christian Doctrines*, p. 331.

[93]For a description of the Robber Council, see A. Grillmeier, Christ in Christian Tradition, pp. 526–529.

[94]The essential portions of the *Chalcedonian Statement* reads as follows: "Following therefore the Holy Fathers we confess with one voice that Our Lord Jesus Christ is one and the same Son, the same perfect in his divinity and the same perfect in his humanity, truly God and truly man of a rational soul and a body, of one nature with the Father according to the divinity and the same of one nature with us according to the humanity in all things like us except sin. Before the ages begotten of the Father according to the divinity but the same in the last days for us and for our salvation born according to the humanity of Mary the Virgin and mother of God, one and the same Christ, Lord, only begotten, in two natures without confusion, without change, without division and without separation. The difference of the natures is not removed through the union but rather the property of each nature is preserved and they coalesce in one person (Greek: *prosopon*) and one independence (Greek: *hypostasis*), not divided or separated into two persons but one and the same only begotten Son, divine Word, Jesus Christ the Lord." The official Greek and Latin text is found in *Conciliorum Oecumenicorum Decreta*, pp. 83–87. For an Orthodox view of Chalcedon and its aftermath, see J. Myendorff, *Christ in Eastern Christian Thought* (Washington: Corpus Books, 1969).

[95]cf. *Conciliorum Oecumenicorum Decreta*, pp. 128, 129. The Letter ("Tome") of Pope Leo of Rome to Flavian, the Patriarch of Constantinople, played a decisive role in the formulation of the Creed of Chalcedon. The "Tome of Leo" can be found, together with other important documents concerning the early christological controversies, in R. A. Norris, Jr., ed., *The Christological Controversy* (Philadelphia: Fortress Press, 1980, pp. 145–155).

[96]An example of contemporary objections to the Chalcedonian formula can be found in Piet Schoonenberg, *The Christ: A Study of the God-Man Relationship in the Whole of Creation and in Jesus Christ* (New York: Herder and Herder, 1971), pp. 61–66.

[97]cf. K. Rahner, "Current Problems in Christology," *TI*, Vol. 1, pp. 149–200; The following articles by Rahner in his *Theological Investigations* series may be of interest to an advanced student: "On The Theology of the Incarnation," *TI*, Vol. IV; "Christology Within an Evolutionary World View," *TI*, Vol. V; "Christology in the Setting of Man's Understanding of Himself and of His World," *TI*, Vol. XI.

[98]This is often called the *anhypostatic* and *enhypostatic* theory: the HUMAN nature is not a person in its own right (*anhypostatic*) but is a person IN the Person of the Logos (*enhypostatic*). P. Schoonenberg attempts to turn Chalcedon on its head by saying that the DIVINE nature is enhypostatic and anhypostatic which entails a novel understanding of the "pre-existence" of Jesus. Schoonenberg's thesis does not appear to be "creative fidelity" to Chalcedon. See P. Schoonenberg, *The Christ*, pp. 80–122.

[99]Pontifical Biblical Commission *Report* as found in J. Fitzmyer, *Scripture and Christology*, p. 57.

[100]Paul VI, "Allocution" at the General Audience of July 3, 1968, in C. Pozo, *The Credo of the People of God*, p. 211. The quote concerns the challenge offered to teachers, theologians, preachers by the *Credo of the People of God*.

[101]For a survey of some contemporary approaches to an understanding of Jesus, many of which demand a reworking of Chalcedon, see, e.g., W. Thompson, *The Jesus Debate*, pp. 115–296, 324–333; M. Cook, *The Jesus of Faith: A Study in Christology* (New York: Paulist, 1981), pp. 133–208. The Pontifical Biblical Commission's 1983 *Report* is basically a summary and critique of a number of christologies upheld by modern theologians: cf. J. Fitzmyer, *Scripture & Christology*, for the *Text* and Fitzmyer's *Commentary*.

[102]By "scholastic" here we mean generally the theology represented by the great teachers around the 13th century, especially Saint Thomas Aquinas.

[103]Pontifical Biblical Commission *Report*, as found in J. Fitzmyer, *Scripture & Christology*, p. 5.

[104]This explanation tallies, so it would appear, with the 1983 statement of the Pontifical Biblical Commission: "The ultimate explanation or rather the mystery of Jesus lies essentially in *his filial relation to God*." cf. Pontifical Biblical Commission *Report*, as found in J. Fitzmyer, *Scripture & Christology*, p. 45.

[105]*Constitution on The Church in The Modern World*, no. 22, Vatican Council II.

[106]W. Kasper, *The God of Jesus Christ*, p. 309.

[107]W. Kasper, *The God of Jesus Christ*, p. 308; see also E. Schillebeeckx, *Jesus*, pp. 254–263.

[108]S. Gregorius Nazianzenus, "Epistulae," 101, 380 in M. J. Rouet de Journel, *Enchiridion Patristicum* (Barcinone: Herder, MCMLVI), no. 1018, p. 381.

[109]Some useful studies on this title are: B. Vawter, *This Man Jesus* (Garden City, New York: Image Books, 1975), pp. 117–134; N. Perrin, *A Modern Pilgrimage in New Testament Christology* (Philadelphia: Fortress Press, 1974); J. Fitzmyer, *Christological Catechism*, pp. 88–89; F. Hahn, *Titles*, pp. 15–53; O. Cullmann, *Christology*, pp. 137–192; J. Jeremias, *New Testament*, pp. 257–276; J. Fitzmyer, *Luke I–IX*, pp. 208–211; V. Taylor, *Names*, pp. 25–35; C. Moule, *The Origin of Christology* (Cambridge: Cambridge University Press, 1977), pp. 11–22; F. Borsch, *The Son of Man in Myth and History* (Philadelphia: The Westminster Press, 1967); H. Todt, *The Son of Man in the Synoptic Tradition* (Philadelphia: Westminster Press, 1965).

[110]J. Fitzmyer, *Luke I–IX*, pp. 208–209; cf. L. Hartman and A. Di Lella, *The Book of Daniel: A New Translation with Introduction and Commentary* (Garden City: Doubleday & Company, 1978), p. 86.

[111]cf. J. Fitzmyer, *Luke I–IX*, p. 209. L. Sabourin, *Christology* writes on p. 22, "There exists no proof, however, that this expression (Sabourin is talking about *son of man* in Aramaic) was used as a periphrasis for 'I.' " However, on p. 24, Sabourin writes that "G. Vermes has demonstrated that, at the time of Jesus or before, the rabbis would use in Aramaic 'son of man' both to designate generically 'a man' or 'any man,' and as a circumlocution for 'I'." J. Jeremias, *New Testament Theology*, p. 261, strongly disagrees with Vermes and insists, as Fitzmyer does, that *son of man* is not a periphrasis for "I."

[112]For a study of son of man in Daniel, see L. Hartmann and A. Di Lella, *The Book of Daniel*, pp. 85–102. The authors' conclusion of their detailed examination of the expression in Daniel 7 is that *son of man* is an apocalyptic symbol for the holy ones of the Most High, i.e., "faithful Israel responsive to the demands of the reign of God even in the face of their present humiliation and suffering, will come into the divine presence in order to receive everlasting dominion in holiness, nobility, and grandeur and so will replace the depraved, brutal, and vile kingdoms of the pagan world which were opposed to the reign of God and to his holy people" (p. 102).

[113]48:2–69:29. A version of the text may be found in R. Charles, *APOT*, Vol. II, pp. 188–281, and in B. Vawter, *This Man Jesus*, pp. 121–122.

[114]R. Fuller, *Foundations*, pp. 39–40.

[115]The two Hebrew terms for *Son of Man* emphasize one or another of these poles: *ben enosh* (strength) and *ben adam* (weakness). Moses, for example, would not be called a *ben adam*; he is a *ben enosh* (*enosh* is from the word for "man," *ish*). I express my gratitude to two of the faculty of Hebrew Union, Cincinnati, who some years ago brought these ideas to my attention.

[116]*The Parables of Enoch* seem dependent on Daniel 7, and pre-Christian Syrian and Palestinian texts stress the meaning of "human, mortal" (cf. J. Fitzmyer, *Luke I–IX*, pp. 208–210).

[117]For an overview of these opinions, see E. Schillebeeckx, *Jesus*, pp. 459–472.

[118]"Until a few years ago the only question was whether Jesus meant himself or someone else when speaking of the *coming* son of man. But today distinguished representatives of critical scholarship point out that Jesus could not have announced the imminence of God's reign, while at the same time expecting a new mediator of salvation before the judgment (Vielhauer, Braun, Kaseman, Bornkamm)." I. Maisch and A. Vogtle, *SM*, pp. 739–740.

[119]N. Perrin, *A Modern Pilgrimage in New Testament Christology* (Philadelphia: Fortress Press, 1974), p. 45.

[120]For a brief account of this opinion and its proponents see J. Jeremias, *New Testament Theology*, pp. 275–276; R. Fuller, *Foundations*, pp. 122–123, speaks about the "distinction between Jesus and the coming *son of man*" but declares that "the *son of man* merely acts as a kind of rubber stamp at the End for the salvation which is already being imparted in Jesus." F. Hahn, *Titles*, p. 31 also says: "There is no express identification of Jesus with the *son of man*, nor is it originally implied."

[121]J. Fitzmyer, *Luke I–IX*, p. 210, opts for this opinion: "Briefly, my own view of the matter is that he (Jesus) probably used *bar enas* in the generic sense (= a human being, a mortal) and that this was later understood in the early tradition in a titular sense and applied to him."

[122]W. Kasper, *Jesus the Christ*, p. 108.

[123]For example, M. Schmaus, *Dogma, Vol. 3: God and His Christ*, pp. 187–188.

[124]B. Vawter, *This Man Jesus*, pp. 129–130.

[125]W. Kasper, *Jesus the Christ*, p. 108.

[126]Some useful studies of Jesus as *Suffering Servant* as understood in this chapter would include: O. Cullmann, *Christology*, pp. 51–82; B. Vawter, *This Man Jesus*, pp. 77–84; G. O'Collins, *Interpreting Jesus*, pp. 132–169; E. Schillebeeckx, *Jesus*, pp. 284–294; J. Fitzmyer, *Luke I–IX*, pp. 211–215; M. Hooker, *Jesus and The Servant* (London: SPCK, 1959); W. Kasper, *Jesus*, pp. 119–121; R. H. Fuller, *Foundations*, pp. 43–46, 66, 115–119; J. Jeremias, *TDNT*, Vol. V, pp. 654–717; J. McKenzie, *DB*, pp. 791–794.

[127]"Until the 18th cent., it was presumed that Isaiah of Jerusalem wrote all 66 chapters of his book." C. Stuhlmueller, "Deutero-Isaiah," *JBC*, 22:2. The reasons for the separate authorship of chapters 40–55 are, according to Stuhlmueller, historical, literary and thematic. (*JBC*, 22:2); cf. C. North, *The Second Isaiah: Introduction, Translation and Commentary to Chapters XL–LV* (Oxford: Clarendon Press, 1964). pp. 1–12.

[128]cf. C. North, *The Second Isaiah*, pp. 20–22.

[129]O. Cullmann, *Christology*, pp. 58–60.

[130]R. Bultmann, *The History of the Synoptic Tradition* (Oxford, 1968), p. 35.

[131]Josephus, *Antiquities*, 12:5, 4; 13:14, 2, narrates that Antiochus Epiphanes, king of Syria (second century B.C.) and the Hasmonean ruler Alexander Jannaeus (the first century B.C.) crucified Jews in Jerusalem; Josephus notes that they were not crucified *after* execution, as was often the case, but while still alive. In his *Wars of the Jews*, II, 5, 2, Josephus speaks of the Romans crucifying about two thousand who had taken part in a revolt around the time of Archelaus. Crucifixion as a form of execution by the overlords had a long history in Israel.

[132]cf. E. Schillebeeckx, *Jesus*, pp. 303, 309.

The Mystery of Jesus   183

¹³³K. Rahner, "Death," *SM*, p. 331 speaks of death as "a rupture, an ending from without . . . But it is also and essentially personal self-fulfillment . . . Death, therefore, . . . is a maturing self-realization which embodies the result of what a man has made of himself during life . . . the fulness of freely produced personal reality . . . At the same time, (death) is the most radical spoliation of man, highest activity and greatest passivity in one."

¹³⁴K. Rahner, "Death," *SM*, p. 332.

¹³⁵W. Kasper, *Jesus the Christ*, p. 117: "The eschatological perspective is very evident in the passages dealing with the Last Supper . . . In their present form these passages are definitely not authentic accounts; they show very clear signs of liturgical stylization . . . What is certain is that they contain at least one saying which did not become part of the later liturgy and which must therefore be regarded as a genuine saying of the Lord." Kasper then quotes the text concerning the fruit of the vine, Mk 14:25.

¹³⁶S. Gregorius Nazianzenus, "Epistulae," 101, 380 in M. J. Rouet de Journel, *Enchiridion Patristicum* (Barcinone: Herder, MCMLVI), no. 1018, p. 381.

¹³⁷cf. S. Th. III, q. 48, a. 6, corpus.

¹³⁸It is the thesis of M. Hooker, *Jesus and The Servant* that theologians had indiscriminately applied Is 53 to New Testament texts. Her book has clearly affected the study of Jesus as the *Suffering Servant of Isaiah*.

¹³⁹cf. E. Schillebeeckx, *Jesus*, pp. 274 ff.

¹⁴⁰Among the works which may be consulted on this subject are: O. Cullmann, *Christology*, pp. 13–50; E. Schillebeeckx, *Jesus*, 441–449; 480–499; J. Fitzmyer, *Luke I–IX*, p. 215; R. Fuller, *Foundations*, pp. 46–4, 67, 125–129, 167–173; F. Hahn, *Titles*, pp. 352–406; M. Schmaus, *Dogma, Volume 3: God and His Christ*, pp. 176–182; H. Kramer, R. Rendtorff, R. Myer, G. Friedrich, *TDNT*, Vol. VI, pp. 781–861.

¹⁴¹For the meaning of prophecy, in addition to the references given above, see, e.g., K. Rahner, "Prophetism," *SM*, pp. 1286–1289; B. Vawter, "Introduction to Prophetic Literature," *JBC*, 12:3–12; J. McKenzie, *DB*, pp. 694–699; P. Beauchamp, "Prophet," *DBT*, pp. 414–419.

¹⁴²B. Vawter, "Introduction to Prophetic Literature," *JBC*, 12:8.

¹⁴³For a concise explanation of *midrash*, see P. Grelot, "The Foundations of Christian Exegesis," in A. Robert and A. Feuillet, *Interpreting the Scriptures* (New York: Desclee Company, 1969), pp. 174–180.

¹⁴⁴cf. R. E. Brown, "Dead Sea Scrolls," *JBC*, 68:103.

¹⁴⁵Since Jesus is the definitive Word of God, there is no such thing in the christian community as a prophet in one's own right, there is no such thing as a priest in one's own right. God's word — his final disclosure, his final word — has been spoken in Jesus, and priest and prophet exist in the christian community only as sharing in the prophetic or priestly role of Jesus.

¹⁴⁶Saint Augustine, *Confessions*, Book X, 27.

¹⁴⁷"(John) contrasts the enduring love shown in the Law with the supreme example of enduring love shown in Jesus." R. E. Brown, *John I–XII*, p. 16. By the expression, "enduring love" John appears to be referring to the Hebrew terms *hesed* (God's merciful Love) and *emeth* (solidity, permanency, enduring). This *hesed* and *emeth* is now Jesus Christ: "And the Word became flesh and dwelt among us, full of grace and truth (Jn 1:14).

¹⁴⁸See K. Rahner, "Christ in the Non-Christian Religions," *TI*, Vol. 17, pp. 39–50; W. Thompson, *Jesus, Lord and Savior: A Theopathic Christology and Soteriology* (New York: Paulist Press, 1980) who urges the study of a *transcultural* Christ, founded on the thought of Thomas Merton and Raymond Panikkar.

¹⁴⁹This is not to say that a sincere, explicit faith in Jesus the Lord with the concomitant sharing in the Eucharist and the Sacraments is not the *full* and powerful sharing in God's plan.

¹⁵⁰The *Pastoral Constitution on the Church in the Modern World*, no. 22, Vatican II, after speaking about Christ the Lord declares: "All this holds true not for Christians only but also for all of good will in whose hearts grace is active invisibly."

¹⁵¹see *Declaration on the Relation of the Church to Non-Christian Religions*, Vatican II, pp. 738–742.

¹⁵²K. Rahner, "Jesus Christ," *SM*, p. 771. See also K. Rahner, "Christianity and the Non-Christian Religions," *TI* Vol. V, pp. 115–134; "Anonymous Christians," *TI* Vol. VI, pp. 390–398; "One Mediator and Many Mediations," *TI* Vol. IX, pp. 169–184; "Anonymous Christianity and the Missionary Task of the Church," *TI* Vol. XII, pp. 161–178; "Observations on the Problem of the 'Anonymous Christian'," *TI* Vol. XIV, pp. 280–294. The question is also treated in Rahner's *Foundations of Christian Faith: An Introduction to the Idea of Christianity* (New York: Seabury Press, 1978), pp. 311–321.

¹⁵³The question of the meaning of the *ultimacy of Christ* is a debated issue in contemporary christology. Some would erroneously reject "christocentricity" (God discloses himself in and through the one and only mediator between God and man, Jesus Christ), for what could be termed a "theocentricity" which for all practical purposes ignores the universal mediatorship of Jesus the Lord. See J. Milet, *God or Christ: The Excesses of Christocentricity* (New York: Crossroad, 1981); see also the sharp critique of J. Pawlikowski's thesis on the equality of the Mosaic and Christian dispensation, *Christ in*

the Light of the Christian-Jewish Dialogue, New York: Paulist, 1982, by an evangelical author, D. Hagner, in his *The Jewish Reclamation of Jesus*, pp. 297–303; J. Fitzmyer refers to this question of the ultimacy of Christ in *A Christological Catechism*, pp. 91–93.

SECTION FOUR: THE KINGDOM OF GOD

[1]Some of the works which may be consulted on this subject are: P. Hunerrmann, "Reign of God," *SM*, pp. 1349–1357; W. Kasper, *Jesus the Christ*, pp. 72–88; J. Jeremias, *New Testament Theology*, pp. 96–121; W. Pannenberg, *Jesus-God and Man* (Philadelphia: Westminster Press, 1968), pp. 225–232, 365–378; E. Schillebeeckx, *Jesus*, pp. 115–229; H. Kleinknecht, G. von Rad, K. Kuhn, K. Schmidt, *TDNT*, Vol. I, pp. 564–593; D. M. Stanley, "The Kingdom of God," *JBC*, 78:93–108; J. McKenzie, *DB*, pp. 479–482; J. Bright, *The Kingdom of God: The Biblical Concept and Its Meaning For the Church* (Nashville: Abingdon Press, 1953); G. Beasley-Murray, *Jesus and The Kingdom of God* (Grand Rapids: Wm. B. Eerdmann's Publishing, 1986); R. Schnackenburg, *God's Rule and Kingdom* (New York: Herder and Herder, 1963); N. Perrin, *The Kingdom of God in the Teaching of Jesus* (Philadelphia: Westminster Press, 1963) and *Jesus and The Language of the Kingdom* (Philadelphia: Fortress Press, 1976); R. Fuller, *The Mission and Achievement of Jesus* (London: SCM Press, 1954), pp. 1–78.

[2]". . . the kingdom of God, more precisely, of the lordship or reign of God, since BASILEIA (*the Greek term for Kingdom*) means primarily the exercise of royal power, sovereignty and dignity, and only secondarily the realm or territory. . ." P. Hunermann, *Reign*, p. 1349; cf. also R. Schnackenburg, "Note on Theological Terminology," *God's Rule*, pp. 354–357.

[3]J. Fitzmyer, *Luke I–IX*, p. 154.

[4]W. Kasper, *Jesus the Christ*, pp. 100–101; cf. Mk 10:29, where it appears there is an identification of Jesus with the Good News; cf. J. Fitzmyer, *Luke I–IX*, p. 153.

[5]cf. R. Schnackenburg, *God's Rule*, pp. 11–74; J. Bright, *The Kingdom*, pp. 17–186; G. Beasley-Murray, *Jesus and the Kingdom*, pp. 17–35.

[6]cf. Ps 72:12–14, 82:3–4.

[7]G. Beasley-Murray, *Jesus and the Kingdom*, pp. 17–18, following Eissfeld and Buber, correctly rejects the notion that Israel could not have thought of God as King until the nation actually had a king, therefore not until the the times of Saul, David and Solomon.

[8]cf. J. Bright, *The Kingdom*, pp. 162–170; G. Beasley-Murray, *Jesus and the Kingdom*, pp. 39–62.

[9]cf. G. Beasley-Murray, *Jesus and the Kingdom*, pp. 43–45; P. Auvray, X. Leon-Dufour, "Day of the Lord," *DBT*, pp. 89–93.

[10]P. Grelot, "Apocalyptic," *SM*, pp. 16–20.

[11]"In apocalyptic thinking still another type of hope was cherished. The kingdom of God is the world transfigured and taken up into heaven. This expectation is still temperately expressed in Daniel, but the "parables" of Enoch, the Ascension of Moses and the Syriac Apocalypsis of Baruch give vivid descriptions of this kingdom and the judgment." P. Hunermann, *Reign of God*, p. 1351.

[12]cf. J. Bright, *The Kingdom*, p. 163.

[13]There is a fundamental truth which is highlighted especially by this apocalyptic world view. Man's freedom is situated. No man is an island. The interrelatedness of all things is an essential element of our being as creatures. Even before any exercise of freedom, one's situation of freedom is intrinsically affected by the universal guilt of humankind, by powers alien to God's rule (anything created has the potential of becoming a destructive idol). In symbolic language, the yearning for God to come and rescue creation is expressing the profound truth of one's situation in a creation which has rejected his offer of love (original sin), a rejection which penetrates into the very constitution of a person and which can only be healed by God's initiative. There is no auto-redemption, there is no possibility of rolling up the sleeves of the human race and transforming this world into the Reign of God (contrary to a form of rugged individualism well known in the western world). God must take the initiative. He must rescue humankind through the inbreaking of his kingly rule. Through him, with him and in him, human beings serve as his loving instrument in the implementation of his reign.

[14]cf. J. Jeremias, *New Testament Theology*, pp. 31–35.

[15]J. Jeremias, *New Testament Theology*, pp. 29, 30.

[16]cf. W. Kasper, *Jesus the Christ*, pp. 78–81.

[17]W. Kasper, *Jesus the Christ*, p. 87.

[18]For a further study of scriptural miracles, see E. Schillebeeckx, *Jesus*, pp. 179–200; W. Kasper *Jesus the Christ*, pp. 89–99; R. E. Brown, "The Gospel Miracles," *JBC*, 78:109–130; J. B. Metz, L. Monden, "Miracle," *SM*, pp. 962–967; P. Ternant, "Miracle," *DBT*, pp. 317–322; W. Grundmann, *TDNT*, Vol. II, pp. 299–317; K. Rengstorf, *TDNT*, Vol. VII, pp. 260; R. H. Fuller, *Interpreting the Miracles* (Philadelphia: Westminster Press, 1963).

[19]". . . what are the evangelists really getting at in reporting the wonders performed by Jesus? Only when that question has been answered can we raise the second- or third-order question as to whether Jesus actually did perform miracles and, if so, which ones;" E. Schillebeeckx, *Jesus*, p. 181. And

The Mystery of Jesus   185

only after we examine the miracles of Jesus can we ask ourselves the question concerning a possible "scientific" explanation of these strange events.

[20]cf. R. Bultmann, *History of the Synoptic Tradition* (New York: Harper & Row, 1968) rev. ed., published in German in 1931, pp. 209–244.

[21]A. Malet, *The Thought of Rudolph Bultmann* (Garden City, N.Y.: Doubleday & Company, 1971), p. 126. Bultmann himself commended Malet's summary of his thought.

[22]A. Malet, *The Thought of Rudolph Bultmann*, p. 127.

[23]A. Malet, *The Thought of Rudolph Bultmann*, p. 127. Notice Bultmann's constant insistence that the evangelists had *primarily* an apologetic purpose in transmitting to us the wonders of Jesus which does not tally with the portraits themselves.

[24]R. E. Brown, "Miracles," *JBC*, 78:126. See Brown's critique of Bultmann's position, 78:116–125.

[25]For example of miracles performed by Palestinian rabbis and Hellenistic wonder-workers, see R. Fuller, *Interpreting the Gospel Miracles*, pp. 21–22.

[26]R. E. Brown, "Miracles," *JBC*, 78:128.

[27]W. Kasper, *Jesus the Christ*, p. 90.

[28]Some would include among the "parable-miracles," the bringing the dead back to life (e.g., the Johannine Lazarus story), the nature miracles (e.g., the walking on the water). cf. W. Kasper, *Jesus the Christ*, p. 90.

[29]Authors based themselves on Thomas Aquinas' teaching that "a miracle is not something done beyond the order of any particular nature . . . something is called a miracle which is done beyond the order of the entire created nature. Only God can do this." S. Th. I, q. 110, a. 4, corpus; cf. q. 114, a. 4.

[30]This is why God's existence cannot be PROVEN through the argument of efficient causality, i.e., if causes are pushed back far enough one must come to an uncaused cause; this is untenable, for the argument is on the level of natural, created causality and the conclusion is the existence of a God who is beyond human causality. Thomas Aquinas rightly called this argument one of the *viae*, an approach to the existence of God.

[31]cf. W. Kasper, *Jesus the Christ*, p. 95.

[32]W. Kasper, *Jesus the Christ*, p. 94.

[33]cf. K. Regenstorf, *TDNT*, Vol. VIII, p. 124.

[34]W. Kasper, *Jesus the Christ*, p. 94.

[35]C. H. Dodd is the most prominent defender of this stance; cf. *The Parables of the Kingdom* (London: Fontana Books, 1961, 2nd ed.), pp. 40–41. For a brief overview of Dodd's contribution to theology, see D. Stanley, "New Testament Eschatology," *JBC*, 78:69 and J. Kselman, "Modern New Testament Criticism," *JBC*, 41:63.

[36]cf. A. Schweitzer, *The Quest of the Historical Jesus* (New York: Macmillan, 1964, 1st German edition: 1906). For an overview of Schweitzer's contribution to theology, see D. Stanley, "New Testament Eschatology," *JBC*, 78:68 and J. Kselman, "Modern New Testament Criticism," *JBC*, 41:35.

[37]cf. J. Jeremias, *The Parables of Jesus* (New York: Scribner's, 1963).

[38]". . . in him (Jesus), God promised himself to the world in judgement and mercy, definitively, supremely and irrevocably. This could be expressed by saying that Jesus by his Cross and Resurrection is the eschatological redemptive event. . ." K. Rahner, "Jesus Christ," *SM*, p. 759.

[39]cf. W. Kasper, *Jesus the Christ*, pp. 77–78; R. Schnackenburg, *God's Rule*, pp. 195–214.

[40]To declare that Jesus employs mental reservation in Mk 13, or that he knew the time of the new age but did not want to know it, or that he knew it by his beatific vision and infused knowledge but not by his human knowledge, all contradict the simple, clear statement of the scriptures. The fundamental difficulty here is that the starting point of christology is not the historical Jesus as painted in the word of God but the philosophical Christ analyzed by Aristotelian logic. For a favorable study of the preceding opinions, see B. de Margerie, *The Human Knowledge of Christ* (Boston: St Paul Editions, 1980); the book is a translation of de Margerie's June, 1977 article in *esprit et vie*.

[41]cf. K. Rahner, "Jesus Christ," *SM*, p. 769; P. Hunermann, "Reign of God," *SM*, p. 1352.

[42]The Transfiguration scene follows immediately upon Jesus' saying that "some of those who are standing here shall not taste death before they see the kingdom of God" (Lk 9:27). J. Fitzmyer, *Luke I–IX*, p. 786, comments that the final saying of Jesus immediately before the Transfiguration (about some who will live to see the kingdom), "preserves much of the futurist eschatological nuance of its Marcan counterpart, even though Luke has suppressed the note of its 'coming with power.' . . . he retains the Marcan relationship of this saying to the coming scene of the transfiguration which is a partial fulfillment of the final saying . . . One cannot help but relate the "seeing of the kingdom" (9:27) by such disciples to their "seeing his glory" (9:32).

[43]cf. J. Jeremias, *New Testament Theology*, pp. 108–121; J. McKenzie, *DB*, pp. 681–684; S. Verhey, "Poverty," *SM*, p. 1260; L. Roy, "Poor," *DBT*, pp. 386–388; W. Kasper, *Jesus the Christ*, pp. 84–86; G. Beasley-Murray, *Jesus and the Kingdom*, pp. 157–164; E. Bammel, *TDNT*, Vol. VI, pp. 888–915.

[44]Concerning Jesus' mission to the Jews, see J. Jeremias, *Jesus' Promise to the Nations* (Naperville, IL.: Allenson, 1958). For an extensive bibliography and analysis of modern Jewish studies on Jesus,

see D. Hagner, *The Jewish Reclamation of Jesus* (Grand Rapids: Academie Books, 1984); for a rather controversial interpretation of christology in the light of Judaism, see J. Pawlikowski, *Christ in the Light of Jewish-Christian Dialogue* (New York: Paulist Press, 1982).

[45]G. Beasley-Murray, *Jesus and the Kingdom,* p. 289.

[46]cf. R. E. Brown, *The Community of the Beloved Disciple*, pp. 40–43.

[47]D. Nineham, *Saint Mark*, p. 201.

[48]T. Hart, *To Know and Follow Jesus: Contemporary Christology* (New York: Paulist Press, 1984), p. 124. Liberation theology is more interested in what Jesus taught and did, in his execution, than in abstract christological debates concerning the nature and person of Jesus; the stress is on the historical Jesus, not on the Christ of the Councils. That there are dangers inherent in such an approach is evident, especially when such a theology is proclaimed in countries where atheistic marxism has made inroads. Nonetheless, "orthodox" liberation theology is a call to practical discipleship much needed in the christian world today. For further readings, see G. Gutierrez, *A Theology of Liberation* (Maryknoll: Orbis Books, 1973), L. Boff, *Jesus Christ Liberator* (Maryknoll: Orbis Books, 1978), J. Sobrino, *Christology At the Crossroads* (Maryknoll: Orbis Books, 1978).

[49]1 QSa 2.3–9 as quoted by J. Jeremias, *New Testament Theology*, pp. 175–176.

[50]cf. J. Jeremias, *New Testament Theology*, pp. 116–117.

[51]cf. W. Kasper, *Jesus the Christ*, pp. 81–83.

[52]Mary is the first to accept Jesus into her life through her representative "fiat." Her blessedness is not in the fact that she is "physically" the Mother of the Lord but because, intrinsic to her Divine Maternity is her faith-filled consent. The Second Vatican Council teaches: "In the course of her Son's preaching she received the words whereby, in extolling a kingdom beyond the concerns and ties of flesh and blood, he declared blessed those who heard and kept the word of God (cf. Mk 3:35; par. Lk 11:27–28) as she was faithfully doing (cf. Lk 2:19, 51). *Constitution on the Church*, n. 58, Vatican II.

[53]As with all the chapters in this introduction to christology, it is impossible to go into depth on any one subject. The literature on *parables* is immense. Some of the works which may be consulted are: J. Crossan, "Parable and Example in the Teaching of Jesus," *New Testament Studies*, Vol. 18 (1971/ 1972), pp. 285–307; J. Jeremias, *The Parables of Jesus* (New York: Charles Scribner's Sons, 1963); *Rediscovering the Parables* (New York: Charles Scribner's Sons, 1966); N. Perrin, *Jesus and the Language of the Kingdom* (Philadelphia: Fortress Press, 1976); F. Hauck, *TDNT*, pp. 744–761; C. H. Dodd, *The Parables of the Kingdom*, rev. ed. (London: Fontana Books, 1961); G. Beasley-Murray, *Jesus and the Kingdom of God*, pp. 108–147; 194–219; P. Perkins, *Hearing the Parables of Jesus* (New York: Paulist Press, 1981); R. E. Brown, "The Parables of Jesus," *JBC*, 78:131–145; J. McKenzie, *DB*, pp. 635–636.

[54]J. Jeremias, *Rediscovering*, p. 10. Jeremias comes to this conclusion by comparing Jesus' parables with "analogous productions from the same period and cultural context . . . comparison reveals a definite personal style, a singular clarity and simplicity, a matchless mastery of construction. The conclusion is inevitable that we are dealing with particularly trustworthy tradition." p. 10.

[55]cf. J. McKenzie, *BD*, p. 635. Jeremias explains: "Jesus' parables are something entirely new. In all rabbinic literature, not a single parable has come down to us from the period before Jesus; only two similes from Rabbi Hillel who jokingly compared the body with a statue and the soul with a guest." *Rediscovering*, p. 10.

[56]"The Jews of Jesus' day despised the Samaritans on both racial and religious grounds . . . So when the parable confronts the hearer of Jesus at the literal level with the combination of *good* and *Samaritan*, it is asking that the hearer conceive the inconceivable." N. Perrin, D. Duling, *The New Testament: An Introduction*, p. 417.

[57]J. Fitzmyer, *Luke I–IX,* p. 707.

SECTION FIVE: THE RESURRECTION

[1]K. Rahner, *Foundations*, p. 271. Among the hundreds who participated in this study via telecomputer, this text from Rahner was constantly challenged. It became evident that "eternal life" on earth was an option many would like to choose; yet with it they wanted eternally perfect — or nearly perfect — health, happiness, love, peace which are not possible in this life. They were, without being able to verbalize it, expressing their yearning for eternal life with the Lord.

[2]The following books on the topic may prove helpful: P. Surgy, ed., *The Resurrection and Modern Biblical Thought* (New York: Corpus Books, 1970); R. Fuller, *The Formation of the Resurrection Narratives* (Philadelphia: Fortress Press, 1980); W. Marxsen, *The Resurrection of Jesus of Nazareth* (Philadelphia: Fortress Press, 1970); N. Perrin, *The Resurrection According to Matthew, Mark and Luke* (Philadelphia: Fortress Press, 1977); G. O'Collins, *The Resurrection of Jesus Christ* (Valley Forge: Judson Press, 1973); X. Dufour, *Resurrection and the Message of Easter* (New York: Holt, Rinehart and Winston, 1975); P. Perkins, *Resurrection: New Testament Witness and Contemporary Reflection* (New York: Doubleday & Co, 1984); P. Benoit, *The Passion and Resurrection of Jesus Christ* (New York: Herder and Herder, 1969); F. X. Durwell, *The Resurrection: A Biblical Study* (New York: Sheed & Ward, 1960); D. Stanley, *Christ's Resurrection in Pauline Soteriology* (Rome:

Pontifical Biblical Institute, 1961); E. Dhanis, ed., *Resurrexit, Actes du Symposium International sur la Resurrection de Jesus* (Vatican: Libereria Editrice Vaticana, 1974). The books by Durwell and Stanely were pioneers in the contemporary study of the resurrection. *Resurrexit* contains two articles in English: B. Ahern, "The Risen Christ in the Light of Pauline Doctrine of the Risen Christian (1 Cor 15:35–37)," pp. 423–435, and R. E. Brown, "John 21 and the First Appearance of the Risen Jesus to Peter," pp. 246–260; articles in other languages are followed by a brief English summary. One of the greatest contributions of *Resurrexit* is the vast bibliography on the resurrection drawn up by G. Ghiberti, covering especially the works produced from 1920–1973. In addition to the above books, the following may be consulted: K. Rahner, J. Schmitt, W. Bulst, J. Schmid, J. Ratzinger, "Resurrection," in *SM*, pp. 1430–1453; R. E. Brown, "Aspects of New Testament Thought," *JBC*, 78:146–159; J. McKenzie, *DB*, 731–734; W. Kasper, *Jesus the Christ*, pp. 124–160; W. Pannenberg, *Jesus-God and Man* (Philadelphia: Westminster Press, 1968), pp. 53–114; P. Hodgson, *Jesus-Word and Presence: An Essay in Christology* (Philadelphia: Fortress Press, 1971), pp. 220–291; H. Merklein, "Resurrection and Christology's Beginnings," *TD*, 32:2, pp. 113–117.

[3]G. O'Collins, *Resurrection*, p. 68, quoting D. Hume, *An Inquiry Concerning Human Understanding*, ed. C. Hendel (New York, 1955), X, p. 138.

[4]The resurrection in itself is meta-historical. However, it is "an *historical* event in its *present* modality, not as an historically observable past fact." P. Hodgson, *Jesus-Word and Presence*, p. 232. As will be seen in the final chapter, Easter is not only a past event, it is a present experience and it is through the present experience that the "original" Easter is illuminated.

[5]cf. P. Grelot, "The Resurrection of Jesus: Its Biblical and Jewish Background," in de Surgy, *Resurrection*, pp. 1–29.

[6]The term *kerygma* is somewhat slippery as should be evident by now. It has three meanings: the proclamation itself, the content of the proclamation and finally, the responsibility of proclaiming. Its most common usage is in the second sense, the "content" of the proclamation, with a wide range of opinions concerning the *essential* content. cf. J. Fitzmyer, *Luke I–IX*, pp. 145–162.

[7]We exclude the late Old Testament books, influenced by Greek thought, which expresses a human being in typical Greek dualistic fashion. cf. Wis 8:19; 9:15.

[8]E. Jacob, *TDNT*, Vol. IX, p. 631.

[9]J. Schmid, "Resurrection," *SM*, p. 1443. Schmid's article is a concise study of the development of the theme of resurrection in the Old and New Testament.

[10]cf. McKenzie, "Man," *DB*, 538–539; also "Aspects of Old Testament Thought," *JBC*, pp. 747, 765–766; E. Jacob, *TDNT*, Vol. IX, pp. 617–631.

[11]J. McKenzie, "Aspects of Old Testament Thought," *JBC*, p. 765.

[12]J. McKenzie, "Aspects of Old Testament Thought," *JBC*, p. 766.

[13]"In Jesus' time no uniform ideas existed about life after death." E. Schillebeeckx, *Jesus*, p. 523; for a description of the varieties of Jewish thought concerning the resurrection of the dead, see pp. 518–525.

[14]cf. Josephus, *Antiquities*, 18, 1, 3 where he speaks of the Pharisees' belief in the resurrection and comments: "on account of which doctrines they are able greatly to persuade the body of the people." Josephus' description of the philosophy of the Pharisees, Saducees and Essenes is given in chapter 1 of Book 18; the first mention of Jesus is in chapter three of the same book giving the impression that Josephus is describing the beliefs of the three principal "sects" of Judaism as they existed around the time of Christ.

[15]Perhaps the core historicity of these events is the cure of someone deathly ill as Jesus himself interprets the cure of the daughter of Jairus (cf. Mk 5:24) and therefore already considered to be in the power of She'ol.

[16]"But the doctrine of the Saducees is this: That souls die with the bodies . . ." Josephus, *Antiquities*, 18, 1, 4. Josephus is using Greek terms to express the Saducees denial of the resurrection.

[17]Jesus speaks of the resurrection only of "those who are judged worthy", apparently affirming that resurrection is only for the righteous. The thought is somewhat clarified by the Johannine Jesus: "Do not be surprised at this, for the hour is coming when the dead will leave their graves at the sound of his (i.e., the Son of Man's) voice: those who did good will rise again to life; and those who did evil, to condemnation" (Jn 5:26–29; cf. Mt 11:22; 10:36; 25:31–46). The rising from the graves can hardly be called "resurrection" for the unjust for they will be sentenced to eternal punishment.

[18]Cited by W. Kasper, *Jesus the Christ*, p. 136, quoting Marcel's *The Mystery of Being*. Gabriel Marcel taught that *fidelity* to the other "actually creates the self." cf. J. Livingston, *Modern Christian Thought*, p. 355.

[19]Cited by W. Kasper, *Jesus the Christ*, p. 83. Concerning the danger of transposing Hegel's understanding of love into theology, see Kasper's note 25 on page 88. For an excellent and concise study of Hegel's understanding of Christianity, see Livingston, *Modern Christian Thought*, pp. 143–157.

[20]P. Grelot, "The Resurrection of Jesus: Its Biblical and Jewish Background," P. de Surgy, ed., *The Resurrection and Modern Biblical Thought*, p. 137, note 73; see also pp. 18–19, 24–25.

²¹cf. P. Hodgson, *Jesus-Word and Presence*, pp. 220–291; K. Rahner, "Resurrection," *SM*, pp. 1438–1440.

²²It is commonly held today that the beloved disciple is not the Apostle John. The beloved disciple who in John's account stands at the foot of the Cross with Mary is not, therefore, the Apostle; cf. R. E. Brown, *The Community of the Beloved Disciple*, pp. 31–34.

²³Manuals of Dogmatic theology used in Catholic seminaries throughout the world were still insisting on the apologetic dimension of the Resurrection and considering it but a postscript to christology up to the eve of the Second Vatican Council; cf. J. Aldama, S. Gonzalez, I. Solano, *Sacrae Theologiae Summa, Vol. III* (Matriti [Madrid]: 1956), where the Resurrection is treated in a short scholion in the tract on the Redemption, p. 312.

²⁴cf. X. Leon-Dufour, *Resurrection*, pp. 6–24; G. O'Collins, *The Resurrection*, pp. 3–17; E. Schillebeeckx, *Jesus*, pp. 346–360; for more extensive bibliography see E. Dhanis, *Resurrexit*, where G. Ghiberti lists 63 specific entries for 1 Cor 15 alone, pp. 660–664.

²⁵cf. G. O'Collins, *The Resurrection*, p. 4.

²⁶For an excellent and concise study of this "becoming" in Jesus, see J. Haughey, *The Conspiracy of God: The Holy Spirit in Us* (Garden City, New York: Image Books, 1976), especially chapter one, "Jesus of Nazareth and the Spirit of God."

²⁷J. Haughey, *The Conspiracy of God*, p. 11.

²⁸cf. A. Oepke, *TDNT*, Vol. II, pp. 333–337.

²⁹cf. A. Oepke, *TDNT*, Vol. I, pp. 368–371.

³⁰It appears more apt to use the expression "somatic resurrection" to denote this radical transformation or transferral into the realm of YHWH, than the term "bodily resurrection" which connotes too often merely a "better type" of body.

³¹cf. W. Michaelis, *TDNT*, Vol. V, pp. 355–361.

³²The apocryphal Gospel of Peter (8:35–40) does describe the resurrection of Jesus: "Now in the night in which the Lord's day dawned when the soldiers, two by two in every watch, were keeping guard, there rang out a loud voice in heaven and they saw the heavens opened and the two men come down from there in a great brightness and drawn nigh to the sepulcher. That stone which had been laid against the entrance to the sepulcher started of itself to roll and gave way to the side, and the sepulcher was opened and both the young men entered in. When now those soldiers saw this, they awakened the centurion and the elders for they were there to assist at the watch. And while they were relating what they had seen, they saw again three men come out from the sepulcher, and two of them sustaining the other, and a cross following them and the heads of the two reaching to heaven but that of him whom they led by the hand overpassing the heavens."

³³The books on the topic of the resurrection given above, deal also with the Easter appearances. Of special interest would be X. Leon-Dufour *Resurrection*, "Stage Two: The Narratives of the Encounter with the Lord Jesus," pp. 61–104 and "Stage Three: The Easter Message According to the Evangelists," pp. 123–194; A. George, "The Accounts of The Appearances to the Eleven From Luke 24, 36–53," in P. de Surgy, *The Resurrection*, pp. 49–73; R. E. Brown, "The Resurrection of Jesus" in *JBC*, 78:152–157. Brown's article has a full page outline of the variant accounts of the resurrection appearances; N. Perrin, *The Resurrection According to Matthew, Mark, And Luke*; H. Hendrickx, *The Resurrection Narratives of the Synoptic Gospels* (London: Geoffrey Chapman, 1984).

³⁴The books listed above on the Resurrection also deal with the topic of the Empty Tomb. The following may also be consulted: J. Delorme, "The Resurrection and Jesus' Tomb: Mark 16, 1–8 in the Gospel Tradition," in P. de Surgy, *The Resurrection*, pp. 74–106; E. Bode, *The First Easter Morning. The Gospel Accounts of the Women's Easter Visit to the Tomb of Jesus* (Rome: Biblical Institute Press, 1970); X. Leon-Dufour, *Resurrection*, pp. 105–124.

³⁵cf. E. Schillebeeckx, *Jesus*, pp. 533–544; W. Kasper, *Jesus the Christ*, pp. 147–154; P. Benoit, "The Ascension," *Jesus and the Gospel*, pp. 209–253.

³⁶Gnosticism is at the root of docetism, for "most of the Gnostic schools were thoroughly dualistic, setting an infinite chasm between the spiritual world and the world of matter which they regarded as intrinsically evil." J. N. D. Kelley, *Early Christian Doctrines* (New York: Harper & Row, 1977), p. 26.

³⁷Speaking of the Ascension, P. Benoit says: "The Lord could, out of his goodness, provide sufficient signs of his departure for the senses of his disciples to perceive." *Jesus and The Gospel*, p. 215.

³⁸"the soul . . . is not really distinct from it (the body) and therefore could only absolutely cease if the soul itself were to cease to exist, and were not immortal, as philosophy shows and the Church's dogma affirms. A substantial relation to matter of this kind, identical with the soul itself and not one of its "accidents," can change but cannot simply cease." K. Rahner, "Death", *SM*, pp. 330–331. The entire article should be studied since it deals not only with death in general but also with the death of Christ. cf. also K. Rahner, *On The Theology of Death* (New York: Herder and Herder, 1961).

³⁹cf. H. Vorgrimler, "The Significance of Christ's Descent Into Hell," *Who Is Jesus of Nazareth*, Concilium, Vol. 11 (New York: Paulist Press, 1966) pp. 147–159. cf. K. Rahner, H. Vorgrimler, "Descent Into Hell," *Theological Dictionary* (New York: Herder & Herder, 1965), p. 124; W.

Pannenberg, *Jesus*, pp. 269–274; W. Maas, "'He Descended Into Hell'", *TD*, 30:1, 43–46. For the scriptural foundation for the "descent into hell" see especially 1 Pet 3:18–20.

[40]"It may be hard to refute in principle those who imagine a scenario with a risen Christ enjoying a new, glorified, bodily existence even though his corpse decays in the tomb. Can we really say that God *could* never bring about such a situation, no matter what? . . . it would seem appropriate that this corpse . . . should share in a glorified existence and belong to the enduring work of redemption . . ." G. O'Collins, *Jesus*, p. 128.

[41]B. Vawter *This Man Jesus*, p. 38.

[42]G. O'Collins correctly says that more insistence should be placed on the theological rather than the historical issues concerning the empty tomb. G. O'Collins, *Jesus*, p. 126.

[43]There may be some probability to the theory advanced by a number of scholars that Mark's account of the empty tomb — the earliest chronologically — may represent a celebration of an annual liturgical feast at the empty tomb by the early Christians. The theory abstracts from the historicity of the empty tomb, but indirectly does support it by again showing the veneration for this sign of the resurrection, without any dissenting voices being heard even from the enemies of Christianity.

[44]R. E. Brown, "The Resurrection of Jesus," *JBC*, 78:151.

[45]E. Schillebeeckx, *Jesus*, p. 529. The entire section on "the third day" should be studied, pp. 526–532.

[46]W. Pannenberg, *Jesus*, p. 105.

[47]We should add the words of Hans Kung, "The idea of a resurrection of the Messiah — still more of a failed Messiah — was an absolute novelty in the Jewish tradition." H. Kung, *On Being a Christian* (Garden City: Doubleday, 1976), p. 372.

[48]Among the works which may be consulted are: W. Pannenberg, *Jesus*, especially pp. 66–73; K. Rahner, "Resurrection," *SM*, pp. 1440–1441; D. Lane, *The Reality of Jesus*, pp. 71–75; X. Leon-Dufour, *Resurrection*, pp. 236–246; W. Kasper, *Jesus the Christ*, pp. 144–154.

[49]"Strict" Whiteheadian process thought denies that the resurrection of Jesus entails the continuation of his subjective consciousness. In Whiteheadian thought, Jesus — as all humans — is not a "person who experiences." Rather, his experiences are his person. At death, these experiences are "prehended" by God, becoming part of God; there is no longer an "individual," a personal self-consciousness. Process thought has excellent insights to offer to theology; however, in its "raw form" it entails a denial of the Trinity, the Incarnation, the Resurrection as taught by the Scriptures lived within the Church. See, e.g., N. Pittenger, *Christology Reconsidered* (London: SCM Press, 1970); Alan Gragg, *Charles Hartshorne* (Waco, Texas: Word Books, 1973), especially pp. 69–72 where the author treats of Hartshorne's understanding of "immortality."

[50]cf. J. Haughey, *The Conspiracy*, especially chapter one, "Jesus of Nazareth and the Spirit of God."

[51]Speaking of Christ's death/resurrection, K. Rahner declares: "By Christ's death his spiritual reality, which he possessed from the beginning and actuated in a life which was brought to consummation by his death, becomes open to the whole world and is inserted into this whole world in its ground as a permanent determination of a real ontological kind . . . By that death his human reality . . . became a determining feature of the whole cosmos." K. Rahner, "Death," *SM*, p. 332.

[52]cf. J. Moltmann, *The Crucified God* (New York: Harper & Row, 1974).

[53]*Constitution on the Church in the Modern World,* n. 39, Vatican II.

[54]Christ as the physical center of the universe is a principal theme of Teilhard de Chardin's thought; see his *Divine Milieu* (New York: Harper & Row, 1965), *Hymn of the Universe* (New York: Harper & Row, 1965). For a study of Teilhard's Christology, see C. Mooney, *Teilhard de Chardin and the Mystery of Christ* (New York: Harper & Row, 1966).

[55]Among the works which may be consulted on this topic are: K. Rahner, "Resurrection," *SM*, pp. 1441–1442; X. Leon-Dufour, *Resurrection,* pp. 217–261; K. Rahner, *Foundations*, pp. 305–311; W. Kasper, *Jesus the Christ*, pp. 154–159; G. O'Collins, *Resurrection*, pp. 117–130.

[56]*Constitution on The Church in the Modern World*, n. 22., Vatican II.

[57]The Supreme Court's decision to legalize abortion does not then justify the killing of the unborn which is against the Law of Christ. Not rarely what is legal may also be immoral. Paul himself realized the expression "freedom from the law" could be interpreted as license (cf. Rom 6:15; 13:10). In difficult decisions, it is the Christian community which through the indwelling Spirit will point the direction to be followed, respecting the supreme norm of a person's *informed* conscience.

[58]*Constitution on The Church in the Modern World*, n. 1., Vatican II.

[59]cf. R. Schulte, "Sacraments," *SM*, pp. 1480–1485.

[60]*Constitution on The Church in the Modern World*, n. 22., Vatican II.

SELECT BIBLIOGRAPHY

(This is a sampling of books which may be useful to those who would like to continue their studies in christology. Additional bibliographies are found in the footnotes at each major topic.)

Anderson, C. *The Historical Jesus: A Continuing Quest*. Grand Rapids: Wm. B. Eerdmans, 1972.

Barr, R. *Main Currents in Early Christian Thought*. New York: Paulist Press, 1966.

Beasley-Murray, G. R. *Jesus and the Kingdom of God*. Grand Rapids: Wm. B. Eerdmans, 1986.

Becker, J. *Messianic Expectation in the Old Testament*. Philadelphia: Fortress Press, 1977.

Benoit, P. *Jesus and the Gospel*. New York: Herder and Herder, 1973.

Boff, L. *Jesus Christ Liberator*. Maryknoll: Orbis Books, 1978.

Bornkamm, G. *Jesus of Nazareth*. New York: Harper & Row, 1960.

Bousset, W. *Kurios Christos*. Nashville: Abingdon Press, 1970.

Bright, J. *The Kingdom of God*. Nashville: Abingdon Press, 1953.

Brown, R. E. and Cahill, J. P. *Biblical Tendencies Today: An Introduction to the Post-Bultmannians*. Washington: Corpus, 1969.

Brown, R. E. *Jesus God and Man*. Milwaukee: Bruce Publishing, 1967.

—————. *The Birth of the Messiah*. Garden City: Doubleday, 1977.

—————. *The Community of the Beloved Disciple*. New York: Paulist Press, 1979.

—————. *The Gospel According to John*. 2 vols. Garden City: Doubleday, 1966 (I–XII), 1970 (XIII–XXI).

—————. *Biblical Exegesis & Church Doctrine*. New York: Paulist Press, 1985.

—————. *The Virginal Conception and The Bodily Resurrection of Jesus*. New York: Paulist Press, 1973.

Bultmann, R. *The History of the Synoptic Tradition*. New York: Harper & Row, 1968.

—————. *The Theology of the New Testament*. New York: Charles Scribner's Sons, 1955.

—————. *Jesus Christ and Mythology*. New York: Charles Scribner's Sons, 1958.

Caird, G. B. *Saint Luke*. Baltimore: Penguin Books, 1963.

Cook, M. L., *The Jesus of Faith: A Study in Christology*. New York: Paulist Press, 1981.

Cullmann, O. *The Christology of the New Testament*. Philadelphia: The Westminster Press, 1959.

De Margerie, B. *The Human Knowledge of Christ*. Boston: Daughters of St. Paul, 1980

de Surgy, P. ed. *The Resurrection and Modern Biblical Thought*. New York: Corpus, 1970.

Dodd, C. H. *The Parables of the Kingdom*. rev. ed. London: Fontana Books, 1961

Dufour, X. *Resurrection and The Message of Easter*. New York: Holt, Rinehart and Winston, 1975.

Duling, D. *Jesus Christ Through History*. New York: Harcourt Brace Jovanovich, 1979.

Dunn, J. D. G. *Christology in the Making: A New Testament Inquiry into the Origins of the Doctrine of the Incarnation*. Philadelphia: Westminster Press, 1980.

Dwyer, J. C. *Son of Man & Son of God*. New York: Paulist Press, 1983.

Fenton, J. C. *Saint Matthew*. Baltimore: Penguin Books, 1963.

Fitzmyer, J. A. *A Christological Catechism: New Testament Answers*. New York: Paulist Press, 1982.

—————. *The Gospel According to Luke I–IX*. Anchor Bible Series, Garden City: Doubleday, 1981.

—————. *The Gospel According to Luke X–XXIV*. Anchor Bible Series, Garden City: Doubleday, 1985.

—————. *Scripture & Christology: A Statement of the Biblical Commission with a Commentary*. New York: Paulist Press, 1986.

Fuller, R. H. and Perkins, P. *Who is this Christ: Gospel Christology and Contemporary Faith*. Philadelphia: Fortress Press, 1983.

Fuller, R. H. *The Mission and Achievement of Jesus*. London: SCM Press, 1954.

—————. *A Critical Introduction to the New Testament*. London: Duckworth, 1966.

—————. *The Foundations of New Testament Christology*. New York: Charles Scribner's Sons, 1965.

—————. *The Formation of the Resurrection Narratives*. Philadelphia: Fortress Press, 1980.

Galot, J. *Who is Christ? A Theology of the Incarnation*. Chicago: Franciscan Herald Press, 1981.

Griffin, D. R. *A Process Christology*. New York: Cambridge University Press, 1977.

Grillmeier, A. *Christ in Christian Tradition*. Atlanta: John Knox Press, 1975.

Guillet, J. *The Consciousness of Jesus*. New York: Newman Press, 1971.

Hagner, D. A. *The Jewish Reclamation of Jesus*. Grand Rapids: Academie Books, 1984.

Hahn, F. *The Titles of Jesus in Christology*. Cleveland: The World Publishing Co., 1963.

Harrington, D. J. *Interpreting the New Testament: A Practical Guide.* Wilmington: Michael Glazier.

Hart, T. N. *To Know and Follow Jesus.* New York: Paulist Press, 1984.

Hendrickx, H. *The Resurrection Narratives of the Synoptic Gospels.* London: Geoffrey Chapman, 1984.

Hodgson, P. C. *Jesus-Word and Presence: An Essay in Christology.* Philadelphia: Fortress Press.

Holladay, C. R. *Theios Aner in Hellenistic Judaism: A Critique of This Category in New Testament Christology.* Missoula: Scholars Press, 1977.

International Theological Commission *Select Questions on Christology.* Washington: USCC, 1980.

————. *Theology Christology Anthropology.* Washington: USCC, 1983.

Jedin, H. *The Ecumenical Councils of the Catholic Church.* New York: Herder and Herder, 1960.

Jeremias, J. *New Testament Theology.* London: SCM Press, 1971.

————. *Rediscovering the Parables.* New York: Charles Scribner's, 1966.

————. *The Prayers of Jesus.* London: SCM Press, 1967.

Kasper, W. *Jesus the Christ.* New York: Paulist Press, 1976.

————. *The God of Jesus Christ.* New York: The Crossroad Publishing, 1982.

Kee, H. C. *Jesus in History: An Approach to the Study of the Gospels.* New York: Harcourt Brace Jovanovich, 1977.

Kelber, W. H. *The Oral and The Written Gospel.* Philadelphia: Fortress Press, 1983.

Kelly, J. N. D. *Early Christian Doctrines.* New York: Harper & Row, 1978.

Klausner, J. *Jesus of Nazareth.* Boston: Beacon Press, 1964 (first published New York: Macmiilan, 1925).

Lane, D. A. *The Reality of Jesus.* New York: Paulist Press, 1975.

Leon-Dufour, X. *The Gospels and the Jesus of History.* Garden City: Image Books, 1968.

Livingston, J. C. *Modern Christian Thought from the Enlightenment to Vatican II.* New York: Macmillan, 1971.

Mackey, J. P. *Jesus the Man and the Myth.* New York: Paulist Press, 1979.

Malet, A. *The Thought of Rudolf Bultmann.* Garden City: Doubleday & Company, 1971.

Marshall, I. H. *The Origins of New Testament Christology.* Downers Grove: InterVarsity Press, 1976.

————. ed. *New Testament Interpretation: Essays on Principles and Methods.* Grand Rapids: Wm. B. Eerdmann's Publishing, 1977.

May, W. E. *Christ in Contemporary Thought.* Dayton: Pflaum, 1970.

McArthur, H. *In Search of the Historical Jesus.* New York: Scribner's and Sons, 1969.

McIntyre, J. *The Shape of Christology.* Philadelphia: The Westminster Press, 1966.

McKnight, E. V. *What Is Form Criticism.* Philadelphia: Fortress Press, 1981.

Moltmann, J. *The Crucified God.* New York: Harper & Row, 1974.

Mowinckel, S. *He That Cometh: The Messiah Concept in the Old Testament and Later Judaism.* Nashville: Abingdon Press, 1956.

Myendorff, J. *Living Tradition: Orthodox Witness in the Contemporary World.* Crestowood: St. Vladimir's Seminary Press, 1978.

————. *Christ in Eastern Christian Thought.* Washington: Corpus, 1969.

Moule, C. F. D. *The Origins of Christology.* New York: Cambridge University Press, 1977.

Nineham, D. E., *Saint Mark.* New York: Penguin Books, 1963.

Norris, R. A. *The Christological Controversy.* Philadelphia: Fortress Press, 1980.

O'Collins, G. *The Resurrection of Jesus Christ.* Valley Forge: The Judson Press, 1973.

————. *Interpreting Jesus* New York: Paulist Press, 1983.

O'Grady, J. F. *Models of Jesus.* Garden City: Doubleday & Company, 1981.

————. *Jesus, Lord and Christ.* New York: Paulist Press, 1973.

O'Meara, T. and Weisser, D., eds. *Rudolf Bultmann in Catholic Thought.* New York: Herder & Herder, 1968.

Pannenberg, W. *Jesus-God and Man: An Essay in Christology.* Philadelphia: Fortress Press, 1971.

Patai, R. *The Messiah Texts.* Detroit: Wayne State University Press, 1979.

Perrin, N. & Duling, D. C. *The New Testament: An Introduction, Second Edition.* New York: Harcourt Brace Jovanovich, 1982.

Perrin, N. *The Resurrection According to Matthew, Mark and Luke.* Philadelphia: Fortress Press, 1977.

————. *What Is Redaction Criticism.* Philadelphia: Fortress Press, 1969.

————. *A Modern Pilgrimage in New Testament Christology.* Philadelphia: Fortress Press, 1974.

Perkins, P. *Reading the New Testament: An Introduction.* New York: Paulist Press, 1978.

_____ . *Resurrection: New Testament Witness and Contemporary Reflection.* New York: Doubleday, 1984.

Pittenger, N. *Christology Reconsidered.* London: SCM Press, 1970.

Pontifical Biblical Commission *Instruction on the Historical Truth of the Gospels* (1964) found in Fitzmyer, *A Christological Catechism,* pp. 131–140

_____ . *Bible & Christology* (1983) found in J. Fitzmyer *Scripture & Christology,* pp.3–53

Rahner, K. *Foundations of Christian Faith: An Introduction to the Idea of Christianity.* New York: Seabury, 1978.

_____ . ed. *Encyclopedia of Theology: The Concise Sacramentum Mundi.* New York: Seabury, 1975. See especially articles on "Incarnation," "Jesus Christ," (I. Maisch, A. Vogtle, R. Pesch, A. Grillmeier, K. Rahner) "Christianity." "Death."

_____ . *Theological Investigations.* Baltimore: Helicon Press, vols. 1–20, 1961–1981, especially "Current Problems in Christology," vol. I, pp. 149–200; "On The theology of the Incarnation," vol. IV., pp. 105–120; "Dogmatic Reflections on the Knowledge and Selfconsciousness of Christ," vol V, pp. 193–215; "Christology in the Setting of Modern Man's Understanding of Himself and his World," Vol. XI, 215–229; "The Quest for Approaches Leading to an Understanding of the Mystery of the God-Man Jesus," Vol. XIII, pp. 195–200; "The Two Basic Types of Christology," Vol. XIII, pp. 213–223.

Reese, J. *Experiencing the Good News: The New Testament as Communication.* Wilmington: Michael Glazier, 1984.

Riggan, G. A. *Messianic Theology and Christian Faith.* Philadelphia: Westminster Press, 1967.

Robert A. and Feuillet, A. *Interpreting the Scriptures.* New York: Desclee, 1969.

Robinson, J. M. *A New Quest of the Historical Jesus and Other Essays.* Philadelphia: Fortress Press, 1983 (originally published by London: SCM Press, 1959).

Sabourin, L. *Christology: Basic Texts in Focus.* Staten Island: Alba House, 1984.

_____ . *The Names and Titles of Jesus.* New York: Macmillan, 1967.

Schmaus, M. *Dogma 3: God and His Christ.* New York: Sheed & Ward, 1971.

Schillebeeckx, E., *Jesus: An Experiment in Christology.* New York: Seabury, 1979.

Schnackenburg, R. *God's Rule and Kingdom.* New York: Herder and Herder, 1963.

Schoonenberg, P. *The Christ.* New York: Herder and Herder, 1971.

Schweitzer, A., *The Quest of the Historical Jesus.* New York: Macmillan, 1964.

Schweizer, E. *Jesus.* Richmond: The John Knox Press, 1971.

Sobrino, J. *Christology At The Crossroads.* Maryknoll: Orbis Books, 1978.

Taylor, V. *The Names of Jesus.* New York: St. Martin's Press, 1962.

Thompson, W. M. *The Jesus Debate: A Survey & Synthesis.* New York: Paulist Press, 1985.

Turner, H. E. W. *Jesus the Christ.* Oxford: Alden Press, 1976.

Vawter, B. *This Man Jesus.* New York: Image Books, 1973.

Wilken, R., ed. *Aspects of Wisdom in Judaism and Early Christianity.* Notre Dame: Notre Dame University Press, 1975.

INDEX

Incarnation
  meaning of, 38
  a dynamic reality, 83, 145
  pattern of God's self–disclosure, 88
  source of miracles of Jesus, 125
Inspiration of Scripture
  definition of, 175, n. 114
Ipsissima verba
  definition of, 22
  rarity of, 173, n. 64
Ipsissima vox
  definition of, 22

Jesus
  existence of, 6–10
  pre-existence of, 74, 75, 84
  as center of cosmos, 164
  as kairos of the Father, 108
  "becoming" in Jesus, 150–151
  fellowship with outcasts, 134
  final word of YHWH, 108–109
  Jesus' understanding of the Father, 46–47,
    117–118
  meaning of two intellects, wills, 87
  foretold in Old Testament, 61–62
  (see "Titles of Jesus," "Resurrection,"
    "personhood," etc.)

Kairos
  definition of, 108
  Jesus as kairos of the Father, 108
Kerygma
  definition of, 188, n. 6
Kingdom of God
  (see "Reign of God.")
Knowledge of Jesus
  self-identity, 88
  of end of world, 129–131
Kurios
  meaning of, 70–71

Late Judaism
  meaning of, 59
Laws of Nature
  relationship to miracles, 123–125
  understanding of, 124
Liberation theology, 134, 187, n. 48
Linguistics
  and christology, 27–28
Literary Criticism
  definition of, 37–38
Lord
  frequency of title in Scriptures, 69
  and "Kurios," 70–71
  and Adonai, 70
  and Council of Nicaea, 75
  and MAR, 70
  and Wisdom Literature, 73
  as emissary of God, 73
  development in early church, 71–75
  importance of title, 69
  meaning at time of Jesus, 70–71
  possible use by Jesus, 71
  the title and the Marcan community, 72
  and psalm 110, 72

Mar
  meaning of, 70

Maranatha
  meaning of, 72
  as stage in development of "Lord," 72
Mary Mother of Jesus
  Immaculate Conception & Assumption, 4
  in Talmud, 10
  as understood by students of "oral" gospel,
    27
  theology compared to icon of Mary, 41
  as Theotokos, 85, 181, n. 89, 91
  the first disciple of Jesus, 135, 187, n. 52
  related to Jesus through faith, 86
Messiah
  use of title by Jesus, 63–67
  and "confession of Peter," 63–65
  and entry into Jerusalem, 67
  and messianic fever, 59–60
  and messianic prophecy, 61–62
  and messianism, 58–59
  and Psalm 110, 66–67
  and temptation narratives, 64–65
  and trial before Pilate, 66
  and trial before Caiaphas, 66
  development of title in early church, 67–68
  history of messianism, 59
  Meaning at time of Jesus, 58–60
  messianic secret, 64
  varieties of mesianism in NT era, 59–60
Messianic Fever, 59–60
Messianism, 58–59
Millenarianism
  meaning of, 60
Miracles of Jesus
  ambiguity of, 125
  and contemporary understanding, 120
  and the reign of God, 118
  as a call to faith, 121
  as "contrary to laws of nature," 123–124
  as fulfillment of salvation history, 122
  as the inbreaking of the kingdom, 122
  biblical terms for, 124
  "definition" of, 124
  disclose wonder of God's Reign, 121–122
  embellished by Gospel authors, 123
  historicity of, 122
  miracles and parables, 123
  raisings from the dead, 53, 123, 144
  respect human causality, 124
  scientific explanation?, 123–125
  theological importance of, 120–122
Mission to Gentiles, 133
Monophysitism,
  meaning of, 84
Monothelitism
  meaning of, 86
Mother of God
  (see Mary, Mother of Jesus; Theotokos)
Mystery
  definition of, 96
Myth
  definition of, 18–19

Nature
  in in thought of Biblical Commission, 87
  meaning of at Chalcedon, 86
  in modern thought, 87
  used analogically, 87
Nestorianism
  meaning of, 85
New Criticism, 27–28